The Leisure Alternatives Catalog

Food for Mind & Body

The Leisure Alternatives Catalog

Food for Mind & Body

Editor-in-Chief: Joseph Allen

Editors: Robyn Greenberg, Rick Harmon, Jean S. Henshaw

Designers: Debra and Don McQuiston

A Delta Special/Publisher's Inc.

A Delta Special

Published jointly by
Dell Publishing Co., Inc.
1 Dag Hammarskjold Plaza
New York, New York 10017
and
Publisher's Inc.
243 12th Street
Del Mar, California 92014

First printing—May 1979
10 9 8 7 6 5 4 3 2 1

Delta® TM 755118, Dell Publishing Co., Inc.

Library of Congress Cataloging in Publication Data

Main entry under title:

The Leisure alternatives catalog.

"A Delta special."
Includes index.
1. Leisure. 2. Hobbies. 3. Recreation.
I. Allen, Joseph, 1944–
GV174.L44 790'.0135 79-83848
ISBN 0-440-54663-X

Manufactured in the United States of America

Staff
Publisher: Richard L. Roe
Editor-in-chief: Joseph Allen
Editors: Robyn Greenberg, Rick Harmon, Jean S. Henshaw
Production editor: Jackie Estrada
Contributing editor: Robert McGarvey
Art direction: McQuiston & Daughter
Project consultant: David Hellyer
Academic consultant: David C. Etter, Ed.D.,
Director, Independent Study,
University of California Extension, Berkeley
Rights and permissions: Patricia Campbell
Operations management: Eugene Schwartz
Business management: Jean Forsythe, Judy Lancaster
Editorial assistant: Charlene Luckie
Research assistant: Paul Scranton
Original design concept and chapter opening art direction: Tom Gould
Design: Don McQuiston, Debra McQuiston, Louis Neiheisel
Illustrators: Kitty Anderson, Joyce Eide,
Debra McQuiston, Louie Neiheisel, Everett Peck
Delta editor: Chris Kuppig
Delta project manager: John McLeran

Typesetting: Boyer & Brass, Inc.
Production Art: Connie Bock, Curt Boyer, Laurie Miller

Contributors
Joseph Allen (J.A.)
Susan Astarita (S.A.)
Rosemary Breckler (R.B.)
Patricia Campbell (P.C.)
Sheridan Crawford (S.C.)
Gregory Dennis (G.D.)
Ann Elwood (A.E.)
Jackie Estrada (J.E.)
Terence K. Fitzgerald (T.F.)
Terry Galanoy (T.G.)
Michael W. Gosney (M.G.)
Candice Goucher (C.G.)
Robyn Greenberg (R.G.)
Elizabeth Hansen (E.H.)
David Hellyer (D.H.)
Belle Heneberger (B.H.)
Jean S. Henshaw (J.S.H.)
John R. Hiza (J.H.)
Bert Hubinger (B.Hu.)
Martin Jakub (M.J.)
Roby James (R.J.)
Arlyne Lazerson (A.L.)
Carrol McBride (C.McB.)
Robert McGarvey (R.McG.)
Donald L. Petersen (D.P.)
Robert Portwood (R.P.)
George Rooney (G.R.)
Susan Silton (S.S.)
Leonard Smukler (L.S.)
Jim Stebinger (J.S.)
Paul B. Taublieb (P.T.)
Mary West (M.W.)
Michael C. Westlund (M.C.W.)
Judith Witty (J.W.)

Acknowledgments
Our thanks to all the many thousands of people who contributed time and effort (and photos, brochures, telephone bills, letters, notes, smiles, and good wishes) during our research for *The Leisure Alternatives Catalog*. We thank the fine group of writers who assembled the text, and the exceptional artists who interpreted the words in pictures.

Special thanks to Dave Hellyer, who got things off the ground, and to Dave Etter, who kept us on the straight and narrow.

A Special Note About the Programs
The data we have compiled for this book have been taken from the most recent literature published by each of the participating programs. We urge you to call or write to the organizations or places before undertaking any long-distance journeys. Changes in programs and costs can and do occur, so please be forewarned.

Contents

To Your Health 91

A healthy body is one of the elusive goals of modern man. Here are some avenues to fitness through nutrition, exercise, rejuvenation, and the rediscovery of healthful living.

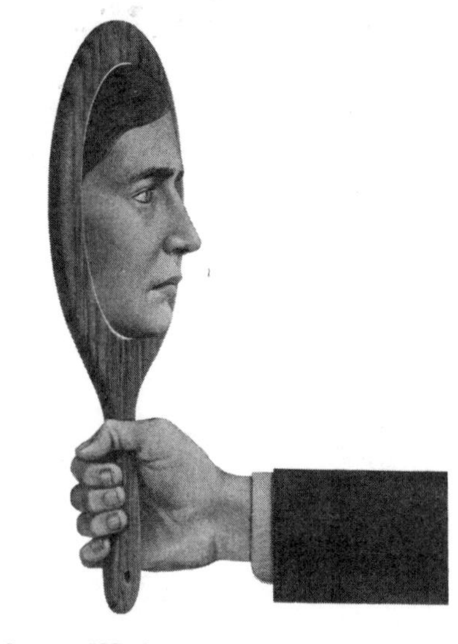

Looking Within 111

Collect your thoughts, examine your psyche, and plunge into the exciting options of self-examination and self-discovery. We offer a range of programs that run the gamut from meditation and physical awareness to spiritualism and massage.

Leisure Learning 133

Afraid you're getting stale? Breathe fresh air into your life by going back to school. The educational programs we provide combine vacation atmospheres with learning opportunities. Here is a wealth of leisuretime learning programs for families, seniors, and adults addicted to knowledge.

The enchantment of the wilderness both beckons and challenges you. We've put together programs that will take you to the tops of mountains, the depths of caves, the shores of distant seas. You'll meet birds and animals, learn outdoor survival skills, and commune with nature.

The thrill of soaring through the sky in a balloon or glider is unlike anything else you'll ever experience. We have programs that take you into the skies and into the seas, with hang gliding, skydiving, scuba diving, and windsurfing. On terra firma, we've got tennis, running, golf, skiing, and martial arts. And mountaineering—Why? Because it's there.

There's nothing so broadening as travel. These treks and voyages were selected because we believe each presents a unique learning experience. These aren't your everyday guided tours. These journeys offer the ultimate: the world itself.

To be able to fill leisure intelligently is the last product of civilization.
ARNOLD TOYNBEE

Introduction: What Is Leisure?

Leisure is something more than spare time, and something less than a life of idleness. It's what happens when two rare commodities coincide: time and money. Not necessarily a lot of time nor a lot of money—but some of each.

Recognizing that you have leisure time available is not as easy as it seems. When there's extra money (for instance), it seems to take care of itself one way or another: it gets spent or invested or hidden in a sock under the mattress. When there's a bit of extra time, it seems to fill itself with chores, catching up, or simply wondering what to do.

But there are some fortunate times when the two come together—ah, but briefly—and confront us. "Here I am," they seem to say, "Here is your leisure time beckoning to you. What are you going to do about me?"

It's not an easy question to answer. How are we supposed to know what to do with leisure? We weren't taught to have leisure; we were taught to work.

We have, in fact, more leisure time than any society has ever had in the history of the human race. Leisure is big business: televisions, tennis racquets, golf clubs, stereos, gardening equipment, campers and RVs, knitting needles, potters' wheels—the list goes on and on.

What we're suggesting by compiling this book is that you consider investing your leisure. Or *re-investing* it, which is probably a better term. We're suggesting that you take that leisure time (and that leisure budget) and do something useful with it. Something enjoyable, to be sure, but something that won't just vanish when it's done.

Look at *The Leisure Alternatives Catalog* as though it were a sort of personal, spiritual investment portfolio. Inspect each of the programs the way you would inspect a company whose stock you were considering buying. Inspect it the way you'd inspect the plumbing in a house; inspect it the way you inspect cantaloupes at the market. Pick the one(s) that are best for you—here and now.

Then act.

Do.

Go.

Learn.

Experience.

Live!

Leisure is one of the best parts of life. That is to say, it should be. If it's not—yet—then try our alternatives. We've found them, catalogued them, and published them just for you.

Artists can color the sky red because they know it's blue. Those of us who aren't artists must color things the way they really are or people might think we're stupid.
JULES FEIFFER

Creating & Collecting

One of the chief differences between man and ape is the remarkable organ found at the end of each arm: the hand. The human hand formed the first weapons and built the first homes. It invented cloth and pottery and art; it enabled us to create civilization.

Our hands are still the principal tools with which we civilize our world. Hands cook our meals and rock our cradles. Hands build cathedrals and colleges. Hands express what is most human as they fashion our tools and our artifacts.

This chapter is about hands, and the wonders they can perform with a variety of raw materials.

Hands can make straw into baskets and dolls. They can make clay into pottery. Hands can turn sand into unimaginably beautiful stained glass. Hands can build houses and furniture.

Hands make the infinite variety of human cuisines—from tortillas to tortonis to turkeys and stuffing. Hands allied with machines record light on film as you shoot photographs.

The pages of Creating & Collecting are packed with the work of hands—perhaps your hands. We proudly present to you 34 pages of what we consider to be some of the world's finest craft and collecting programs. As you read through this chapter, you'll find a dazzling array of subject matter, ranging from antiques to zucchini gardening.

We've located these programs so that you can participate in them. Not one of them will exclude you just because you're an amateur. Not one of them will bore you if you are something more than an amateur.

Here are programs and people who will help you make things from wood and glass, from fiber and clay. Here are gourmet cooking instructors who'll help you upgrade your Steak Diane, stuff your tamales, or stir-fry your water chestnuts.

Here are photographers who will teach you how to capture a baby's first smile, the stark grandeur of the sea, or the pearly drops of dew on a spring rose.

Here are weavers who'll see you through your first tapestry. And glass-blowers who will show you how to capture the ineffable fire of light in a stained glass window.

And here are artists who will give free rein to your most hilarious fantasies in painting, drawing, or sculpture. Artisans who will teach you the intricacies of serigraphy, lithography, and calligraphy.

And here are the quintessential green thumbs—those gifted human beings who'll teach you how to keep a Boston fern alive, or how to cultivate your own food organically.

Release the genie you hold inside you. Train your hands to do your bidding. Now that we've compiled all these programs for you, you've no excuse not to.

Vegetable assemblage by Joyce Eide

Little by Little

Antique Fever

Great furniture designs are timeless; they are copied over and over again for the delight of millions. The names of great furniture designers and notable periods have become standards of taste in interior decorating: Chippendale, Sheraton, Hepplewhite, Queen Anne, Empire, Louis XV.

But there's an important difference between a Chippendale chair and a Chippendale-style chair. That difference is Thomas Chippendale, who died in 1779; there haven't been any real Chippendale chairs since then—which puts the real thing at a fancy premium.

With antique fever sweeping the country, what better place to learn "what's what" and "who's who" in this special world than at the Smithsonian Seminar in American Antique Furniture.

The connoisseurship program undertakes the analysis of masterpieces of furniture craftsmanship and art as milestones of design and beauty. Lectures present pieces of antique furniture for illustration, along with color slides of great museum and private collections. The principal lecturer is Oscar P. Fitzgerald.

For the antique collector, one topic is of major concern: the detection of forgeries and fakes. After all, it's not an easy task to tell a Chippendale copy made in 1801 from the real thing made a mere 25 years earlier. The Smithsonian program gives good counsel in fake detection.

Participants will tour reconstructed rooms of the original Smithsonian building (completed in 1855), nicknamed "The Castle." They will also amble through the Diplomatic Reception Rooms of the Department of State, the Henry Francis du Pont Winterhur Museum, and the stately Lindens—the oldest house in Washington, D.C. (although it was originally built in Massachusetts).

Programs last for five days, and include sessions on topics such as "The Years of Transition from Medieval to Classical," "Furniture of the Federal Period," and "The Golden Age of American Furniture." Time is also devoted to the care, repair, and conservation of fine furniture.

In addition to the program at the Smithsonian, the participant will have bountiful free hours to explore the wonders and byways of the nation's capital. For the museum buff, there's the National Gallery, the Museum of African Art, the *National Geographic* Explorer's Hall, and the Corcoran Gallery.

For the theater enthusiast, Washington offers a variety of possibilities, including the Kennedy Center for the Performing Arts, the National Theater, Ford's Theater (newly restored), and the Folger Theater (a Shakespeare legend).

There are no prerequisites for this course, and there is no college credit offered. Participants in the connoisseurship program do so out of love and a quest for knowledge. The price may rise slightly from current levels, but is set at press time at $350, including hotel. Transportation to Washington is, of course, extra.

Advance reading lists are mailed to each participant to help the seminars begin with a background of common knowledge. —J.A.

Smithsonian Institution
Selected Studies Program
Washington, D.C. 20560

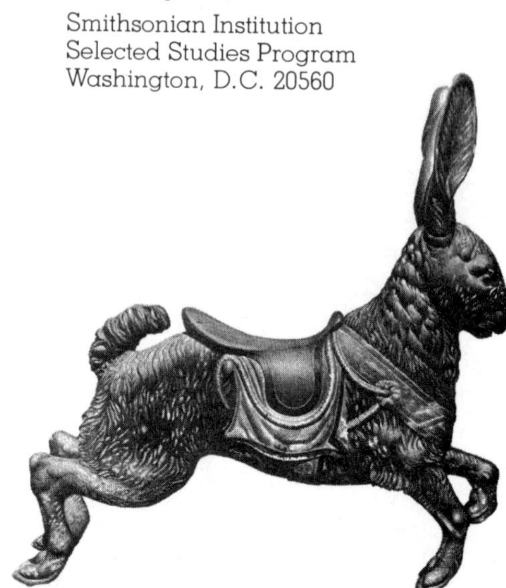

Quarts of Quartz

Join Don Ricardo de Leon on an eight-day excursion across miles of Mexico rarely seen by Americans. Transportation, hotels, meals, lectures—all are included in the package price of $235.

Here's the run-down: Day One—You'll fly into Leon from Mexico City and the day will be spent visiting the markets, small onyx shops, and silver jewelry centers. Day Two—Off to Guanajuato, where you'll receive a guided tour of the local museum, parks, and well-known souvenir and artisan markets. Days Three, Four, and Five—Ghost towns and gems are your goals as you trek high into the Sierras, enjoying the wilderness and marveling at the silent mystique of abandoned towns and mines. The area abounds with rare quartz crystals (they're free!). Day Six—On the road to San Miguel Allende, where you'll talk with local jewelers and survey gem centers for bargains on unset stones. Day Seven—Your destination is Queretaro, where you'll discover a wealth of polished and uncut amethysts, opals, etc.—at the best prices yet. Day Eight—You've come full circle, with plenty of stories to tell and who knows what to show!

Each registration includes a student membership to the Instituto IMLE, an international study center in Leon, Guanajuato, which certifies academic credit and offers special courses in Spanish. —M.G.

IMLE
Hidalgo 206
Leon, GTO
Mexico

Capture a Kaleidoscope

The perfection of nature is nowhere more evident than in the brilliant symmetry of the butterfly's wing. And the avid collector of such creatures is certainly a devotee of the rare and fascinating species native to Sri Lanka (formerly Ceylon). Gemini Tours has organized a butterfly safari *par excellance* for collectors and for shutterbugs.

It's deluxe-class throughout this seven-day excursion, beginning with your stay at the Inter-Continental Hotel in Colombo. You'll visit Ratnapura, nicknamed the "Gem Capital" (rock-hounds, take note), and then set off in search of *Troides helemus*, *Kalima pilachus*, and *Pelipides agna agna*. You'll see species with names like Painted Lady, Red Admiral, and Blue Tiger. All told, you'll probably spot as many as 100 different varieties.

You'll also visit Buddhism's first Holy City (Anuradhapura), view the oldest historically authenticated tree in the world (the Bo Tree, planted 2500 years ago as a sapling), and visit dozens of gardens, temples, museums, and other historic sites.

Gemini's prices are quoted in the currency of Sri Lanka; your bank can supply the current exchange rate. —J.A.

Gemini Tours Limited
No. 73, Dharmapala Mawatha
Colombo 3
Sri Lanka

Stamp of Approval For the stamp collector, the *sine qua non* of the hobby is the Philatelic Foundation, which offers the education of a stamp collector's dreams. Course offerings include "Postal History of the Confederacy," "The Drama of Postage Stamp Creation," and "1861—A Year of Change." All courses are audio-visual packets, and you may rent them.

The Philatelic Foundation
270 Madison Avenue
New York, NY 10016

Money Money Money Know your booby heads from your sycees? Members of the American Numismatic Association know them well—and they'll assist you with your Paduans, your Bungrowns, and your Fantasy Money for good measure. Sophisticated pennypinching, nickelpinching, etc., for the avid coin collector.

American Numismatic Association
P.O. Box 2366
Colorado Springs, CO 80901

Antique Attack Got a yearning to spend a summer "antiquing"? Then do it in style—with knowledge at your fingertips. Do it with the folks from Joseph Stanley Ltd., who conduct "antiquing" binges worldwide. Venice, Florence, Dublin, Oxford, Spain, Morocco—you name it and they've got it (if, of course, it's worth having).

Joseph Stanley Ltd.
181 West Bridge St.
New Hope, PA 18938

It is completely unimportant. That is why it is so interesting.
AGATHA CHRISTIE

Call It Gustatory

Edible England

Oh! To be in England. The theater, Westminster Abbey, the Tower of London, New Bond Street, the sparkling cuisine.

Hold it! The sparkling cuisine? Are we thinking about the same England?

The England of greasy, soggy fish? The England of day-old shepherd's pie? The England of boiled everything? That's sparkling?

Not exactly, but the well-known shortcomings of English cuisine itself have created an interesting gastric phenomenon in London. No city as cosmopolitan, as sophisticated, and as busy as London can exist forever on soggy fish—as you might guess.

Tourists have been reporting for years on the wonderful *foreign* restaurants in London. The waves of Indians and Pakistanis have brought with them the distinctive spices and herbs of the sultry subcontinent. The Asian peoples of the British Empire have established a stakeout on Chinese food (from eyewateringly hot to festive Cantonese) that puts Singapore to shame.

And London is alive with restaurants of all climes and ilks—Armenian, West Indian, French, Italian, Thai, Tunisian, Austrian, Jewish, Indian, Argentinian, Chinese, Moroccan (you get the picture).

Edible England is a program which sets as its goal acquainting you with this United Nations of food. And, of course, they'll sneak you into some of the good (yes, Virginia, there are some good ones) English-style restaurants as well. There you'll feast on saddles of lamb, standing prime ribs of beef, and good ol' Yorkshire puddy.

Prepare yourself for tutorials on topics to make the mouth water and the stomach growl: "The Great Beers of Britain," "French Wine," "Italian Wine," and "The Great Cuisines of the World." And prepare yourself for that amused tolerance which England has made into its own hallmark. "If you don't want to go to a Greek restaurant tonight, Martha, then go somewhere else—Turkish restaurants abound here too." The program is handled by providing all participants with lists of places to eat—you pick what you want, when you want it. None of the standard gourmet tour, "Tonight ve vill eat Coquilles St. Jacques."

While you're pondering Edible England, let us slip in some pecuniary details: to wit, about $650-$750 per person, depending on exchange rates and time of year. The price includes hotel, breakfasts, a river trip to the Naval Observatory at Greenwich, wine and beer tastings, gourmet information, a gourmet feast the last night, etc. No travel included, because, love, you're all going from different places, aren't you?

And when you get back, you can bring all your friends a nice tin of chockie bickies. —J.A.

University of Wisconsin
Dr. Lorin Robinson
Dept. of Journalism
River Falls, WI 54022

Bon Appetit!

The best way to learn a language, so they say, is to live it—total immersion, like a fundamentalist baptism. And there's no doubt that the best way to learn to cook is to, well, cook. Those two principles provide the operating idea of Yetabo.

Yetabo is headquartered in a picturesque country French home in the Burgundy region of France. The name of the townlet that Yetabo calls home is Pailly, and it looks very much like it must have two or three hundred years back.

What Yetabo offers is an avalanche of everything French, what might legitimately be called a "total learning experience." You learn the language in sessions that last five or six hours a day. You learn fine French cooking from master chefs, along with the art of French menu planning. And last, but certainly not least, in this famous province—you learn wine, wine, and more wine.

You'll learn to distinguish a Puligny Montrachet from a Pouilly Fuisse from a Chablis Fourchaume Premier Cru. You'll learn to prepare potage aux epinards, riz creole, saute d'agneau, and crepes Suzettes. Perhaps best of all, you'll learn enough of the French language to get you across what Yetabo calls the "psychological barrier."

Prices are in French francs, but run $400-$500 per week per person. Monthly rates are also available. —J.A.

Yetabo
Pailly, 89140
Pont-sur-Yonne
France

The Raw and the Cooked

Despite its folksy-sounding name, the Cooking Kitchen is a veritable university of cooking skills. Its faculty is distinguished and quite sizable, as cooking schools go. Its curriculum is varied both in subject matter and format. You can, for instance, study cooking in "A Touch of Class" for a single lecture session lasting one morning. Alternatively, you can take one of many gourmet trips with Ms. Bell lasting up to a week.

The thrill that tingles the cooking enthusiast as he/she reads the Cooking Kitchen's brochure is a delicious experience. It's akin to being in a wonderful toy store. You'll take that, that, and that, please—and maybe one of those as well.

The "appetizers" and "entrees" of the Cooking Kitchen range from "Coffee, Coffee, Coffee" through "Hunter's Harvest" (a lesson in cooking wild game). The possibilities continue with "The Flavor of Italy," "A Harvest of Herbs," and such inscrutables as "Oriental Express."

As you read through the Cooking Kitchen's brochure, though, the most attractive part is that it sounds like everyone who works there is having a ball. And that's more tempting than anything else I can think of. —J.A.

Judith Bell's Cooking Kitchen
3940 W. 50th
Minneapolis, MN 55424

Southern Fried Join the ranks of Atlanta's top cooks at Rich's Cooking School, located deep in the heart of the Old South herself. If you know anything about Southern cookin', you know that learning the arts from these people ain't just whistlin' Dixie.

Rich's Cooking School
Forsyth & Alabama Sts.
Atlanta, GA 30303

Haute Stuff Everyone who is anyone knows that Beverly Hills is a center of *haute cuisine*. You can't have that much money concentrated in one place without good food following close behind. Study the Beverly Hills good life with the Lillian Haines Institute of Culinary Arts—it's got real pizzazz.

The Lillian Haines Institute
of Culinary Arts
P.O. Box 5248
Beverly Hills, CA 90210

Antipasto to Zuppa Inglese
Italy. The word means many things to many people—but to most people it means *food*. And a gourmet tour of Italy with Canterbury Travel is almost too much to describe. *Tutti, tutti.*

Canterbury Travel, Inc.
Kent Green P.O. Box 159
Kent CT 06757

Boston Baking An intimate cooking school in Boston—La Cuisine—provides the answers to a gourmet cook's dreams. Courses such as Baking 1 and Baking 2, Gastronomy, French Provincial Cooking. Ah, soft shell crabs, croissants, champagne sherbet, and lobster souffle.

La Cuisine
92 Charles St.
Boston, MA 02114

We may live without poetry, music and art;
We may live without conscience, and live without heart;
We may live without friends; we may live without books;
But civilized man cannot live without cooks.
EDWARD BULWER-LYTTON

Queen of Wok and Roll (Egg)

If you pale at the sight of a Big Mac . . .

If one more Hamburger Helper would send you to the funny farm . . .

Then you're ready for Oriental cooking. And Jeanne Tahnk.

Jeanne, a queen of wok and roll (egg), performs her culinary wonders on Fletcher Street in Winchester, Massachusetts. In five weeks, she can transform you from a mere fryer-of-eggs into a cordon bleu of Chinese cuisine—all for a paltry $60 (including cost of food).

You will learn, among other arcane arts, the mysteries of Pekinese, Cantonese, Mandarin, and Szechuan cookery. When someone cries "What's for dinner," you can respond "Mandarin pancakes, moo goo gai pan, Buddha's delight, and glazed banana candy." If that's not enough, you can silence all complaints with a serving of "ants crawling on a tree."

Jeanne holds several diplomas from famed Taiwanese cooking schools. And when she runs out of moo-shi pork or won ton, she can switch with ease to Japanese cookery (complete with raw fish).

Anyone for drunken Cornish hen? —D.H.

Jeanne Tahnk School
of Oriental Cooking
9 Fletcher St.
Winchester, MA 01890

Rome Gourmet Adventure

Come to Rome and take a bite of the city home with you. That's right, a bite. That's what participants in the seven-day Rome Gourmet Adventure do.

But, important as eating and wine tasting are to all Roman holidays, this Gourmet Adventure goes one step further—not only do participants sample the rich Italian culinary delights, they also learn to cook them. Sixteen hours of cooking classes are included in the package, with instruction taking place at Rome's Lo Scaldavivande Cooking School. Students quickly learn not just to eat gnocchi, fragalotta cake, pasta, and the rest of the Italian cuisine, but to make every course themselves. Better still, classes conclude with a lunch, featuring cuisine prepared by class members and topped off with a tasting of celebrated Italian wines.

Ample time is also provided for exploring Italy's non-culinary delights, and tour members who wish to skip the cooking classes will be taken on guided jaunts through Rome instead. Cost for the seven days—including cooking classes, air fare, and hotel accommodations—is about $855. —R.McG.

E & M Associates
667 Madison Ave.
New York, NY 10021

I Wanna Go Back . . . Poi and grass skirts are not really where it's at in Hawaii—notwithstanding travel brochures. NIU International will educate you in the food, culture, and fashions of the erstwhile island kingdom. And, of course, there's nothing to stop you from getting in some beach time, too.

International and Special Programs
Northern Illinois University
De Kalb, IL 60115

1 from Column A Grab your wok, and let Karen Lee help you do the rest. Her courses in Chinese cooking give you the basics: handling the cleaver, chopping, shredding, slicing, mincing, stir-frying, deep-frying, steaming—and keeping cool.

Karen Lee Chinese Cooking Classes
142 West End Ave.
New York, NY 10023

Lady Mady's Kitchen Cooking with Mady teaches you the basic skills of gourmet cooking. Mady herself keeps classes quite small so that individual feedback is possible. New England pot roast to poached salmon to chicken breasts Albufera.

Cooking with Mady
20 Bramble Brook Rd.
Ardsley, NY 10502

Pick It, Cook It, Eat It Specific cooking needs specific instruction. How would you fancy a course called "Only Cheesecake"? Or how about "Bride's First Dinner" or "The Complete Chicken"? The Classic Cook has it all—and you can pick exactly what you want to learn.

The Classic Cook, Ltd.
Station Square
Pittsburgh, PA 15219

Spice Up Your Life

Variety is the spice of life, they say. Judith Ets-Hokin is living proof of it. Founder of a cooking institute in San Francisco, Judith offers five-day cooking packages, particularly geared to out-of-towners, throughout the year. The course menu reads like a grand international restaurant: French, Italian, Chinese, American, and Viennese dishes, plus instruction in boning, pasta making (her specialty), and bread making.

Having studied under two famous American chefs and graduated from English, French, and Italian cooking schools, Judith endows her classes with this same diversity. She firmly believes that good cooking is a "creative activity," which sparks students to plunge into experimental recipes.

Classes combine both demonstration and participation, depending on the subject of the day. Meals are served whenever the schedule calls for preparing a full menu. Most likely you will have a chance to try your own creative hand after watching Judith prepare such specialties as lasagna or French bread.

If you're lucky enough to pass through this fabled city and find your way into the school's culinary

camaraderie, we guarantee that you'll find the atmosphere congenial to your gustatory senses. Situated in a renovated Victorian storefront, the school is part of a veritable culinary paradise: cooking school, specialty food shop, cookware store, and restaurant.

Judith believes that quality—the best equipment and ingredients—combined with simplicity is the essential component of fine cooking. She urges students to grow whatever they can—advice which she herself follows in maintaining a garden of fresh vegetables, herbs, and fruits.

Learn it all while you gather around the large cooking area surrounded by natural wood shelves filled with delectable goodies. Watch American dishes which you might never before have heard of take shape: jambalaya, apple Betty, Philadelphia pepperpot soup. You'll be encouraged to interrupt with questions, and cautioned against being intimidated by recipes.

Judith also directs a $35 12-lesson correspondence series designed for hooked cooks too occupied or too far away to get to San Francisco. And a brand-new reducing course, consisting of eight three-hour sessions, looks at the reasons why people become overweight and includes demonstrations of low-calorie meal preparation.

There are no prerequisites for joining either the correspondence or regular programs. Classes remain small—usually 8-14 at a time—and the cost for most classes is $15 for each three-hour session.

When Judith says, "Let your dishes take on your personality, by varying seasonings, adding your own extras—that way you make a statement that is you," you'll realize this isn't some run-of-the-meal program. —S.S.

Judith Ets-Hokin Culinary Institute
1802 Bush St.
San Francisco, CA 94109

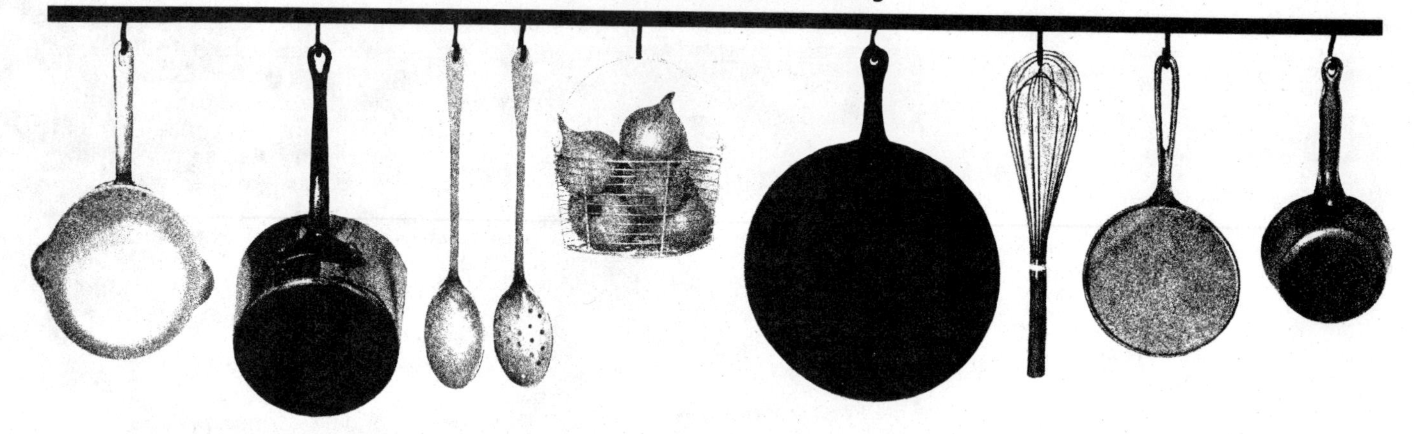

The How of Chow

Culinary Arts, A School of Fine Cooking in Baltimore, offers a broad array of unique classes and clinics taught by highly qualified carriers of the gourmet flame.

The Directors, Bonnie Rapoport and Anne Barry, hold the coveted Grande Diplome from the world famous Cordon Bleu School of Cookery. They maintain an honorable stature in fine food circles, with writings featured in area publications, frequent appearances on local and national television, and consultation work for restaurants across the country. A cookbook is in the works featuring recipes from the curricula of Culinary Arts.

Offerings in the Culinary Arts program range from basic techniques for true beginners to the most sublime cuisines for sophisticated cooks. Guest teachers, some of world-renown, are frequently featured, and the growing staff is allowing expanded course diversity. Germain Sharretts, recognized gourmet teacher in the New England area, has joined the Culinary Arts program, offering classes based on regional menus of France and Italy, a baking series, a course on North African Cuisine, and several clinics.

All lessons are given on a demonstration basis, each including a complete menu plan. Technique in handling food and equipment is stressed repeatedly. Each demonstration concludes with a buffet meal for all. —M.G.

Culinary Arts Cooking School
5701 Newbury St.
Baltimore, MD 21209

***The cook was a good cook,
as cooks go;
and as cooks go she went.***
SAKI

What's Cooking?

Ever wield a zucchini corer? How about a mushroom fluter or an asparagus peeler? If you haven't, give the folks at The Complete Cook a call. They will gladly make the proper introductions.

Offering a full range of courses for novices and polished cooks alike, The Complete Cook's specialty is the guest chef. With instruction handled by local restaurateurs and imported "name" chefs, The Complete Cook's menu of courses is geared to guiding the student from the soup through the nuts. Along the way, stops are made to cover egg roll wrappings, cake decorating, the magic of the food processor, Kosher-style Oriental cuisine, vegetable breads, and the Greek picnic.

Demonstrations at The Complete Cook—of that zucchini corer, for example—are free. Fees for classes start at $11 and head upward, with 15 hours of instruction by those imported princes and princesses of the kitchen pegged at $175. —R.McG.

The Complete Cook
222 Waukegan Rd.
Glenview, IL 60025

A Week in New York with Annemarie

If there was ever a perfect culinary guardian angel in New York, that angel would have to be Annemarie Huste, the cheery proprietress of Annemarie's Cooking School. As you tour the Big Apple with Annemarie, you can feast on tidbits of her illustrious acquaintances as well as on her cuisine.

A former food editor for the *Saturday Evening Post*, Annemarie was chef to Mrs. J. F. Kennedy, and to master showman, Billy Rose.

Annemarie will show you the intricacies of three great national cuisines: French, Italian, and Chinese. She will also educate you in the all-important concept of overall meal harmony. Her own concept of cooking instruction has been published as "cooking dynamics" in two cookbooks, and you will be privy to her secrets from hors d'oeuvres to final cheese board.

You'll visit the wholesale flower market and take lessons on making centerpieces. You'll stir-fry Chinese vegetables and meats under the guidance of the remarkable Dee Wang. You'll learn the art of buying fresh produce, fine sausages, herbs and spices.

And after you've eaten and learned your way through a week with Annemarie, you'll get a decorative diploma. Who could ask for anything more? —J.A.

Annemarie's Cooking School
164 Lexington Ave.
New York, NY 10016

Culinary Wizardry

If you had your ruby slippers on, you could just click your heels together and go straight to Kansas. But perhaps Kansas isn't exactly what you had in mind. Well, whatever.

You now have a better choice, due to the arrival on the travel scene of a new pack of wizards who term themselves The World of Oz. And do they have a gourmet tour for you! Hoo-hah!

They went straight to the source for this one. While you're staying at the Montfleury Inter-Continental Hotel at Cannes, you'll eat at restaurants and from menus selected for you by Simone Beck (Julia Child's coauthor on *Mastering the Art of French Cooking*). You'll study with master chef Dominique Ferriere at the thirteenth-century Chateau du Domaine St. Martin. You'll take lessons from Jean Paul Robert, who won the 1977 Grand Prix Escoffier. Then it's off for an afternoon with Josef Rostang, master chef at the internationally famous La Bonne Auberge. Finally you'll study with Mme. Beck herself at her home in Grasse.

It's not cheap, as you might expect. But it is magical. And if you don't like the food—there's no hope for you. —J.A.

The World of Oz
3 E. 54th St.
New York, NY 10022

Gourmet Olé

One of the most ecstatically delicious programs in the culinary world is headquartered in the historic mountain province of Guanajuato, Mexico—the last bastion of Spanish occupation in Central America during the Mexican struggle for independence.

Now this province is known for San Miguel Allende, for the picturesque ciudad of Guanajuato itself, and for the pleasures of IMLE (Instituto Moderno de Lenguas Extranjeras) in Leon. IMLE is the spiritual home of Mexican-food gourmets, and its offerings may very well be the revelation of a lifetime to those unfortunates who have not yet fallen captive to this great cuisine.

As a student at IMLE, you'll spend seven glorious days in the kitchen. How can a day in the kitchen be glorious, you may ask? You'll find out quickly enough as you hobnob with chamorros (pork shanks and sauce wrapped in corn husks and baked), sincronizadas, Yucatan tamales (made in banana leaves), salbutes, and panuchos. You'll learn what a real Veracruz sauce is, and you'll experiment with seafood in ways that will knock 'em dead back home.

Hotels are first class all the way. The food is only as spicy as you make it (since you're the apprentice chef). The scenery is breathtaking. The cost is within anyone's reach. By the way, IMLE publishes a monthly periodical: *Poor Ricardo's Almanaque*; at $6 per year, it's a steal. —J.A.

Instituto Moderno
de Lenguas Extranjeras
Av. Hidalgo Num. 206
Leon, GTO
Mexico

Grape Scott! Two rivers in Germany give their names to light, fruity wines: Moselle and Rhine. With this tour you'll bicycle through the two viniferous valleys, sampling lore and history and the inevitable hock.

Hike-Ski Tour Vermont
RFD 1
Chester, VT 05143

Cholesterol Begone! Vegetarian cooking can be tasty—and everyone knows the health value of avoiding meat. If you want to develop the vegetable side of your table (yucky cholesterol, begone!), try Creative Vegetarian Cooking. Courses in overweight cooking are also available.

Creative Vegetarian Cooking
P.O. Box 35906
Los Angeles, CA 90035

Duck Soup Hearty winter soups in Southern California? At a culinary center called "A Matter of Taste" anything is possible—as long as it's gustatory. Ongoing courses in northern Italian food, and seasonal classes at Christmas.

A Matter of Taste
514 N. La Cienega Blvd.
Los Angeles, CA 90048

Food for Thought New Yorkers will delight to find out that the New School for Social Research has gone into the food business—at least the food teaching business. With its customary aplomb and expertise, as you might guess. French, Italian, Chinese—the works.

New School for Social Research
66 W. 12th St.
New York, NY 10011

A dessert without cheese is like a beautiful woman with only one eye.
ANTHELME BRILLAT-SAVARIN

Seeds & Weeds

Rooftop Jungles

Even though the Dodgers are no longer around, there's still at least one good reason to live in Brooklyn. It's called the Brooklyn Botanic Garden.

To believe this, you'll need to read the BBG's catalog yourself. You'll notice immediately that, in keeping with the Garden's character, this modest leaflet overflows with the joy of its creators. For example:

Scrounging for a Rooftop Garden

A course designed to test the imagination! The class will cover the basic principles of how to make a roof garden at the lowest cost possible–a feat which may be accomplished by practicing the art of scrounging in and around the city.

If your aspirations run higher than rooftops, BBG will train you to become a "street tree pruner," which gives you license to do something not even the Mayor of New York dares to do: trim out the deadwood.

For every month of the calendar, BBG has a unique offering. In February (for example), with all the boroughs locked in the icy fist of winter, the BBG offers "Bonsai for Beginners." Not only will you learn "Japanese techniques for creating miniature tree forms," but you can take your plants home in Japanese containers to boot.

In March, the ground still harder than a Brooklyn cabbie's heart, BBG—with spring in the offing—will teach you all about city vegetable gardening: which vegetables will do well with a minimum of space, and how to plan a small garden for a succession of crops, with plants and seeds included for home use.

And "whan that Aprille with his shoures sote the droghte of Marche hath perced to the rote," the BBG is ready with another bag of delights. You may learn, for example, how insects survive the winter, where they build their homes, and how to identify them. Or you may marvel, as the editors did, to learn that bacteria and algae, and fungi and slime molds (not to mention liverworts), are really plants without flowers.

Nor is one's pleasure in all this love of nature diminished one whit by the ridiculously low cost of all this fun. For annual members ($15), the levies are even more nominal. Example: "Orchid Growing for Beginners" is a mere $12, and a smashing $9 bargain for members—orchid plant included!

For some delightful reading—especially before a warm fire on a winter's night—send for this slight but scintillating brochure.

This is no mere catalog. It is a celebration of nature. —D.H.

Brooklyn Botanic Garden
1000 Washington Ave.
Brooklyn, NY 11225

Green Thumbs for Sale

If you are a gardening enthusiast, who has never been able to sit in a lecture room without getting the jitters, the University of Guelph's home-study courses in plant growth and design may be your answer. Bringing Mother Nature's grace into your home is the object of all three "Creative Self-Learning Courses," each of which includes a filmstrip, hand-held viewer, cassettes, and printed text.

Their "Flower Arranging" course provides a general background of design concepts, supported by a step-by-step visual presentation of actual flower arrangements. A number of the particulars discussed and illustrated are: containers, care of cut flowers and foliage, and the proper use of roses, fruits, and vegetables.

The "Plant Propagation for the Homeowner" course, which includes eight filmstrips for $50, may be exactly what you need to put an end to the plant carnage taking place in your home. You'll learn all the tricks necessary to successfully keep your plants alive.

Finally, if you want to do more than just keep up with the Joneses, try the course in "Plant Use in Home Land-scape." You'll learn how to take care of your evergreens, your flowering trees and shrubs, and your perennials. —M.G.

Creative Self-Learning
Independent Study Office
University of Guelph
Guelph, Ontario NIG 2W1
Canada

Garden of Earthly Delights

Every city has a residential section where the gardens are, well, a tradition. In the spring, those gardens paint the earth's joy in palettes such as even rainbows cannot rival.

Those gardens don't just happen; they are the products of hard work and solid knowledge. If you want to develop that knowledge, you might consider the "Intensive Gardening and Horticulture Workshop" offered by The Farallones Institute in Occidental, California.

The setting is rural and relaxed, but the schedule is demanding—and rewarding. You'll cover both vegetable and flower gardening, of course. You'll also investigate composting and drip irrigation (so that's how some people always have perfect flowering peaches!). There'll be lectures on floriculture as a cottage industry (what a wonderful way to start a business).

For those among you with milkmaid fantasies, there'll even be a section on home dairies and haying. Who knows?

The program is residential, and runs for a month, so don't plan on any quick-and-dirty weekend lectures. When you finish up at Occidental you can hang out your shingle as a gardener. Count on it. It's $500, including room and board. —J.A.

The Farallones Institute
15290 Coleman Valley Rd.
Occidental, CA 95465

Branching Out You probably thought the LPGA had something to do with women who play golf—didn't you? Well, in this case, it doesn't. It's the Living Plant Growers Association, "dedicated to furthering an interest in and production of indoor foliage and other potted plants." That's a pretty specific goal, and the LPGA has some concrete approaches to it. For example, their International Foliage Plant Seminar held each autumn, or their "Plant of the Month" newsletters. They also sponsor horticultural exhibits at various locations and publish plant care booklets. Got a black thumb? Let LPGA turn it green.

Living Plant Growers Association
P.O. Box 289
Encinitas, CA 92024

Lily Lore "Consider the lilies of the field . . ." If ever there was a single flower more closely allied to the entire Western tradition, knowledge of it escapes us. The lilies of France, Easter lilies, tiger lilies. The North American Lily Society is a compendium of "lily-ana." The Society maintains a valuable library and an unparalleled slide collection for your delectation. They'll bring you up to date on the latest breeding procedures and on disease prevention. They also provide a seed exchange. But most spectacularly, they have lily shows locally and internationally.

North American Lily Society
Box 40134
Indianapolis, IN 46240

Lily-of-the-Valley said
She guessed she was a sleepy-head;
But she got up and dressed for town
In her new green tailored gown.
FLOWER CHILDREN

The Shape of Things

Miles Ahead

Have you ever spoken with an interior decorator who thought that he was the world's only true arbiter of good taste? There's a good deal of tongue-clucking and tasteful head-shaking from those paragons, and they wear facial expressions that tell you they've been eating antacid tablets by the gross.

It's to save you from such ethereal and disapproving persons that the Inchbald School of Design was formed 19 years ago. According to the founder, Jacqueline Inchbald Thwaites, "there has been a tendency to elevate the art of creating one's own environment into something so esoteric that the average person shrinks from competing. This is ridiculous."

Healthy attitude, that.

What the Inchbald School sets out to do is to offer principles of interior and exterior design and decoration—and encourage their students to go from there. The philosophy of the Inchbald School is similar to that of the greats in modern design: Eames, Mies van der Rohe, Gropius.

Simply stated, Inchbald thinks good design makes an environment (home, office, or whatever) that you will enjoy, rather than one that the neighbors will automatically admire.

The curriculum is simply designed, following the principles the School instills. There are courses in Fine & Decorative Arts, Garden Design, Design & Decoration, and Interior Design. The Garden Design segment is affiliated with the Royal Horticultural Society.

Realizing that different folks require different strokes, the School offers several types of instruction. You can take an intensive one-year course in everything, for instance. The one-year course has been increasingly popular with students from all over the world. But if you have less than a year to spare, you might select a ten-week course in Design and Decoration, or an alternate ten-week course in Garden Design, replete with field trips to period and contemporary gardens in and around London.

If you have even less than ten weeks (sigh, like most of us), there's still a place for you at Inchbald. There are five-day courses in several disciplines.

Whatever your needs, and whatever the time you have available, Inchbald is expanding its repertory of offerings yearly, and you'd do well to write for their current literature. Even the brochure is a paragon of readable prose and easy design.

A particularly attractive portion of the Inchbald curriculum is their one-year course leading to a diploma in Fine Arts. It is an intensive course, designed to give students an introductory knowledge of architecture, painting, and sculpture, with a more substantial insight into the decorative arts, furniture, silver, ceramics, and glass. Lectures on jewelry and dress are also included. Courses like that are such stuff as dreams are made of.

The longer courses at Inchbald would require residence in London (one-year, ten-week courses). The short courses (five-day) are easily compatible with vacations. Prices are quoted in pounds Sterling, and vary widely with various courses. —J.A.

Inchbald School of Design
7 Eaton Gate
London, SWWI 9BA
England, UK

One must not always think that feeling is everything. Art is nothing without form.
GUSTAVE FLAUBERT

Fashion It Yourself!

Where *is* the fashion industry heading? Nobody knows for sure, but students at the Parsons Evening Division have a huge jump in answering that question—and just about every other question in fashion, design, and the rest of the applied arts.

Affiliated with Parsons School of Design, one of America's most celebrated art schools, the Parsons Evening Division provides part-time and evening students with a smorgasbord of classes in all fields of design, including textiles, theater costuming and lighting, photography, and interior decorating.

Intrigued by shoe patternmaking? Parsons Evening Division offers three courses. Perplexed by makeup? There's a course at Parsons. Same goes for fashion coordination, floral settings, handbag patterning, jewelry design, and the operation of a boutique.

Geared for beginners and the more experienced alike, courses are often taught by working professionals. Costs vary, but most courses fall in the $100-$150 range. —R.McG.

Parsons School of Design
Evening Division
66 W. 12th St.
New York, NY 10011

Fanciful Fashions

How would you like to rub *haute couture* elbows with the likes of Christian Dior and Yves St. Laurent? If your answer is Oui! then dig out those dusty old *parlez-vous Francais* books and get cracking. The Paris American Academy in Paris, France, has a four-week workshop/seminar that will seduce your fashion fancy.

Workshops are structured to develop the special talents and abilities of each individual. Design principles and contemporary fashion trends are explored. Live nude drawing and basic illustration courses prepare you to carry out your ideas.

Seminars are conducted by a wide range of speakers including famous designers, style house consultants, and costume museum directors. Students are encouraged to speak with the lecturers.

And once you've created what has to be the most revolutionary style since "the mini," The Fashion Workshop will tell you how to market and promote your merchandise. Included in this part of the course will be fashion vocabulary, trade terminology, and the study of designers and their influence on trends.

Courses are taught in both French and English, and "Survival French" is taught every morning for half an hour. Housing is provided and counseling in all aspects of French life is readily available. —B.H.

Paris American Academy
9, Rue des Ursulines
75005 Paris, France

On the Rhode Mention the field of design and a small state springs immediately to the minds of those in the know. The Rhode Island School of Design is where it's at. Has been, and will be. Their continuing education programs are breathtakingly wide in scope and credentials.

Office of Continuing Education
Rhode Island School of Design
2 College St.
Providence, RI 02903

Clarissa's Couture The Clarissa School will prepare you for a career in fashion sewing or fashion design. You'll learn to visualize designs, to cut patterns, and to tailor correctly. You'll learn fashion stitchery and custom techniques. Part-timers and one-timers may find the courses a bit heavy.

The Clarissa School
107 Sixth St., 7th floor
Pittsburgh, PA 15222

Interiors Interior design and fashion design are the two fortes of the Traphagen School of Fashion. Programs are geared to those who have a high school education. Some very distinguished graduates grace their catalog—and they are in the right location.

The Traphagen School of Fashion
257 Park Ave. South
New York, NY 10010

You Wanna Be in Pictures? Draping is what fashion designers do in the movies. And it's just one of the things you'll learn to do at the Mayer School of Fashion Design. You'll also learn patternmaking and grading, and basic dressmaking. No-nonsense skills, these.

Mayer School of Fashion Design
64 W. 36th St.
New York, NY 10018

Fiber & Clay

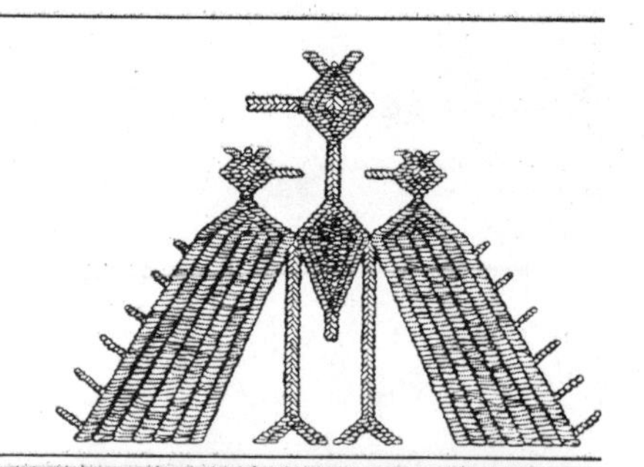

Dream Weaver

If ever a rainbow was caught by the hands of a mortal and made into an artifact, that artifact would have to be a Central American textile. The colors in such fabrics are vibrant to the extreme—giving the unmistakable impression that they have a life of their own.

As you watch an Indian weaver fashion intricate and age-old designs on a primitive backstrap loom, you begin to appreciate this folk art that has survived invasion, cultural decline, poverty, and isolation—to remain as young and dynamic as it must have been a thousand years ago. And as you watch such weavers at work, it's easy to commune with the past, because the same looms and techniques have been in use since well before Columbus shook a rattle in his cradle.

Gordon Frost's Study Tours are instant sellouts whenever they are scheduled. Why? Because they are magical trips to a lost civilization. Because there in the jungles and the mountains of Guatemala lurk arts and craftsmen of such sophistication and skill that the days of the Maya once again seem imminent.

The tour leader, Gordon Frost, has been a collector of Guatemalan folk art for years, and has spent considerable time in the lesser known regions of Guatemala. He takes small groups of 15-20 participants to see and feel a bit of the noble past. According to Frost, "Because the Indian art made for foreign markets only weakly reflects the quality and intimate spirit of the Indian art made for personal use," the tours visit people and places seldom reached by tourists.

Chichicastenango may be your picture of Guatemala, but it is not Gordon Frost's. When you visit that small country with Mr. Frost, you will spend time with the Mam Indians of the Chuchumatanes Mountains, the Quiche-Maya of the Department of Quezaltenango, the Cakchiquel Indians of the Department of Solola, and others. An effort is made to survey as many unique Indian groups as possible.

You'll see the making of traditional pottery, in addition to the above-mentioned backstrap and footloom weaving. You'll see Indian dances with full masks and costumes. And you'll get to know the Pre-Columbian culture of Central American Indians as you never thought you'd be able to.

The tours take two weeks, and are planned with the good offices of Pan Am. The rate per person, from Los Angeles, is $1095, plus applicable taxes. University credit will be offered in 1979 and 1980 by the University of California at Santa Barbara.

Because the tours are popular, and because there is only one Gordon Frost to lead them, book your space early. And take along some discretionary capital to bring home your own remembrances of the magic lands you'll see and the ancient peoples you'll visit. In the words of one recent participant, "To return to the reality of the Christian-Judaic world afterwards was a shock." —J.A.

Gordon Frost Guatemalan
Folk Art Collection
23616 Fambrough
Newhall, CA 91321

A Stitch in Time

Sewing and stitching comprise one of the oldest and most widespread handicrafts in human development. And the Center for the History of American Needlework takes precisely this long view of things. Their lectures and workshops are unique in the world (as far as we can tell) and start back at the very beginning. Their course, "Needlework and Textiles in Women's Lives," begins with Paleolithic times and works its way to the present, emphasizing the historical, mythological, and cultural associations of fiber media.

The main thrust at the Center is, of course, American needlework, and the folks at CHAN have done the subject up proud. Lectures are available in "Ethnic Needlework and Textiles in American Life," "The Tools of Needle and Textile Artists," and "American Needlework and Needlewomen." There's even a workshop devoted to "Textile Awareness."

All lectures and workshops are traveling shows, and can be engaged for a nominal fee plus traveling expenses. The Center, which is a nonprofit educational institution, encourages memberships as well, with all funds going to the support of this fascinating and worthwhile endeavor. —J.A.

Center for the History
of American Needlework
P.O. Box 8162
Pittsburgh, PA 15217

Lots of Pots

At the end of a six-mile dirt road on the slopes of Mt. Blitzen in central Nevada lies a mecca of free-style ceramic learning. It's called Tuscarora, and it was founded a little over 100 years ago as a silver boom town. Today, the silver mined out long ago, the citizens of Tuscarora have devoted themselves to the timeless art of pottery.

Classes are conducted in a studio that is itself a Buckminster Fuller geodesic dome. Hours of relaxing are invested in trout fishing, hiking, and backpacking (or ice fishing and cross-country skiing in the winter). Clean air and sagebrush plains dominate the Tuscarora environment.

Eight students are accepted at a time, for a fee of $565/month. The fee includes everything—even room and board. Much of the food is grown on the school's organic farm.

Facilities include kickwheels and handbuilding tables, a clay mixing and storage room, and a variety of kilns. No formal instruction is given. Instead, each student is counseled individually by the expert staff, headed by Dennis Parks, an internationally known ceramicist and potter. College credit can be arranged for time spent at Tuscarora. Some fellowships are available, and funding is derived partially from the National Endowment for the Arts and the Nevada State Council on the Arts. —J.A.

Dennis Parks
Tuscarora Pottery School
Tuscarora, NV 89834

From Rags to Riches The Weaver's Shop inhabits a building that originally had two products made within its walls: sewing machines and coffins. That was back in 1866. About 100 years later it became a haven for weaving mavens—which it remains.

The Weaver's Shop
39 Courtland St.
Rockford, MI 49341

Yes, Virginia A scientific approach to clay and potting is the tour de force at Glenville State College. You'll learn about the plasticity of water at various temperatures, about drying shrinkage, and about firing shrinkage. You'll work with electric kilns, as well as gas, raku, and test kilns. A complete summer curriculum in ceramics.

Glenville State College
Glenville, WV 26351

Deck the Halls Ask a Dallas fiber-fan. He'll tell you. Las Manos is the only word in "Big D" for weaving, macrame, and embroidery. Of particular interest to some may be their workshops in "Quickie Things to Do for Christmas."

Las Manos Inc.
12215 Coit Rd.
Dallas, TX 75251

A Rash of Weaving Lily Bohlin is a weaver well known for her "fantastic gift for colour." Her unusual warps, her mixings of colors, and her innovative approach to the weaving of hangings mark her as unique. Let some of that rub off on you.

Lily Bohlin's Weaving School
and Studio
1021 Government St.
Victoria, BC
Canada

Throwing Headquarters

Dave and Cathy Robinson may have found Paradise in Henniker, New Hampshire. Their Craney Hill Pottery Works is located on eight-acre, mostly wooded property with a year-round stream and a splendid view of distant hills. And there, amongst the idylls of the woods, they throw pots. And they teach others to throw pots.

In the intensive one-week courses offered at Craney Hill, each participant receives individual attention. Dave Robinson will analyze your present throwing ability and then work

out a personal program for "rapid improvement." In some cases this entails going back to basics and getting a fresh start.

Tuition is $80/week. Various types of lodging can be selected by participants—ranging from cabins to tents to motels. You may take your meals with the pot-throwers for $15/week; otherwise there's a supermarket a mere 20 miles away where you can stock up on your own.

One note: pot-throwing is the only subject of instruction at Craney Hill. The Robinsons have concentrated exclusively on this aspect of ceramics. —J.A.

Craney Hill Pottery Works
Craney Hill Rd.
Henniker, NH 03242

You must begin with an ideal and end with an ideal.
SIR FREDERICK G. BANTING

Fiber Fascination

Ancient peoples lavished much of their artistic energy on textiles. Recently excavated tombs in such areas as Peru and the Middle East have shown us the sophistication our forbears attained when it came to cloth and tapestry.

For those interested in learning about such ancient crafts as weaving, rug design, tapestry, quilting, and batik, Vassar College offers an ideal summer program. Workshops are taught by accomplished artisans; class size is severely limited so that the emphasis can remain on individual instruction.

And, let's face it, Vassar has a certain historic charm of its own, quite aside from fiber. Poughkeepsie, Vassar's hometown, is situated in the lush greenery of the middle Hudson River Valley. As you sit at your loom on a rainy day, you'll hear those Knickerbocker bowlers crashing and Rip van Winkle a-snoring.

Vassar is located just about halfway between Albany and New York City, and transportation in all forms is handy. The fiber arts staff adheres to the high quality of instruction that has made Vassar a standout in American education for years. —J.A.

Vassar College
P.O. Box 370
Poughkeepsie, NY 12601

As the Wheel Turns

If you're not already a potter or a ceramicist, you might want to quickly turn into one when you read about Steamboat Village.

Like some other excellent pottery havens, Steamboat Village has excellent potter's wheels, a gas-fired downdraft kiln, wedging tables, and so on. Clay and glaze are available, and the instruction, conducted by Dr. Herb Schumacher of the University of Northern Colorado, is top-notch. Emphasis is placed on developing each person's skills and design sensitivity.

But the clincher is the location and the hospitality. There you'll be, high in the clean air of the Rocky Mountains, residing in one of the state's most renowned lodges, two miles south of famous Steamboat Springs. Your hosts are Birthe and Sven Wiik, world-class Scandinavian innkeepers.

Relax in the sauna. Then, when you're looking for air or inspiration, take to "them thar hills." Hike. Swim. Fish. Play tennis or volleyball or soccer. And pot, pot, pot. —J.A.

University of Northern Colorado
Dept. of Fine Arts
Greeley, CO 80639

Criticism comes easier than craftsmanship.
ZEUXIS

A Tapestry of Technique

For most Americans, a "weaver" is someone who changes lanes too often on a highway. But to the Mannings, a weaver is one who weaves—as in cloth.

Getting back in touch with the skills of bygone days has enjoyed quite a vogue over the past five years or so. It was probably sparked by the Bicentennial celebrations we all heard too much about. Artsy-craftsy programs sprung up in community colleges like spring weeds.

But the Mannings Studio is no spring weed. No, sir. The Mannings Studio has been operating for 30 years now. They seem to be 30 years well spent.

The student who signs up for a "beginning weaver" course at the Mannings will cover such subjects as "warping," "sleying," and "threads and sett." The advanced weaver will find a fantasyland of threads and yarns, in addition to a course covering "pick-up," "laid-in," and "double weave" techniques.

If it was good enough for grandma, sonny, it's bloody good enough for me. —J.A.

The Mannings
RFD 2
East Berlin, PA 17316

'Tis wise to learn;
'tis God-like to create.
JOHN GODFREY SAXE

Stalking the Primitive Pot

Ever wish the world would just go away? Have a picture of yourself as a cave-dweller with no worries? Wish things would uncomplicate themselves and life would revert to Stone Age simplicity?

In case the above fantasy sets your blood to stirring, we have a program you should find to your liking. It's a week-long, live-in workshop in primitive pottery making and firing. You'll learn simple toolmaking and how to process clay by hand. You'll also learn to improvise fuelstocks (wood, straw, even dung). Best of all, you'll learn primitive firing techniques for oxidized, mottled, and blackware in open bonfires and pit fires.

You'll learn to build rudimentary kilns from scavenged materials. By the time you're finished, you'll have the experience and the knowledge to make and fire pottery without the assistance of complex technology—with limited means and materials and at relatively little (or no) cost.

Academic director is Dr. J. A. Cummings of the University of Wisconsin at Whitewater. Courses are taught at the Pigeon Lake Field Station by Kurt Wild. Your week's excursion into primitive pots will cost about $112-$115. —J.A.

Mr. Kurt Wild
Art Department
University of Wisconsin
River Falls, WI 54022

Pottery Pastures

Picture Pat Proctor priming potmakers on the pleasures of porcelain. Certainly tongue-twisting but not by any means inconceivable.

Tucked away on a hill, overlooking a mountain range and small lake in Camden, Maine, is Pat Proctor's home. That's not all. Adjacent to this serene countryside residence is a pottery studio, equipped with kick wheels, spacious work areas, and large glazing and handbuilding areas.

For two- or three-week sessions, from 9 a.m. to 9 p.m. Monday through Friday, Pat Proctor invites you to cover your hands with clay and just plain enjoy yourself. A private teacher and production potter who has studied under several professional potters herself, Pat guarantees personal interaction and instruction to each of the five students comprising every intimate session.

She'll challenge you with stoneware and porcelain, wheel throwing, hand building, and sculpture. She spends a half day with each student, whether she/he is beginning or advanced. Your expectations will be met in every possible way. Costs for the two- and three-week sessions in July and August are $200 and $300, plus materials.

Neither price includes living accommodations. But arrange to stay in a motel or inn nearby. Find out why Pat Proctor doesn't hesitate describing this as a "green vacation." —S.S.

Pat Proctor
Kosmer Pond Rd.
Camden, ME 04843

Wood & Glass

A Touch of Glass

There are certain periods in western civilization that are marked artistically by accomplishments in glass. The splendor of the Gothic period in France is most astonishingly evident to today's viewer in the glowing jewel box of La Sainte Chappelle in Paris—a 360-degree vision of brilliant stained glass.

In similar fashion, many of the greatest artworks of the period we now call Art Nouveau are glass—the famous Tiffany lamps, and the twisting intricacies of Lalique sculpture are only representative samples.

Glass is a great artistic medium in the hands of some people, and Pilchuck Workshops are a gathering of such people. It is, indeed, the only school in the United States with glass as a primary concern—and at Pilchuck glass might even be said to be an obsession.

The School is located in a remote and rural setting in the state of Washington. Teachers and students live and work together, sharing ideas about the techniques and aesthetics of glass. Individual and cooperative work periods for the students, demonstrations by the faculty, and slide lectures all stress the development and quality of artistic ideas rather than the production of commercial objects.

Open only during the summer, Pilchuck offers intensive work sessions focusing on the craft of hot glass, on architectural glass design, and other related artistic disciplines. Students learn by both watching the instructors work, and by executing their own projects. Such sessions are augmented and enriched by the presence of visiting artists and guest lecturers.

The instructors are as talented and well-known a group of glass artists as could be found. Their works have been shown and collected by the Metropolitan Museum of Art, the Whitney Museum, the Museum of Contemporary Crafts, and the Corning Museum of Glass—not to mention the Smithsonian. Those same instructors have been the recipients of many awards, including Guggenheim and Fulbright Fellowships, the Tiffany Foundation grant, and individual grants from the National Endowment for the Arts.

The names of the courses are further guides to the "no nonsense," conscious artistic discipline of Pilchuck: Molten Glass, Furnace Construction, Stained Glass Workshop, Glass Blowing, Architectural Glass, Glass Aesthetics.

The history of glass is a story of romance and beauty, and there are few—if any—art forms as alive and as intense as glass. No other art form creates with light and form in as pure a way. That fact is what led Dale Chihuly and a small group of followers to found Pilchuck in 1971. Chihuly is Chairman of the Glass Department at the Rhode Island School of Design, in case you're interested in credentials.

If you are interested in working at Pilchuck, contact them for prices and for schedules. And if you're interested in working with glass, Pilchuck is a one-of-a-kind opportunity. —J.A.

Pilchuck Glass Center
4532 East Laurel Dr., N.E.
Seattle, WA 98105

Country Carving

Craft skills have been historic lifelines for diverse cultures—but they are fast disappearing in an increasingly technological world. But back in the western hills of North Carolina, life goes on—just like it always has.

The idea behind Country Workshops is "to carve a link between traditional cultures and a new, human-scaled society." The program consists of intensive workshops taught by master craftsmen of the "old school." High standards, understanding natural materials, and technical excellence are emphasized.

Each workshop is five days long and is limited to 10 or 15 participants. Subjects for the upcoming year include Log Building (Peter Cott, instructor); Country Woodcraft (Drew Langsner, instructor); and—interestingly—Kudzu Textiles (Ann Foster, instructor).

Fees for each workshop amount to $160. The living conditions are woodsy: no electricity and no plumbing. And, in case you plan to use the gas station across the street, we are informed that there are "no public accommodations close by." —J.A.

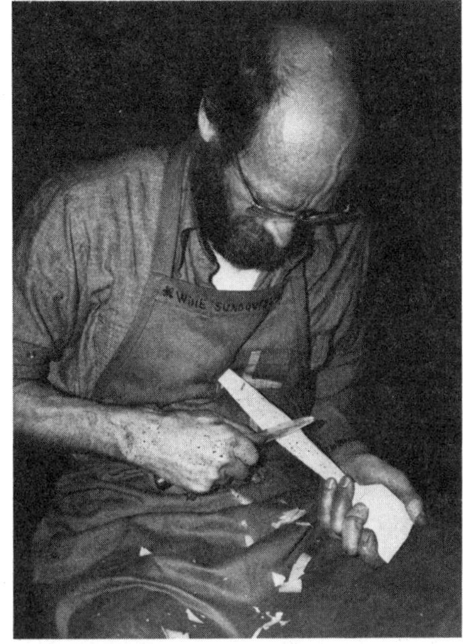

Country Workshops
Rt. 3, Box 221
Marshall, NC 28753

Cornerstones

A civilized culture has to have made great technological strides to have produced Cornerstones, a center for people who want to design and build their own houses—and perhaps change their lifestyles in the process.

Cornerstones is a college for owner-builders, providing the information and experience necessary for designing a personal and economical residence.

A student first takes one of the basic courses, either New House Construction or Retrofitting Old Houses. Then those planning to build in the near future may join the Design Workshop, conducted by the staff architect, to practice their new knowledge and complete a finished design.

The Hands-On Carpentry Experience is the third and final element of the program, in which students work with Cornerstones instructors during the summer, building passive solar houses.

Many students become quickly involved with their own building project, so the school facilitates cooperative, wholesale buying of building materials as well.

With a library and bookstore on the premises, students are at once in touch with both practical instruction and the writings of authorities on building. —D.P.

Susan Black Wing
54 Cumberland St.
Brunswick, ME 04011

Wooden Images

When the setting sun signals the end of a working day, insurance salespersons, doctors, office clerks, and housewives gather eagerly at the John Harra Woodworking Studio in a spacious New York City loft. Here they complete the oak desk they have always secretly desired to build. They design the wall unit they were once tempted to buy, but could never afford.

Run by a former premedical student, John Harra, the studio changes from a professional cabinetmaking shop during the day, into a lecture room and workshop at night. Harra's 17 years of experience with wood, and his confident belief that people can build anything they want to, stirs enthusiasm within his students, who spend 10 weeks of instruction or longer using the studio's 10,000 square feet.

In this relaxed setting you'll learn about hardwoods, softwoods, and plywoods, about shopping for lumber, about routers and jigsaws, power nailers and table saws. Design is instrumental in the learning process. If you have a design in mind, Harra and his assistants will help you effect it. If you don't, they will brainstorm with you and suggest a design that appeals to you and is within a reasonable price range.

When students are not pounding nails or putting final touches on their projects, they can be seen conversing over coffee in front of a Franklin stove. The creative ambience of the studio allows them to discuss future coffee tables or repair jobs on their front doors at home. Whatever projects they're mulling over, students at the workshop are proving John Harra's theory: "Two hands, ten fingers, and six billion brain cells can't all be there just to sell underwear."

Prices for the course are approximately $150 tuition and $20 shop fee (for 10 four-hour sessions of instruction). —S.S.

John Harra Woodworking Studio
39 West 19th St.
New York, NY 10011

Culture is something that has made man something other than a wrinkle on the face of the universe.
ANDRE MALRAUX

Carve Yourself a Niche

Mention "Manhattan" to most outsiders today, and the vision aroused is one of muggings in Central Park, dog droppings underfoot, and taxi-clogged streets. It's certainly not a vision of earnest people sawing boards, operating woodturning lathes, or carving delicate patterns in walnut or mahogany.

But that's the scene down on 32nd Street in New York City at a place called The Woodsmith's Studio. In one corner, a psychotherapist from St. Vincent's Hospital puts the crowning touches on a small teakwood writing table. (The platform bed she planned to build wouldn't fit into her tiny West Side apartment.) Across the room, a newspaper delivery supervisor perfects the finish on his dream: a rolltop desk of wormy chestnut. Nearby, a telephone installer delicately chisels an eagle in a block of wood.

Throughout the week they come—men, women, and kids—to shed formality, roll up their sleeves, and get sawdust in their hair. The Studio offers all comers "basic woodworking skills that last a lifetime," says Doug Geller, one of two bright young men who run this unique enterprise. Doug learned to revere wood while apprenticed to a Shaker craftsman, who taught him the gentle, patient art of fashioning wood with hand tools. Jerry Gerber, co-director, also has his own custom cabinetry shop.

Doug and Jerry think of woodworking as a rare hobby "because it brings both utility and beauty into the small acts of our lives." "Anyone who has ever joined two boards, refinished an old chair, or whittled a stick has felt the attraction—even enchantment—that lies in a piece of wood," says Doug.

Students progress logically from simple techniques—such as sawing a board—to more exacting tasks, such as fitting a drawer. Personal guidance is assured, with an average ratio of one instructor to three students. Special classes are offered for boys and girls seven through ten years of age.

"If you've never seen your child sawing, sanding, or hammering away, you're in for a surprise," says Doug. "The happiness of a young woodworker—not just playing with tools, but engaged in a real project—can be a revelation."

Studio instructors working with kids have found that the idea of making something useful for the family often has great appeal to the youngsters. Projects include spice racks, bookcases, picture frames, tables, magazine racks, stools, and stands for the television—projects they attack with "great intensity and delight as they progress through the different techniques."

For the undecided who would like to look before enrolling, there are free lectures on Saturday afternoons at one. Ten-week courses ($155 for 25 hours of instruction) are offered in woodturning, picture-frame making, woodcarving, furniture finishing, and cabinetmaking. Two-week "mini" courses at the same cost and total number of hours, but at a more intense pace, are also available.

Knowing about this unique effort to bring beauty into "the small acts of our lives" somehow makes one forget the dog droppings. —D.H.

The Woodsmith's Studio
142 E. 32nd St.
New York, NY 10016

O young artist,
you search for a subject
—everything is a subject.
Your subject is yourself,
your impressions,
your emotions in
the presence of nature.
EUGENE DELACROIX

Log It as a Winner

When the B. Allan Mackie School says it is the only school of its kind—you'd better believe it. Log building may not be much in demand these days, but the Mackie School is seeing to it that the requisite skills get a fair shake at surviving.

Log building—in case you're wondering—means exactly what you might expect it to mean. The Mackie School offers studies suitable for the following groups of participants: (1) those who plan to follow careers as log builders; (2) those who intend to build a deluxe log house of their own; (3) professional log builders pursuing in-service and advanced studies.

You supply all your own tools, and two textbooks are required reading. The demand for the course is apparent from the fact that the main textbook, *Building with Logs*, is in its sixth edition. The subsidiary text is *Notches of All Kinds*.

Beginners should plan to spend nine weeks learning fundamentals; some advanced courses last only four weeks. Fees are $100/week (not including housing). You could do worse than to bring your kids up in a log house—ask Abraham Lincoln. —J.A.

B. Allan Mackie School of Log Building
Box 1205
Prince George, B.C. V2L 4V3
Canada

A Chip off the Old Block

You can get some idea of the style of this course from the name of the town it's in: Bishop's Waltham, Hampshire. If it sounds straight out of Jane Austen or Trollope—well, just maybe it is.

According to the current proprietor, Mike Law (Harrison and his sons started the business in 1830, and have been gone for some time now), the setup is very informal. Participants can stay at the Workshop or in a local hotel.

The Workshop adjoins the Law house. It is well heated, they assure us, and has a thick carpet of wood-shavings underfoot. There are always at least five lathes set up and working, ranging from those almost 100 years old to the most modern Coronets and Arundels "of the type you probably use at home."

All tools, wood, polishes, etc., are provided; you supply your own overalls. Time is spent on curing wood first, since wood is the essential raw material. Then it's on to bowling and faceplating and such. The attitudes of the establishment are again in evidence in statements like "sandpaper does not enter into our thinking . . ." Ahem!

Then, in Law's own words, "at 6:00 p.m. Friday, you will be so tired of the sound of my voice, that you'll be glad to call a halt." It's a two-day affair with the lathe. Prices vary with international exchange rates, but should stay within the range of $120-$135. —J.A.

Thos. Harrison & Sons—Woodturning
Hoe Farm House/Hoe Road
Bishop's Waltham
Hampshire S03 IDS
England, UK

The bow was made in England: of true wood, of yew wood, The wood of English bows.
SIR ARTHUR CONAN DOYLE

Gimme Shelter Thwarted by real estate prices? You might try the Shelter Institute's alternative to overpriced housing. They suggest you build it yourself—and they'll tutor you in the "whys and wherefores": framing, wiring, plumbing, the works.

Shelter Institute
38 Centre St.
Bath, ME 04530

Get Stoked Get out that lathe and start straightening up that mess in your workshop. When you get back from Gordon Stokes' course in woodturning, nobody will be able to turn you off!

Gordon Stokes
202 The Hollow
Bath, Avon
England, UK

Children of Child When next you're in Essex, you woodworking enthusiasts, you might just stop in at the Old Hyde—the haunt of Peter and Margaret Child. Peter has the tools and the knowhow for you (and they say Margaret is one of the finest cooks in the area). Classes and tools for craftsmen woodturners.

Peter Child
The Old Hyde
Little Yeldham
Halstead, Essex
England, UK

Carving Correspondence The family crest over the mantel is carved in a deep, rich mahogany. Picture it, and picture the satisfaction you'll get from creating it from a piece of unshapen wood. A first-rate wood carving school, wot? And it's all by mail!

F. W. Miles
23 Rands Estate
Preston, Hull, Yorkshire
England, UK

Doing It All

Paradise Regained

Two years ago, UNESCO (United Nations Educational, Social, and Cultural Organization) decided to publish a report on innovative art programs worldwide. They chose five schools as outstanding; one of those was Canada's The Artists' Workshop. When you're looking for credentials, that's about the best there is.

You'd probably expect such a school to be elitist, selective, highly professional—a gathering place for the world's art establishment. You'd expect the hallowed halls of such a school to be foreign ground for somebody who just always wanted to learn to sketch.

Wrong.

In the words of the Workshop's brochure, "We delight in beginners too and the complete duffer is as welcome as the student who is already exhibiting, performing or being published." Unusual? Yes, unusual.

But The Artists' Workshop is an unusual enclave. It seems to be that most rare of all birds: a school dedicated to art, rather than to artists.

And there are precious few fields of artistic endeavor which go ignored at the Workshop. They offer studies—for rank beginners to seasoned professionals—in acting, ceramics, color, craftsmanship, dance, design, drama, drawing, fibre arts, film, art history, history of photography, painting, movement, poetry, photography, portraiture, pottery, quilting, sculpture, theatre, writing, and yoga. And that's only hitting a few of the high points, m'dear.

"Beginners are more than welcome in almost all courses at the Workshop and no one should feel reluctant to come if they are just starting or starting again. However we have found that in certain areas beginners are more comfortable in courses especially designed for them." Those areas are acting, drawing, painting, jazz dancing, photography, sculpture, and watercolor.

If The Artists' Workshop begins to sound like Paradise Regained, it may be just that for the budding, but blushing artist-to-be. It's a totally unpretentious atmosphere, with something to learn at every turn of the hallway. And, since all the arts are treated with the same candor and professionalism, you are likely to find yourself flowering in several fields at once.

The Artists' Workshop is one of three institutions which make up The Three Schools of Art. The others are The New School of Art and the Hockley Valley School. The three together also operate The Poor Alex Theatre, which is used by all three schools for presentations, and which houses several annual film festivals—among them a truly outstanding Japanese Film Festival.

The attitudes of the Workshop may be best summed up by Stephen Leacock: "Personally I would rather have written *Alice in Wonderland* than the whole *Encyclopaedia Britannica*."

Prices for programs vary. —J.A.

Three Schools
296 Brunswick Ave.
Toronto, Ontario M5S 2M7
Canada

Grist for Your Mill

The Brookfield Craft Center occupies a restored eighteenth-century grist mill and a nineteenth-century barn situated on opposite banks of the Still River in the western Connecticut countryside.

With such a setting, this nonprofit organization attracts America's best-known craftsmen and artists. The school welcomes both beginners and advanced students, and emphasizes a spirit of exploration. It offers classes in weaving, clay, enamel, stained glass, jewelry, felt, porcelain/white stoneware, natural dyes, quilting, textile art and design, silkscreen, Japanese toys, basketry, wood carving and many, many other topics.

Special fund-raising events, exhibits, and slide lectures are conducted regularly. You may want to call the Center at (203) 755-4526 for a current schedule. Membership, with a nominal fee, is required of all registrants other than for one-day classes. Class length varies from one to ten all-day sessions, and may cost from $20 for a one-day session to $125 for ten sessions (Monday through Friday).

A weekend class in Cloisonne Enameling is described in the summer schedule as an "Examination of various methods to approach cloisonne: IT construction, fabrication of cloisonne patterns, flat and formed work, securing enamels by various mechanical connections and methods of finishing . . . $52 for 3 all-day sessions." —D.P.

Brookfield Craft Center
P.O. Box 122
Brookfield, CT 06804

Absolutely Divine!

Examine your bankbook again. For a chance to develop painting, drawing, and photography skills in a sixteenth-century Italian monastery, you might suddenly find unexpected resources.

The University of New Mexico's Continuing Education program annually sponsors summer excursions to a mountainside monastery overlooking the town of Terni. Until the early nineteenth century 20 friars prayed daily here in La Romita monastery. Still surviving from this earlier ambience are the grand Umbrian hills with great white oxen pulling plows, bells sounding from neighboring monasteries, and cuckoo birds singing in surrounding olive groves.

Open to beginning and advanced students 18 and over, the 33-day program involves full days of artistic activity, either in La Romita's chapel studio or on location. Enhancing individualized painting and drawing instruction are pertinent sessions in art history. Photography students focus on black-and-white prints, taking full advantage of the location's subtle lighting for design and composition features.

The impressive $2000 price tag includes: all land and air transportation, accommodations, meals, a week in Florence, and bus tours of Rome, the hill towns, surrounding monasteries, Romanesque churches, and art galleries.

Be sure to take full advantage of the La Romita site itself. Examine a seventeenth-century Trinity painting over the church altar, or the cloister garden flanked by boxwood and blueberry bushes. Chances are you'll start resembling the Capuchin mendicant friars who founded the monastery by begging for a year's stay. —S.S.

University of New Mexico
Continuing Education
Bureau of Conferences and Institutes
Albuquerque, NM 87131

New England Style If you have a yearning to do it all—and do it in beauty—think about doing it at Goddard College, amidst the splendor of a New England summer. Their Summer Art Community offers every craft you can think of—and some you can't.

Goddard College
Plainfield, VT 05667

Illustrious Luminaries Crafters, unite! Wesleyan Potters, Inc. has brought together a regular summit meeting of craft luminaries, and they'd be pleased as punch to have you join them as well. Their catalog will fill you in.

Wesleyan Potters, Inc.
350 South Main St., Rt. 17
Middletown, CT 06457

No Needles Here Haystack is a friendly place where small groups congregate to learn about crafts. Fabrics, ceramics, graphics, metalsmithing, jewelry, weaving, woodworking, and everything else you can imagine.

Haystack Mountain School of Crafts
Deer Isle, ME 04627

The Old Country If you want to study arts and crafts where arts and crafts originated, you've got to go to Europe. Northern Illinois University has an array of programs to make a peacock blush. Programs also cover the map in a Grand Tour fashion.

International and Special Programs
Northern Illinois University
DeKalb, IL 60115

Les Beaux Arts La Rive Gauche, she beckons you. Spend a summer in France at the Paris American Academy on the Rue des Ursulines in the Quartier St. Michel. Study peinture, la langue francais, serigraphie, danse, musique—or any of the other fabled beaux arts. And if your tummy gets the best of you, you can even study cooking. Vive la yum-yum!

Paris American Academy
9 Rue des Ursulines
75005 Paris
France

Survival of the Fittest From novice to seasoned pro, Evolution Art Institute offers programs to please and educate in basic crafts. Blacksmithing leads the list, together with stone studies, woodworking, loom building, stained glass, and (mysteriously) masks. Evolve your artistic bent into something glorious.

Evolution Art Institute
6030 Roblar Rd.
Petaluma, CA 94952

The Craftsman of Venice A free-form home for art is what the Venice Studio seeks to provide. It is a fertile place where imagination grows rapidly to keep up with fast-paced skills development. Main fields of concentration are painting, drawing, and sculpture (including wood, bronze, and portrait sculpture). International staff.

Venice Studio
346 Sunset Ave.
Venice, CA 90291

A Prince of a Frog

New England is a bastion of individualism and tradition. When you visit New England, you cannot avoid yearning for the days when life was simpler, skills were stronger, and time was more readily available.

Well, sir, that atmosphere has never disappeared at Frog Hollow.

The Vermont State Craft Center at Frog Hollow is a repository of both skill and initiative—and its wealth of knowledge and spirit is available in classes for all ages. The emphasis is on traditional crafts, the ones so much now in vogue.

Courses are available for young students, for parents and children, or for adults. Within the three categories, course offerings are much the same in title, with content varied for the different groups. Typical course offerings (which vary, depending on who's teaching at the Center when you're there) include "Decorative Papers for the Holidays," "Melon Basketry," "Woodcut Printing," "Bobbin Lace Workshop," and "Throwing and Handbuilding (Pottery) for Teenagers." Prices are modest. —J.A.

Frog Hollow Craft Association
Middlebury, VT 05753

Crafting in the Valley

Now here's a group of people who've gotten together something like a utopian situation. Peters Valley's population consists of practicing craftsmen exclusively—and each one has to be elected by a jury of his peers to qualify to move in.

But you don't have to be elected to visit. In fact, visiting and studying are mightily encouraged. Peters Valley seems deadset to please everyone. They offer two-day seminars, a full summer session, an internship program, weekend workshops, art galleries for the inartistic—and a resident program. Whew!

Areas covered are numerous and a bit arcane at times: ornamental blacksmithing, regular blacksmithing, ceramics, jewelry, enameling, photography, textiles (batik, yes, batik), woodworking, and puppetry. Scattered among their topical offerings are courses in making musical instruments, in pit-firing techniques, in papermaking, and in pinhole photography. By the way, new craft skills are apt to appear at Peters Valley as soon as they are discovered.

Go ahead, treat yourself to total immersion in craftsmanship—and to a setting reminiscent of cooler, greener, more peaceful days.

Exact schedules and prices were unavailable at press time, but contact them and they'll fill you in. —J.A.

Peters Valley
Layton, NJ 07851

Mountain Magic

Quadna Mountain in Northern Minnesota may not appeal to many during the deep freeze of winter, but when summer strikes, the area proliferates with potters, actors, painters, weavers, photographers, writers, and craftsmen. The reason? They come to the Summer Arts Study Center for one- and two-week sessions. Anyone may attend; there are no prerequisites.

Mother Nature does not go unattended either. The emphasis at the Quadna Center is to do two things: experience life in a different manner—through nature—and explore whatever creative vein you have chosen. Students have the option of staying at the Quadna Lodge, or of pursuing the gypsy life by camping out in the Quadna Camp Grounds at bargain basement prices.

Arts and crafts are stressed, including courses such as gum printing in photography—a revived turn-of-the-century pigment printing process; pottery techniques including raku, bonfire, salt, and stoneware firing; fiber design exploring off-loom possibilities; jewelry making specializing in pewter casting; quilting; and stained glass.

A three-credit class, normally one

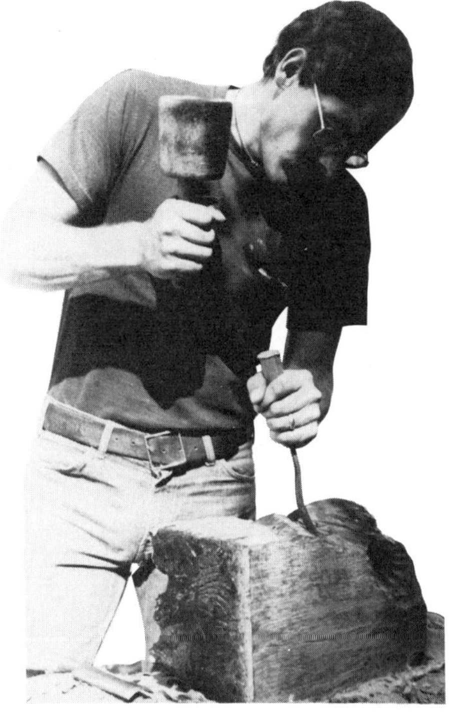

week in duration, runs about $70, but there may be minimal additional course fees. Or additional courses. It would be hard to stop with just one. —S.C.

University of Minnesota Extension
1128 La Salle Ave.
Minneapolis, MN 55403

Down in the Valley

Let your creative juices flow down Trail Creek. The nonprofit Sun Valley, Idaho, Center for the Arts and Humanities will captivate the artist within you. For scenery, facilities, and diversity of course offerings, Sun Valley can't be beat.

Beginning and advanced photographers take informal workshops designed for those interested in photography as a possible life's work. You'll use a fully equipped communal darkroom, and you'll share the pleasure of working closely with and listening to weekly lectures by major

contemporary artists in the field.

Don't give up hope if the environment sounds fantastic but photography bores you. The ceramics studio, professionally equipped and always open, allows students to combine personal effort with stimulation from master craftspersons. You'll use electric, stoneware, salt, and raku kilns, involving yourself in all aspects of clay. Workshops with artists-in-residence provide constant interaction and exposure to a variety of techniques.

If your body is your artistic medium, the Center offers instruction in numerous dance forms to adults and young people at beginning and advanced levels.

Scholarships and college credit are available to all participants. The two-day to ten-week workshops average 12 students, and prices range from $50 to $1000. Who knows, the fine atmosphere at Sun Valley might even convince you to settle there for awhile. —S.S.

Sun Valley Center
for the Arts and Humanities
Box 656
Sun Valley, ID 83353

Brooklyn's Best

One of the most elaborate instructional art programs at any American museum is in Brooklyn. When you come right down to it, there are a lot of good folks from Brooklyn—Howard Cosell notwithstanding. Nowhere else in the world, for instance, could the budding artist have studied over the past few years with the likes of Max Beckmann, Ben Shahn, William Baziotes, Rufino Tamayo, David Levine, William Kienbusch, and Reuben Tam.

There's far too much at the Brooklyn Museum program to think of seriously treating it here. What we can hope to convey is the amazing breadth of the program (painting, graphics, sculpture, ceramics, furniture construction, jewelry), and the sensible alternative formats. You can opt for weekend programs, part-time programs, full-time programs, or internships. There are classes for adults and classes for children and classes for those in between (high school).

The prices charged by the Museum are generously low—and well within the reach of any interested party. The only way to get all the details is to get all the details; write for the catalog and be amazed yourself. —J.A.

The Brooklyn Museum Art School
188 Eastern Parkway
Brooklyn, NY 11238

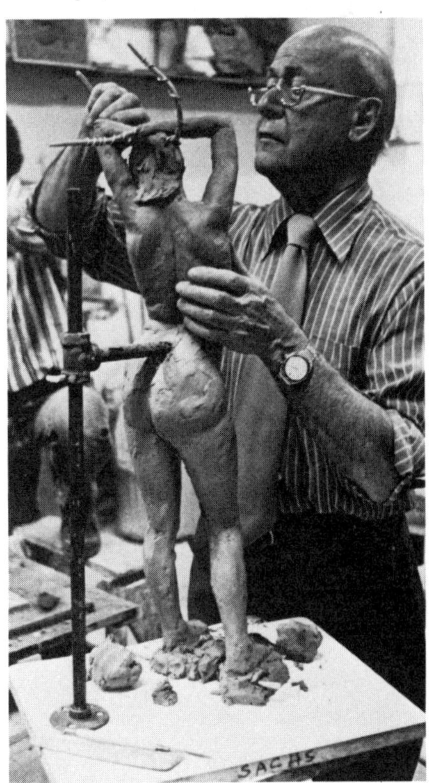

The Creative Corps

What are the things that make life worthwhile? Your first answers are likely to be the obvious: family, good job, good health. But when you probe deeper, what are the things that enrich a life already on an even keel?

For a growing number of Americans, the answer is personal creativity. How can that creativity express itself? In photography; in ceramics; in basketweaving; in painting; in stained glass—in the thousand and one things you can do with your hands and mind to create something that is distinctively your own.

There is no fuller curriculum of these artisan skills anywhere than at the California College of Arts and Crafts. Structured like many other institutions of higher learning, the College offers regular daytime sessions leading to regular degrees. It also offers an incredibly rich extension program structured so that a broad spectrum of the population can avail itself of the riches listed in the catalog.

There is no economical way to list the range of the College's offerings. The concept is so ecumenical that it includes courses in kite-making, in low-budget video technology, in enameling and photo portraiture, in modeling—even in Chinese landscape painting. It might be easier to list the courses not offered by the College, but even that would require such analysis and research that it's not practical.

The College is fully accredited, but is devoted entirely to education in art. The rainbow-like diversity of offerings gives students an opportunity to experience their own areas of interest in relation to many other possibilities, and to change their minds without changing schools.

The major facilities available at the College include: a ceramics center, drawing studios, an environmental design department, a filmmaking department, glass facilities, a graphic design and illustration center (what used to be called commercial art), metal arts and jewelry studios, painting studios, printmaking studios (etching, lithography, relief, screen, and letterpress printing), a sculpture studio (foundry; also wax, plaster, and clay), photography darkrooms, a television studio, three weaving studios, and woodworking studios.

Three summer sessions are offered each year, in addition to the extensive extension program. Chances are if you're interested in any handicraft topic, the College has something to offer you.

Fees are based on units taken ($120 per unit); consequently your involvement can range considerably in total price. A random check through the catalog shows that a great majority of courses in regular session are three units each ($360).

Extension courses may be taken for credit or just for fun, and prices vary—with credit courses costing more in order to accommodate testing, record-keeping, etc. A running check indicates that most extension courses fall into the $100-$140 price range. No prices include travel or accommodations.

The only way to appreciate the College fully is to write for your own packet of information. Go ahead. Do it. —J.A.

California College of Arts and Crafts
5212 Broadway
Oakland, CA 94618

Create, artist! Do not talk!
GOETHE

Basking in Banff

One of the most sophisticated and complete crafts and visual arts programs in the western hemisphere is to be had amid the splendor of the Canadian Rockies at the Banff Centre in Alberta.

The Banff Centre has offerings for all age groups and skill levels, but it serves as a focal point for professionals and artists of the highest calibre. The air at the Centre is heavy with talent and knowledge, and as clean as only mountain air can be.

Now nearly 50 years old, the Centre offers an encyclopedic program; we couldn't begin to list all their subject areas. Among them are lithography, drawing and painting, sculpture, ceramics, plaster and clay, photography, weaving and textiles, papermaking, and clothing design. One of the nicest parts is that the Centre offers other programs for other members of the family (theatre, opera, dance, business management).

And for those of you who are vacationing away from crafts—or who think crafts are for other people—there are always those fast, firm, silvery trout darting around in perfect sylvan streams.

Offerings are concentrated in the summer months for obvious weather reasons. There are some winter offerings for those with snowshoes. Prices are best obtained from the latest catalog, and converted to US dollars at current exchange rates. —J.A.

The Banff Centre School of Fine Arts
Box 1020
Banff, Alberta T0L 0C0
Canada

A Vintage Port

One of the finest and most exclusive gatherings of craftsmen and artists to be found anywhere is sponsored by a nonprofit cultural foundation called Centrum. It's called the Port Townsend Summer Arts Season, and it concentrates on a master painting class and studio arts workshops.

A Centrum-sponsored event is definitely a star-studded occasion. When they schedule a master painting class, for instance, it's really staffed by a master painter. In 1978 it was Elaine de Kooning—one of those rare modern painters whose canvases easily command five-digit prices. De Kooning's work is exhibited at all major museums, and she holds professorships at 16 colleges. Needless to say, the competition to study at Port Townsend is stiff.

The studio arts workshops are similarly high-class. Topics are liable to change from year to year but typically include "Printing Without a Press," "Book Arts," "Calligraphy," "Weaving with Simple Looms," and "Flags and Banners."

If you can get in, you're very promising indeed. —J.A.

Centrum
Fort Worden State Park
Port Townsend, WA 98368

Go East Young Man!

Don't let the name fool you. The University of Northern Colorado is in Florence, Italy.

Sure, UNC's main campus is in Greeley, Colorado. But, forsaking the advice of that city's namesake, Horace Greeley, dozens of UNC students annually pack their bags and head *east* to the school's Florence campus, La Poggerina. With accommodations available for about 70 students per academic quarter, La Poggerina's facilities are also open to non-UNC students including European natives.

Placing its stress on intercultural learning experiences, UNC's slate of courses is studded with such gems as "Workshop in Stained Glass" and "Oil Painting Studio." Other art courses provide opportunities to learn the ancient art of iron-mongering, to discuss philosophies of art with local craftsmen, and to practice intaglio and relief print making—all in the exhilarating Florentine environment. Mastery of Italian is not a prerequisite, and most courses involve extensive use of local facilities such as museums, churches, and historic sites.

Courses are now offered in the spring, summer, and fall quarters, with many instructors drawn from the local community. —R.McG.

University of Northern Colorado
Program in Comparative Arts
Center for Non-Traditional and
Outreach Education
Greeley, CO 80639

He is the greatest artist who has embodied, in the sum of his works, the greatest number of the greatest ideas.
JOHN RUSKIN

Valley of Unaddled Ids

Far from the madding crowd, in the gentle wilds of the North Georgia mountains, in a place called Rabun Gap, lies The Hambidge Center for Creative Arts and Sciences. "The way is beauty" wrote Mary Crovatt Hambidge, philosopher-artist and founder of the Center. We couldn't agree with her more. At the Hambidge Center you will be as much an apprentice to nature as to any of the resident artists, scientists, and writers. In this quiet valley, you may once again discover the creative potential that has lain dormant within you for years. Simply put, it is a place where addled ids can come unaddled.

You'll find the rather traditional curriculum of weaving, spinning, and potterymaking. You can become environmentally aware through courses that aim to help you "develop a basis for a personal universal view." Also offered are courses in the arts—music, painting, poetry apprecia-tion—and an intriguing new category called "Creative Process." These courses promise to usher you into The Age of Creation, an era of intuitive, holistic knowledge. Here the focus will be on "Concepts of Community in the New Age," "Personal Unfoldment as a Creative Being," and "Adventure in Consciousness."

What really sets The Hambidge Center apart from the commonplace multitudes of arts and crafts centers is the physical geography. At Rabun Gap there's a bit of nearly everything nature has to offer, about 600 acres of it: mountains, valleys, fields, streams, waterfalls, forests, and all the flora and fauna you can absorb. "In this little cove," says a Center brochure, "there are areas seldom visited by man . . . The property includes a working farm, grist mill, a flock of sheep (providing wool for spinning and weaving), a 15-room weave shed, a 'Tree House' pottery studio with ten potters' wheels and a gas-fired kiln, a photo lab with two enlargers, painting studio, concert and exhibition space, a central guest house for workshop participants, and several studios of artists and scientists."

If you are 18 or over, you can stay at The Center for $40 overnight, or $225 per week. Breakfasts are cozy do-it-yourself affairs, and meals for both vegetarians and meat-eaters are available. No pets, and smoking only by sufferance. —D.H.

The Hambidge Center
P.O. Box 33
Rabun Gap, GA 30568

Simply Enchanting!

Toss aside summer plans for working or attending your local summer school and spend eight exciting weeks in the "Land of Enchantment" indulging your creative character. The Santa Fe Workshops of Contemporary Art, a nonprofit educational organization dedicated to serving the needs of the "New Generation," sponsors a summer program rich in artistic content.

Offering sessions throughout the year with continuous enrollment and credit possibilities, the Workshops are open to beginning and advanced students alike. Classes are designed to develop individual potential, stressing each artist's personal relationship to the object.

Topics of concentration are painting, photography, drawing, silk screen, sculpture, weaving, and yoga. In all genres, individual vision, outward form and inward feeling, and the production of direct and non-imitative art are prominent themes in the overall teaching approach.

In addition to these workshops, a two-day Living Image Seminar open to all participants aims at freeing the creative flow of images and stimulating individual expression. Topics such as "The Hero Journey" and "Dreams as a Positive Catalyst for the Artist" are explored.

Cost for this inviting summer program, which runs from June 19 through August 13, is $500 or $62.50 a week. —S.S.

Santa Fe Workshops of
Contemporary Art
P.O. Box 1344
Santa Fe, NM 87501

Flying the Snowbird

Picture yourself sitting in an open-air pavilion surrounded by snowcapped mountains listening to Tchaikovsky's "1812 Overture." Or would you rather be *in* the orchestra? Or perhaps out hiking in those mountains? Whatever your artistic desires, the University of Utah Snowbird Summer Arts Institute has it all.

Painting, drawing, weaving, jewelrymaking, photography, sculpture, and music are taught at all levels. Professors and guest artists are available during evening "Conversations with the Artists," complete with slide shows and refreshments. Art exhibitions, nightly concerts, student recitals, and trips into the beautiful Snowbird village are all a part of the Institute experience.

The mountains of Little Cottonwood Canyon provide an awesome environment and a varied subject matter for the student, and short hikes to the surrounding alpine meadows, forests, streams, and mountain peaks are easily made.

Many of the art workshops may be taken for two-, four-, or six-week periods. Courses may be taken for credit or noncredit, and tuition is approximately $70 per course. Scholarships are available. —B.H.

The University of Utah
Snowbird Corporation
Snowbird, UT 84070

Art in Jersey "I studied art in Jersey" may be the mark of excellence in the future, if the Newark Museum has its way. Their course offerings include such wonders as photo silk screen printing, calligraphy, and wire sculpture.

The Newark Museum Arts Workshop
43-49 Washington St.
Newark, NJ 07101

Southern Comfort Callanwolde is a fine arts center with an eye to completeness. In addition to classes in such crafts as stained glass and textiles, they offer literary arts, performing arts, and visual arts to the willing student. In a beautiful Georgia mansion.

Callanwolde
980 Briarcliff Road, NE
Atlanta, GA 30306

Family Affair Midwestern artists and crafters, take note. The Birmingham Bloomfield Art Association offers a catalog of courses that will stun the reader with its completeness: printmaking, sculpture, painting, photography, pottery, jewelry, cloisonne, and much more. Programs for kids as well.

Birmingham Bloomfield
Art Association
1516 S. Cranbrook Rd.
Birmingham, MI 48009

Tarheel Crafters The Blue Ridge Mountains of North Carolina are the perfect setting for the Penland School—six miles from the nearest town: the thriving metropolis of Spruce Pine. Classes are severely limited in number and extremely concentrated. All crafts.

Penland School of Crafts
Penland, NC 28765

The lyf so short,
the craft so long to lerne.
CHAUCER

The Peaceable Kingdom

Dig out your drop spindles, telescopes, and a copy of *The Indian Tipi: Its History, Construction and Use*. Then take a trip to the Peaceable Kingdom, located on 152 acres of land where the Blackland Prairies meet the wooded Post Oak Savannah.

There you will learn about spinning and weaving, astronomy, and tipi construction. You will take courses in Beekeeping, Organic Gardening, Blacksmithing, Medicinal and Edible Native Plants, Primitive Survival Skills, and Pottery.

The Peaceable Kingdom School was created "to provide technical training, facilities, tools and professional reputation" to students interested in learning arts and crafts. Dedicated to a spirit of creative versatility, its bucolic setting provides a quiet and peaceful working atmosphere.

The staff consists of permanent resident craftspeople, whose activities include practicing their art, class instruction, farming, construction, and general maintenance. Guest instructors are often invited to teach special classes such as Poetry, Buttermaking, Horseshoeing, and Wood Sculpture. Students are invited to request special classes.

The Peaceable Kingdom offers Spring and Fall sessions, with classes lasting anywhere from one day to a four-month blacksmith apprentice program. Tuition varies depending on the length of the courses you choose to take. —B.H.

The Peaceable Kingdom Foundation
Washington-on-the Brazos, TX 77880

A Bountiful Harvest

Picture yourself designing a sunburst in stained glass. You look up from your rapt concentration, and pause briefly to appreciate your surroundings. You are in an eighteenth-century farmhouse deep in the Green Mountains of Vermont. As you look outside into the shade of venerable maple trees, you might drift back in time 100, 200—even 300 years.

Perhaps stained glass doesn't just set your blood to racing. If not, Fletcher Farm has other offerings: weaving on the loom and off, needlework, spinning and dyeing, lampshade construction, drawing, pottery, early American decorative arts, woodcarving, silver jewelry design—and rosemaling.

Rosemaling, you know. It's a variety of Norwegian folk art transplanted to this country with the influx of Scandinavian immigrants 150 years back.

Fletcher Farm is absolutely fully equipped in all fields of traditional crafts. In fact, they are so fully equipped and so professionally staffed that most schools will give you credit for your studies at Fletcher Farm (if you make your arrangements in advance, of course).

Sponsored by the Society of Vermont Craftsmen, Fletcher Farm operates year-round, but has an extra-intensive summer program for those part-time crafters. Food is good. Prices vary with the course and time invested, but there are some scholarship dollars available. —J.A.

Fletcher Farm Craft School
Ludlow, VT 05149

Sitting Pretty

Across the living rooms of America, there's a recurrent pipe dream that can now be realized. All you folks who dream of going out in the garage and really *making* something—now's your chance.

The Craft Center in Worcester, Massachusetts, offers programs in furniture design, woodworking, and furniture refinishing. With the instruction offered here, you can take your Aunt Georgina's dining room set, remodel it, refinish it, and move it into your own house. You can design and make a wine rack that fits under the kitchen counter. You can build a real four-poster bed with a soft, hand-rubbed finish.

The furniture design program, employing traditional joinery techniques, encourages the creation of unique pieces of furniture for home use. Other subjects covered are carving, turning, and finishing.

The Craft Center also offers courses in silk screen printing, enameling, stained glass, ceramics, jewelry design, weaving, and photography. All are excellent, but the furniture program is really spiffy.

Tuition is so low it's not worth mentioning—so we won't. Write for their brochure. —J.A.

Craft Center
25 Sagamore Rd.
Worcester, MA 01605

Ranch Style

By the time you reach Snowmass, the hills will be lush green and the sky an exquisite blue. In the late afternoon, an occasional summer shower will make the aspens whisper.

You have come to this rustic ranch on an alpine meadow to learn, from masters, some of the many skills taught every June, July, and August. If ceramics is your thing, Daniel Rhodes (or someone equally expert) will teach you modeling, coil building, and other techniques. For the woodworker, there are classes in laminating, bending, and various facets of furniture making. Guest artists such as Clinton Cline will show you the secrets of intaglio etching, modern and traditional.

For the fiber artist, there is instruction in applique, trapunto, and stitchery. You may discover how to create yarn by spinning, then how to color it with vegetal dyes. With your own yarn you may weave a tapestry on a loom that you have fabricated from branches. And should you wonder what to do with all the things you create, there are sessions on marketing.

The nonprofit Center sits at 8000 feet, just eight miles from Aspen. With its eight rustic, turn-of-the-century log cabins (once part of a working ranch), the Center looks like a set from *Gunsmoke*. —D.H.

Anderson Ranch Arts Center
P.O. Box 2406X
Aspen, CO 81611

Hallowed Highlands

Here's a chance for you and your family to do some real communing: with nature, with each other, and with the creative urges within you. The Haliburton School of Fine Arts offers summer and fall programs for virtually every age bracket.

Programs begin in mid-June and run through approximately the first of October, yielding a full season of family learning and family joys. The beauty of the Ontario Highlands, with its lakes, streams, and hills, combined with the excellent lodge and campsites, offers an opportunity for participants to combine a family fine arts experience with a spectacular nature holiday.

Children's programs concentrate on "macro" views of various arts: music, theatre, pottery, handicrafts. Programs for adults encompass such a variety of topics it is hard to imagine that anyone could feel left out. Courses run the artistic gamut, from fabric painting to photography, from theatre performance to stained glass, from fresco painting to stitchery.

Fees vary widely for classes, depending on materials used and facilities needed. A course in earthenware runs $100; a course in children's theatre costs $15. —J.A.

Haliburton School of Fine Arts
P.O. Box 339
Haliburton, Ontario K0M 1S0
Canada

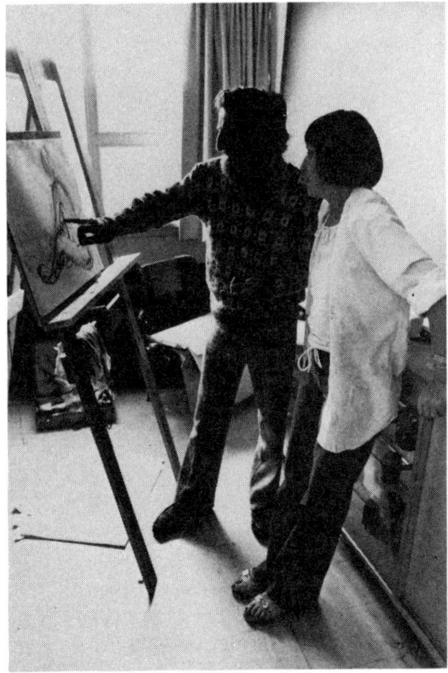

Proud Beginnings Located in the Appalachians of the Ohio River Valley, the Cedar Lakes Crafts Center offers an attractive setting for its intensive five-day workshops in arts and crafts. The area is one where crafts have flourished through generations spanning hundreds of years.

The Crafts Center
Cedar Lakes
Ripley, WV 25271

Superior on Superior Make a splash in art this summer at the Grand Marais Art Colony on the shores of beautiful Lake Superior. Study painting, drawing, sculpture, or ceramics in the spacious Colony studio—a former church. Programs are all formulated and conducted under the auspices of the Minneapolis College of Art and Design.

Grand Marais Art Colony
Minneapolis College of Art and Design
200 East 25th St.
Minneapolis, MN 55404

Decathlon of Arts Study art and take the kids along to Lake Placid in upstate New York. The Lake Placid School of Art offers summer workshops in photography, watercolor, ceramics, jewelry, and dance—with young people's programs to match. And that gorgeous ex-Olympic setting is frosting on the cake.

Lake Placid School of Art
Saranac Ave.
Lake Placid, NY 12946

Lenses & Light

Thru the Lens

Get out your Nikon, your Leica, your Canon. Haul out your Brownie, your Instamatic, your SX-70. Whatever you use to snap those pix, dust it off and pack a bag.

Thru the Lens Tours may be something the world has been waiting for—at least it seems that way to us. Tourists throughout time have yearned for ways to preserve their fleeting visits to monuments of grandeur. To that end, it seemed, the entire traveling population of the eighteenth and nineteenth centuries carried sketch pads and charcoals. Landscape painters were forever being commissioned to record the splendors of the Alps, or of the Rhine castles, or the brilliant autumns of the Vienna Woods.

Then along came the camera, and suddenly the touring world was snapping fuzzy pictures instead of sketching. New homemade compositions were everywhere combining such unlikely items as the Chateau of Versailles and Uncle Henry's thumb, or Mavis and the baby waving hello from Hadrian's Tomb.

That was fine for a time, but soon the enchantment wore off and people began to yearn for better mementos than off-kilter snapshots. What did they do? They bought better cameras, better film, better prints, tripods, etc., etc. The product? Much finer pictures of Versailles and Uncle Henry's thumb.

And now—we think we have the answer. Thru the Lens Photographic Adventures will see to it that you arrive home with really memorable photographs of where you went. And "where you went" may be just about anywhere. The latest brochure lists tours to Turkey, Greece, Portugal, Norway, the Western Pacific, Chile, Guatemala, Ancient Kashmir, Iceland, Switzerland, the Rocky Mountains, and the Himalayas—to name a few.

The itineraries range from one- and two-week domestic trips to longer tours in Latin America, Europe, Africa, Asia, the South Pacific, and the Orient, and all are designed to provide maximum opportunities for good photographic results.

Escorts and instructors are expert photographers, and a program of professional instruction and advice is offered to all participants. The goal of this program is to simplify the mechanics of photography and heighten the creativity of the individual.

Groups are small to allow individual attention and freedom of movement. Travel is at a leisurely pace to permit time for picture stops and appreciation of local cultures. Care is taken to be in the right place at the right time for best lighting, and special events such as native dances and local costume displays are prearranged.

Prices vary with destinations and length of trips, but the tours offer you APEX fares when available, which shows that their heart is in the right place.

If you want a packet of information, write to them. All their brochures are illustrated with photographs taken by nonprofessionals on their own tours—so you'll get an idea of what you may take home. Happy shuttering! —J.A.

Thru the Lens Tours, Inc.
P.O. Box 4516
12501 Chandler Blvd.
North Hollywood, CA 91607

Picture Yourself...

If nothing exciting has developed lately, get out of the dark(room) and take a hike. That is, with a famous photographer. The University of California Extension, Santa Cruz, has numerous Spring and Summer Photography Workshops that should make your shutter click!

Photograph life in the deserts and mountains of Baja California. Hike along the Eel and Mattole Rivers through the heart of the Redwoods. Trek through the Mojave's "Lonesome Triangle." Canoe through 73 miles of wilderness lakes in the spectacular back country of Canada's Cariboo Mountains! These are just a few of the workshops available.

All the while you will be accompanied by an expert photographer. Depending on the trip, attention will be focused on exposure techniques, composition, use of natural light, visual perception, use of filters and special lenses, or development and printing techniques.

For the less adventurous, various courses are also offered at the university. But for the rest of you, get your hiking boots out. Be prepared to provide your own camera and film, and to make you own food, lodging, and transportation arrangements. Costs vary depending on the length of the workshop. —B.H.

University of California
Photography Workshops
University of California Extension
Santa Cruz, CA 95064

Nature Photography Up Close

As you pack your bags for this one, write a note for the babysitter explaining that you're "going up to Whispering Pine Lodge at Pickerel Lake for some time with John and Kitty Kahout." Plan to come back satiated with scenery, clean air, good food—and a whopping good dose of photographic technique.

There are three basic six-day courses, and between them they cover a surprisingly large area. First there's the Scenic Course, designed to sharpen your skill in capturing the beauty and splendor of outdoor scenes. The course covers composition, camera technique, lighting, etc.

The Close-Up Course will enable you to explore and enjoy the enchanted world of close-up photography in the wilds. Capture that dewdrop on that dogwood petal!

The Creative Course helps you improve slides already taken—with cropping, retouching, blocking light areas, work with Kalvar, 3M colors, and Diazochrome among the topics covered.

Sound complete? It is. And reasonable as well, with the six-day package, including everything, at $230 per person. —J.A.

John Kahout's School of Photography
318 N. Catherine Ave.
La Grange Park, IL 60525

Beyond the Image Apeiron is a place where the meaning of visual images, their emotional and intellectual effect, is of central importance. You may study photography here, but it will always be placed within the larger context of art and art history. A fascinating approach offers unlimited horizons.

Apeiron Photographic Workshops
Silver Mountain Rd.
Millerton, NY 12546

Trip the Lightworks Lightworks started out in a chicken coop near Chicago, but it never was for the birds. Now at home in Minneapolis, Lightworks offers intense one-week sessions on photography, generously dosed with close student-teacher interaction.

Lightworks
25 University Ave., SE
Minneapolis, MN 55414

History in the Making Study the history of photography while you're creating its present, at the Photographers Place. Courses in nineteenth-century photography, the period of 1900-1940, and postwar pix. Improve your technique with a group of pros whose names you'd recognize in a minute.

The Photographers Place
Bradbourne, Ashbourne, Derbyshire
England, UK

Camera Treks One of the most enchanting—and challenging—photographic programs anywhere is under the aegis of Tod Papageorge. Go to the cradle of Western civilization, Greece, with this son of the Aegean.

Panopticon Summer Workshop
187 Bay State Rd.
Boston, Mass. 02215

Au Naturel Nature photography is a field as rewarding as it is specialized. Ever wonder just how people shoot the beads of dew on a rose? The quizzical looks on racoons' faces as they wash their hands? You can study wildlife and nature photography with Larry West and John Shaw, in locations from Central America to Northern Canada.

Nature Photography Workshops
1090 Crestview
Harrison, MI 48625

It is, in fact, hard to get the camera to tell the truth; yet it can be made to, in many ways and at many levels.
JAMES AGEE

The Baron of Black and White

One of the most specialized seminars we've encountered is also one of the most fascinating—and most darkly romantic. Ron Rosenstock's brochure on Photographic Workshops in Ireland is right out-front: "This workshop is for those seriously interested in the art of black-and-white photography and in the culture and geography of Ireland."

Sounds quite limiting, doesn't it? Perhaps—until you consider that Ireland has the reputation for some of the most majestic seascapes in the world. It also has more unspoiled stately homes than England—and feudal castles that would chill the marrow of any invader.

Rosenstock's workshops are held at Summerville, a 16-room stone house overlooking Clew Bay in County Mayo (a fireplace in each bedroom for coziness). Mr. Rosenstock also teaches photography at the Worcester Craft Center (Worcester, Massachusetts), and has taught his subject for over ten years. He is widely published and has quite an illustrious background, indeed.

Suddenly, black-and-white images of Ireland seem a full universe of opportunity. —J.A.

Ron Rosenstock
91 Sunnyside Ave.
Holden, MA 01520

Wilderness Wonders

The Place: T Cross Ranch, pardner, situated between Yellowstone and Grand Teton National Parks. Not too shabby. Local wildlife includes bighorn sheep, mountain lions, moose, elk, eagles, coyotes—need we continue?

The Program: Small workshops with Boyd Norton, whose vision of the Rockies has been published by the Sierra Club, Viking Press, Rand McNally, and others. You may even have his work on your coffee table this minute. Before he took up photography, by the way, he was a nuclear physicist. But as anyone in the know can tell you, there are a lot fewer photographers fit for *National Geographic* than there are nuclear physicists in the world. So Boyd went for the noble. When you see his turf, you'll know why.

Equipment: Bring your own cameras and equipment. Bring your own film. Bring backpacking gear, sleeping bag, snake rope, whatever. Food is provided. Since workshops are timed to coincide with spring wildflowers and fall foliage, weather may be nippy—a word to the wise.

Total cost is $485 plus your transportation. Seminars are limited to 20 persons each—and they fill up rapidly. Check the current schedule for times, and be sure to check the recommended equipment list to see that your camera is up to par. Then reach out for immortality. —J.A.

University of the Wilderness
29952 Dorothy Rd.
Evergreen, CO 80439

Each day, as I look, I wonder where my eyes were yesterday.
BERNARD BERENSON

Mainly Photography

All I can think of since I read the Maine Photographic Workshops brochure is going to Rockport, Maine, this summer.

It seems like a true mecca for photographers—a place where genuinely serious students of the craft can hone their creative skills. And if you long for a sense of community with students of like interests, the Maine Workshops just might be what you're looking for. There's likely no better place to find an accomplished mentor and a circle of interesting fellow students.

MPW talks about improving "each photographer's visual voice," about island photo expeditions around Penobscot Bay, about classes limited to six, ten or fifteen, and about workshops with the top black-and-white, color, and cinema photographers in the country.

They offer a 5½-day "Crash Course" each week from June through September; a Basic Photography class for those able to spend two weeks; and many workshops such as Half-Tone Dot Printing, Audio-Visual Presentations, Filmmaking, Color Perception, Dye Transfer Color Printing, and on and on.

Write them for a copy of their catalog. If the photographs alone don't turn you on to a working vacation in Rockport, you ought to turn in your Pentax. —D.P.

The Maine Photographic Workshop
Rockport, ME 04856

Island Images

If the gracious life and the welcoming manner of the legendary South survive at all in these harried, hurried times, it is in the coastal islands of Georgia. Those same coastal islands that are the timeless home to the likes of Porgy and his woman, Bess.

In these unique photographic workshops, you'll be studying with Bill Weems, who is a special photographer for *National Geographic*, and a nature photographer of much repute. You'll be guided by Jean Milmine, who is an experienced birder and naturalist.

So get ready to catch those skeeters on that honeysuckle. You'll see brother alligator lazing down a slow-moving bayou. You'll visit heron and egret rookeries. And you will see beaches like you never knew existed in such white, trackless perfection.

And one night, with a modicum of catfish luck, you'll creep up amid the noise of the waves to the ageless ritual of the great loggerhead seaturtle, dropping her eggs into the scooped-out sand. And as she lumbers back into the surf and the deep, you will realize two things: she is at one with eternity, and you, by gum, you've got the best damned photograph of your ever-lovin' life!

Trip size is limited to 15, and leaves from near Savannah. Cost for the one-week program is under $300, but you must provide your own cameras and your own insect repellant—swat! —J.A.

Wilderness Southeast
Rte. 3, Box 619
Savannah, GA 31406

Canyon Portraits

A scenic drive to Cedar Breaks, Utah, to witness a showcase of rainbow-colored cliffs marks the beginning of a photographer's ten-day dream. The Canyonlands Nature Photography Expedition offers 20 serious students special opportunities to shoot spectacular canyonlands in the American Southwest.

Accompanied by a professional photographer and author, students explore Bryce Canyon junipers, and lavender sediments reminiscent of those inspiring the imaginative lenses of Ansel Adams and Edward Weston. Schedules of activities at all sites depend on weather, lighting, fall color, and group interests. Individual discussion and critique with instructors, analysis of photographic composition, evening slide presentations, and breathtaking hikes enhance the daily photographic sessions.

Mornings are ideal for shooting the yellow interwoven canyons of Zion Park; evenings offer the opportunity to capture Capitol Reef's fertile river canyons and desolate plateaus. Accommodations in deluxe tent camps offer sufficient time to roam alone and shoot moist pines after rainfall.

Participants must be familiar with photography fundamentals, but are free to work with 35mm to large cameras, in black and white or color. Cost is about $600 without transportation to Cedar Breaks. The late September dates promise fall hues and hints of winter, so plan to give yourself an early Christmas present. —S.S.

Nature Expeditions International
599 College Ave.
Palo Alto, CA 94306

Art comes to you proposing frankly to give nothing but the highest quality to your moments as they pass.
WALTER PATER

The Arts

Civilization. We live in it; we study it; we create it incessantly. But civilizations other than our own—other than the today, the here, the now—that's another problem. We only know them from their testimony: their writings, their art, their dances, their music—all passed down among generations or across miles.

This chapter is devoted to an exploration of civilizations and their testimony. In particular, it is devoted to an appreciation of that testimony we call "Art."

What are the arts? Dance is a foot-stomping, hand-clapping, high-leaping celebration of the body. Music is the language of the soul, with the wisdom to know that words don't matter. Theater is a forum for exploring the complexity of human emotion. Art and architecture are living reminders of the past, of the pinnacles of human experience.

What is it that takes the breath away in great art? It is the artist's ability to speak directly to generations of people he never knew on subjects of universal interest. It is the communion with strangers long dead, as you view their artifacts or listen to their music. It is the perfection of the artist's palette or technique; it is the soaring height of the dancer's leap; it is the warmth of the cold white marble carved to become Michelangelo's Pieta.

Explore these and other facets of art with us. Know that our adventures in the arts are in six categories: dance, music, writing and literature, drama, film, and art and architectural history.

And as you wander with us, remember that the essence of art appreciation is the experience of ravishment at the hands of the artist. Even the most tired blood should stir at the sight of the Pyramids at dawn. Even the most cynical eye should dew over as the pitiful old King Lear breathes his last on the heaths of stages worldwide.

So click those castanets! Tune that fiddle! Gaze at paintings commissioned by popes and kings. Go to the Parthenon at night and breathe the air of centuries of art and human accomplishment.

We have a flying carpet here the likes of which Sinbad only hoped for. Through the programs in the chapter, you can soar across centuries and cultures. You can taste greatness, and share the longings for immortality that unite people of all ages and all places.

Give wings to *your* soul. It's the finest thing you could possibly do for yourself.

Media assemblage by Tom Gould

Kick Up Your Heels

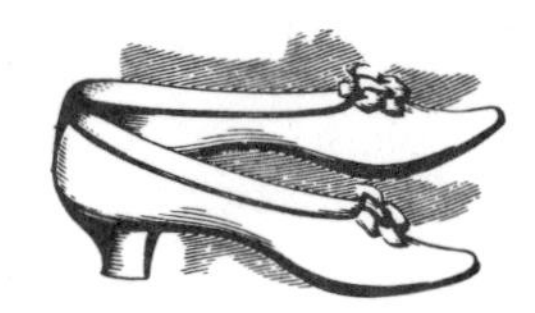

Summertime, and the Dancing Is Easy

Some things *sound* so good in and of themselves that you know they've *got* to be, and The Country Dance and Song Society has just that kind of ring to it—one that tells you pleasing times flow from its soul.

The Society, which dates back to 1915, refers to itself simply as an association of people dedicated to the enjoyment, preservation, and study of English and American traditional dance, music, and song. Pinewoods Camp, near Plymouth, Massachusetts, is the Society's summer retreat, where six weeks of activities are offered in a remarkably soothing setting for the harried and near-harried among us.

Two "Dance Weeks"—a feature of the camp for almost 40 years—offer modern renderings of country, contra, and square dancing, as well as morris and sword dancing. Classes are rich in information, as leaders and teachers vary in backgrounds from university professors to guitar pickers, from Juilliard School graduates to Appalachian storytellers. Morning dance presentations set the tone for each day, and evening wingdings allow students to practice what they've learned in open-air pavilions surrounded by pines. The rhythms of the musicians who accompany each session will surely carry along the newest toe-tapper and hand-clapper in the crowd.

"Chamber Music Week" is for amateur musicians interested in exploring early music. Classes are given in wind and string instruments, Renaissance and Baroque dancing, and voice. "Folk Music Week" emphasizes British and American folk instruments and songs, ranging from ballads to sea chanties to traditional regional styles of music. This is certainly for anyone who misses an old coffeehouse folk scene and wants a bit more than nostalgia.

The Society makes it possible for adult music and dance enthusiasts to introduce their children to the Anglo-American tradition in a "Family Week" experience. Teachers here are skilled at working with young dancers and singers, and the fine old art of story-telling is practiced nightly for all ages.

A regular membership in the Society costs $10. A week at the Pinewoods Camp ranges from $155 (Family Week) to $185 (Chamber Music Week), with reduced rates for children. Pinewoods also runs a handy sales room specializing in books and records on folk music and dance, so that campers can continue their exploration of the work they begin at the camp.

Traveler's checks, restaurant line-ups, or rushing to a show? Forget it! The "feel" you get from the Country Dance and Song Society of America is a happy one. You'd expect that from a group of people whose chief purpose is to get together to sing and dance. —R.J. & C.McB.

Pinewoods Camp
Country Dance & Song Society
55 Christopher St.
New York, NY 10014

For the good are always the merry,
Save by an evil chance,
And the merry love the fiddle,
And the merry love to dance.
WILLIAM BUTLER YEATS

Disco Kid

Another Saturday night at the disco. And what excuse can you tell your friends this time—that you cut your legs while shaving and it's too painful to walk, let alone dance? Sooner or later the naked truth will be discovered—that you don't know how to dance. Make it easy on yourself. If your feet say no and your hips lock in place when the music starts, then let Jo Jo's Dance Factory fire up your dance routine and condition your inactive body.

Classes are taught at all levels in jazz ($4.50 per lesson, $40 for a card of ten), ballet ($4 per lesson, $35 for a card of ten), hustle ($7.50 for a single class, $30 for five classes, $50 for five classes for couples), and latin percussion ($65 for the four-week course).

Jazz man and artistic director Jo Jo Smith was the dance consultant for *Saturday Night Fever,* and all the

dancers who performed in the film were selected from the Factory. (At Jo Jo's, one never knows when fame and fortune will strike.) Smith's credits also include the Broadway hit *West Side Story,* in which he had a role as a dancer, singer, and actor. He choreographed the off-Broadway hit *Your Own Thing* and the Fifth Dimension's act for their Caesar's Palace engagement.

So tap your feet and snap your fingers—you gotta start somewhere. —S.C.

Jo Jo's Dance Factory
1733 Broadway at 55th
New York, NY 10019

Fiddle-dee-dee

If you're ready to experience a change of pace from the disco routine, a week-long class in traditional dance in Appalachia could prove a most attractive alternative. The Augusta Heritage Arts Workshop is a community-sponsored arts project in Elkins, West Virginia, that promises to give its participants a revived sense of cultural pride in the mountain heritage of Appalachia.

On the workshop's agenda is instruction in such diverse traditional dance offerings as flatfooting, Appalachian clogging, morris and contra dancing, and calling for community dances. Professional musicians provide lively traditional music for all dance sessions, incorporating fiddles and dulcimers into the performance of old-time mountain tunes.

Prices for the workshops vary, depending on whether or not you're a West Virginia resident. Costs range from $60 for folk dancing to $370 for musical instrument construction. The workshops are set to run for a month, beginning in early July.

The communal atmosphere of the classes, the clapping and footsteps that fill the air—these are the moments and memories that participants share at the Augusta Heritage Arts Workshop. —S.S.

Folk & Traditional Dance Classes
Augusta Heritage Arts Workshop
P.O. Box 1725
Elkins, WV 26241

Dancing on a Pillow

There are very few dance institutions that are not "all one way or the other." If they're into ballet, then they shun modern. If they're modernists, they find ballet irrelevant. Not so at Jacob's Pillow.

First off, the school at Jacob's Pillow was founded by Ted Shawn. To dance enthusiasts, the name means ecumenism among the branches of dance. And following Shawn's precepts, the focus at the Pillow is on *all* forms of dance: ballet, modern, ethnic, tap, jazz—and a bit of mime.

The faculty is illustrious, and together they represent the experience of several major companies (the Joffrey, Ballet Russe, Netherlands Dance Theater, Alvin Ailey, and others). Jacob's Pillow is in its 47th year in the Berkshires. It is situated in the midst of 100 wooded acres, with many of its buildings dating back 300 years.

Nearby, newcomers to the Berkshires have gathered: the Tanglewood Festival, the Berkshire Theater Festival, and the Williamstown Theater Festival. With Jacob's Pillow, they comprise one of the richest cultural experiences available in summertime USA.

Schedules run from the end of June to the beginning of September. —J.A.

Summer School
Jacob's Pillow Dance Festival, Inc.
Box 287
Lee, MA 02138

Come a Courting In an atmosphere of lute and ensemble music, you can easily allow yourself to be carried away to another era. The Early Music Workshop provides expert instruction in Renaissance court dances of England, France, and Italy. You can dance in the first week in August for five days. Cost is $90 for five days, and room and board is available nearby.

Early Music Workshop
Creative Arts Center
West Virginia University
Morgantown, WV 26506

Dance, If the Spirit Moves You
In the beginning, Man danced his praise to the gods. Today, we still think of dance in a spiritual sense. Loyola Marymount University holds a course on liturgical dance in which you can learn the theory of this form and regularly participate in the dance activity. Interested? Cost is $100 for 14 weeks. Write them for the details.

A Course in Liturgical Dance
Division of Continuing Education
Loyola Marymount University
Loyola Blvd. at West 80th St.
Los Angeles, CA 90045

To Russia with Love—er—NYU Treat yourself to the glamorous experience of the Russian ballet—in Moscow or in Leningrad—on an NYU study tour. Perhaps you have always dreamed of attending live performances of the Bolshoi and Kirov. Now you can visit the foremost ballet schools and meet in discussions with leading cultural and dance figures. Travel costs and tuition for eight days: $795. Write for dates.

The Ballet World in Russia
World Campus Program
New York University
Division of Liberal Studies
2 University Place
New York, NY 10003

Going Through the Motions
Have you ever felt like dancing the exotic temple dances of South India? Or, perhaps you'd like to try your nimble toes at period dances of the 17th century. Or do you simply feel like being stately in a minuet? No matter what kind of dance tickles your fancy, the Valley Studio is the place to receive instruction. Dance in the midst of tree-covered hills and rock-studded ridges.

Dance/Movement Classes
The Valley Studio
Route 3
Spring Green, WI 53588

Serb Yourself

If you want the benefits of a Balkan dance experience without putting in years of study, you can sign up for a Yugoslavian Folk Dance Festival Tour. All you need to be is a folk.

The Slavic-American Society sponsors the Yugoslavian Folklore Institute in the resort town of Arandjelovac, some 50 miles south of Belgrade. There, each summer, an intensive two-week program of Balkan dance is held. The dance classes, taught by the area's experts, are said to be so good that many of the graduates are now teaching Balkan dance in their own homelands.

The Institute combines dancing with a pleasant immersion in local cuisine, customs, and culture. There are optional trips to monuments, evening dance parties, concerts with local residents, and visits to nearby kafanas (coffee bars) and villages.

If you are a true folklore buff, you can plan your tour of Yugoslavia to coincide with an eight-day visit to the Zagreb Folklore Festival, billed as the most spectacular festival of genuine folklore in Europe. The festival includes displays of folk art and over 150 public dance performances within a single week. Accommodations for folk dance students are in the old summer home of a Serbian prince.

Tax-deductible membership in the Society is $15 annually. The cost for the Folklore Institute is $400, the tour of Yugoslavia $620, and the Zagreb Festival $230. Air fare is not included. —R.J. & C.McB.

Yugoslavia Folk Dance Festival Tours
Slavic-American Society
3661 Grand Ave.
Suite 202
Oakland, CA 94610

Be Square

Arrive Sunday afternoon at the trout farm, dance that night in square dance attire, and mingle with square dance zealots from different parts of the country. On hardwood floors, you'll surely dos-a-dos the week away. You'll get to know your callers, too, at a midnight whirlpool session or a rubber raft afternoon in the Chattooga. If it's square dancing you want, plus a week of supplementary fun, Andy's Square Dance Inn and Trout Farms provides it all for you.

Eighty participants gather in April, August, and November for the New Dancers, Basic Caller, and Advanced Caller programs. Activities in these workshops are geared to the beginner who needs personalized training. You'll learn to "allemande left," "courtesy turn," "wheel and deal," and "swat the flea." Each program includes instruction in rounds and squares and offers nightly film features and optional nature hikes, guided by hosts Jerry and Becky Cope. The last-evening party is known as "San Juan Carnival Time." Dancers dress in costumes with a Spanish flair and dine on authentic San Juan recipes.

Dancers choose accommodations from inn rooms with televisions to cottages overlooking Trout Lake to campsites alongside the road. Chef Harry, Becky's dad, is there to see you are well taken care of, with homemade rolls and special family recipes for good, southern cooking. Cool mountain temperatures and fresh Georgian air promise to rejuvenate all evening strollers. Prices range from $55 to $140 per person for a full program. —S.S.

Andy's Square Dance Inn
& Trout Farms
P.O. Box 129
Dillard, GA 30537

By Leaps & Bounds

Dance is the primary performing art. It is the granddaddy of all the others: theater, music, pantomime. Dance is the embodiment of the rhythm of life.

The American Dance Festival, in residence at Duke University, is a gathering of dance eagles unmatched at any other American location. The faculty and participants read like a who's who of American dance: Martha Graham, Bella Lewitzky, Twyla Tharp, Alvin Ailey, Eliot Feld, Erick Hawkins, Merce Cunningham. The courses of study embrace all major forms: modern dance, ballet, jazz technique, ethnic dance.

And the magic begins with the very young and the inexperienced. Although the festival prefers its participants to have had some previous training, it will tutor dancers of virtually all levels of expertise. There is simply no other source of dance instruction to equal it in these United States. The Festival provides a "huge palette to give students and public what they won't get the rest of the year," according to *The New York Times*.

While participating in the Festival, you'll immerse yourself in movement, form, composition, technique, and—above all—rhythm to an astounding extent. You'll take classes in improvisation, repertory, and kinesiology. You'll be exposed to injury problems of dancers, therapeutic massage, and anatomy. You'll be able to enroll in ethnic dance classes to learn the African styles of Katherine Dunham and the Indian Bharata Natyam of Balasaraswati.

For six weeks, the East campus of Duke will become a scene of rejoicing in movement. It will release such energy and grace that Durham, North Carolina, will seem like the Moscow of Diaghilev. There will be performances by the Eliot Feld Ballet, the North Carolina Dance Theater, the Twyla Tharp Dance Foundation, Pilobolus, and the Paul Taylor Dance Company—to name just a few.

Whether you are there to dance or just to admire, you'll begin to understand the almost monastic devotion which young dancers give to their art. You'll appreciate the sweat and the years of stretching that enable a fleet of feet to soar.

Concurrent with the Festival, the Loblolly Summer Arts Program will be conducting workshops, classes, and performances in music, opera, and theater. There are also several regularly scheduled film series on campus. Over the Fourth of July weekend, a major Folk Festival will be staged at Eno River Park, featuring bluegrass music, clogging, storytelling, crafts, and traditional foods.

And that's about as fine as you can get—anywhere. —J.A.

American Dance Festival
1860 Broadway
New York, NY 10023

Feet, Do Your Stuff

Do you feel like an Isadora Duncan, but are trapped within the body of an ordinary mortal? Do the words *en pointe, arabesque*, ball change, and the swing mean nothing to you? Then the New School's Choreographer's Theatre (CT) is the program for you. CT will take the Alvin Ailey rejects and Martha Graham hopefuls, without protest. Its magic words are "open to all." One need not be a prima ballerina in order to enroll. CT is, quite simply, a good place to begin.

The CT faculty is no batch of ingenues, however. They are drawn from both CT members and the Laura Foreman Dance Theater, the first professional modern dance company to be made Artists-in-Residence at a New York university.

A wide range of movement is offered—from the rigors of classical ballet training to the upbeat, uptempo jazz dance found in Broadway shows. The spectrum of dance at the New School extends to dance therapy, pantomime, and workshops in improvisation and sensory awareness. Classes run about $115. —S.C.

Choreographers Theater
Dance Dept.
The New School
66 West 12th St.
New York, NY 10011

Will you, won't you, will you, won't you, will you join the dance?
LEWIS CARROLL

Dancing on High Points

Ever wanted to dance on a mountain top? You've probably never given it any thought before. But now that that lovely image has flashed through your mind, perhaps we can get you to step right in and kick up your heels to a Rocky Mountain sky.

The way to do it is through a program called, naturally enough, Dance in the Mountains, which springs to life each summer in the tiny Colorado town of Crested Butte. With the Rockies supplying a backdrop that no set-maker could hope to match, students learn ballet, modern dance, and mime in one of two 30 × 40 foot outdoor studios used as classrooms.

The three-week course is staffed by visiting professionals with varying backgrounds in the world of dance. The program caters to applicants from the age of 12 on up but prefers those who have had the equivalent of three years' previous dance experience. Students can take up to four different classes each day, and the session culminates with a full school performance in conjunction with Crested Butte's Arts and Crafts Fair.

Dancing is conducted on a Monday-to-Friday basis, with weekends free for local exploration. Costs for the program range from $275 to $600, depending upon room, board, and class arrangements. Crested Butte, which lies about 125 miles southwest of Denver, also offers a full range of outdoor sports, from hiking to tennis, to help fill the student's leisure hours. —C.McB.

Dance in the Mountains
Dancer's Workshop
P.O. Box 173
Crested Butte, CO 81224

Just Plain Folk

Eat, drink, dance (not to mention sing, play instruments, and learn crafts), and be merry ought to be the motto of the Stockton Folk Dance Camp.

Six full days of study-fun for both beginners and advanced dancers is offered this summer. In addition to the six hours of classes (covering such topics as folk dance, lore, rhythm, and motion), there are daily free swims, ethnic song sessions, castanet lessons, nightly "all-request" parties, and a final talent night and costume show. Whew!

The camp offers an amazingly varied international staff of native dancers. Some of the dances represented include Russian, Scottish, German, Turkish, Mexican, and American square, to name just a few.

There are two Folk Dance Camp sessions: mid to late July, and the end of July to early August. Cost is $190 per person for room, board, tuition, and fees ($110 will cover just the latter two). A deposit will hold a place for those energetic enough to tackle this dance experience. —P.C.

Stockton Folk Dance Camp
University of the Pacific
Stockton, CA 95211

Polynesian Pitter-Patter

Dance some *sa-sa* (group precision dances) and several *mauluulu* (action dances performed to songs) in Samoa. Take the opportunity to learn the basics in the men's slap and knife dances. Try your hand at the *soke* and stick dance in Tonga, and attempt the men's and women's seated dances in Fiji. The *otea*, *tamure*, and *tapa* dances will be a breeze by the time you reach Tahiti.

GoodTravel Tours has assembled a South Pacific encounter trip that is not for every dancer or traveler. If "Club Med-type" comfort is what you have in mind, GoodTravel will openly discourage you. Here you can live in thatched huts and sup with the peoples of the Pacific. Or, if you prefer a slightly more pampered vacation, you can stay in a nearby hotel. In either case, you will learn Polynesian dances and experience their music. Here you will make friends, not merely visit.

The World of South Pacific Music & Dance—a 24-day learning vacation—will be brought to you in living cultural color. And above all, you will leave with the memory of dances, some of which have never been seen in the United States.

Trips run in June, July, August, and October, and the cost is $1348 for land and $848 for air fare. A color and sound film will be made of all dances, and is available, at cost, to participants. Sightseeing is also included. —S.C.

The World of
South Pacific Music & Dance
GoodTravel Tours
5332 College Ave.
Oakland, CA 94618

The Joy of Movement

The Joy of Movement Center is one of New England's leading centers for instruction in dance and movement. It is dedicated to the principle that such activities can and should be enjoyed by everyone, not just by professionals.

The combinations of subject matter available at the Center make bizarre juxtapositions. You could, for instance, take a triad of courses like ballet (Department of Traditional and Contemporary Dance), weight control (Department of Movement and Exercise), and tai chi (Department of Martial Arts). Odd combinations, but logical. They all have to do with a healthy, fit body in motion.

There are also offerings in other areas of movement: ethnic dance, creative dance, massage training, mime. And in a delightfully eccentric departure from the dance norm, the Joy of Movement Center offers drawing courses that concentrate on the body in motion.

For the person who is not inclined toward the classical technique, nor toward ethnic traditions, nor toward modern dance in its stagey embodiment, the Center also offers disco dancing. So if you've always wanted to tango or rhumba or mambo, you won't be disappointed. All classes cost $40. —J.A.

Dance & Movement Classes
The Joy of Movement Center
536 Massachusetts Ave.
Cambridge MA 02139

Dance by the Light of the Moon If square dancing is your hobby, why not make it into a complete vacation? Kirkwood Lodge offers six full nights of square- and round-dance fun on maple hardwood floors. Workshops are held from June to October by a "staff" of callers from Abilene, Texas, to Birmingham, Alabama, and Muscatine, Iowa. Golf, water skiing, fishing, and swimming facilities are located on the premises. Prices depend upon the type of accommodation you choose. So allemande left!

Attn: Square Dance Vacation Manager
Kirkwood Lodge
Lake Road 54-24
Osage Beach, MO 65065

Get Your Mixed Pickles! *Mixed Pickles* is not a specialty item you might find on a gourmet-lover's shelf, but is rather a magazine put out by folk dance folks. It is the best source of information on clubs, trips, and special folk dance events in these United States. Those whose interests range from belly dancing and Yugoslavian festivals to neighborhood folk dance cafes should have this periodical on their rack. Yearly subscriptions are $5.

Mixed Pickles
Attn: Raymond La Barbera, Editor
P.O. Box 500
Midwood Station
Brooklyn, NY 11230

Pace Yourself Beginning dancers need a relaxed, supportive atmosphere in which to learn. More advanced devotees need opportunities to perform and choreograph compositions. Sun Valley Dance Center offers instruction to adults at both the beginner and advanced levels. Ballet, modern, and jazz dance is supplemented by courses in body maintenance, tai chi chuan, and choreography. Single classes for three weeks are $75; for six weeks the price is $100. Write for dates.

Summer Dance Workshop
Sun Valley Center
Box 656
Sun Valley, ID 38853

And hand in hand, on the edge of the sand, they danced by the light of the moon.
EDWARD LEAR

Prick Up Your Ears

A Fest That's No Jest

The Spoleto Festival has a major drawback: there's too much to do and you can't take it all in. For the historic city of Charleston, South Carolina, becomes a treasure trove of the performing arts for three very full weeks in late May and June.

The driving force behind the two Spoleto Festivals (there's also one in—surprise—Spoleto, Italy) is Gian Carlo Menotti, one of today's most illustrious Italian operawrights. Menotti is a man of enormous talent and energy, and it's nearly impossible to keep up with him and his festival. One feels like a child in Willy Wonka's chocolate factory: there's so much candy you can't decide which to eat.

How is it possible, for instance, for attendees to choose between concurrent performances of *La Traviata*, a pair of Menotti one-acts (*Martin's Lie, The Egg*), and a performance of Luchino Visconti's film, *L'Innocente*? It's not a choice that a person ought to have to make. It's like being told you can have any *one* fur coat from Neiman-Marcus—it's just not bearable.

In the first place, you have to get by the historic splendor of Charleston itself. It remains the most beautiful of all Southern cities—and one of the most redolent of historic confrontations. Fort Sumter still guards the harbor like a Civil War ghost. The grace and charm of antebellum homes still dominate the Old Quarter. And the artistic population is astonishing in its proportions.

It just ain't fittin'. Even if you can map your way through each day, you're bound to be exhausted before you get through. Imagine seeing the Dance Theater of Harlem before lunch, a country music jamboree when you should be napping, and a couple of massive art exhibits on your way to a performance of Janacek's overpowering Glagolitic Mass. What kind of music would you hear in your dreams after a day like that?

One thread to help you through this cultural maze is the excellent lecture series which dominates the learning experience at the Festival. You might hear a lecture by the members of a brass quintet, for instance, or a talk on the restoration of the jewel-like Dock Street Theater by a local architect.

We recommend the Spoleto Festival to those for whom decision-making is no major problem. If you are one of those people who can pick and choose between 25 courses at a Thanksgiving dinner, you'll do well. And, of course, you can see everything there is to hear and see at Charleston—and love it—and then dash over to Spoleto, Italy, to pick up the pieces you missed. Mama mia! That's it!

Or, in operatic parlance, "Gran Dio! O ciel!" —J.A.

Spoleto Festival USA
P.O. Box 157
Charleston, SC 29402

Dueling Dulcimers

Music.
Country music.
Down-home country music.
Making down-home country music.
Making instruments that make down-home country music.

We're talking about the Augusta Heritage Arts Workshop, a program that can take you to the roots of some of the root music of this country.

Held each summer in the scenic mountains of West Virginia, the workshop bills itself as an adventure in folk art, music, dance, and folklore. Chief among its sessions is a five-week course in musical instrument construction and a three-week stint learning Appalachian music.

The instrument construction course ($310 for state residents, $370 out-of-state) centers on the design and construction of hammered dulcimers, mountain dulcimers, and five-string banjos. Resident instructors and visiting instrument-makers guide students from concept to completion, and even touch on the topic of repair work, should your creation go wrong. The Appalachian music course ($105 in-state, $135 out-of-state) offers instruction in old-time instruments like the fiddle, banjo, guitar, hammered and mountain dulcimers, and the autoharp. Students also learn vocal styles and songs from "old masters" in the field.

Those who attend may choose to take room and board at the college or camp on their own in the nearby Monongahela National Forest. —C.McB.

Appalachian Music/Musical Instrument Construction
Augusta Heritage Arts Workshop
P.O. Box 1725
Elkins, WV 26241

The Vienna Agenda

It used to be that Mozart's *Requiem* conjured up images of Europeans sporting powder wigs and nodding off while sitting on a church bench.

But NYU's World Campus Program has changed all that. Two travel seminars, Opera in Vienna and Budapest (ten days for $1150), and The Music of Vienna (nine days for $720), offer everyday folks the chance to expand and enrich their cultural experiences by attending exciting performances and gathering together in seminars with established musicians and critics.

In April, the Vienna agenda includes concerts at the Staatsoper and Volksoper, touring the Schonbrunn and Belvedere Palaces and the Kunsthistorisches Museum (have they got Brueghels for you!), and visiting the Austrian National Library.

Next stop: Budapest. Three days of sampling Hungarian cuisine in out-of-the-way gypsy cafes, scanning music archives, and attending performances at the famed Hungarian State Opera House.

Jaunts to Salzburg with Robert Sherman, program director of WQXR and music critic for *The New York Times*, will be included in the January/February Music in Vienna excursion.

Just think: you'll be humming a Strauss waltz instead of a Streisand tune while sudsing in the shower. —S.C.

World Campus Program
New York University
Division of Liberal Studies
2 University Place
New York, NY 10003

Organ Orgy

Organs are like sterling—they're only brought out for company. Imagine, however, that you are invited to the unveiling of the world's most beautiful organs—organs that were sprinkled throughout Holland, Germany, and Austria and that are housed in castles and churches. All the elements for a veritable transport in time are present: the stunning, high sweep of the architecture, the ornate religious icons, and the deep resonance of the chords. A whole host of organists, vocalists, and instrumentalists perform, on schedule, for you. The organs date as far back as the Gothic period, and the music is strictly Renaissance and Baroque.

Westminster Choir College of Princeton, New Jersey, arranges a grand tour that is guaranteed to make you feel like royalty. Go with the experts to the sources of European organ culture. The price of $1250 for the two-week tour covers transportation, accommodations, demonstrations, and sightseeing. Graduate credits are included at no additional cost.

It sure beats Sunday choir with Mrs. Maple at the pipe organ, listening to Hymn 43 for the third time this month. —S.C.

European Organ Culture Tour
Summer Sessions Office
Westminster Choir College
Princeton, NJ 08540

High-C Adventures

Michael Barclay, it would seem, is one of those lucky people who got to grow up and live out his childhood dreams.

At the age of ten, resplendent, no doubt, in a shiny new suit, he was led through the doors of the Metropolitan Opera House in New York for his first taste of the world of arias and divas, of Wagner and Verdi, of exquisite costumes and magnificent voices. And for young Master Barclay, it was love at first sight.

During the next 15 years, he estimates he went back to the Met over 1000 times to listen, learn, and grow more in love with his beloved opera. Today, across the continent and in opera-loving San Francisco, Barclay is one of the art's great aficionados—working as critic, commentator, lecturer, and leader of a unique organization called Opera Education West.

Under the umbrella of this group, Barclay personally leads opera study tours each year to the great opera centers of the world. His journeys have included the Munich Opera Festival, the Wagner Festival in West Germany, the Salzburg Festival, the Glyndebourne Festival, Florence Musical May, the Vienna Opera Festival, the La Scala Bicentennial, four annual tours to the Metropolitan and New York City Opera companies, and rounds to San Francisco Opera performances. On his upcoming roster are newly created tours to France, Holland, Russia, Hamburg, East and West Berlin, Seattle, and Santa Fe.

These speciality tours feature the very best in accommodations, top-quality tickets for the many productions included in each visit, opportunities to meet and mingle with opera stars and personalities, side trips to the cultural highpoints and scenic locations, and in-depth lectures by Barclay on the opera, cast, conductor, composer, etc. of that evening's performance.

Trips vary greatly in length and cost. The Santa Fe opera holiday is scheduled for six days (six performances) at a cost of $825, while a 24-day, 21-opera extravaganza in Germany and Austria runs $3200. Other samplings are the Munich Festival (14 days, 14 operas, $2300), San Francisco (seven days, seven performances, $950), and New York (nine days, nine operas, $1171). A no-frills option (meaning lesser hotel accommodations) is available with most trips and reduces the cost by several hundred dollars. The listed prices do not include air fares.

Besides the trips, Barclay conducts—through the Opera Education West organization—opera appreciation classes on general and specialized subject areas in Berkeley and San Francisco. To date, over 10,000 people have attended his lectures, which are held in conjunction with the spring and fall seasons of the San Francisco Opera. The San Francisco lectures are available on tape cassettes for new and experienced opera buffs across the country. —C.McB.

Opera Education West Tours
400 Yale Ave.
Berkeley, CA 94708

Opera in English is, in the main, just as sensible as baseball in Italian.
H. L. MENCKEN

Classical & All That Jazz

Most of us invest more time in a job than we do in ourselves. We're too interested in that next sale, next deadline, or next paper before our interest in music. And we wouldn't know how to proceed if free time just happened to appear.

One answer to this dilemma is the music history and appreciation correspondence courses that are offered through UCLA's Life Long Learning Program: an individualized learning experience that is like being on your own in a class of one.

Investigate how musicians transform their emotions into the jazz experience. The History of Jazz course moves from the idiom's African and Caribbean roots through rock 'n' roll, New Orleans jazz, boogie woogie, and swing and bebop. The cassette tape course includes more than 200 musical cuts, and is a mini jazz library in itself.

Classical concert goers who love the highbrow stuff but don't know why it sounds the way it does can listen carefully to examples of melody, harmony, and other aspects of music in the Introduction to Music course.

Courses are $75 to $95, with text and cassette costs excluded. Course work is submitted by mail to assigned instructors. —S.A.

Music History & Appreciation Courses
Lifelong Learning Program
University Extension
University of California
Berkeley, CA 94720

Merry Melodies

You've left theaters humming the tunes, had stars in your eyes, and had toes twitching to dance. The memories of a good musical linger on and on in your memory—but what do you really *know* about them? Did you realize that they are a unique art form, known the world over as "The American Musical"?

How would you like to have Vincente Minnelli, director of *An American in Paris*, *Gigi*, *Meet Me in St. Louis*, and *Brigadoon*, take you behind the scenes and tell you about the whimsies and calamities that went into the filming of his musicals? All this and more is open to you through the College of Continuing Education at the University of Southern California.

Speakers in past sessions have included Stanley Donen (director of *Pajama Game*), Nanette Fabray (who sang the lead in *High Button Shoes*), Lawrence Kasha (producer of *Seven Brides for Seven Brothers*), and Gene Kelly (actor-dancer in *Singing in the Rain*). Noncredit cost is $65; credit cost runs $140/unit.

There are also classes in opera that will take you to view three performances of the New York City Opera Company. The fee of $100 includes tickets. —R.B.

Music Programs
College of Continuing Education
CES
University of Southern California
Los Angeles, CA 90007

Opera's Home Sweet Home

Lovers of opera often wonder where Verdi and Puccini lived and whether their surroundings inspired the creation of their great works. Such wonders are what E & M Associates explore on their 13-day Musical Tour of Florence, Parma, Siena, and Milan. You will see La Scala and the Parma Opera House, the Toscanini Memorial, and the famous Sienese Music Academy. This could be the vacation you've been "wondering" for so long. Write for their brochure.

Italian Mosaic Musical Tour
E & M Associates
667 Madison Ave.
New York, NY 10021

Making These Seats Pay Off

Surely you have sat in orchestra seats and felt you were still missing out on what was being performed. Unlike learning how to tie shoelaces, music appreciation does not come easily to most of us. Subtle variations between pieces and styles often go unnoticed. The New England Conservatory, one of the most respected music institutions in this country, offers several history of music courses in its summer school program. Now you can explore exotic tunes of India or familiarize yourself with the music of our own time, the 20th century. Tuition is $100 per credit. Write for their catalog.

Summer School
New England Conservatory of Music
290 Huntington Ave.
Boston, MA 02115

Music, the Common Thread

Leningrad, Kiev, Moscow, Odessa. Verona, Salzburg, Munich. Monte Carlo, Paris, Strasbourg. Aspen, Santa Fe, New York. What do these cities have in common aside from sitting on the face of the globe? They are all the sites of proposed opera festival tours offered by Daily-Thorp Travel. You choose where you want to be, and a tour is bound to go there. The experience is costly but, believe it or not, waiting lists do occur. You had better write and reserve early this year.

Worldwide Opera Tours
Daily-Thorp Travel, Inc.
654 Madison Ave.
New York, NY 10021

Esterhazy Evenings

A toast to class—as in a classy program concerning classical music in classic surroundings.

We write of the Classical Music Seminar presented in Eisenstadt, Austria, each summer under the auspices of the University of Iowa's School of Music. What makes this seminar unique is both its setting and its approach to its subject.

Eighteenth-century Austria was one of the cultural centers of the Western world, counting Haydn, Mozart, and Schubert among its sons. The seminar is designed to deepen one's understanding of that rich period through musical experiences set in the locale and atmosphere in which many composers actually worked and performed. Much of the program takes place in Eisenstadt's Esterhazy Palace, a structure that was a magnificent cultural showcase.

The seminar makes room for both players of music and those who merely enjoy listening to it. You may choose to take part as a "participant" or an "observer." Participants attend all seminar offerings and are coached by an American and Austrian faculty in master classes. Observers attend but do not play in master classes.

The two-week program costs $1195, which includes room, board, sight-seeing trips, and charter flight from Chicago. —C.McB.

Classical Music Seminar
The University of Iowa
311 Jessup Hall
Iowa City, IA 52242

Lisszten to This

All periods of music have had their share of astounding virtuosi. The 18th century, for example, had its keyboard genius in Scarlatti and its string wizardry in the legendary Paganini.

But perhaps the most colorful virtuosi belong to the deeply romantic 19th century, when the brooding genius became the model of the instrumentalist—as did the wild-living, wild-loving heroes of then-current literature (of which Heathcliff was one of many). Of this type of artist, there is but one archetype: Franz Liszt. His deliciously Hungarian music lives on in the repertories of symphonies worldwide.

The International Festival of the American Liszt Society celebrates this musical genius, this enigmatic monk, this Casanovan lover. Lectures, as well as recitals, are the highlight of this festival, sponsored by North American and Soviet Liszt buffs and specialists. You can learn about the influence of literature on Liszt's compositions, his interest in piano technique, and the music publishing industry in his day. This immodest but delicious outpouring of music comes alive once each year. Write to the Society for its dates, location, and program. —J.A.

The American Liszt Society, Inc.
Attn: Fernando Laires, Pres.
Peabody Institute of the
Johns Hopkins University
Conservatory of Music
Baltimore, MD 21202

Over the piano was printed a notice: Please do not shoot the pianist. He is doing his best.
OSCAR WILDE

Desert Song

Opera in New Mexico may seem as unlikely as tumbleweeds in New York City but, sure enough, the Santa Fe Opera Festival opens every summer with a selection of live works that rivals the Met's. Grand Ol' Opry, it ain't. You might, instead, hear Strauss' *Salome* or Puccini's *Tosca*.

Each year, the University of Denver sponsors an In-Residence Studies in Opera program during the week of the festival. The rigors of academic study are not shunted, though participants are not cloistered in classrooms. The program's approach is to study operatic works, meet with the people at Santa Fe who perform them, attend live performances, and review what has been seen and heard.

In-Residence Studies attracts opera buffs from all over the country, as does the festival. Opera friendships are continually being made, as an intensely focused community of singers, opera lovers, and casual observers evolves. Classes meet on a daily basis for lectures. Cost, including tuition, tickets, and books, runs about $350. Lodging is in nearby motels. There may be time for things nonopera, but don't count on it.

Reservations must be made early. In-Residence Studies keeps its students coming back for more. —S.C.

In-Residence Studies in Opera
Lamont School of Music
Colorado Seminary
University of Denver
University Park
Denver, CO 80208

The Moving Finger Writes

Magical Mystery Tour

"Blast! Holmes. Three weeks on their trail and I still can't make sense of it."

"Steady, Watson. The clues are everywhere."

"Clues? What clues, Holmes? Just another bunch of bloomin' Yank tourists if you ask me. No great mystery here."

"Ah, but you're wrong, Watson. Think back, where have our American friends been in the past three weeks?"

"Standard visitors' run, I'd say. Some guided trips around town, a play, a visit to the countryside, Madame Tussaud's waxworks, the 'Old Bailey several lectures and discussions."

"Yes, Watson, but look closer. Where did those trips take them?"

"Well, there was Whitechapel and Mayfair."

"And who do you associate with them?"

"Why, Whitechapel was Jack the Ripper's home territory, of course. And Mayfair was the headquarters for the dashing crook J. R. Raffles and the aristocrat detective Lord Peter Wimsey."

"Precisely, Watson. And where else did they go?"

"They were also in Dame Agatha's area, where Miss Marple and the Belgian Poirot did some of their best detective work. Not to mention several of *our* old haunts. Brought back some memories, that did."

"Correct again, Watson. And where did they spend their time at Madame Tussaud's?"

"In the Chamber of Horrors, among the world's most famous collection of real life criminals."

"And the play, Watson. What sort of play was it?"

"A mystery, old boy, a mystery."

"And the lectures? What did the lectures deal with?"

"Well, there was one with a detective and one with a crime writer. By Jove, Holmes! I see what you're onto. Of course! That's why they were at the 'Old Bailey' court and out at that country house asking which butler did it. It's a bloody mystery tour, isn't it?"

"Yes, Watson, and further deductions tell me that the venture is sponsored by the British Study Center of the University of Wisconsin. The tour, I'm told, costs as little as $1200 American, plus air fare."

"Brilliant, Holmes, as usual. Tell me, what put you on to them?"

"Elementary, my dear Watson. It was the trench coats. No one in his right mind would wear a trench coat in London in August." —C.McB.

British Mystery Tour
British Study Center
Attn: Dr. Lorin Robinson
Arts & Sciences Outreach
University of Wisconsin
River Falls, WI 54022

Bronte by the Brook Cambridge. Famous throughout the world for its university, and an inspirational environment for those who pursue the task of studying. Brookside College. It looks onto the brook from which it takes its name. Most Americans never get the chance to experience this world that nurtured such men of distinction as Milton, Newton, and Russell. Now those with an interest in English literature of the 18th, 19th, and 20th centuries can enroll in intensive four-week courses here during the summer months. Classes are supplemented by tours to such historical sites as the Bronte, Keats, and Hardy Museums and Stratford-upon-Avon. Accommodation is arranged with English families living in Cambridge.

Courses in Modern English Studies
Brookside College
3 Brookside
Cambridge
England, UK

Heading South—and West
When you lay your pen down and the desire to "get away from it all" strikes, remember that there's more than tumbleweed and desert in New Mexico. There's Santa Fe, and the Santa Fe Workshops of Contemporary Art, which focus on poetry and short-story writing. You can attend painting, drawing, and sculpture classes at no extra cost. The eight-week summer tuition (mid-June through mid-August) is $500, or $63 per week. Limited scholarship funds are available.

Santa Fe Workshops of
Contemporary Art
Box 1344
Santa Fe, NM 87501

Basic Ingredients Just what makes a good story—defying the believable, challenging the imagination, adding a touch of strangeness to your character? And what makes for a good poem? The Creative Writing Workshops at the Hambidge Center can help you to analyze the writer's craft—both in poetry and fiction—in class and individual sessions. Workshops run for a week in June, July, or August. Calling all stories—finished and unfinished!

Creative Writing Workshops
The Hambidge Center
P.O. Box 33
Rabun Gap, GA 30568

Grammar, which knows how to control even kings.
MOLIERE

Where Buffalo Roamed

The Institute of the American West works on a grand scale. It must. Its subject is the American West, and there are few expanses of land so rich in history, art, and literature.

The Institute functions as an interdisciplinary humanities program that conducts yearly seminars that reflect national and universal themes. On its advisory board are scholars on American history and popular culture, writers, and artists, all dedicated to exploring the American past.

The Institute's most recent conference focused on the writer and the West, and brought together 16 experts for a series of panel discussions, workshops, and informal gatherings. The focal point was the themes and visions of writers who wrote about the West, and the ways in which those themes have been integrated into popular culture (movies, for example). We're told that the four-day '78 session (at a cost of only $40) spawned the theme for the Institute's 1979 program, Open Space and the West. —C.McB.

Institute of the American West
Sun Valley Center
Box 656
Sun Valley, ID 83353

Pros and Poetry

If you long for an environment in which your mind can meditate solely on the writing of poetry or prose, and if you are willing to devote a year to this commitment—then you will find your dream at the Naropa Institute.

The Institute, located in Boulder, Colorado, has developed an approach to education that encourages the integration of intellect and creativity.

The one-year Poetics Certificate Program gives students the opportunity to work closely with advisors who are accomplished, practicing writers. During this period, the apprentice writer works toward completing his/her own book of poetry or prose.

In the winter and spring quarters, the emphasis is placed on the students' individual writing. During the summer, the course offerings expand to include the Visiting Poetics Academy and a weekly poetry reading series.

There is much support and encouragement at the Institute, with its small-school environment, intimacy of activities, and common purpose between instructor and student. —R.B.

The Poetics Program
Naropa Institute
1111 Pearl St.
Boulder, CO 80302

All Lit Up

If you were intent on studying Jane Austen or Charles Dickens and you could go anyplace you choose—where would it be? If you are serious, there's no doubt that you'd pick Oxford University. It has a certain ring of authenticity to it, doesn't it: "I read Dickens at Oxford, old chap—and you?"

Oxford's reputation didn't come out of thin air, you know. It's been built up over five centuries (when Oxford was young, so was Chaucer). If you fancy going back to the source for your literature studies, Oxford's the spot.

Northern Illinois University's British Literature at Oxford program allows you considerable latitude in the subject matter you study while you're there. It also provides you with tickets to performances at the Royal Shakespeare Theatre in Stratford-on-Avon, and access to the mother of all English libraries, the Bodleian.

You can elect any period from the Restoration to the 1920s. There are concentrated courses in certain major figures—Dr. Johnson is one. There's a view of the ridiculous and the sublime: Wilde and Pater. As a matter of fact, there's just about anything you'd want. Cost: $1175, plus air fare. —J.A.

British Literature at Oxford
International Programs Office
Attn: Dr. Orville Jones
Lowden Hall 107
Northern Illinois University
DeKalb, IL 60115

Women's Writes

If you can read this, then you are alive. If you are alive, then you have lived. And no two lives are ever exactly alike. Therein lies the roots of becoming a writer. Ever tried? Sure, you've dreamed about writing a book about your life. Everyone has. But the International Women's Writing Guild wants to help women open up their minds and put their unique lives onto paper. If you have the desire to write, they want to inspire you to get on with it.

They invite women from all backgrounds to participate and begin to write at their annual Conference/Retreats. On the West Coast these are held at Vallombrosa Center in Menlo Park, near San Francisco. That is the old estate of the Hopkins family of railroad builders. On the East Coast, the Writing Conference/Retreats are held at Skidmore College, Saratoga Springs, New York.

Conferences are for beginners as well as professionals. They cut across all walks of life. The Guild is dedicated to the growth of human potential. It aspires to expand women's perceptions in order to stimulate creative energy and to motivate them to express their ideas through the art of writing. —R.B.

International Women's Writing Guild
Caller Box 810
Gracie Station
New York, NY 10028

Take to the Hills

"A free gift of the spirit running loose in the mountains." In the words of Gurney Norman, author and native of East Kentucky, that's what the Appalachian Writers Workshop is all about.

The Hindman Settlement School in Hindman, Kentucky, is, for two weeks each summer, the place where the traditions of Appalachia are kept alive—at least in the field of literature. The published works by the writers who host this program tell the workshop's story, from Harriet Arnow's *The Dollmaker* (which follows the lives of Kentucky hill people through their contact with an industrial mill) to James Still's *Hounds on the Mountain*, Wilma Dykeman's *Return the Innocent Earth*, and Cratis William's *The Southern Mountaineer in Fact and Fiction*. Each author here clearly speaks and writes about what he or she knows and loves—that is, Appalachian life and lore.

The workshop is open to all interested writers, although you must submit a sample manuscript for admission. Informal sessions on the novel, short story, poetry, and essay are included, and you may concentrate on Appalachian subjects during the second week of the workshop.

Cost is $50 for tuition; $30 for room and board. Auditing fee is $5 per day. Housing is available, and enrollment is limited to 50.

So take to those hills, and write! —S.C.

Appalachian Writers Workshop
Hindman Settlement School
Hindman, Knott County, KY 41822

I love being a writer. What I can't stand is the paperwork.
PETER DE VRIES

Childhood Delights Bedtime stories and picture books are surely one of the highlights of being a young child. Turning pages, ever so slowly, to gaze upon pictures or to drink in the simplicity of the words. It is the adult, however, who writes and illustrates children's books. And Uri Shulevitz, famed author and illustrator of young people's literature, is available to guide you in your task. A workshop to explore a highly visual approach to the picture book is now being offered. One- and two-week options run from $130 and $225. Write for dates and location.

Workshop in the Writing & Illustrating of Children's Books
The Shulevitz Workshop
563 S. Burlingame Ave.
Los Angeles, CA 90049

Indulge in Some Port Port Townsend may not be on your list of places to be this summer, but you might want to consider it now. Centrum, in its fifth year of sponsoring creative and performing arts activities, is calling all writers for its Poetry Symposium and Seminar in Fiction. Here is a setting for serious talents to grow—where forests of cedar, fir, and madrona provide a backdrop for several miles of sandy beaches. You can huddle in the midst of this natural world and do what you do best—that is, write. Admission is competitive, but the faculty is distinguished. Cost varies, depending upon which seminar(s) you attend.

Poetry Symposium/Seminar in Fiction
Centrum
Fort Worden State Park
Port Townsend, WA 98368

A Change of Scene Divorce yourself from American language and culture—even if you are a writer—and expose yourself to a new setting. Oxford, England, for example, or any place for that matter where Antioch International Summer Seminars are held. Artists become writers and writers become artists in workshops that stress both experimentation and professionalism. You design your own program and work toward its objectives with a staff member. July and August are the times. Have you packed already?

Antioch International Summer
Writing Seminars
Antioch College
Yellow Springs, OH 45387

I never travel without my diary. One should always have something sensational to read on the train.
OSCAR WILDE

Write-O

The people in Blighty who "work" with the English language are gathering together to show curious Yankees just how it's "done" there. For three and a half weeks, Americans with an interest in mass media will meet with broadcasters, journalists, and other mass communicators to discuss how media and advertising compare 'twixt the United Kingdom and the United States.

Organizations to be visited include the BBC studios, Reuters News Service, the London *Times*, and the London Broadcasting Company. Your hosts will include representatives from the *Sun* and *Guardian* newspapers, a lawyer whose specialty is Britain's restrictive libel laws, a gentleman who will discuss Scottish journalism and Scottish sensibilities, and a lecturer from the University of York who will speak on British culture as it is affected by British mass media.

When not into the whos, whats, whens, and whys, the group will visit St. Paul's Cathedral, the Royal Shakespeare Theater, and the famous Foyles Bookstore.

The tour is sponsored by Northern Illinois University, and will run from mid-June to mid-July. The cost of $900 covers tours, admission tickets, some meals, and travel within the British Isles. Overseas transportation is not included. —T.G.

Mass Media in Britain Program
Attn: Dr. Orville Jones
International Programs Office
Lowden Hall 107
Northern Illinois University
De Kalb, IL 60015

Take Me to Your Reader

Got a novel lurking in the back of your mind? How about a simple magazine article? Or a musical comedy? If you're a writer who has not yet encountered the fame you deserve, you might find this writers' workshop to your taste.

First of all, you ought to become a member of the National Writers Club. Joining is a simple matter—$29.50 for your first year. You'll get a wide assortment of services and privileges—including manuscript appraisal and *Authorship*, the club's periodical.

But one of the big pluses is the annual workshop. There you'll meet the people who can help make your talent what it ought to be. Last year's meeting was attended by several prominent magazine editors on the prowl (*Family Circle*, *Mademoiselle*, *Reader's Digest*).

The workshops are also meeting places for successful writers with advice for up-and-comers. Clive Cussler (*Raise the Titanic*) and William Hosokawa (*Thunder in the Rockies*) have attended in the past. Seminars are also held on the technicalities of writing (copyrights, agents, etc.) as well as on genres (novels, short stories, TV). Price is under $100, excluding transportation. —J.A.

Annual Writers' Workshop
The National Writers Club
1450 South Havana
Suite 620
Aurora, CO 80012

Do It Write

All grown up, but still have an eye for kids' stories? Well, literature for little folks is a booming business these days, and some of the most talented authors in America have been trying their hand at it.

The Society of Children's Book Writers has chapters in major cities and serves as a voice for wee folk book writers and illustrators across the nation. Membership and conference participation is open to anyone with an interest in children's literature—published or not. Each summer at SCBW's Santa Monica conference, writers and illustrators gather to hear discussions by the pros on mystery, nonfiction, fantasy, and science fiction writing geared for small ones. Individual manuscript critiques are also availablo.

Tuition is $115 for nonsociety members. Tax-deductible society membership dues are $20. The annual conference is cosponsored by the University of California at Los Angeles's Extension Department. Participants may earn three quarter units of credit. —S.A.

Writers' Conference in
Children's Literature
Society of Children's Book Writers
P.O. Box 296
Los Angeles, CA 90066

With Pen in Hand

Can you imagine Leo Tolstoi writing nonsense verse? Emily Dickenson writing a gothic novel? T. S. Eliot writing a human interest story for *People* magazine?

Of course not. Different writers have not only different styles, but different genres. And the world of Writing (with a capital W) is a world made up of hundreds of specialties.

One school that seems to realize this fact in its writing program is the Rhinelander School of the Arts, where writing is taught in a no-nonsense, craftsmanly series of genre courses. Summer workshops at Rhinelander offer you the specific writing skills you'd like to develop. No umbrella-like creative writing courses here.

You can take courses in poetry, fiction, or article writing. You can take courses in humor, science fiction, or children's literature. Or you can get into the business end of writing with such offerings as Small Magazine Production, Writing the Newspaper Column, and Writing and Publishing Local History.

One of the most fascinating offerings is the Yarns of Yesteryear Workshop, specializing in the writing of personal memoirs, family histories, and folklore. Pack your typewriter and go. Tuition for one week is $60. —J.A.

Writing Workshops
Rhinelander School of the Arts
University of Wisconsin, Extension
719 Lowell Hall
610 Langdon St.
Madison, WI 53706

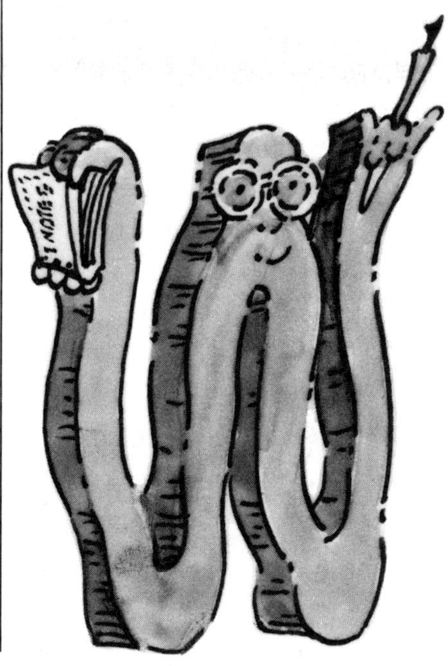

Easy Writer

Everyone gets the idea sooner or later that he/she could be a great writer. Housewives who knock out great meals are suddenly knocking out novels. Power-wrench operators go home at five to knock out magazine articles, and even plays.

To guide those amateurs and pros who aspire to these realms, the Artists' Workshop offers intensive writing courses in glamorous downtown Toronto. Conducted at the noted Canadian Three Schools complex are courses in writing children's stories, creative journalism, the keeping of diaries, the structure of plays, creative writing from personal experience, and workshops in selling materials to the marketplace.

As one successful writer noted, "Everybody knows the 26 letters of the alphabet. All you have to do to make a million is put them down in the right order." Here is a place to learn as you write that winning piece. —T.G.

Writers' Workshops
Three Schools—Artists' Workshop
296 Brunswick Ave.
Toronto, Ontario M5S 2M7
Canada

On Stage, Please

Midsummer Night's Stage

Beats there a heart that at some time hasn't longed to be on stage, grandly and gloriously spouting the lines of one of Shakespeare's great plays to a breathless audience?

Or, have you secretly wished that, just for once, you could whisk backward through time to experience Renaissance living?

There is a place in our world where you can retreat into drama and a Renaissance way of life. For you can study and move inside Shakespeare's writings and Renaissance culture in an idyllic academic retreat on the campus of Southern Oregon State College.

Oregon in the summer! You will spend your days and evenings watching Shakespeare, Moliere, and Brecht, surrounded by towering Douglas firs. Rivers, lakes, and mountains will be close at hand to lure you away between the plays and discussions.

Not one play or merely two, but a seven-play season is here for you to enjoy. Four Shakespearean, one 17th-century, and two modern productions, seven days a week.

So you're not rich? Who said it costs a fortune to travel back in time? You will be staying in excellent dormitory accommodations, and your meals will be at a reasonable cost. Southern Oregon State College is cosponsoring this Institute of Renaissance Studies with ten other colleges and universities. And this means that while the heart of the program is centered in Ashland, different phases of the program will be scattered among campuses along the west coast. It's enough to make your heart sing, when you realize you can stretch your studies into an entire festive Renaissance summer that reaches from Spokane, Washington, to Santa Barbara!

And if you don't enjoy performing on stage? Well, there's a lot more to theater than acting. There is writing and rewriting, and there is learning about direction and production that pull a play together and make it work.

In the From Script to Stage session, you can meet with members of the festival company (actors, directors, dancers, musicians) to gain insights into their performances. And in other sessions you might delve into the plays and come up with religious undertones for discussion.

There's only one way to get the full picture of all these Renaissance flavors, and that is to write to the folks who sponsor this Festive Campus and Institute of Renaissance Studies. —R.B.

Institute of Renaissance Studies
A Festive Campus
Attn: Prof. Homer Swander
P.O. Box 14403
University of California
Santa Barbara, CA 93107

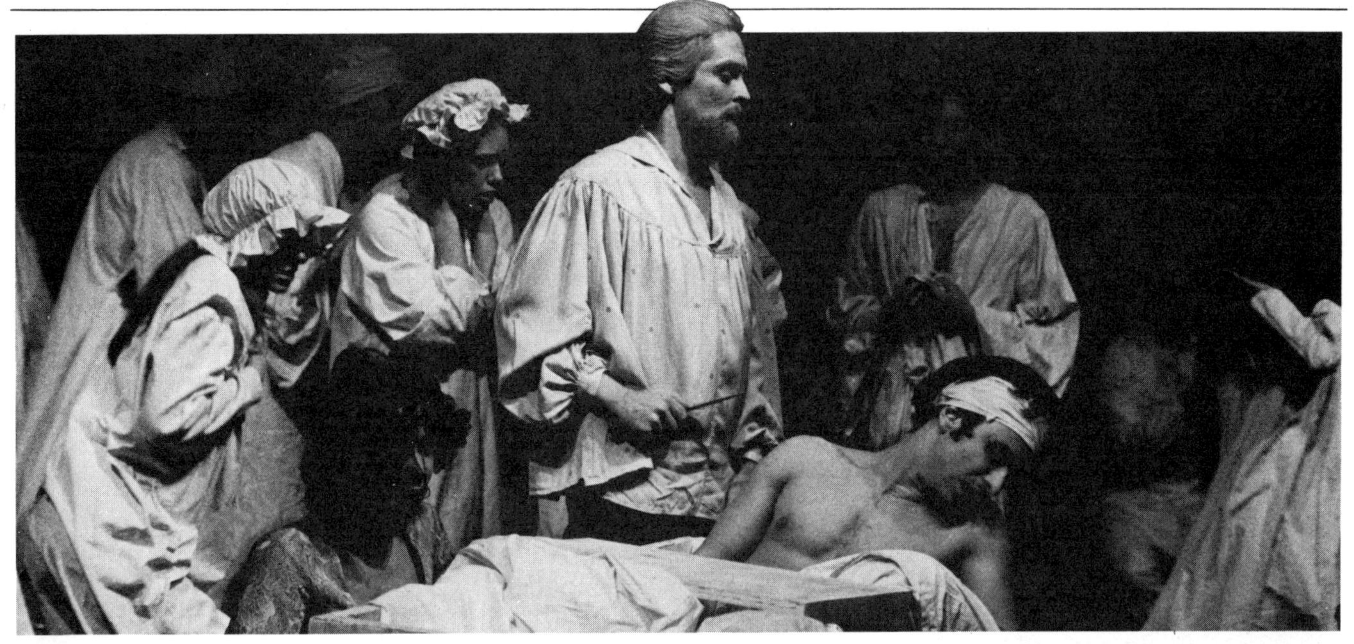

Get Your Act Together

The stage! The movies! Many of us think we could get up there and do it better. If only we hadn't already embarked on another career. If only we could drop everything and try to make it in the world of the dramatic arts.

It may come as a surprise, but you *can* get your feet wet at the American Academy of Dramatic Arts, a respected educational institution devoted to artistic excellence. The school counts among its alumni Edward G. Robinson, Robert Redford, Rosalind Russell, Spencer Tracy, Grace Kelly, and TV's David Hartman.

How can you do it? By enrolling in evening school, Saturday school, or summer programs at the Academy's eastern division in New York or western headquarters in Pasadena. The curriculum covers basic principles and practices and provides a chance to get professional training at a convenient time—for a modest cost.

Even if you don't wind up with credits in major productions, the payoff—a solid background in the dramatic arts—is great. Individual evening offerings include scene study, movement/dance, makeup, auditions, singing, and musical theater. The summer school curriculum focuses on movement, singing, speech, vocal production, rehearsal, and performance. Summer school tuition is $375. Per course evening fees range from $115 to $165. —S.A.

Evening School/Saturday School
American Academy of Dramatic Arts
EAST: 120 Madison Ave.
New York, NY 10016
WEST: 1610 East Elizabeth St.
Pasadena, CA 91104

Clowning Around

Vault right out of the humdrum into the Big Top! And where could you find a bigger top than on an outdoor stage? Valley Studio has two of them, and its rich curriculum includes instruction in the techniques of Greek tragedy, pantomime, puppetry, masks, voice, clowning, juggling, and stage combat. There are enough drama and movement courses here to suit any performer's taste.

Located in a valley surrounded by tree-covered hills 40 miles west of Madison, Wisconsin, Valley Studio is also the home base for the Wisconsin Mime Theatre, as well as a center of information for an international mime community. The studio offers weekend workshops during the fall, winter, and spring. Five two-week summer sessions and an apprentice program consisting of a two-year sequence are also offered. Academic credit may be arranged. Fees range from $100 for a two-week summer session to $1600 for a 28-week apprentice program. Cost covers tuition, room, and board. —M.W.

The Valley Studio
Route 3
Spring Green,
WI 53588

A Play Thing

Facing a season of cultural discontent? Perhaps you're seeking some theatrical catharsis to relieve your cultural pangs. What better place to go when in need of dramatic transfusion than swinging old London, where 50 or so theatres may be open on any given night?

The University of Wisconsin's British Study Center is offering a 21-day package tour of London's theatre scene that includes tickets to nine performances, plus discussions with respected professionals who pull aside their backstage curtains to share an insider's view of their craft.

London's claim to being a theatre capital is hard to refute, especially when its riches range from the Royal Shakespeare Company to avant-garde productions in which the audience becomes a part of the play itself.

The cost of the tour (which includes five free days to explore other facets of London's culture), varies according to the number of participants, but $1000 should cover your air fare, bed, and breakfast for 20 days.

All the theatre that you can absorb is waiting for you. —T.F.

The British Theatre
British Study Center
Attn: Dr. Lorin Robinson
Arts & Sciences Outreach
University of Wisconsin
River Falls, WI 54022

I didn't like the play, but then I saw it under adverse conditions—the curtain was up.
GROUCHO MARX

Be Mime

Mime. As in pant-o-mime.

What can we say about mime? We can say that mime cannot be said, it must be shown. We can say that mime is the absence of these things that you now see—these words. We can use cute definitions to say it: "mime is moving expressively" or "mime is mirroring exactly." We can say that mime is an ancient art made new again by contemporaries like Charles Chaplin and Marcel Marceau. We can say that mime is the work, indeed the life, of a man named Samuel Avital, who is the chief reason for saying all we have said so far.

Samuel Avital, a Moroccan Jew raised with the mystical beliefs of the Kabbalah, has extensively studied (under Marceau, for one) the art of mime. Since 1971, he has run Le Centre du Silence, a school of mime in Boulder, Colorado.

Avital's school and his theory of teaching readily call to mind such adjectives as "unique," "intense," and even "mystical." He sees the learning of his craft not merely as a course, but as a way of life itself. He believes that the true art of mime can come only from a pure soul, one that is totally committed to the art. He seeks, expects, and demands dedication from his students.

The teaching sessions at Le Centre du Silence run for two-week periods in the fall, winter, and spring of each year. Two four-week courses are held during the summer. Classes meet five days a week for a total of 30 hours, with the addition of practical assignments, improvisations, and compositions. Among the topics explored are isolation/undulation techniques, motion/stillness, parallels, animal work, and masks. Morning meditations and evening gatherings are additional components of the program.

A sampling of Avital's techniques is seen in one of his exercises for learning "space awareness." With eyes closed, students attempt to run across a floor covered with people without kicking anyone. You can see how such a feat would, indeed, take a special awareness.

Classes are limited to 12 to 18 members for maximum individual instruction. The cost for the two-week sessions is $350, while the four-week course is $450. Neither amount includes room or board. Prospective applicants should send a picture of themselves and a short letter stating their inner motivation for the work.

Avital has also written a book (*Mime Work Book*) about his philosophy, work, and school. Its 158 pages are filled with mime demonstration photos and creative exercises, and it is required material for those attending his class sessions. It might also make interesting reading for others inclined toward the subject. —C.McB.

Le Centre du Silence Mime School
P.O. Box 1015
Boulder, CO 80306

You need three things in the theatre—the play, the actors, and the audience, and each must give something.
KENNETH HAIGH

Stage Crafts

We all have a bit of the actor in us. It's only occasionally that we let it out to play. A part in the school play or home movies is about as far as most closet Othellos and Desdemonas ever get.

But the mystique of the theater need not pass us by. There are many little theater groups throughout this land, and now there is an exceptional chance to learn about stage techniques in an adult education program at the Goodman School of Drama at De Paul University in Chicago.

The school, reputed to be one of the finest professional training grounds in the United States, has developed a series of classes for adults with an interest in theater. Three levels of acting classes (improvisation, scene study, and advanced scene study) are offered, along with two courses in voice and speech, two in stage make-up, and one in stage movement.

The program, taught by Goodman professionals, can introduce or refresh your memory in the principles and practices of the theater. Evening and Saturday morning sessions are $90 per course. —C.McB.

Goodman School of Drama
Adult Education
De Paul University
804 W. Belden
Chicago, IL 60614

The art of acting consists in keeping people from coughing.
SIR RALPH RICHARDSON

Theatre of the Sun (Valley, That Is)

Good theatre has an impact on the audience that is overwhelming. You don't come out of a well-produced play marveling at the costumes or the sets—you come out marveling at the world you have just seen.

But those worlds that hide behind proscenium arches don't just happen; they are the careful creation of legions of skilled and dedicated craftsmen. At Sun Valley Center's Theatre Workshops, you can work at perfecting any of the myriad skills that create the mirage of the stage.

If you've a yen to, you can study stage make-up. Or ensemble acting techniques may grab your fancy —with improvisations, theatre games, and memory exercises. Or, if you're not into serious drama, you can opt for Sun Valley's cabaret classes.

Classes are conducted under the aegis of the New Haven Ensemble Company (which spends the academic year at Yale). With these theatrical gurus, you can pursue the art of stage direction, tumbling and stage combat, or children's theatre.

And there are, of course, productions each summer. You may find yourself walking the boards as Hamlet or Ophelia under those azure Idaho skies. Break a leg! —J.A.

Theatre Workshops
Sun Valley Center
Box 656
Sun Valley, ID 83353

The Ghost of Shakespeare Past The Age of Shakespeare is very much alive today, and students of drama have come to recognize that a true assessment of Shakespeare's works is best achieved by the *combination* of study and theatre experience. Here is a unique opportunity to explore Elizabethan drama and literature in Shakespeare country. The course runs from mid-July to mid-August. Bed, board, tuition, and theatre tickets ran about $960 last year. To go or not to go—that is the question.

Drama & Theatre in the Age of Shakespeare
Attn: Ms. G. Bartlett
Dept. of Extra-Mural Studies
Mason Croft/Church Street
Stratford-upon-Avon, Warwickshire
England, UK

Extend Yourself Theater games extend the actor's powers of concentration and observation, and increase involvement with fellow players. New stage realities develop. Viola Spolin developed a body of theater techniques to transcend the traditional approach to teaching the actor. Six-week intensive summer programs are offered at her school in Hollywood. It's time you developed your character!

Spolin Theater Game Center
6600 Santa Monica Blvd.
Hollywood, CA 90038

Behind the Scenes For those who aren't theater majors and don't know good acting from bad, you can learn how to discriminate here. For those who are gifted or somewhat-less-than gifted actors, you can work on creating new characters. If you have sat for years and marveled at what is happening on stage, you can now examine the elements of a performance that excite the audience. USC offers all this and more in a potpourri of theater courses designed to lure those with an interest in the stage. Costs are reasonable, credit options are available, and new offerings are on the drawing board all the time.

"On Stage" Courses
College of Continuing Education
Division of Academic Programs
CES 200
University of Southern California
Los Angeles, CA 90007

Pictures in Motion

Reel Applications

Mass media are a pervasive part of our daily lives. They provide information and entertainment—on screens, on billboards, on paper, and over the air.

The Summer Institute of the Media Arts in Cambridge, Massachusetts, is an attempt to explore media—film and video in particular. And from all appearances, it is an excellent attempt. The Institute's programs are not meant to be merely art appreciation courses or history of film studies. Their scope goes well beyond that, into the realm of theory, technique, and practical application.

The intensive three-week workshops and seminars that make up the heart of the program are held on the campus of Tufts University, just six miles from downtown Boston. The school's faculty consists of well-known artists and critics in the field: directors, producers, animators, holographers, photographers, and university professors. In addition, guest artists and guest lecturers are often incorporated into the program.

On the production end, courses include filmmaking, videotaping, and animation. Seminars focus on such topics as the anthropological film, film analysis, screenwriting, directing, and third world cinema.

Students become acquainted with 8mm (single and double system) and 16mm film, black-and-white and color video, and 35mm slides. Actual films are scripted, directed, and shot by students in groups and individually. The school prides itself on teaching practical techniques and contemporary methods of critical analysis.

Classes are held for five full days each week and are supplemented by evening instruction. Class size is kept between 15 and 30 to allow for individual attention. College credit is available.

Tuition for the three-week courses is $375, with an additional $75 lab fee required for those offerings associated with production. Room and board arrangements can be made with Tufts. —C.McB.

Summer Institute on the Media Arts
University Film Study Center
18 Vassar St.
Cambridge, MA 02139

Photography is truth. And cinema is truth 24 times a second.
JEAN-LUC GODARD

Catch It at Cannes

Great Caesar's ghost! Have you ever dreamed of living in a villa on the French Riviera, five miles from Cannes, and mingling with the greats of the film industry? No, this isn't a dream! You can make the trip with students of the University of Pennsylvania—and you don't have to be a student.

During the three weeks of the famous festival, where actors, directors, critics, producers, distributors, exhibitors, investors, and film buffs come to discuss the latest films from all over the world, you can attend showings from morning to midnight in the dozen or so small theaters in Cannes.

The audience around you will be as exciting or as exotic as the films you will see. And the nights on the Riviera will be starry and warm.

Seminars and special events will be held at the Chateau de La Napoule. Although you must make reservations and pay for your own round-trip flight, the living is easy once you arrive. $195 pays for three weeks of accommodations at the villa. This does not include meals. There is a $50 autobus fee to carry you to Cannes and back on all those lovely days and nights. —R.B.

A Cannes Experience
Attn: Joan Campbell
College of General Studies
Summer Session
210 Logan Hall/CN
University of Pennsylvania
Philadelphia, PA 19174

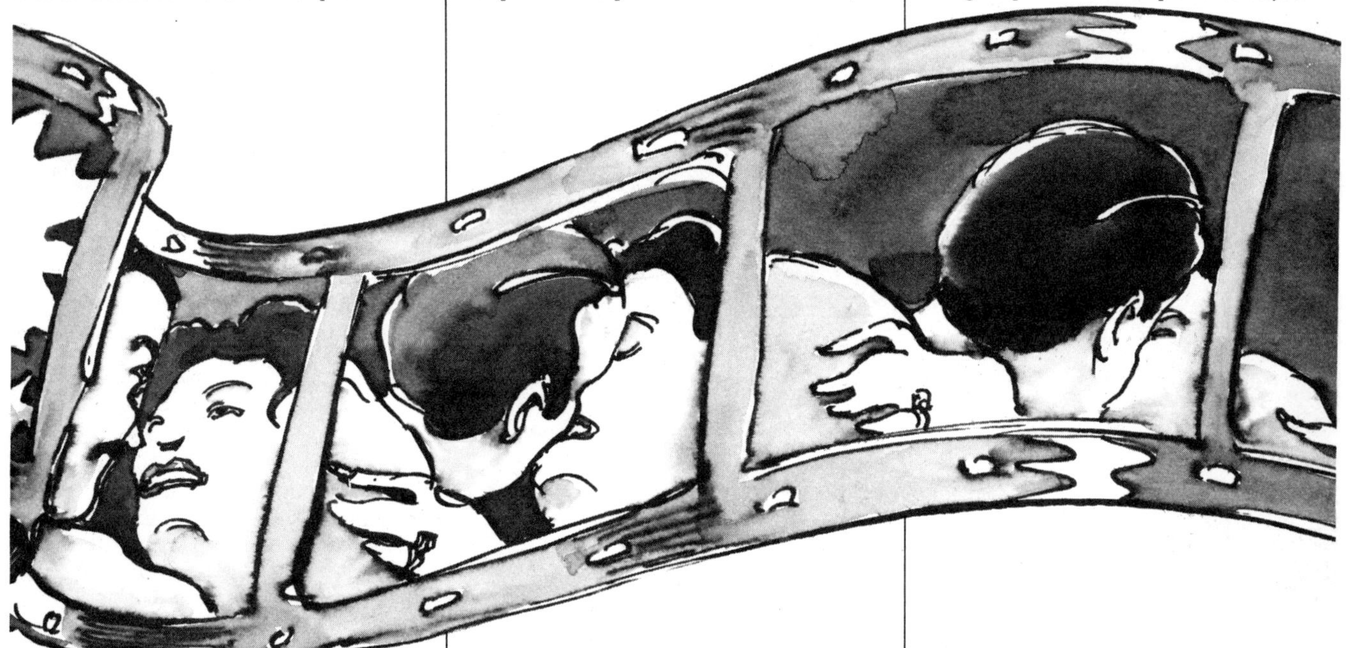

Hollywood Afloat

Here's a cruise with a twist, and it's hardly a lemon—especially if you're into movies and the folks from Hollywood who make them.

The American Film Institute sponsors an annual Caribbean cruise that is open to the public on a first-come, first-serve basis. Those who sign on leave from Fort Lauderdale aboard the Norwegian luxury liner *Royal Viking Sea* and spend seven sunny days on a trip to St. Thomas and St. Maarten.

What separates this cruise from your normal run-of-the-ocean experience is the AFI connection, which means that participants get a close-up look at the world of the cinema. Highlights of the week include: screenings of a dozen classic feature films as well as shorts from talented young directors, and a chance to hobnob with at least four Hollywood stars who make the cruise with you. (Charlton Heston was on deck for the last one, but the seas were calm this time around.) A series of discussions on the past, present, and future of the movie art is also presented.

Your ticket, which entitles you to all cruise amenities, depends on the accommodations that you select. Prices go from a high of $1850 down to $856, on a per person, double occupancy basis. —C.McB.

American Film Institute Cruise
Don Ton Associates
2061 Business Center Dr.
Suite 107
Irvine, CA 92715

Cinematic Samurai

The Japan Society, founded in 1907 and located in New York City, is an association of individuals actively engaged in bringing together the peoples and cultures of Japan and the United States. One of the key methods the group uses to carry out its objectives is an ongoing film program that has brought the best of the Japanese cinema to these shores, allowing Americans to experience and familiarize themselves with Japan's most important actors and directors. Many of the films make their US debuts under the society's auspices.

Recent offerings included a series of 21 films dating back to 1934 titled "Unknown Masterpieces of the Japanese Cinema" and a program of Japanese comedies ranging from silent film days to the present. The society has also sponsored a film retrospective by Kon Ichikawa, one of the country's master directors, and an extensive presentation of the works of Sachiko Hidari, once one of Japan's greatest actresses and now among its most promising directors.

Japanese cinema is noted for its emphasis on humanism and has been a vital force in cinematic development. The Film Festival Program confirms this position, and offers serious filmgoers a rare opportunity to experience it. —C.McB.

Film Festival Program
Japan Society, Inc.
333 East 47th St.
New York, NY 10017

Cinema, Southern Style

"Filmmaking in the Deep South?" you might ask. "There is none," you might be quick to reply. Wrong, for the Alabama Film-Makers Co-op has recently dedicated itself to putting cameras into every hand that wants to hold one.

Super 8mm, 16mm, and video camera instruction is now available. The Co-op presently sponsors 13 statewide programs and is in the process of building its own studio. Seminars and workshops focus on production equipment, film theory and appreciation, the history of the cinema as an art form, and editing and directing. All classes are conducted by experienced staff members.

The Co-op attempts to encourage beginning and experienced film-makers to use the film medium as a form of self-expression. Classes are open to the general public at a reasonable cost. With this new southern accent, American cinema may never be the same. —T.G.

Alabama Film-makers Co-op
4333 Chickasaw Dr.
Huntsville, AL 35801

Reach for the Stars

Filmmaking. Reely, whether you hanker to make your own, or just want to know how it's done, the University of Southern California presents the opportunity for a close-up of the fundamentals of movie-making, as well as a chance to quiz the makers and stars of great American movies.

You can start with the wide-angled Introduction to Filmmaking, for this class covers cinematic technique, budgeting, and scriptwriting. You can advance to the Professional Film-making Workshop, where students take a project through production. Or, study the manipulation of space in a course on composition and design in film, and scrutinize the visual architecture in *Citizen Kane*, *The Maltese Falcon*, *Red Desert*, and *8½*.

In the Theatrical Film: From Concept to Screen course, guest professionals will discuss the producer's responsibilities and how studios actually select their film projects. In The Greats of American Musicals, you may meet Vincente Minnelli, Nanette Fabray, or Gene Kelly in lecture, interview, film clip, and question-and-answer sessions.

Classes run for 8 to 11 weeks. Fees range from $65 to $280. —M.W.

Screen Programs
College of Continuing Education
CES
University of Southern California
Los Angeles, CA 90007

Oldies but Goodies

Are you a film buff who can sit back and recall almost every film, good or bad, that was ever released? Do you want to see more "oldies and newees," and share your interest with other kindred souls?

There is no better way to do these things than to join the American Film Institute. A wide range of programs on film from all eras is offered, and you can sit back and discuss its history and development with people "in the know."

The Institute sponsors several guest lecturers during the year, but it attracts its largest crowds for its film series programs. You could find yourself rubbing shoulders with some of the greats and near-greats in the darkened AFI theater. AFI's diverse program ranges from Clark Gable to Italian Neo-Realism to Greek Cinema.

You may also take the opportunity to view hundreds of shorts and documentaries, tour screening rooms, or attend demonstrations of television and film production equipment.

Viewing a film can be more than just a night out on the town. Now you can take in the whole of an industry. —R.B.

The American Film Institute
The John F. Kennedy Center
for the Performing Arts
Washington, DC 20566

A picture shows me at a glance what it takes dozens of pages of a book to expound.
IVAN TURGENEV

Shooting with the Stars

Sherwood Oaks is the name, and celluloid's the game. Drawing on the legendary talent banks of Hollywood, this experimental college offers a soup-to-nuts program in all phases of filmmaking, acting, and writing.

But it's not your run-of-the-mill film school. Not by a long, long shot. The smarts you'll get from Sherwood Oaks are the smarts that are currently dominating the entertainment industry. Their roster of speakers reads like a membership list of the Academy of Motion Picture Arts and Sciences.

And nothing is lost. They keep all their lectures on tape for the enrichment of future classes of students. Their tape library tells a large part of their story. As of this writing, more than 500 cassettes were available to registered students, including talks by William Goldman, Robert Altman, Francois Truffaut, Gene Kelly, Robert DeNiro, and Lily Tomlin.

The library also offers scripts of important films—scripts that are not available elsewhere. Among those on file are *Taxi Driver, Close Encounters of the Third Kind, Annie Hall,* and *Foul Play*. There are 350 others.

But the real essence of Sherwood Oaks is the class structure. Let's zoom in and try a couple of brief close-ups.

Acting classes during the 1978-79 year were conducted by some quite illustrious teachers and actors: Comedy Acting taught by Jack Riley (*The Bob Newhart Show*), Advanced Acting taught by Clu Gulager, and Acting Workshops taught by Perry King and David Proval.

But say you're not into acting. Say you're the type who wants to stand behind the camera. Try Sherwood Oaks' Cinematography Seminar, taught by Michel Hugo (*One Is a Lonely Number, They Only Kill Their Masters*). In this seminar you'll cover the equipment and the techniques you'll need to be a cinematographer: 35mm cameras and lenses, film reports, stocks, lab printing processes, front and rear projections, and special effects.

Or maybe you're a critic. Then you might be interested in the New Films Seminar. Here's a chance for you to get a sneak look at films that may be big hits of the coming months. And you'll hear lectures and commentaries by people connected with making them. Films previewed during the past year included *The Boys from Brazil, The Big Fix, Comes a Horseman,* and *Paradise Alley*.

Sherwood Oaks' purpose is, quite simply, to create a talent bank of professionals for the future. The stars of tomorrow may well be sitting in classes with you. But don't think that you must want a film career to benefit. You can attend classes here with nothing more in mind than just shooting better home films or improving your company's approach to audio-visual materials.

Many seminars are one-day affairs, but the majority of classes stretch over a period of weeks. Prices and schedules vary widely, based on the availability of suitable instructors.

And after you enroll, don't be surprised if you meet Orson Welles strolling through the halls or William Peter Blatty scribbling notes between classes for his next smash screenplay. After all, this is Hollywood. —J.A.

Sherwood Oaks Experimental College
6353 Hollywood Blvd.
Hollywood, CA 90028

The Atelier Approach

Lights! Camera! Action! Amidst the pine trees of upstate New York . . .

Pine trees? New York?

Hey, haven't you heard? The Gray Film Atelier in Hoosick Falls, New York, is *the* place to study filmmaking. The Atelier is an independent studio with an excellent apprenticeship program. Shooting, screenwriting, directing, researching, editing, producing, and distributing (and sometimes even acting) are among the filmmaking tasks Atelier students have an opportunity to master.

Apprentices jump right into the thick of it by working on a filming assignment during the first week of study. First assignments focus on inexpensive super-8 film and equipment. Apprentices later advance to working on professional Atelier productions in the 16mm medium.

It should be pointed out that the Atelier is a school for those with a pretty serious interest in the art of filmmaking. The program entails some degree of commitment: the basic period of study is one year and the tuition is $1750. But if you are looking for a film program in which your involvement is both direct and intense, then the Gray Film Atelier is for you. —P.C.

The Gray Film Atelier, Ltd.
P.O. Box 70
Hoosick Falls, NY 12090

The Reel Thing

Rockport, Maine, is certainly no Hollywood, and fishing harbors are not known for their glamour. But for the frazzled and dazzled cinematographer, the Maine Photographic Workshops (MPW) could be just the salve for the harried eye.

Every summer, accomplished filmmakers, directors, cameramen, and other working film professionals attend one- and two-week workshops in directing, production, lighting, and technical aspects of filmmaking. If, however, you are a serious student or hobbyist in film, you may opt for a slot as an auditor.

Either way, you are sure to engage in plenty of dialog, critique, and practicum. Workshops in the past have been led by cinematographer Vilmos Zsigmond (*Close Encounters, Deliverance, McCabe and Mrs. Miller*), and director Mark Rydell (*The Rievers, Cinderella Liberty, The Long Goodbye*).

See a raft of good films, as they are screened by workshop leaders. Or shoot or screen your own films, before you sit and view the others. MPW is not a formal school, and no degrees are granted. Serious photographers will find courses in color, film production, and audio-visual techniques that can be applied to nature and commercial photography, as well as photojournalism. —S.C.

Rockport Film Workshops
The Maine Photographic Workshops
Rockport, ME 04856

You Oughta Be in Pictures

Remember that time you walked out of the local Bijou, firmly convinced that you could make a better movie than the one you just saw? Well, here's your chance. A genuine Hollywood producer from a genuine Hollywood studio will teach you everything you need to know to become another George "Star Wars" Lucas or Francis "Godfather" Coppola, in your own reel life.

Danny Rouzer has been involved in film and theatrical productions since 1942 and has worked at several major Hollywood studios. He is offering courses that blend together the technical, artistic, and business aspects of filmmaking. Instruction is offered in cameras and lenses, lighting, cinematic tricks, sound, editing, budgeting, and financing. Graduates can seek employment or utilize their skills on such occasions as hometown weddings, graduations, and Bar Mitzvahs.

The complete course for $350 runs for two weeks. For those not from Tinseltown, there will be opportunities to visit Disneyland, the beaches, and homes of the stars and producers of the industry. —T.G.

Danny Rouzer Studio
Motion Picture Production Services
7022 Melrose Ave.
Hollywood, CA 90038

Treasures Left Behind

Orient Yourself

Let's suppose you're off on a trip to the Far East, hoping to learning something about its art treasures, firsthand. Let's also suppose you've been allowed to bring someone with you—an expert to aid you in your quest.

Let's further suppose that Michael Ridley, Esq., is available to make the journey with you. Mr. Ridley, F.R.A.I., F.S.A. Scot., F.R.A.S., is the keeper of Oriental art and antiquities at the Bournemouth Museums and Art Galleries. He has traveled extensively throughout South East Asia, the Far East, and Japan. He specializes in the development and spread of Buddhist art and is also the author of three books in the "Art of Religion" series.

Do you suppose Mr. Ridley might just be able to give you an insight or two into Far Eastern art during your trip?

The answer to that one is: you bet your pagodas he could. Well, Mr. Ridley is, in fact, available for expert advice in the Far East—just as dozens of other men and women with equally rich backgrounds are available for trips all over the world. That is, if you do your traveling on one of Swan's Art Treasure Tours.

Swan, an English company represented in North America by Esplanade Tours of Boston, will take you to most any of the earth's treasured places and provide you with on-the-spot expertise that is intended to make your trip a rich and rewarding experience. Their group of lecturers, built and expanded during the company's quarter century of business, is unrivalled in its field.

There are few spots of artistic interest in the world that Swan doesn't cover, and even fewer treasures within those domains that aren't on their list. A sampling of their offerings would include the art treasures of France, Spain, England, Italy, Portugal, Poland, Transylvania, Bulgaria, Moravia, India, Pakistan, Afghanistan, Nepal, Bhutan, Sri Lanka, Malaysia, Java, Hong Kong, Thailand, Burma, Bali, Singapore, Japan, Moscow, Leningrad, North Africa, the Middle East, Turkey, Mexico, and Central and South America.

To be sure, at the root of it all, Swan is in the tours-for-tourists business, just as thousands of other travel companies are. But their approach isn't the standard hit-the-high-points program that most touring outfits sell. Their design is to appeal to a more sophisticated audience, one filled with travelers who truly intend to learn and investigate as they go.

Though lectures are included on all tours, there is no force-feeding of information. If a work of art or a period of style interests you, your expert will be glad to provide a lengthy explanation. But if you'd rather wander off on your own, then please be their guest.

Tours are limited to a maximum of 32 people, and they last anywhere from two to four weeks. Most prices fall within the $1500 to $3000 range.

That little something extra—call it a touch of class—seems to separate Swan's Art Treasures Tours from the rest of the pack. —C.McB.

Swan's Art Treasures Tours
Esplanade Tours
Gen. Sales Agents for
Swan (Hellenic) Ltd.
38 Newbury St.
Boston, MA 02116

Anglo-Arto-philia

Unstuff yourself from a chair! Why browse over books about the great art collections of England when you know photographs can never really depict the grandeur of the art works housed in galleries and old mansions? England is only a flight away, and through the University of Wisconsin's British Study Center, you can join a group tour and view the art collections of London.

For 21 days, you will be immersed in art and art history, touring the National Gallery, the Tower of London, St. Paul's Cathedral, and some of the great old houses of the region. You will feast your eyes on many of the world's most famous masterpieces, while experts show and tell all. You will also take architectural walks, visit art book shops, and explore the streets of London on your own.

Since the dollar and the pound are playing tiddly-winks at this time, the total cost can only be estimated to average $1000-$1100. This includes air fare (round trip from Wisconsin), 20 nights' accommodation with breakfast, guided sightseeing tours, admission tickets, transportation by private bus on all visits outside central London, lectures, and a study guide program. —R.B.

The Art Collections of London
British Study Center
Attn: Dr. Lorin Robinson
Arts & Sciences Outreach
University of Wisconsin
River Falls, WI 54022

You Gotta Have Art—and Business

Art and business may not appear to be ideal bedmates. About like spinach and ice cream, you might think.

But the fact of the matter is there's an interdependence between these two fields. And that's one of the reasons we'd like to recommend The New Academy for Art Studies in London for their fresh approach to the history—and the business—of art.

In one of three ten-week programs between October and June, you can get a firm groundwork in the study of both the fine and decorative arts. The course focuses on painting, sculpture, architecture, furniture, ceramics, glass, and metalwork and includes a critical investigation of the businesses that are connected with the arts—auction houses, art galleries, and museums.

Among the program's features are a project tracing the history of taste and patronage in England, visits to important private collections not generally accessible to the public, discussions at the studios of contemporary artists, and lectures by over 60 visiting experts.

The program may be of special interest to art graduates but is by no means limited to them. A serious desire to study the arts is the only prerequisite. Write for costs. —C.McB.

The New Academy for Art Studies
12 Lonsdale Rd.
London, W.11
England, UK

When in England...

As almost any archaeology student will tell you, classroom study is valuable, but firsthand examination of genuine historical sites can be invaluable. For individuals wishing to combine the study of a rich archaeological heritage with an overseas vacation, a unique program sponsored by the University of Wisconsin's British Study Center provides just such an opportunity.

"The Roman Presence in Britain" is a three-week tour of England and Scotland that enables both archaeology and history buffs to study roads, settlements, forts, and walls left by the Romans during their 400-year occupation of Great Britain. The program includes tutorials that brief participants on the sites visited on the tour. Museums housing art collections from that period will also be featured.

Fourteen of the 21 days will be spent touring the countryside by bus. In addition, students will explore London, Edinburgh, and the two cities that remain walled from Roman times, York and Chester.

While transportation fares make exact costs impossible to determine, students will pay an estimated $1100, which includes all tuition costs and round-trip air fare from New York to London. —G.R.

The Roman Presence in Britain
British Study Center
Attn: Dr. Lorin Robinson
Arts & Sciences Outreach
University of Wisconsin
River Falls, WI 54022

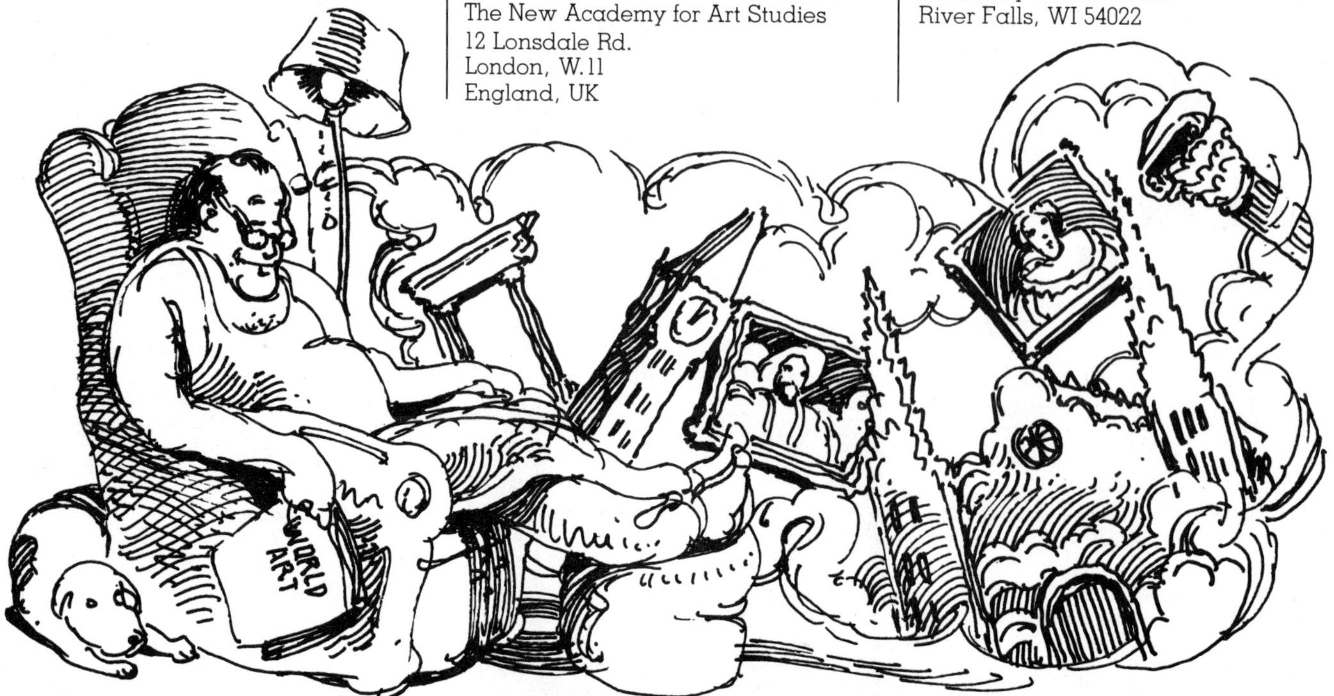

Louvre It Up!

You awaken to the sound of bells, dress quickly, and dash down the ancient staircase for your morning croissants. Satisfied with breakfast, you stroll along the Boul' Miche, window-shop a bit, and greet your friends along the way. All this while you're on your way to school.

Class is assembled and you troop over to the Louvre to look at some of the most famous French paintings of the past two centuries. Your professor, an art historian, enlightens you on the significance of what you are seeing. You learn that next week, your class will visit a famous French contemporary artist in his studio, to watch him paint and learn about his art.

This exquisite dream can be a reality. The Paris American Academy offers a series of courses in the history of French art, from the Romanesque period to the 20th century. Lectures are given in English, and visits to many museums and galleries in and around Paris are included. You can enroll in the Academy for credit or take the courses for your own pleasure and edification.

Write to find out costs and dates. Bon voyage! —A.L.

"History of French Art" Courses
Paris American Academy
9, Rue des Ursulines
75005 Paris
France

A painting in a museum hears more ridiculous opinions than anything else in the world.
EDMOND DE GONCOURT

There's No Place Like Rome

On the unofficial cultural exchange, we Americans get Gucci, Pucci, and Alfa-Romeo. But these Italian goodies do not replace the real richness of Italy—the art and architecture that one confronts face to face in Rome.

An extensive hotel chain in the Eternal City has put together a series of excursions known as the "Italian Mosaic Tours." Designed for Italian art and architecture buffs, these four tours touch on the ancient, early Christian, Renaissance, and Baroque periods of the city. Rather than view a mere facade, one studies foundations and floor plans. In place of the minutes one usually takes to see masterpieces, half-days are set aside. The Colosseum, Palatine Hill, the Pantheon, the Roman Forum, the Catacombs, St. Peter's, Borghese Gallery, and dozens of other sites are visited. Similar tours are also available to historic Tuscany, Venice and the Veneto region, and Sicily.

"Inside" commentaries on art periods and regions by local guides will enlighten your sensibilities. Italian Mosaic Tours have been organized for groups in the past, but E & M Associates are planning tours for individuals in the future. Check with them for their current tour information and for specific costs. —T.G.

Italian Mosaic Tours
E & M Associates
667 Madison Ave.
New York, NY 10021

Holy Land Lore

Dilettantes need not enquire. The Institute for Antiquity and Christianity is for serious-minded individuals desiring an earnest study of the origins of the Western cultural heritage.

The Institute provides extensive opportunities for continuing education in its lectures, exhibits, and study trips focusing on the ancient Near East, the classical culture of Greece and Rome, and the biblical world of Judaism and Christianity.

An example of the Institute's programs is its lecture series entitled "Archaeology and the Bible," an eight-part presentation that examines how archaeology illuminates the historical background of the Bible. A second example is their escorted archaeological tour of Egypt and Israel, which includes visits to some of the most spectacular monuments of the ancient civilizations. The tour, led by local guides and complemented by Institute lectures, offers an in-depth look at the history of these lands from the pyramids to the walls of Jerusalem.

Those wishing to take part in the Institute's activities, or to aid them in their research work, may do so by becoming a member at a cost of $25. —C.McB.

The Institute for Antiquity and Christianity
Claremont Graduate School
831 Dartmouth Ave.
Claremont, CA 91711

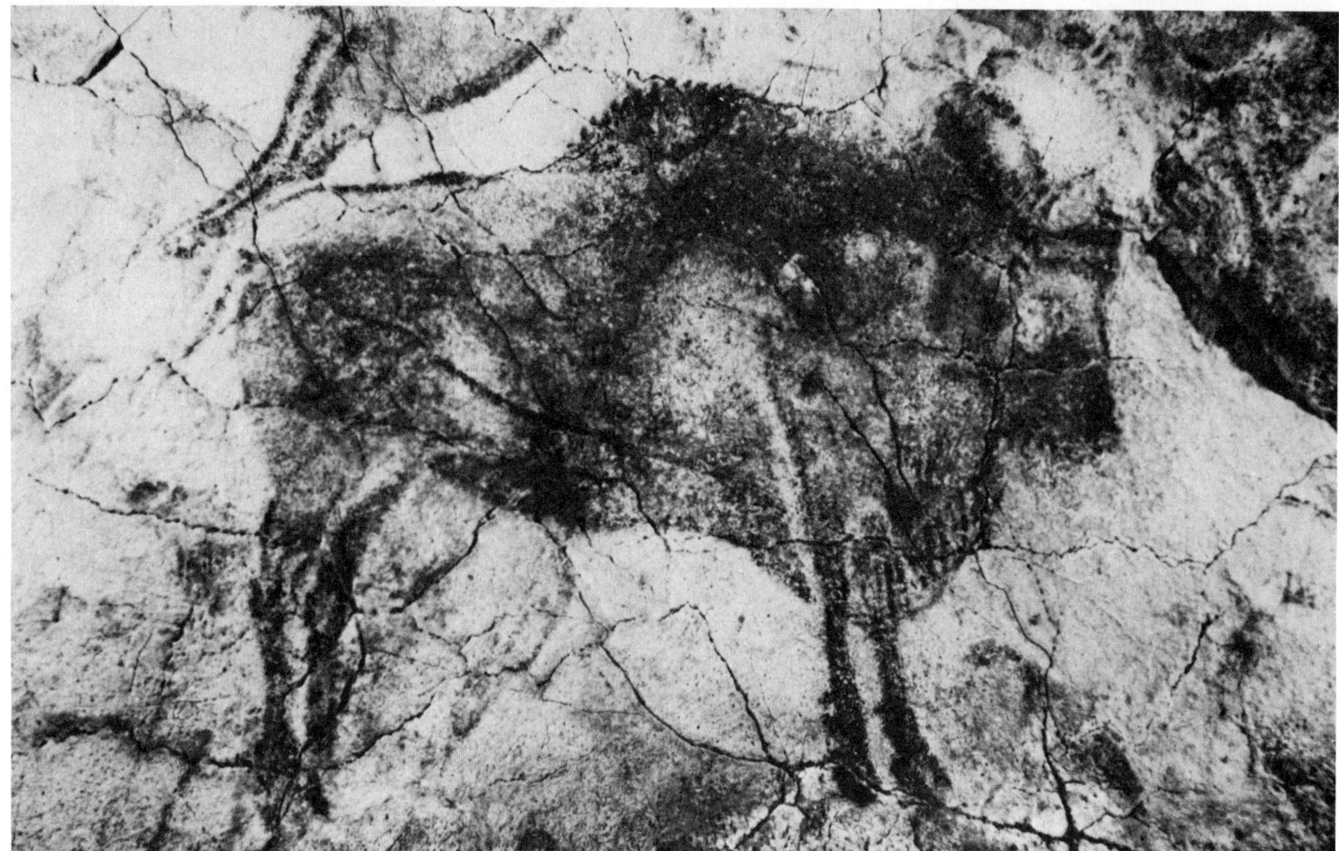

Ancient Galleries

If you have ever yearned to visit the Perigord Caves of the Dordogne Valley, then you know instantly what we are talking about—the site of paintings, done 14,000 years ago, by Paleolithic man. If you have yearned, then you recognize what a rare journey you are being invited to join. Project Earliest Man is an art tour that takes you backward through time, while you travel in all the best comfort and graces of our modern day.

You will observe bison, horses, and other animals painted on walls by artists of long ago who were sensitive to the demands of anatomy. Look for the muscles of the bison, and at the proportions between hunter and prey. These paintings will jar loose your conception of "primitive" man as a shaggy creature with a mere rudimentary brain.

You will also have time to ponder the mysteries of Stonehenge, whose structure reveals a sophisticated understanding of astronomy by Stone and Bronze Age inhabitants. You will continue on to Castle Combe, a restored and picturesque medieval village. Dinner and accommodations will be in an elegant manor house.

You will be accompanied throughout your tour by experts in prehistory, cave art, and European culture. Lectures by some of Europe's foremost experts will be included. Such specialists could include archaeologist Trevor Rowley of Oxford University or the Secretary of the Council for British Archaeology.

But burial tombs and ancient galleries are not all this tour has to offer. While visiting these sites, you will live in equally extraordinary accommodations—towering castles, elegant chateaux, and quaint country inns. You will dine on the finest gastronomy of Europe, such as truffles and pate in the Perigord.

You will visit London and Oxford and tour the Loire Valley. You will lunch at a 400-year-old pub in Wales. You will reach Cognac, where the world's finest brandy is produced. Backward in time you will go, to the Basque country, where the origin of the people is neither French nor Spanish.

The cost of the tour is $2500 per person, air fare excluded. Sanctuaries or truffles, anyone? —R.B.

Project Earliest Man
Society Expeditions
P.O. Box 5088
University Station
Seattle, WA 98105

Flo with the Arts

Dreams need never languish or die. If you have yearned for the opportunity to feast on art, you can stave your starving at remarkably low fees in the lovely Tuscan countryside at La Poggerina, a converted seminary near the town of Figline Valdarno.

There, under a University of Northern Colorado Program in Comparative Arts and on a true Renaissance campus, you may join in the study of classical art, the history of architecture in Florence, Renaissance painting, medieval Tuscan art, and the Baroque period. Field trips will take you to the Tower of Pisa, Arezzo, and the Temple of Minerva, a Roman edifice dating back to the first century after Christ.

Your accommodations include meals, and you will live as a student, perhaps mostly in blue jeans. Although you must write for tuition costs, full pension comes to around $10 per day. Where can you beat that? Students may be from outside the UNC and may enroll for either undergraduate or graduate level academic credit. The program runs three times a year—spring, summer, and fall. Long underwear may be needed in winter, but bring your suit for bathing in the summer. —R.B.

Comparative Arts
in Florence Program
Attn: Dr. James Cobb
Center for Outreach Education
University of Northern Colorado
Greeley, CO 80639

The Art Before the Course

Some people never leave home. Indeed, their thoughts, daily routines, and learning experiences are strictly good ole USA.

Not a chance that this description characterizes the involved adults who sign up for the NYU World Campus Program. These folks study art and architecture with the experts in the world's major centers for such treasures.

C. Bruce Hunter, a noted authority and author of the *Guide to Ancient Maya Ruins*, both teaches the course on Mayan archaeology and escorts the travel/study tour of archaeological sites around Mexico City. Scholars in Italy will explain Rome's five civilization layers and Florence's position as seat of the Renaissance. Leading architects, preservationists, and landscape artists in Japan will cover pre- and post-modern architectural development. World Campus participants should plan to be away about nine days at a cost of approximately $700 to $800.

NYU's weekend program reflects the same spirit of learning with specialists, but in areas closer to the university's home base. Architect Richard Crowley, supervisor of the historic survey of the Hudson Valley's Rhinebeck area, is seminar leader for this architectural tour. Crowley has access to many residences usually closed to the public view. Or, if art is more to your liking, you can join art historian Margaret Grayburn on her tour of impressive art collections in Boston. The weekend price of $170 includes lodging, meals, transportation, lectures, reading lists, and materials. —S.A.

World Campus Program
New York University
Division of Liberal Studies
2 University Place
New York, NY 10003

Weekend Seminars Program
New York University
School of Continuing Education
2 University Place, Room 21
New York, NY 10003

A Capital Find

Please bite your tongue and don't think cynical thoughts when we tell you there are some real pros in Washington, DC, ready to give you the tour.

No, we don't mean *those* guys. Our group consists of art specialists who work for the National Fine Arts Association, experts in art tours of the nation's capital.

There are several things we like about the NFAA tours. One is the emphasis on American art and architecture, an area often lost in the highfalutin' shuffle of world aesthetics. America has a rich heritage in art, and Washington, DC—and its surrounding environs—offer an exciting share of it.

Another is the multiplicity of the tours themselves, focusing on the city's great galleries and museums (among them the Hirshhorn, Corcoran, and Renwick), the mansions of Old Georgetown, and nearby historic spots like Annapolis and Fredericksburg.

And, too, an NFAA guide is really an "expert," not just someone with a memorized script. Each guide has a degree in fine arts, art history, or a related field, and most of them have at least one graduate degree. Furthermore, guides attend a six-month training course and are continually encouraged to keep abreast of new developments in their fields.

NFAA tours are for parties of 25 and up, and the costs are reasonable. They'll even plan special itineraries to suit your group's needs. —C.McB.

Art Tours of the Nation's Capital
National Fine Arts Associates, Inc.
5402 Duval Dr.
Washington, DC 20016

Buy Old Masters. They fetch a much better price than old mistresses.
LORD BEAVERBROOK

C. PECK

The universe is full of
magical things patiently waiting
for our wits to grow sharper.
EDEN PHILLPOTS

Insights into the Elements

Ten thousand years ago, while our ancestors still lived in caves, a night-gazing human being observed that the stars move from one side of the sky to the other. He concluded that they must be controlled by a great power unknown on earth. Magic.

Plants grow from the womb of the earth when the great sky god sends rain. Magic. Unspeakable power is lodged in the hearts of noble beasts. Magic.

And then came the great advance: some prehistoric genius attempted to control the elements. He killed the lion he worshipped and dressed in its skin, giving himself the lion's magic. He danced in a circle around a smoky fire in that bloody lion's skin—and so began the transformation of magic into science.

No, scientists do not dress up in lionskins. But they do pursue the same goal: they try to harness the universe and subdue it to the will of mankind. Yet modern science, for all its sophistication, still stands in awe of the universe it tries to understand.

We invite you to share in that awe, and in that rapidly advancing sphere of knowledge called "Science." We've grouped our invitations into five sections. In the first, you'll sample the marvels (and the oddities) of the waters. You'll follow whales with the American Cetacean Society on their journey to breeding grounds, and you'll study the ageless sea turtle with the Caretta Research Project on one of Georgia's barrier islands.

Our second section will guide you in an exploration of the past. You'll look through the remnants of other civilizations in your search for monuments and shards—worldwide.

And then you'll take a closer look at the wonders of earth and space. You'll begin under the ground—where our ancestors resided—with the study of caves. And you'll soar upward to the stars with the Adler Planetarium.

Our fourth section is a look at the past and the future from a different viewpoint: energy and technology. You'll learn about people who are reemploying yesterday's technologies in programs that go back to the basics: the basics of homestead-ing. And you'll see the strides we're making (and hope to make) in such fields as solar energy.

And from there, it's but a short hop to today's developing natural science: ecology. From the Grand Tetons and Yosemite to Zion—and out into the wildernesses of the world—you'll explore the unending chain of nature, and the balance between natural communities and today's modern world.

True, we're not heavy on magic in this chapter. But we are heavy on respect—which is the same thing in some ways. And when you come right down to it, there *is* magic at the other end of a telescope and in the ocean and in the remote natural corners of the world.

Precious magic.

Illustration by Everett Peck

Curiosities of the Sea

No Doubt About This Spout

One way to have a "whale of a good time"—while learning about science—is to join up with the American Cetacean Society's whale-watching trips during the annual migration of the great gray whales from the Bering Sea to the lagoons of Baja.

These creatures, the largest and best known of the whale species, can put on quite a spectacle for visitors. You do have to keep your eyes glued to the water, for the whales come to the surface every so often in order to breathe. There is an exhalation or spout delivered a moment after the nostrils break the surface. The spout is usually 10 to 15 feet high in a single column that divides slightly at the top.

Camera buffs find this quite a challenge, as the gray whale often "spy-hops" (whale language for "peeking") just as you are changing your film. But then again, you may be lucky and have him breathe right in front of you, giving you a picture you will be raving about for years to come.

Whether you choose to go down for just one day ($14.00 for ACS members, $16.50 nonmembers) or take the eight-day excursion ($485 members, $510 nonmembers), there will be scientists along to instruct you in what you are seeing and to show slides that will enhance the knowledge you gain on this trip.

The sportfishing boat *Bold Contender* is used for the six-hour whale outings. It has a roomy bow for viewing and is equipped with a full galley on board for your dining and drinking convenience.

If you choose the longer voyage, you will travel on *The Searcher*, a modern, well-equipped vessel—your floating hotel. On this voyage you will travel to San Ignacio Lagoon, "the home of the friendly whale." Shore parties will explore some of the more remote areas of the lagoon.

If you are truly adventurous, bring along your wetsuit, mask, fins, and snorkel, and swim in water with unlimited visibility—alongside sea lions and fish.

Trips are accompanied by experienced American Cetacean Society whale-watch guides who will enlighten you with tales about the gray whale, its biology, and the natural history of its environment. Besides the gray whales, there will be California sea lions, possibly elephant and harbor seals, and a variety of bird life.

Expeditions are scheduled in January and February of each year. You need to be a bit nimble for these trips, because you will be hopping in and out of small skiffs. And don't forget your seasickness pills—if that is your inclination. —R.B.

Whale-Watch Outings
American Cetacean Society
P.O. Box 22305
San Diego, CA 92122

Shiver Me Timbers

The wind is howling at 35 knots. Your fingers are so numb that you can't hang on to the foresail line. Your nose is red and runny. The mainmast makes a 45 degree arc with every roll of the ship.

"Hey," yells your instructor, "shinny up the mast and take care of that jammed halyard."

You decline. Heartily.

"I'll flunk you if you don't."

You do it. And not surprisingly, you do it well.

Instructor? Flunk? Yes, because you're a student sailing on the schooner *Harvey Gamage*. Not only do you learn how to unstick stuck halyards, but you study oceanography, maritime history, and navigation.

You'll sail from St. Thomas to the Bahamas, and you'll work in marine labs and visit wildlife sanctuaries along the way. You'll learn how the barracuda became a barracuda—and why he doesn't like cold water—in your Biology of Fish class.

Dirigo Cruises teamed up with Long Island University and put together this semester at sea. The "Seamester" lasts for two months during the spring and fall of each year, and it is fully accredited. The cost for the program in 1978 was $3100.

But I doubt whether you'll be thinking about that paperwork on your desk when you're 90 feet above deck, swaying like some misplaced Tarzan, trying to unjam a jammed halyard. —J.S.H.

Semester at Sea
Dirigo Cruises
39 Waterside Lane
Clinton, CT 06413

A Whale of a Deal

Hmmmm, how to open this piece? Well, we could do the Captain Ahab bit. Throw in a few "ahoys" and "shiver me timbers."

Naw, too obvious.

How about the Jonah angle? Three days in the belly of, and all that.

No. Don't like that one either.

Perhaps the used-car salesman approach: "Have we got a whale of a deal for you!"

Uh, uh. Too corny.

Oh, we'll just go straight with it. After all, it is one of the best of whale watching programs. No need to try anything snappy.

Whales are great big, almost always gentle, ocean-going mammals who have gotten much recent public exposure as a threatened species. The viewing of these creatures has enjoyed a tremendous boom lately. Adventures International runs four different whale trips each year—three to Mexico and one to Hawaii.

The thing that makes their trips stand out from the bunch is the emphasis they put on learning about—and not just looking at—these massive creatures. Well before the adventure begins, participants are sent bibliographies and are encouraged to heighten their experience by perusing these selected books and articles. Once underway, slide shows and informal lectures allow for even deeper insights into the whale's daily activities.

The nine-day Hawaiian tours costs $495, plus air fare. The eight- and nine-day Mexican tours range from $550 to $600. —C.McB.

Whale-Watch Adventures
Adventures International
4421 Albert St.
Oakland, CA 94619

Wait Until Dark

You know about all-night diners, all-night discos, and all-night DJs. But what about all-night turtles? Bet we've got you there.

The Savannah Science Museum conducts the Caretta Research Project at the National Wildlife Refuge on Wassaw Island, perhaps the most unspoiled of Georgia's barrier islands. The object of the project is to learn more about the habits of the Atlantic loggerhead sea turtle (*Caretta caretta*), a threatened species.

As a week-long participant, you will spend each night patrolling beaches, searching for the huge female loggerheads which crawl ashore to deposit their eggs between late May and July of each year. Turtles will be tagged, measured, and observed. Your research team will be headed by a leader who will share his knowledge of field techniques and turtle habits.

Participants pay $120 (which includes room and board) for this opportunity to participate in scientific research. The only qualification is that you be enthusiastic about islands and turtles—and, they might add, be willing to stay up all night to prove it. —C.McB.

The Caretta Project
Savannah Science Museum
Attn: Gerald Williamson
4405 Paulsen St.
Savannah, GA 31405

The Whale that wanders round the Pole
Is not a table fish
You cannot bake or boil him whole
Nor serve him in a dish.
HILAIRE BELLOC

Ocean Notions

You'll have a whale of a good time on an Oceanic Expedition. It's guaranteed—because most of the trips spy on cetaceans.

But whale watching alone is not the goal. Instead, Oceanic Expeditions afford lay-people the opportunity to join in research programs conducted by scientists. Take the orca expedition, for example. Killer whale myths are terrifying, but ungrounded. Participants in the two-week expedition that focuses on the behavior of orca herds—or pods—quickly learn that huge as killers are, they pose no threat to us.

Worry not. Enthusiasm alone is all you need to join. Participants in Oceanic Expeditions are assigned useful tasks that do not require a technical background. Photographing whales, for example, could be one of your tasks, as a photo library is indispensable to the science researcher, and all you need to know is how to press the shutter button.

Gray whales, too, are the subjects of Oceanic Expeditions. Try the one-week whale-watching adventure off Mexico's Baja peninsula, the heart of the grays' breeding ground. Using inflatable boats, participants venture into the sheltered lagoons where the whales mate and rear their young—and where photographic opportunities are unexcelled.

Want a species with a bit more spice? How about the eight- to twelve-day shark study, where Jaws and his kin are your focus? Under the leadership of a marine biologist, tour members can live aboard the *Quest*, a 40-foot ketch, and roam the South Pacific in search of sharks. Better still, and for the courageous, you can dive into the waters for close-up scientific observation of the sharks.

Bird rookeries, sponge beds, tidal pools, and the like are the tamer coastal treats offered during the eight-day Crystal River, Florida, adventure. Field study and specimen collecting occupy much of the time on this trip, which is conducted by a noted biologist/naturalist.

Additional Oceanic Expeditions include East Coast whale watches, snorkeling in Hawaii, marine science on Maine's coast, and a six-day course in emergency medicine at sea. Program cost varies with length and destination. The two-week orca study is tabbed at $600, for example. Twelve days of South Pacific shark watching costs $660. All programs also require membership in the Oceanic Society at a $12 annual fee. —R.McG.

Oceanic Expeditions
The Oceanic Society
240 Fort Mason
San Francisco, CA 94123

The sea, like a great sultan,
supports thousands of ships,
his lawful wives.
These he caresses and chastises
as the case may be.
FELIX RIESENBERT

Join the Marine

If the sea's your thing, WIMSC is the place to be. Unscramble that alphabet soup and what you have is the Wallop Island Marine Science Center on the south Atlantic coast of the Delmarva Peninsula, where Maryland and Virginia meet. It's the site of dozens of American University summer field courses in marine and environmental sciences. Courses run the academic gamut from introductory marine science to advanced graduate-level probings of the deep.

Beginners, for example, flock to the Introduction to Oceanography course. At-sea assignments and field trips are mixed with classroom discussions of the chemical and geological aspects of the oceans.

Marine ichthyology, anatomy of chordates, and marine botany await the more advanced. Background courses in biology and geology are often prerequisites for these offerings.

Amateur naturalists, sportsmen, and other interested citizens are welcome. Most courses run three weeks, and the cost per program is about $275 for tuition, with an additional $200 for room and board. —R.McG.

Field Courses in Marine & Environmental Science
Division of Continuing Education & Summer Sessions
The American University
Washington, DC 20016

The Young Man & the Sea

You've always wanted to be a part of a Cousteau expedition. Never mind that you get seasick. Never mind that you can't scuba. You'll scrub decks. You'll even stand watch at night. You just want to take part.

Your chance has come. Every summer, Jean-Michel Cousteau, son of Jacques, holds Project Ocean Search research expeditions. The expeditions study oceanography, marine ecology, pollution, and other topics. You can pursue your own research, and you can receive academic credit from the University of Southern California's College of Continuing Education.

Anyone over 16 can apply. If you scuba, great. If not, there'll still be plenty of jobs to do as a part of the team of marine scientists, staff, and divers that accompanies the ship.

Projects for 1979 have not been finalized as of this writing, but 1978 expeditions visited the Caribbean, the South Pacific, and islands off the coast of South Carolina and Southern California. Projects range from ten days to one month, and costs vary from $600 to $3400. —J.S.H.

Project Ocean Search Expeditions
Jean-Michel Cousteau Institute
P.O. Drawer CC
Harbour Town
Hilton Head Island, SC 29928

Keeping Pace with the Herd It's late December or January, and you just happen to be in the Southwest. You're a bit tired of taking trips to the desert, and you want some kind of adventure you can't busy yourself with back home. Well, the Gray Whale spends Christmas in the Southwest, too, and you can follow the last leg of its journey to its breeding grounds off Baja California. San Diego Natural History Museum whale-watching trips keep pace with the herds, and what a reasonable idea for an afternoon—only $4.50 for adults.

Whale-Watch Trips
San Diego Natural History Museum
P.O. Box 1390
San Diego, CA 92112

Some Bodies You Should Know Oceans cover 70 percent of the earth, yet maritime concerns are generally not included in the education of most Americans. You might well be acquainted with the terms of the Versailles Treaty. But how long can you speak on the subject of bodies of water? Sea Semester attempts to give scientific and practical experience in the marine and nautical sciences. The 12-week program is divided into shore ($950, excluding room and board) and sea ($2050) components.

Sea Semester
Sea Education Association, Inc.
P.O. Box 6
Church St.
Woods Hole, MA 02543

One Fish, Two Fish, Red Fish, Blue Fish Driftwood identification, intertidal flora and fauna, and coastal navigation are just some of the short courses offered by Seatauqua. Beach walks, films, and lectures explore the Oregon coast. Write for their brochure.

Marine Science Center/Seatauqua
Oregon State University
546 SW Smith Ct.
Newport, OR 97365

All Decked Out The deck of a sailboat could be the best spot from which to learn about the marine environments of Lanai, Maui, and Molokai, Hawaii. Marine Life Mini-Expeditions are for those who want to go beyond casual sails along the shore. Trips run in late May to early September and are sponsored by the Waikiki Aquarium.

Marine Life Mini-Expeditions
Sea Trek Hawaii
47-696-1 Hui Kelu St.
Kaneohe, HI 96744

The Fabric of Oceans Of all the 50 states, none is more sea-oriented than Hawaii. In Hawaii, the ocean is "more than a constant visual horizon; it is the fabric of Hawaii's sciences, culture, and life style." What better place, then, to study the ocean than in this site of beaches, bays, and lagoons? The Introduction to Ocean Studies program is an intensive ten-week experience that focuses on ocean sciences as well as basic maritime skills. The all-inclusive cost for the program in '78 was $2267.

Summer Introduction to Ocean Studies
Hawaii Loa College
45-045 Kamehameha Hwy.
P.O. Box 764
Kaneohe, HI 96744

Wet Your Feet with This The Virgin Islands, Block Island, and Cozumel, Mexico—what do all these sites have in common? They are the locations of the marine biology field work courses offered by Suffolk County Community College. Students learn field techniques and the collection/preservation of marine organisms. A science background is not essential, although students are required to submit a paper on their observations at the end of the trip. Costs are: $400 for the Virgin Islands (11 days in January), $194 for Block Island (5 days in August), and $371 for Mexico (7 nights in January). Happy classifying!

Field Courses in Marine Biology
Attn: Prof. Henry Keatts
Eastern Campus
Suffolk County Community College
Riverhead, NY 11901

Porpoises in Need (of Protection) We think of whales, dolphins, porpoises, and seals as permanent residents of our waters, but behind the scenes, their future lies somewhat in question. Nineteen marine-related organizations, ranging from the Oceanic Society to the International Fund for Animal Welfare and the Cousteau Society, sponsor a protection workshop in this marine mammal controversy. Specialists will identify and discuss key issues, and interested citizens as well as scientists are invited. Whale-watch trips, accompanied by a marine biologist, are also scheduled. Registration fee is $25 per person. (Meals and lodging are extra.) Whale-watch fee is $5. Write for the dates for this year's conference.

Marine Mammal Protection
New England Workshop, Inc.
c/o Provincetown Center for
Coastal Studies
P.O. Box 826
Provincetown, MA 02657

In Pods We Trust

Looking for a whale of a time? Try watching in Mexico's Baja California where, in the quiet lagoons, whale pods still frolic and give birth to their young. But, exciting as whale watching can be, one must also be aware of the whales' delicate ecosystem and avoid disturbing their environment. Piet and Carolyn Van de Mark, experienced Baja hands, will gladly initiate you into the rites and *rights* of whale watching, as their Baja Frontier Tours are designed to meet a variety of vacation needs—from weekend whale-watching adventures to an eight-day Baja safari that allows exploration of onyx mines and ancient desert structures.

Some tours offer hotel accommodations, while others feature camp-style living. All, however, revel in Baja's treasures.

Cost hinges on tour length and the type of accommodations you choose, but most of these Baja vacations range between $400 and $800. Custom tours, with higher price tags, are also available. —R.McG.

Baja's Frontier Tours
Attn: Piet & Carolyn Van de Mark
4365 New Jersey
San Diego, CA 92116

Not-So-Ancient Mariners

A morning of note-taking on the behavior and acoustics of whales is part of the curriculum of seabound students on the 144-foot sailing vessel *r/v Regina Maris.* Several times each year the ship slips away from Boston Harbor, bound for oceanographic research in waters cold or tropical. The professional crew of scientists on board is accompanied by students who swab the decks and collect data for the study in progress. Participants can learn celestial navigation and marine mammology, firsthand.

Students and scientists on the *Regina Maris* bobbed about the Galapagos Islands last summer, studying tuna-porpoise-seabird relationships. That data will aid policy-makers in protecting porpoises that are caught in the fishing nets of tuna fleets.

Students pay $2800 to participate, have had one year of college biology under their belts, and possess a strong interest in oceanography. The *Regina Maris* sets sail under the sponsorship of the Ocean Research and Education Society, a nonprofit group whose goals are aimed at generating knowledge of the ocean environment. The Society is a membership organization. Members can share in the experiences of the *Regina Maris* through a weekly newsletter and can enjoy a day sail a couple of times a year. —J.W.

r/v Regina Maris
Ocean Research &
Education Society, Inc.
51 Commercial Wharf 6
Boston, MA 02110

In Search of Monuments & Shards

Unearth Some History

"Come on, grandpa. Come on. Tell us."

The old man's eyes took on a twinkle.

"Tell us again how you became the greatest archaeologist of them all."

He shifted his legs and looked down at the two little boys. He folded his elbows on his knees and his face broke into a smile.

"All right, if you really want me to. It was way back in 1979 that I got my start. I was a young man then, and I heard of this program that had recently started out in California, at Berkeley, a program they called University Research Expeditions. The idea was for just plain folks—like I was then—to join in with archaeologists and those kind of people and go off and dig up the earth.

"We had to pay to go along, mind you, anywhere from $400 to $1400, if I remember right. But that was OK. They used our money to cover the expenses on the projects, so it was going for a good cause.

"Well, they had some strange and exciting digs back then. You could go off to a place like Labrador, Canada, and investigate late Eskimo sites. You could assist in preparing an archaeological map of the Theban Necropolis in Egypt. You could dig for fossils in Nevada, or excavate a medieval African town in Ghana. Italy, Iran, Brazil—by golly, there wasn't anywhere they didn't go. And the nice part was that you were doing important stuff on those trips. You were helping scientists discover how societies got started, how they developed, why they disappeared. You could travel and learn with folks from 18 to 80.

"So I took one of those trips—down off the coast of South America to study some pottery—and the bug bit me. No, I don't mean any kind of insect; I mean the discovery bug. It got in my blood. It took me and shook me.

"Next thing you knew I was joining those university expeditions all the time. Oh, it wasn't always fun and games, of course. But if you had the bug like I did, you didn't mind. They wanted people like me, people with a love of history and archaeology and a willingness to participate. They didn't want any tourists.

"And from there it just grew, boys. I got to doing more and more digging. They couldn't hold me back. Mountains, jungles, deserts—I had to explore them all. And I did, and they led me up here," he said, sweeping his hand across the great glass dome of their spaceship as it neared the Martian ruins. —C.McB.

University Research Expeditions Program
University of California
Berkeley, CA 94720

Layer by Layer

How good are you with a spade? A hand trowel? A paint brush? Got a whim to go digging down through the alluvial soil, to assist in uncovering 10,000 years of continuous inhabitation by man?

Where? Not in Egypt. Not in darkest Africa. In Illinois. It is all part of the Northwestern University Archaeological Program which enables laymen to assist in the excavation of sites. For at least 8000 years before Christ was born, individuals were busily leading their lives along the river valleys of Illinois.

The dig, known as the Koster Site, has been excavated down to a level of 35 feet, unearthing village built upon village. The villages are called "horizons," and outlines of permanent houses on prepared terraces have already been uncovered.

What can you hope to gain, aside from dirty hands, blisters (maybe), and a few pieces of clay or tools? Well, you would contribute to the study of the origins of the first people who came to America. And you might help to answer questions about their ability to read the heavens and cultivate their lands. Oh so many answers lie buried beneath layers of dirt! Join up now and dig deep. —R.B.

Archaeological Program
Northwestern University
P.O. Box 1499
Evanston, IL 60204

Sites to Behold

A list of areas associated with archaeological sites would not normally include Arkansas. And true, Arkansas has not yielded archaeological findings of international acclaim. But the state's historic past is now being preserved through a unique program—sponsored by the Arkansas Archaeological Survey—in which amateur and professional archaeologists work together in an educational and productive atmosphere. The program is ideal for archaeology buffs who do not have the cash or the inclination to seek archaeology sites abroad.

The program is divided into two areas. The Field Training Program in Archaeological Techniques, begun in 1964, is desianed to provide the layman with experience in excavation, site survey, and laboratory processing under professional supervision. The field sessions last from 9 to 20 days and are held at different sites throughout the state. The Certification Program for Lay Archaeologists concentrates on formal and extended training in various aspects of archaeology outside of an academic degree program. Both programs allow lay archaeologists "to perform a real service toward achieving the goals of preserving the past for the future."

The registration fee for either program is merely $5. Participants must join the Arkansas Archaeology Society, and membership dues are $1.50 for one entire year. —G.R.

Arkansas Archaeological Survey
Coordinating Office
University of Arkansas Museum
Fayetteville, AR 72701

Excavating for a Find

We will abstain from asking if you "dig" this one, for the excavations at Tel Dan provide an excellent environment for folks in pursuit of archaeology.

The project is sponsored (and here is a mouthful) by the Nelson Glueck School of Biblical Archaeology of the Hebrew Union College/Jewish Institute of Religion in Jerusalem. The school has engaged in important archaeological work in Israel since 1963, and Tel Dan is their latest project. Dan is a Biblical settlement at the foot of Mount Hermon and was one of two cities where Jeroboam set up the worship of the Golden Calf after Solomon's death.

The school seeks 80 volunteers each summer to work under the direction of Syro-Palestinian archaeology specialists. In addition to training in basic field techniques, participants are enrolled in an Archaeology of the Land of Israel course. The digging at Tel Dan has already uncovered a rich portion of the city's past, and the long-term excavation plan for the area promises still greater discoveries.

Volunteers can earn three hours of academic credit for this $400, five-week excavation. The program, however, is worth many times that amount in the experience gained from unearthing history itself. —C.McB.

Excavation at Tel Dan
Hebrew Union College/
Jewish Institute of Religion
Nelson Glueck School
of Biblical Archaeology
40 West 68th St.
New York, NY 10023

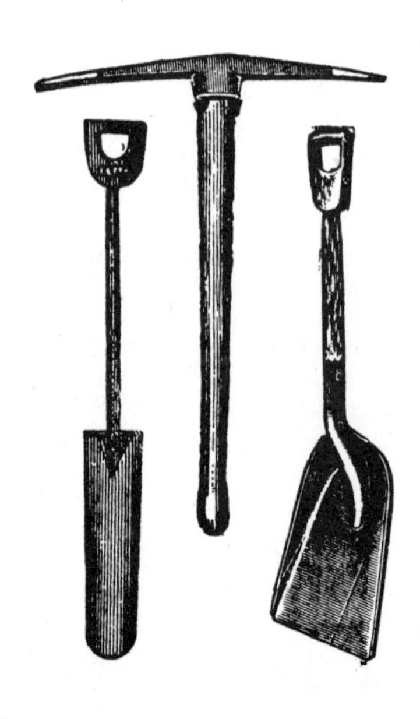

Meet Me in Old Sturbridge

You've heard hundreds of "good news/bad news" jokes, but at Old Sturbridge Village Field School in Historical Archaeology, the administration brags that the good and bad news are very much the same. The "good news" is that you'll have the opportunity to participate in all facets of the archaeological process. The bad news: you'll *have* to participate in all facets of the archaeological process. Students are expected to be fully involved in all phases of the program—in research, excavation, lectures, and seminars.

The training here is solidly archaeological. Even before arriving at the school, participants are required to digest three archaeological tomes. But the real work begins at the village itself—an outdoor museum that recreates a rural New England community of the period 1790 to 1840. In the first week, participants attend orientation classes. Before you hit the dig site with your shovel in hand, OSV wants to make certain you know what you are looking for, and why.

With the close of the initial week, students move on to the old Stratton Tavern, the current dig location. A large 18th century farmhouse in Northfield, Massachusetts, the building served as both a roadside tavern and a home residence. This dual aspect of the site is an archaeologist's dream, as the details of complex cultural interactions are unearthed.

The day begins at 8 a.m. at the dig with full-scale excavation work. That's pick-and-shovel time, and it lasts until lunch. In the afternoon, a rotating schedule comes into play. Students are assigned tasks ranging from cleaning artifacts through logging the day's discoveries. At the day's close, it's time for dinner and, afterward, a lecture or seminar.

Since the student body is limited to 24 participants per summer, there is a good deal of interaction between student and faculty. In fact, many faculty members are among the cream of the profession's crop.

While at Stratton Tavern, students are housed at the nearby Deerfield Mt. Hermon schools. Full access to school recreational facilities is granted, and the same goes for Dudley College, where students stay during orientation week.

Cost for the seven-week program is about $725, inclusive of room, board, and tuition. Academic credit can be arranged for some students. But current academic affiliation is not a prerequisite. —R.McG.

Archaeology Field School Program
Old Sturbridge Village
Sturbridge, MA 01566

Antiquities are history defaced, or some remnants of history which have escaped the shipwreck of time.
FRANCES BACON

Dig This!

Who began the King Tut craze? Steve Martin? Nope, it was the archaeological team that unearthed the boy prince and his brethren. Sign up with an archaeological dig, and a few shovel strokes later you, too, may discover critically important data.

It's easy to dig what's happening at the Archaeological Institute of America. AIA annually puts out a bulky listing of global archaeological opportunities—digs—where students, volunteers, and paid staff are needed.

For beginners, the place to start is at a field school, where the rudiments of digging methods are taught. Here, too, the variety is great. Some schools pay you to attend; others require you to pay. Volunteers, however, are sought by nearly every dig the world over.

Digs *do* change annually. But each year's list of sites is enticing, with extensive field work going on in the US as well as in England, Canada, Crete, Yugoslavia, and so on down the list. Next year's line-up is sure to be as long. Can you dig it? Write the AIA for a copy of their current Fieldwork Opportunities Bulletin. —R.McG.

Archaeological Institute of America
53 Park Place
New York, NY 10007

In the elder days of Art,
Builders wrought with greatest care
Each minute and unseen part;
For the gods see everywhere.
HENRY WADSWORTH LONGFELLOW

Think Old

We often encourage the old to think young. But here's a program that wants the young to think old! Old as in ancient. And old as in archaeology.

The Association for Cultural Exchange in England has built its British Archaeology program around an integrated session of class work, field trips, and actual excavation experience at sites throughout the British Isles. Each summer, the 45-day session lures college students and recent graduates to Britain for a serious sampling of old-world archaeology, as well as a chance to work alongside European counterparts.

The program begins in Salisbury with two weeks of intensive lectures, seminars, and individual projects. Students partake of field trips, which include most of the major archaeological sites in southern Britain—Stonehenge, Woodhenge, Avebury, Durrington Walls, West Kennet Long Barrow, and Silbury Hill. The collections of the Devizes, Avebury, and Salisbury museums are visited as well.

A three-week period of practical excavation training follows, with students working six days a week at selected sites. The session concludes with a week at London's Astor College, where excavation reports are prepared and submitted.

The cost for the program is $895, which includes room and board as well as plane fare from New York. —C.McB.

British Archaeology Summer Seminar & Excavations
Institute of International Education
809 United Nations Plaza
New York, NY 10017

Have Dig, Will Travel

It is possible to accompany an archaeology expedition without being associated with the National Geographic Society or the Leakey Foundation. If you're an aspiring archaeologist or just someone who's interested in the subject, Earthwatch has an expedition for you. A nonprofit organization designed to encourage public involvement in the sciences, Earthwatch sponsors a wide variety of archaeological expeditions each year.

Researching prehistoric art in the highlands of Kenya, exploring mammoth graveyards in South Dakota's Black Hills, and studying nomadic sites in the Judean Hills of Israel were among the 45 expeditions included in Earthwatch's 1978 program.

Anyone from 16 to 75 can sign up for an expedition, and all that's required is "good sense and good humor." Participants share the costs of the expeditions, most of which last two to three weeks, and can opt for academic credit from participating institutions. Special skills or education is not required, as volunteers "learn by doing" on the expedition.

Total fees range from $600 to $1000 and include meals, accommodations, and equipment. —G.R.

Archaeology Expeditions
Earthwatch
10 Juniper Rd.
Box 127
Belmont, MA 02178

The Face of the Earth & Beyond

Glacial Estates

The Yosemite Natural History Association's Field Seminars will take you up, up, and away to observe the wonders of Yosemite that, until now, you may only have explored vicariously in books or on TV. And the opportunity is there to get yourself back into shape, along with a little backpacking experience on the side.

You might want to aim for the field study tour of the Clark Range. This is one of the most rugged, majestic, and primitive areas in the park. It is usually admired from afar, but now you can visit the range for six days and five nights, exploring its western and eastern sides, observing the rich variety of the granite composition. You'll see unspoiled lakes, forests, and meadows and you'll learn about the ecological relationships of the area.

Or, maybe you'd rather choose something a bit more unusual, like the Ice and Rock Field Study Expeditions. On these one-day hikes, the climbing will sometimes be strenuous, but the pace will be easier. And you will have the opportunity to examine rocks and glacial structures.

Speaking of glaciers—there is also a field study tour that will take you scrambling out over the McClure Glacier to study its structure, motion, and growth. You will be above 10,000 feet, but you will be assisted by an experienced ice-climber. Your group will move to a Mt. Lyell base camp for three more days of climbing. And for a fee, mules will pack in your gear.

We hope all this huffing and puffing activity hasn't scared you off—because there are nice cozy astronomy sessions for you, too. There is one called Stars Over Yosemite, which will be held for five majestic nights at Glacier Point, where stargazing is superb and the sky overhead is free of reflected car-light beams. Classes start at 7 p.m. and run through to 10 p.m., and the instrument to be used in this outdoor classroom is the Celestron 8 telescope.

You will learn basic star and constellation names and locations, and hear the myths about them as well. You will also study meteors, meteorites, fireballs, comets, and asteroids. No UFO's are being contemplated, however.

If you want something inspiring but even tamer—the Weather Field Study Seminar is for you. Yosemite is an excellent laboratory for this three-day course, as nearly every weather phenomenon occurs in the park, and the effect of weather on vegetation and land forms can be observed at every season.

The seminars run June through August, and the cost is $50 per seminar. Credit fees are optional. —R.B.

Field Seminars
Yosemite Natural History Association
P.O. Box 545
Yosemite National Park, CA 95389

Fire and Ice

If geology is your thing—and we're willing to bet it holds a fancy or two for you—Iceland just might be your place. And if Iceland *is* your place, then Twickenham Travel folks may be the ones you want to take you there.

Iceland is still a land in creation. Its volcanic landscapes provide an unparalleled opportunity to study volcanic activity and earthquake phenomena. Geologists find unique sites created here by old lakes, glacier fronts, and outwash plains.

Twickenham runs a variety of tours to this island republic that are designed for educational or research groups. They'll guide you through the geology, biology, and geography of Iceland's unusual terrain, or they'll work with you to arrange a tour suited to your group's needs.

On their list are 8-, 15-, 22-, and 29-day glacier expeditions, as well as 15- and 22-day glacier and volcano treks. The tours are led by experts and require a minimum of ten persons per party. —C.McB.

Iceland: Island of Challenge
Twickenham Travel Ltd.
2 Chester Row
London SW1W 9JH
England, UK

Ice is the silent language
of the peak;
and fire the silent language
of the star.
CONRAD AIKEN

Going Under

Geology's grand for studying the land,
But speleology's a rave if you're stuck
in a cave.

At the National Outdoor Leadership School you'll get a taste of both of these sciences, with a good dose of wilderness training to boot. It's a rare treat for those with a touch of geologist-cum-adventurer in their hearts.

NOLS's 37-day geology course is held in the Wind River and Absaroka Ranges in Wyoming. These two chunks of the rugged Rocky Mountains vary markedly in their makeup—from crevassed glacier to ancient volcano.

Speleology, of course, is the study of caves, and NOLS's 35-day wilderness and speleology course is unique in its field. Conducted in the Bighorn Range in northern Wyoming, the first 20 days of the session are spent "above ground" learning such skills as camping and wilderness conservation. At the session's completion, participants enter the subterranean world of La Caverna des Tres Charros, moving through crawlways, practicing vertical and horizontal caving techniques, and learning equipment selection. Both courses run for a month and cost $815.

NOLS offers a rugged classroom curriculum, both above and below the ground. —C.McB.

Wilderness Speleology/
Geology Courses
National Outdoor Leadership School
Box AA
Lander, WY 82520

The Ice Tour Cometh

It's another sweltering summer day and, you're musing, you'd do *anything* to cool off. Well, here's your chance—go climb a glacier.

Those huge ice mounds are beckoning, and Wildernorth will gladly make the necessary introductions, serving as your guide in the process. One-, two-, and five-day glacier treks to Alaska are Wildernorth's standard fare, and all trips include an orientation designed to familiarize newcomers to life on the ice. Geologists and experienced mountaineers accompany the tours as well, and learning by doing is integral to Wildernorth's approach to the ice caps.

Slide-illustrated seminars on glacier formation and evolution are included in some packages. An optional three-hour instructional photo-flight over the spectacular glacier system is also available. You'll see icefields and glaciers in all stages of evolution, ogives, nunataks, horn peaks, deep cirques, and glacial lakes.

Cost of Wildernorth's packages ranges from $35 for a day tour to $700+ for an eight-day romp through the Katmai Volcano and the Valley of Ten Thousand Smokes. Campground accommodations, technical equipment, and meals are included. —R.McG.

Glacier Exploration/ Backpacking Trips
Wildernorth
Mile 102 Glenn Hwy.
Palmer, AK 99645

Star Struck

How does three weeks of studying British stars sound? Naw, not the Beatles, the Stones, or Sir Laurence Olivier. The kind we have in mind here light up the sky, not the stage. We're talking about astronomy and a most unusual opportunity to learn about it in and around London.

The Brits, you know, have been associated with astronomy for a long, long time. Their roots in it go back to the Stone Age and the famous stone circle in Wiltshire known as Stonehenge, which is thought by many to be an actual astronomical instrument.

Should you sign on for this program, which is offered through the British Study Center of the University of Wisconsin, you'll visit Stonehenge as well as many other buildings and sites that tie in to the country's study of the heavens. Your list will include The Royal Observatory at Greenwich, The Science Museum, The Observatory at Herstmonceux, The National Maritime Museum, and The Royal Society.

Tutorials, planetarium talks, films, and field trips are conducted by both staff and guest lecturers. The program costs $650 (plus air fare) and includes a tour of London. Lots of free time is left over to study some of the city's "other" stars. —C.McB.

The History of Astronomy in Britain
Attn: Dr. Lorin Robinson
Arts & Sciences Outreach
University of Wisconsin
River Falls, WI 54022

Twinkle, Twinkle

What could be more pleasant in life than stargazing—lying outside on a clear, starry night marveling at the universe above. But aside from locating the Big Dipper, most of us don't know much about the stars themselves.

For those who chance to be in the New England area and who want to learn more about the stars, the Boston Museum of Science offers a wide selection of courses in astronomy. The courses range from those geared to the amateur astronomer to those for the more advanced stargazer.

Celestial navigation, the selection and use of telescopes, and naked-eye astronomy are just some of the offerings in this planetarium series. Courses for adults are held on weeknights and generally meet for eight-week periods. The standard course fee is $40, with discounts for museum members. Space in all courses is limited.

For those who don't wish to take an extended course, the museum offers a variety of 35-minute daily lecture/ demonstrations in the planetarium, with different shows being offered each season. The museum also shows science and science-fiction films every Friday night. —G.R.

Astronomy Courses
Museum of Science
Science Park
Boston, MA 02114

The Outer Limits

Welcome to the world of pulsars, neutron stars, and dreaded black holes. This is not the turf of Darth Vader—not even of Rod Serling. This is the real thing—astronomy and the many worlds beyond our own—and such topics await your study at Chicago's Adler Planetarium.

Adler's annual array of courses is perhaps as varied as the stars themselves. Stars and Stellar Evolution, for example, explores black holes and other topics germane to the birth and death of stars. For mariners, there are treats, too. Learn celestial navigation, and never again will you dock in Hawaii when your destination is San Diego. For amateur astronomers and perhaps voyeurs, there are courses in constructing telescopes.

Most courses—which run for about six weeks—cost $25. College credit can be arranged in connection with some offerings. —R.McG.

Astronomy & Navigation Courses
Adler Planetarium
900 East Achsah Bend Dr.
Chicago, IL 60605

Sky—what a scowl of cloud
Till, near and far,
Ray on ray split the shroud:
Splendid, a star!
ROBERT BROWNING

Harnessing Sun, Wind, & Water

The Alternative to It All

Remember the 1973/74 energy crisis with its ever-lengthening lines at gas stations and its soaring gasoline prices? Hard to forget, right?

Hard to forget, too, were the questions provoked by that shortage: are future crises inevitable, and what will our energy future be?

If you mix together equal parts of social awareness, ecological concern, and interest in alternative technologies, what you create is the Goddard summer-long program in Social Ecology. While no pat answers are promised, Goddard does provide a step in the right direction: instruction in the facts—the facts of energy.

Mystifying as "social ecology" might sound, it's really a very simple concept. "Not merely a study of technology," says Goddard, social ecology is "an attempt to discover how people can break down the patterns of man's exploitation of nature." As a consequence, the program's agenda is laden with discussions on energy—because today's energy problems stem in large measure from man's exploitation of finite resources. Renewable alternatives are at the top of Goddard's list. The sun and the winds, for example.

The home base for the Social Ecology program is Cate Farm, a 40-acre proving ground for myriad technologies. Integral to the operation is a solar-heated greenhouse, an 1800-watt wind generator, smaller windmills, and several more esoteric contraptions.

In the classroom, students are given a theoretical backbone with lectures on the present/coming crisis in energy, wind power, solar specifics, and energy efficient shelters. But energy is not the only theme. Discussions focus on biological agriculture, for example. What's that, you say? That's a course that delves directly into food production on farms and explores the sound agricultural principles that are associated with such production.

In line with its aim of examining alternative technologies and life styles, the Social Ecology program weaves mandatory work assignments into the course's fabric. To that end, every student is required to put in four working hours of farm chores each week.

There is considerable diversity in the backgrounds of participants. Cost for the 12-week program is about $2300, inclusive of room, board, and tuition. College credit is available, as is financial aid. —R.McG.

Summer Program in Social Ecology
Box SE-4
Goddard College
Plainfield, VT 05667

Animal Farm

Most city kids don't have a corn-raising Uncle Ned in Nebraska, a crazy cousin Sam homesteading in Idaho, or an Aunt Minnie breeding goats in Oregon.

Which is by way of saying that most city kids don't get to partake in a standard city kid's dream—living on a farm.

Through an unusual learning experience called the Brooklea Farm Project, that opportunity now exists, primarily for those in the 17-to-21 age bracket.

Brooklea, located in Washington County in upstate New York, is not a "come out on Sunday and pet the cows" place. It is a real, live working farm. Those who take part in the project/school actually live there and provide the manpower to make it run.

Students pay just over $1700 for the privilege of spending three ten-week periods (from September to June) learning such arts as sheep shearing, alfalfa seeding, tractor driving, maple sugaring, and goat milking. The program is presented through classes, field trips, apprenticeships, and films, with a large emphasis on practical experience. General areas covered include animal and plant sciences, farm equipment, homesteading, and wilderness training. —C.McB.

Brooklea Farm Project
R.D. 2
Fort Ann, NY 12827

Farmers in the Dell

Self-sufficient life styles have been making a comeback in recent years, and more and more people are turning to homesteading. Although homesteading sites are no longer "free for the taking" as they were in 19th-century America, the opportunity to live independently and in harmony with the land still exists.

Jefflin Farm, a school of homesteading and intermediate technology in New York, believes that "anyone can build their own home and grow their own food once they have the basics in mind." And basics is what Jefflin is all about.

Each spring and summer, Jefflin Farm offers two-week, limited-enrollment courses to teach people the basics of homesteading. The farm's goal is to get homesteaders off to a good start based on sound knowledge, thereby eliminating costly errors.

The first week is devoted to organic gardening and animal management. Students learn erosion prevention, care of the soil, crop harvest, and storage. The care of animals (poultry, pigs, sheep, goats, and rabbits) is also taught, with the emphasis on proper health care and shelter.

The second week focuses on home building and alternative energy. Jefflin subscribes to Plato's maxim that "before he dies, every man should build a house." Selecting of lumber, framing, wiring, plumbing, and using solar and wind energy are covered.

Students at Jefflin Farm stay at nearby camping facilities. The cost of the course is $125 per week or $235 per session. —G.R.

Jefflin Farm
School of Homesteading &
Intermediate Technology
R.D. No. 1
Barton, NY 13734

Ee-i-ee-i-o

The simple life isn't so simple. If you plunge casually into a small, alluring family farm situation, you may just wind up on the fast track to financial ruin.

Ask Maynard Kaufman. He knows the pitfalls of homesteading and the ways around them. An associate professor of religion at Western Michigan University, Kaufman puts in half his time on one of those farms, where he's assisted by his wife, Sally. The homestead, a 100-acre spread just north of Bangor, confirms the fact that rural self-sufficiency is attainable—with hard work and knowhow. Better still, you're welcome to come learn how to do it yourself.

Under the sponsorship of Western Michigan, Kaufman annually offers courses in the realities of homesteading. For openers, there's Homesteading Theory. Plow through that and you're ready for the practicum session, where participants live and work on the farm.

Does this sound like your cup of carrot juice? Kaufman's courses are open to both traditional and nontraditional students. Nine months on the farm—inclusive of room, board, and tuition—costs about $1500 for Michigan residents, $2150 for nonresidents. —R.McG.

Environmental Studies/
Homesteading Program
Western Michigan University
Kalamazoo, MI 49008

To own a bit of ground,
to scratch it with a hoe . . .
this is the most satisfactory
thing a man can do.
CHARLES DUDLEY WARNER

Cream of the Crop Hayfields, pastures, and garden space. Henhouses, greenhouses, and rabbitries. Pigs, draft horses, goats, and sheep. If the image of an old-time farm has appeared in your mind, you are on the right track—for this is what the Center for Resourceful Living is all about. This 52-acre farm in the heart of the Berkshires offers one of the richest samplings of farm production/alternative life style courses, from dairy and poultry production to field, orchard, and woodlot plants and small farm management. Participants may register for one or two semesters, and credit is available. NASC and Massachusetts students are given preference.

Center for Resourceful Living
Attn: Howard Schechter
North Adams State College
North Adams, MA 01247

Sol Survival A new global energy ethic is emerging, slowly but surely. On a Solar Trek, you can examine this ethic within a practical context, focusing on building construction and human life styles. You will meet with educators, designers, and conservationists. You will travel to Toronto, Ontario, Montreal, and northern Vermont to visit solar heated, ecological homes and their inhabitants. The fee of $285 for the week-long trek covers transportation and accommodations. Sunshine can really do much more than simply brighten up your day.

Solar Trek
Canadian Nature Tours
1262 Don Mills Rd.
Don Mills, Ontario M3B 2W8
Canada

Home Sweet Homestead A western homesteading experience is not merely a chance to tend an outdoor garden; it is an opportunity to be self-reliant and work with materials gathered from the land. Western Door has obtained a mountain plot near the Ashley National Forest in Utah, and you can join them in their work toward the completion of this homestead. Perhaps you were one of those "summers-on-the-sidewalk" city kids who dreamed about life on a farm. Here's your chance to live out those daydreams while you study homesteading, shelter construction, and wind/solar power. The course is held in June, July, and August. Cost is $475.

Wilderness Homesteading
Western Door Wilderness School
172 N St.
Salt Lake City, UT 84103

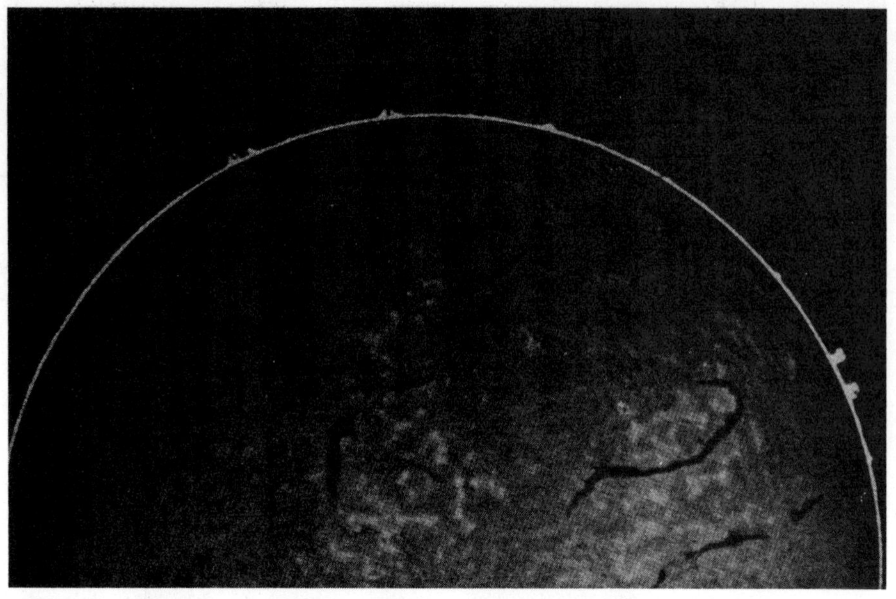

Get Energized

We can think of few areas today that hold as much promise for mankind as solar energy. By now, most everyone favors the general idea. A glance at your last heating bill may show that even you are not really resistant to the idea.

But few people understand the concepts and technology of solar energy, and this lack of information has undoubtedly led to its snail's-pace advance into our modern society.

So it is encouraging to hear of the New England Fuel Institute and its program designed to shed some light, if you will, on the topic of solar energy. Their basic five-day solar heating technology course aims to instruct the interested general public—including homeowners, landlords, building managers, students, and tradespeople—in basic solar heating technology, installation, and maintenance procedures.

The course is conducted at one of the most up-to-date solar facilities in the country. Some 60 percent of the session is devoted to "hands-on" utilization of the solar equipment at the Institute's on-site training laboratory.

Both day and evening sessions of the one-week program are available at a cost of $150. No previous technical or solar energy experience is required.

The Institute, which is licensed by the Massachusetts Department of Education, also offers a four-week, 160-hour solar heating installation and maintenance course for those involved in the field. Cost is $500. —C.McB.

New England Fuel Institute
Solar Energy Education Division
P.O. Box 888
20 Summer St.
Watertown, MA 02172

Cool It (or Heat It)

With winters getting ever colder (and colder), and utility bills getting ever higher (and higher), the concept of solar energy attracts more and more attention.

In case you're not up on the lingo, there are two types of solar energy installations. There's the active installation, which uses high technology such as solar energy converters, photovoltaic cells, etc. Then there's passive installation, which emphasizes correct placement of windows, insulation, etc.

It's the passive design that receives emphasis at the annual Passive Solar Conference, sponsored by the US Department of Energy and presented by the American Section of the International Solar Energy Society.

At the conference, you'll be able to attend workshops on topics like Passive Cooling/Passive Heating, Designing the Solar Building, and Attached Solar Greenhouses. You'll hear lectures and presentations by scientists and practitioners from all over the world.

You don't need to be wise in the ways of solar energy to participate. All you need is to be forward-looking enough to worry about what's going to happen when the oil runs out. Workshops average about $20 each. —J.A.

Passive Solar Conference
American Section of the International Solar Energy Society, Inc.
c/o American Technological University
P.O. Box 1416
Killeen, TX 76541

Do What's Appropriate

Slowly, we are seeing some of the seeds of the '60s take root. Most never made it. But a few took hold and sprouted, bearing the fruit of change.

The Farallones Institute is a California-based nonprofit organization that focuses on what they call "appropriate technology": those living systems that do not rely on nonrenewable resources but that do emphasize decentralization and individual participation. Farallones folks are concerned with solar heating, small stock raising, intensive gardening, and recycling. In other words, they are into living as near to the natural as possible.

The Institute addresses itself to the problems caused by our dwindling resources. It recognizes our "need to develop a set of alternatives to the present plug-in, flush-and-forget, high technology spiral that we, as Americans, have adopted as the only means to a good life." Their staff includes biologists, architects, agronomists, solar designers, horticulturists, and craftspeople who are based at the Institute's two centers: their rural center on an 80-acre ranch north of San Francisco and their urban center in Berkeley. Both are working and living areas for community members, as well as classrooms for participants.

Among the extended workshops offered are Habitat Construction and Solar Systems (four weeks, $450), where members learn about the construction and low-cost approach to building a solar heating system. In the

Residential Program (five weeks, $500), participants assume an active role in horticultural activities from growing vegetables and flowers to pasture management and haying.

Their educational programs encompass one- and two-day workshops, year-long resident apprenticeships, and regular classes. The emphasis is on "hands-on" learning in practical skills and the application of appropriate technologies to daily living. —C.McB.

The Farallones Institute
Rural Center
15290 Coleman Valley Rd.
Occidental, CA 95465

Power to the People

Gasoline will soon hit a buck a gallon, and your home heating bills will go up, up, up. But there is a new light at this tunnel's end, and the Domestic Technology Institute can show you the way.

Energy conservation and renewable energy resources—solar, waste conversion, and the like—are DTI's staples. Exotic as those approaches may seem, DTI's workshop program aims to inform the general public about these emerging energy solutions and, in the process, to point out the ways in which they can be applied in your home at minimal cost.

There is, for example, a five-day workshop in community energy technology, in which there is an intensive look at solar energy. A brief glimpse can also be had in a two-day solar greenhouse construction and operation workshop. Other offerings include low-cost solar heating and cooling and energy conservation.

All workshops are open to you, the consumer, and the stress is on the practical. Special rates are available for groups and low-income individuals, and workshops can be designed to meet the needs of specific groups. —R.McG.

Energy Conservation Workshops
Domestic Technology Institute, Inc.
2520 West Cedar Dr.
Lakewood, CO 80228

Some Like It Hot

Solar energy is an idea whose time has come, for while the earth is gradually being drained of its energy sources, the sun remains a resource virtually untapped by man.

Although solar power has long been a popular concept, only in recent years has it become a practical one as well. One of the most comprehensive educational programs on solar energy is the International Solar Energy Conference and Fair held each spring in El Paso, Texas. El Paso is an ideal site for the five-day event as it is the city with the highest level of solar radiation in America and it is the site of a developing solar energy industry.

The conference is designed for public consumers and consists of lectures and exhibits focusing on the practical uses of solar power. The 1978 conference included sessions on home energy conservation, current solar legislation, and water cooling/heating system technology. The conference also included a series of lectures by international experts on the development of solar energy in other countries. Write for details on this year's conference. —G.R.

International Solar Energy
Conference & Fair
West Texas Council of Governments
The Mills Building, Suite 700
303 N. Oregon St.
El Paso, TX 79901

The sun was shining on the sea,
Shining with all his might:
He did his very best to make
The billows smooth and bright—
And this was odd, because it was
The middle of the night.
LEWIS CARROLL

The Web of Life

At Home in the Field

There you stand, next to an eminent ecologist, peering into the smoky bowels of one of Hawaii's great volcanos. He leans toward you and points to a crack in the great hole's northern wall. "We'll begin our study there in the morning," he says.

Now you are falling backward into the warm waters of Jamaica, dropping down among the fish and flora of one of the world's finest diving grounds. The scuba gear feels snug and light. You pick up a hand signal from the two oceanographers swimming alongside you and begin paddling downward in the direction of a tower of red coral that is to be your objective.

The stuff of dreams? Or Monday night travelogs? Not so, friends. These are facts of life, thanks to an organization called Earthwatch, a nonprofit group that wants and needs your participation to make these scientific adventures happen.

The basis of Earthwatch is a simple one: scientists require money and assistance to carry on their studies, and laymen are often willing to provide both. So why not join them? Well, Earthwatch is doing just that, allowing scientists the opportunity to work on special projects in their fields while offering everyday people a chance to learn from contact with the professionals. Earthwatch has matched the learned and the willing for field studies in 19 states and 44 different countries around the globe.

Earthwatch participants are drawn from all segments of society, and they range in ages from 16 to 75. Students wishing to gain valuable scientific experience outside of school have joined research teams to investigate the ecology of tropical forests in Costa Rica. Teachers have gained new knowledge of the environs of Tapezco by tending traps and collecting specimens of brilliantly colored butterflies and salamanders. Businessmen have broken their daily routines by joining investigations of the lakes of Lapland, Sweden. Retired men and women have continued their educations on the Barnacle Reefs at Black Rocks, North Carolina.

Prospective members can peruse an Earthwatch catalog listing dozens of expeditions that will be undertaken during the coming year. Each one is tax-deductible, and the programs range from $500 to $950 for a two- to three-week excursion. The fees cover the expenses of the research team and include food, accommodations, field gear, and supplies. Members are expected to provide their own air fare and travel expenses.

Prior experience and special skills can prove helpful, but they are not required for most trips. (An expedition to study the iguanas of the Galapagos Islands asked that its members have "a tolerance for close contact with lizards.") More important is a desire for adventure, a sense of humor, and an ability to cooperate with others in often difficult and unexpected circumstances. Tourists need not apply. Earthwatch is looking for modern-day explorers. —C.McB.

Earthwatch
10 Juniper Rd.
Box 127
Belmont, MA 02178

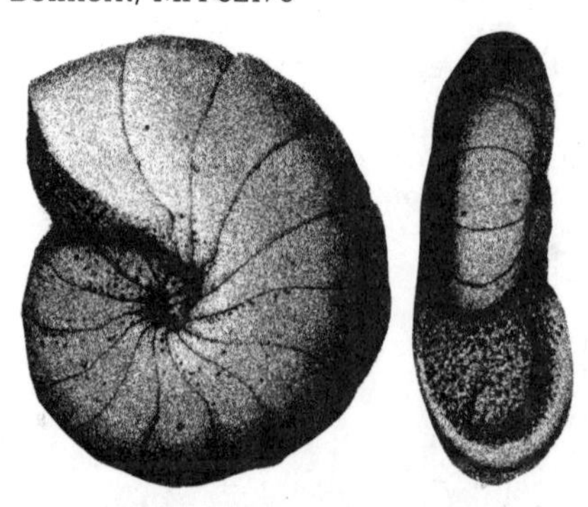

Great, wide, beautiful, wonderful world,
With the wonderful waters
round you curled,
And the wonderful grass
upon your breast,
World you are beautifully dressed.
MATTHEW BROWNE

Wild Moorland Charms

Who knows? You might meet the spirit of Robin Hood as you wander along the misty Pembrokeshire Coast, explore the woodlands of Epping Forest, or ramble about the wild moors of Malham Tarn. For all of these adventures are part of the weekly ecology field sessions of the Field Studies Council, and they all take place in England.

You can choose a week along the Pembrokeshire Coast and the off-shore islands, observing and studying marine ecology and breeding sea-birds. Or you can go to Epping Forest, where you will study the problems caused by soil erosion, noise and water pollution, and various types of leisure activity.

A totally different kind of field study session can take you only a short distance away to Flatford Mill, where you will be able to examine East Anglian vegetation in and after the Ice Age. Or, if you are truly romantic, you may choose to travel to the far north of England, to the Malham Tarn Field Centre. Here, in a region apart from civilization, you may uncover its hidden charms: its wild moorlands, its sometimes bleak, sometimes lush valleys, it waterfalls, becks, and rushing rivers. Write for costs and dates. —R.B.

Field Studies Council
Information Office
Preston Montford
Montford Bridge
Shrewsbury SY4 1HW
England, UK

Students of the Sequoias

Ecology students normally spend a good portion of their time in "the laboratory"—defined by Webster as "a place providing opportunity for experimentation, observation, or practice in a field of study." Similarly, the Yosemite Natural History Association defines California's Yosemite National Park as a "remarkable natural laboratory of plant and animal life and spectacular geology."

Each year the YNHA conducts a series of field seminars designed for the study of botany and ecology in a beautiful outdoor setting. The seminars last from three to five days and cover specific aspects of ecology. The park's giant sequoias, plant life in alpine or subalpine zones, and the use of plants by Indians of the Western Sierra Nevada are among the topics offered.

Most seminars are approved and accredited by the University of California, Berkeley, Extension Studies Department. The YNHA staff for these seminars is comprised of natural history instructors from California colleges and park ranger/naturalists.

While the seminars include some lectures, a majority of time is devoted to field observation. Participants camp out near the seminar sites.

The basic seminar fee is $50. The cost for credit is somewhat higher. The course fee also includes a camping permit. —G.R.

Field Seminars
Yosemite Natural History Association
P.O. Box 545
Yosemite National Park, CA 95389

In Native Haunts

As fireflies disappear in morning light, so, too, are many species of plant and animal vanishing from our modern world. There is still time to seek them out in their native haunts, to study and observe them. And the University of California, Berkeley, invites you to do so on their ecological research expeditions. You will track, record, observe, and describe the roles and habitats of animal communities in selected ecological study zones.

Trips are available to New Caledonia, Oceania, where on Grand Tere, an island off the eastern coast of Australia, you will be engaged in the study of over 2600 species of native flora. In Ecuador you can explore plant/insect relationships and view the Dalechampia, a twining vine which flaunts huge white and purple flowers and belongs to the poinsettia family.

East Africa offers you the chance to study alpine plants of Mount Kenya and to see most unusual, giant butter-cups. Guatemala will overwhelm you with its rich assortment of tropical birds, mammals, reptiles, and amphibians in regions ranging from sea level to cloud forests. And Kenya—ah, here you will study three species of monkeys on a primatology project.

A modest contribution (fully tax deductible) subsidizes the expense of the research and covers meals, transportation, and lodging. —R.B.

University Research
Expeditions Program
University of California
Berkeley, CA 94720

Teton Titillation

For the general public, the study of science has often held negative connotations, Memories of high school teachers droning on about obscure theories and principles emerge from the dark corners of one's mind. Smells of formaldehyde and other nose-twisting gases, claustrophobic laboratories, and fat, dull textbooks—all the things that paint a bleak picture—are often recalled.

But we are here to tell you, today, that the study of science doesn't have to be that way. It can be fun and stimulating, and it can be presented in a magnificent setting—and it is, in the Teton Science School Summer Seminars.

The school resides in one of America's grandest natural locales, the land of the Grand Teton National Park in Wyoming. Here sweeping granite peaks rise above pristine lakes, dazzling alpine wildflowers, glaciers, and herds of moose and elk. It all makes for a classroom like none you have ever experienced before.

Specialists (among them college professors, park administrators, and local experts) accompany students to camps high in the Teton back-country. Once there, participants study such subjects as alpine flora, Teton-range geology, and the structure of colorful mushrooms and fungi.

A sampling from a recent brochure includes the study of earthquakes and volcanoes, forest practices, vascular flora, terrestrial insects of Jackson Hole, fossils of the Green River formation, and aquatic ecology of Grand Teton National Park.

Books become a secondary source of learning in these five-day seminars, having been replaced by the best teacher of them all—direct observation and investigation. The school offers Snake River float trips as a key part of its agenda.

The program, which runs from June through August, is open to the general public at a cost of $12 per day. Students are expected to provide their own food and equipment for extended back-country trips. College credits (at $10 per quarter unit) are also available.

The Grand Teton Summer Seminars may be the perfect formula for curing those old "I hate science" blues.—C.McB.

Grand Teton Summer Seminars
Teton Science School
Box 68
Kelly, WY 83011

Far from the Madding Crowds

Your average laboratories they aren't, but what better place can there be to research and study the whys and wherefores of forests, mountains, deserts, and rivers, than in those very places themselves?

The Wilderness Studies Program of the University of California, Santa Cruz, traveled last year to Death Valley, Sequoia National Park, and the Ruby and Sierra Mountains. They also paddled down the Snake River. While there, naturalist-led groups analyzed plant migration and man-made changes in the wilderness. They backpacked and studied a spring desert in bloom. They ski toured and explored the interdependence of climate and land communities. Groups were kept small for close interaction between expert and student, and "learning by doing" was stressed.

The costs last year ranged from $70 to $350. Course duration varies from one to four weeks, and it's possible to earn University of California Extension credit on the trip. Be sure to have a good working combination of legs and lungs—these trips aren't equipped with sedan chairs. Get in touch with them soon—enrollment is limited. —J.S.H.

Wilderness Studies Program
University of California
Extension Office
Santa Cruz, CA 95064

Park Place

There aren't any tulips to tiptoe through in Zion National Park, but a brief glance at their field seminar brochure reveals that their walks are much more exciting.

The panoramic setting of the park will serve as your outdoor classroom for whichever of the seminars you choose. Sessions last for five to six days, and evening "happenings" are held as well.

On their "steeped in nature calendar," you will find a wide range of ecology adventures. You can study the birds of the "Dixie Corridor," one of the most unique faunistic areas in Utah, lying between the high southern end of the Great Basin and the lower northern end of the hot desert.

Other sessions will introduce you to the colorful varieties of trees, shrubs, and flowers in the park, invertebrate animals (which covers the aquatic, terrestrial, and aerial forms), and the collection and identification of freshwater algae and other aquatic plants found in the streams and water sources of Zion.

A special study of the diverse ecosystems of Southern Utah—ranging from the hot desert (elevation 2350 feet) to alpine tundra (elevation 11,307 feet)—will be made. You will also have plenty of opportunity to observe insects, spiders, snakes, lizards, frogs, and toads—but only if you choose.

The credit fee is $53; noncredit is $35. —R.B.

Zion National Park Field Seminars
School of Continuing Education
Southern Utah State College
Cedar City, UT 84720

There's More Than Spuds in Idaho

Three hundred years ago, the United States loomed as a vast wilderness. Wilderness acres today, however, are few in number, and fewer still are those of us who have experienced the excitement of true wilderness living.

But for students seeking to answer the call of the wild, there is a special route—the University of Idaho's program in wilderness ecology, where participants spend two weeks prowling the Selway-Bitterroot area.

No more than 24 explorers are accommodated each summer, as use of the area is limited in order to preserve its natural state. Students enroll in botany or zoology classes that include horseback treks through the 6000-foot terrain. Instruction is given by university professors, and each student is required to compile a project reflective of his/her experiences by the course's completion.

Fee for the course is $225, inclusive of tuition, food, and equipment. Participants must have completed their junior year of college or have secured the permission of the instructors. The Wilderness Ecology program is scheduled on a year-to-year basis, and its offerings hinge upon the availability of funding. —R.McG.

Wilderness Ecology Program
Special Programs Office
University of Idaho
Moscow, ID 83843

Ecology has become the political substitute for the word "mother."
JESSE UNRUH

Look to your health:
and if you have it,
praise God,
and value it next to a good conscience,
for health is the second blessing
that we mortals are capable of:
a blessing that money cannot buy.
IZAAK WALTON

To Your Health

What with rich foods, sedentary jobs, and the stress of urban life, it's no wonder that we find it such a struggle to stay fit.

Our bodies just don't understand what to do with potato chips and onion dip and beer. Our digestive tracts are puzzled by the onslaught of red meat, ice cream, starch, cholesterol, frozen vegetables, and preservatives. It's no accident, mind you, that antacid tablets do such a business.

Staying fit has not historically been an American problem. The people who made this country great had no way of predicting the extent of the problem we face with posterior spread. And if anyone had suggested to our ancestors that they start their mornings with 12 minutes of Royal Canadian Air Force exercises, he'd have been shut away somewhere out of sight.

But however unexpected, the problems are very real. We're a nation suffering from flab, varicose veins, cigarette smoke, smog, high blood pressure, lack of exercise, job anxieties, traffic nerves, atherosclerosis, and a variety of other life style maladies.

If your body is yelling "Uncle"—or even if it's just a mite uncomfortable, we may be able to make a helpful suggestion or two. Not that we're doctors, mind you.

What we've done is to research the topics of fitness and health and to report some of the approaches that seemed most interesting. Because we're not doctors or nutritionists, we've not been able to rule on the medical value of any of these programs. What we've used as our criteria have been variety, uniqueness, and accessibility.

Some of the programs you'll read about in "To Your Health" are mainline, backbay, old-reliable, high-ticket spas. You'll recognize them as you read, and in many cases their reputations precede them. Others, though, are a bit out of the way, or a bit smaller, or a bit less orthodox. What we've tried to bring you is something akin to a spring bouquet of approaches to bodily health.

Consequently you'll find here a distinct bias toward variety. We've found herbal retreats and yoga retreats. We've located homeopathic flower essences, hot springs, mud packs, and cleansing fasts. We've located a real wealth of vegetarian programs in a wide variety of locations. And we've uncovered a full spectrum of possibilities in weight reduction.

What we hope to do in "To Your Health" is stimulate thought. Before you get into the shower tonight, pause for an honest look in the bathroom mirror. Take a deep breath and try not to cough. If you like what you see—and you like how you feel—terrific. If not—quick, read this chapter.

And be sure to check with your physician before signing up.

Photography by Gordon Menzie

Body & Soul

Healthy and Whole

Holistic medicine is one health of a good idea. If for you it's an idea whose time has come, you might try a visit to the Wholistic Health and Nutrition Institute in Mill Valley, California.

Holistic health is an approach to preventive medicine that emphasizes the maintenance of a physical, psychological, and spiritual balance in the individual. Using a combination of educational programs, clinics, and counseling by skilled professionals, WHN aims at helping people to take stock and then take charge of their own health care—and later perhaps to help others do the same.

If you want only the personalized program, you can start with the health evaluation, consisting of three clinic visits over a two-week period. As an educational experience, this one is unprecedented in its uniting of modern medical technology with a focus on the individual's attitudes and life style. The first clinic visit orients you to an understanding of what the health evaluation has to show you and includes such medical tests as blood work, lung capacity, and urinalysis. The second visit delves further, with iridology (using the study of the iris of the eye to diagnose diseases or chemical imbalances), personology (the exploration of the interfaces between the mind and the body), and a medical review. The third visit provides nutritional guidance, stress reduction methods, and homeopathy (stimulating the body's own natural healing forces). Through it all, you'll practice self-assessment and keep a diet diary, and at the end of the evaluation you can choose to go more deeply into one or another of the programs WHN offers. The cost of the health evaluation is $250.

If you want to continue to develop your learning into certification as a Health Resources Consultant, or to combine WHN classes with college credits from New College of California or Columbia Pacific University, you can by arrangement with WHN. (Continuing education credit for physicians and nurses is also available through a cooperative relationship with Brookwood Hospital.)

Classes are available in natural medicine, psychology, physiology, nutritional science, parapsychology, herbal healing, massage, holistic birth control, homeopathy, women's physical and mental health, stress management, iridology, and orthomolecular psychiatry. Biofeedback methods are used to encourage the development of instincts about yourself and your physical and mental needs. Cost of courses range from $6 to $40. Most courses are discounted for members of the Institute, so it might make sense to join if you're going to take a number of them. They range in length from one day to several weeks, depending on the content. —R.J.

Wholistic Health and Nutrition Institute
150 Shoreline Hwy.
Mill Valley, CA 94941

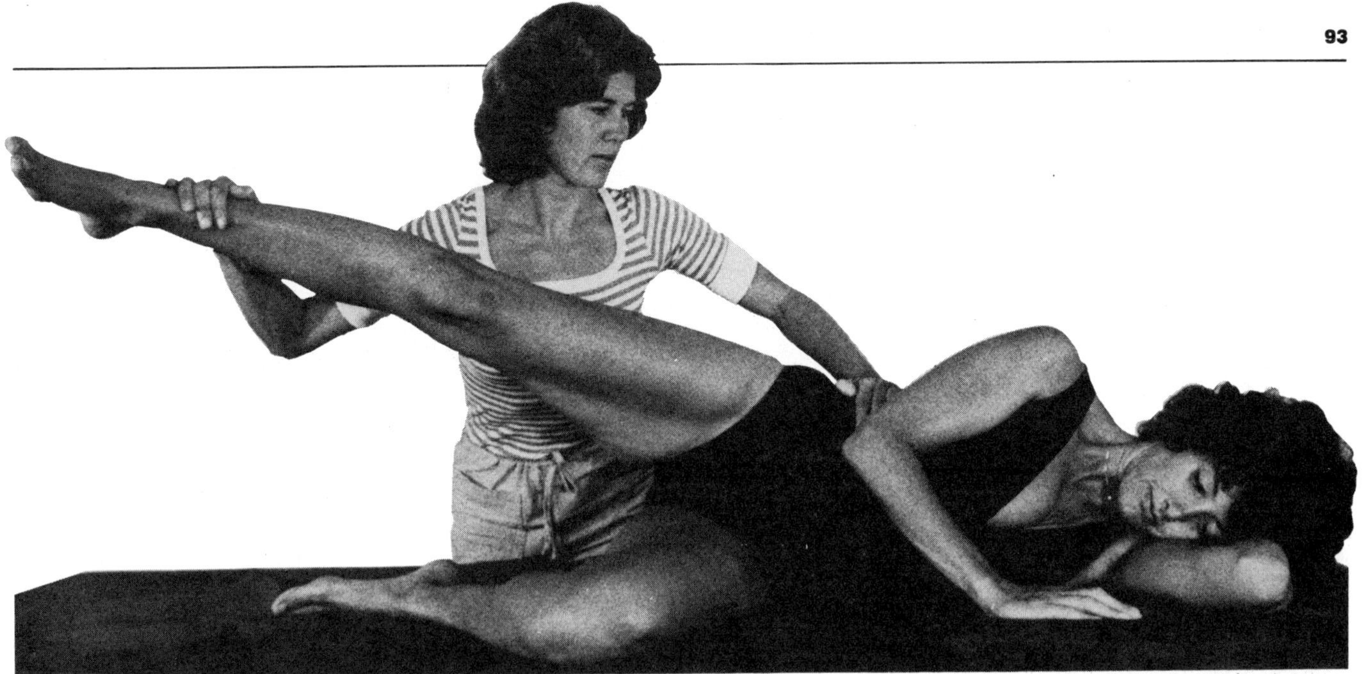

Healthy Touches

5:30. You're stuck in a traffic jam on the freeway. The engine is about to overheat, there's nothing but static on the radio, and the jerk in back of you decides to lay on his horn. It's the appropriate end to a rotten day. You arrived at work late, someone had taken your parking space, and you spilled coffee in your lap just before your meeting with the Big Boss.

5:35. Having determined that your state qualifies as "emotionally strained," you quickly review the principles of your Touch for Health class.

5:38. You touch the frontal eminences of your forehead with the first two fingers of your hands, right and left at the same time. With your fingers applying constant light pressure you go over in your mind what's bothering you.

5:40. You release the pressure and mentally review the problem without applying pressure to your forehead.

5:42. Your head seems clear and the strain is gone. As the traffic begins to crawl along you're once again grateful to the Touch for Health Foundation and the self-use classes you took from them. Through the principles of ancient Oriental acupuncture/acupressure combined with Western developments, they have taught you to diagnose and care for your own body. —E.H.

Touch for Health Foundation
1174 North Lake Ave.
Pasadena, CA 91104

Salad Days

There are hotels that specialize in golf. There are hotels that specialize in tennis. There are those that favor skiing, and there are those that favor gambling. But we've yet to come across a hotel that specializes in vegetarianism—that is, until we learned of Fannie Shaffer's Vegetarian Hotel.

Besides good eats ("fresh vegetables and fruits, delicious crisp salads, and home baked whole-grain breads and cake"), Fannie offers the usual recreational activities such as golf, tennis, horseback riding, ping pong, and handball. But she also offers the unusual—lectures on health and nutrition under the "tree of knowledge," and classes in yoga and calisthenics. There are also woods to hike in, arts and crafts to create, and folk dancing to learn.

Children are welcome, as are any special diets. (If you're not allowed to eat it, Fannie won't serve it to you.)

Open May to October, the hotel's weekly rates are $101 to $186 per person, depending on the number of people to a room and the type of accommodations. —J.S.H.

Fannie Shaffer's Vegetarian Hotel
P.O. Box 457
Sullivan County Catskills
Woodridge, NY 12789

Mother: It's broccoli, dear.
Child: I say it's spinach, and I say the hell with it.
(Caption to cartoon)
E.B. WHITE

For the Health of It Health is a balance between rest and activity, according to the Foundation for Natural Living. And they've opened an in-patient therapeutic-learning healing center that practices this belief. While at the Pacific Healing Sanitarium patients themselves participate in the design and management of their own health program in an attempt to achieve this balance.

Pacific Healing Sanitarium
The Foundation for Natural Living
54 S.E. 127th Ave.
Portland, OR 97233

Be Your Own Keeper "Meadowlark is neither a hospital nor a rest home," say the folks of this nonprofit "community" of health. It "is a place where we may learn and apply principles of effective living. Here at Meadowlark we are a family, learning and applying the ways of wholeness, of peace, of health." It is a place "where one may learn to help himself to health, to high-level wellness, by practicing under guidance, tested techniques for living."

Meadowlark
Friendly Hills Fellowship
26126 Fairview Ave.
Hemet, CA 92343

A Place in the Sun The Orange Grove Health Ranch in Florida offers fresh fruit, fresh food, and fresh air—not to mention fresh orange juice most of the year. And there's more. Live there for at least one day and you'll hear lectures and group discussions on health and natural living. Rates start at $15 per day for room and food.

Orange Grove Health Ranch
Rte 4, Box 1225
Arcadia, FL 33821

Whole and Wholesome

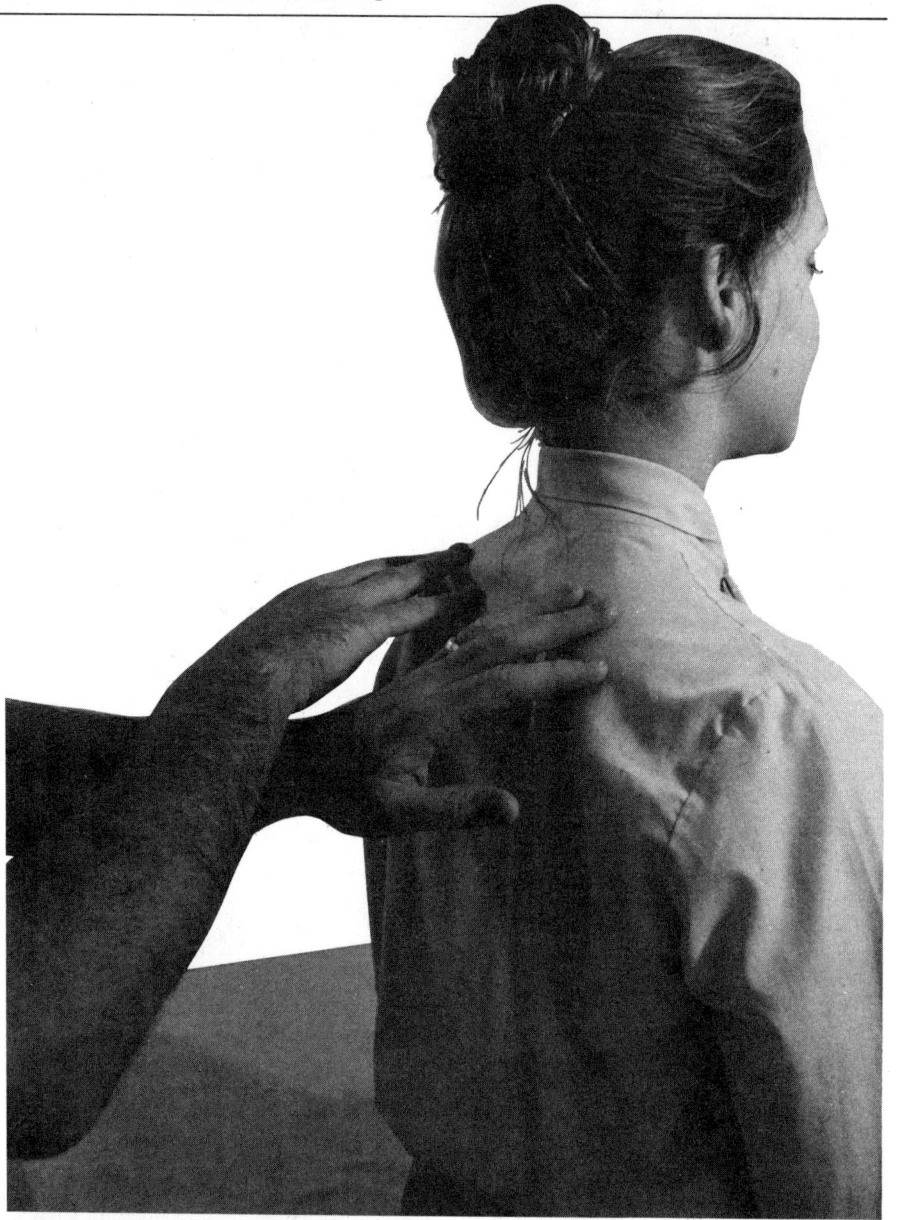

Some years back when Benjamin Franklin stepped out into the fury of a thunderstorm to discover electricity, it's doubtful his vision included Polarity Therapy.

At the Rochester Center for the Healing Arts located in Rochester, New York, Polarity Therapy is just one of the many new-age courses, lectures, and workshops the Center has to offer.

The concept of the Center, a nonprofit organization, is that when an individual understands health as a state of harmony and balance and assumes responsibility for his own well-being, he can actually play an important role in insuring his own health while assisting in the healing process.

Polarity Therapy, offered by the Center both in workshops and in seminars, approaches disease from the perspective that it's caused by blocks and imbalances in the electromagnetic currents of energy that circulate throughout the body. These blocks result in tension, pain, and disease, and the Polarity practitioner removes these blocks by using the positive and negative polarities of his hands.

The Center also recognizes the importance of diet in the creation of a healthy individual and offers a number of programs in this vein.

There's a series of lectures by a noted author, titled "What's That You're Eating?" and the Center offers a course in nutrition that explores the role of natural foods and examines the myths surrounding the use of protein.

The use of herbs as an alternative to traditional healing practices is the subject of one series of lectures. Those in attendance will learn how to use herbs in relieving illness and how to find and prepare herbs.

From the Butsu-Gan Ko-Sei School of Acupuncture in Kyoto, Japan, comes Dr. Hung, who presents a short course in the five-element theory of acupuncture as a means for increasing the circulation of energies throughout the body.

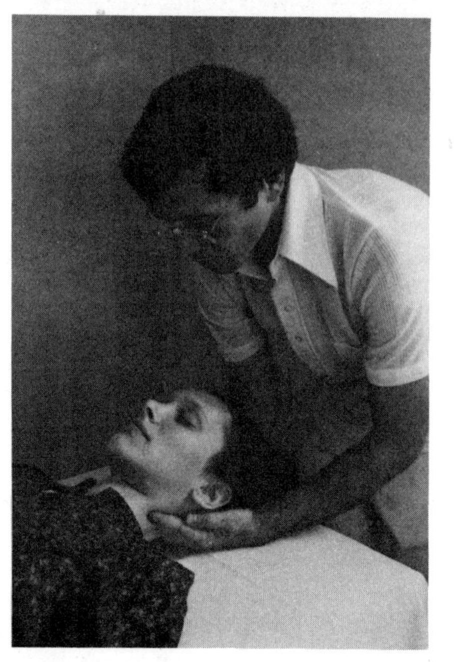

Teaming up with the Rochester Museum and Science Center as part of its bridging-the-gap approach to new-age and traditional health care, the Center offers a two-part lecture series that examines a wide range of relevant issues, including "Mind-Body Interaction in Health and Disease," "Humanistic Medicine and Medical Ethics," and "Advances in Modern Medicine: A Double-Edged Sword."

Membership is tax deductible and costs $10 per year. Members receive 20 percent discounts on most fees for programs, are allowed to attend the semimonthly meetings, and are given priority registration privileges. —P.T.

Rochester Center for the Healing Arts
304 Oxford St.
Rochester, NY 14607

I never resist temptation, because I have found that things that are bad for me do not tempt me.
GEORGE BERNARD SHAW

Certified Wellness "One of the most precious assets a person can have is good health. Good physical and mental health can make the difference between a happy life and a miserable one." To encourage people to work toward achieving and maintaining good health, UCSD Extension has planned a series of courses designed to cover the rudiments of physical and mental well-being. "Upon completion of the course work, participants are awarded a certificate, tangible proof of their commitment to themselves and their future."

Certificate in Well-Being
University Extension, X-001
University of California, San Diego
La Jolla, CA 92093

It's Not Nice to Fool with Mother Nature "Death begins in the colon." Not a pretty thought, and the San Diego Natural Health Offices want to do something about this autointoxication. The Offices believe in cleansing the colon, then following a good nutritional program so that the lungs, glands, and eliminative organs "can do their proper work and keep the body in a healthy condition."

San Diego Natural Health Offices
4459 Morrell St.
Pacific Beach, CA 92109

Healing Waters "Prior to the arrival of white settlers, these Sacred Healing Grounds were used by the Apache Nation," says the Healing Waters brochure. "Today, our 200 acres of hotel, hermitage, and hot springs facilities are available for retreats and seminars which aid in the development of body, mind, and spirit."

Healing Waters
P.O. Box 847
Eden, AZ 85535

Herban Renewal

Rx for: (fill in your name)

Take one herbal retreat at the Oak Valley Herb Farm in the Sierra Nevada mountains of Northern California. Learn to make salves, tinctures, syrups, cough drops, and herbal massage oils. Wander through 160 acres of woods and meadows. Experience a three-hour herb walk and eighteen hours of intensive classes. Collect wild and cultivated herbs from hills and gardens and learn to prepare your own first-aid kit. Study Bach flower remedies, kinesiology, and foot reflexology. In between studying and collecting, relax with massage, discussion, hiking, swimming, or sauna.

Continue taking this Rx for as long as needed. The three-day retreats are offered once a month, May through September. The cost is $40, which includes kit materials, vegetarian meals, and optional indoor sleeping.

Other "medications" available are "Woman's Herbal Studies," "Growing, Harvesting and Using Herbs," and "Advanced Medicinal Herb Course."

For mild cases a half-day herb walk in the spring and early summer (for $2) may be sufficient.

Caution: may be habit forming. —E.H.

Herb Retreat
Oak Valley Herb Farm
Star Route
Camptonville, CA 95922

Yoghurt is very good for the stomach, the lumbar regions, appendicitis, and apotheosis.
EUGENE IONESCO

. . . and Astrological Birth Control

You can have your back cracked, your feet massaged, or your future charted. You can learn Chinese healing massage or the 31 exercises for cultivating the Ch'i force.

The House of Life in San Diego, California, offers a wide-ranging series of holistic health classes, lectures, and workshops woven together to provide an avenue for total physical, mental, cosmic, Karmic, and general good health.

There's iridology, where an eyeful means that by examining your iris a qualified practitioner can not only determine what ails you but can also identify any imbalances in your whole system.

As far as your back goes, there's nonforce spinal manipulation. and among the other 20 courses and workshops there's the study of foot reflexology—the art and science of restoring vitality through massage of the feet.

Learn to control one corner of destiny with astrological birth control, or attend a lecture where the topics range from colon therapy to nutrition.

This varied selection of new-age programs is taught by experts in their respective fields. Costs range from $1 for the lectures to between $15 and $70 for the workshops and classes. —P.T.

House of Life
3970 4th Ave.
San Diego, CA 92103

Aging Backwards

Horizons: Lost & Found

If you've dreamt for years of a sort of paradise into which you could sink, enjoy yourself, pamper yourself, and emerge happier, healthier, more spiritually content, and even a better person, then try Shangri-La. It's not in the middle of the Himalayas any more; it's in Bonita Springs, Florida.

Shangri-La was established to let people get away from it all—but in such a way that they can eventually get *to* it all. That's why the founders, the Cheathams, named it after James Hilton's famed place of peace, a place so unhurried and spiritually renewing that the aging process stopped.

Shangri-La offers a total health program, including lectures, exercises, pool classes, and a diet tailored to making the individual attain and stay in superb physical condition. The emphasis is on natural methods—thus, no drugs, "miracle cures," or therapies are used. Instead, organic vegetarian foods, life-saving relaxation, and guided exercise give the guest—whether for a day or a season—a natural way to healing many physical and psychological problems.

Among the artificial and unhealthy things the staff of Shangri-La frowns on are canned or frozen foods, animal products, cigarettes, and alcohol. As a matter of fact, fasting is encouraged, though by no means required, and guidance is given to those who want to fast during their stay. The exercise programs are curtailed, if necessary, for the fasters.

The emphasis here is also on education. Books are available in such areas as anatomy, family planning, ecology, exercise, fasting, gardening, immunization, psychological inspiration, natural hygiene, health, and vegetarianism. The widespread reading complements the regular lecture program in all phases of natural health.

The resort's programs include secluded men's and women's sunbathing facilities, a swimming pool, watercycling to get around the tropical waterways in the Bonita Springs area, shuffleboard, organic gardening, yoga, ping pong, weightlifting, and exercise classes. Films are also shown. The resort covers more than eight acres of land and contains a complete jogging track for those so inclined. Six different residence buildings provide a variety of settings for the guests, and each building is named after a person who contributed prominently to the search for good health or the simple life.

A cooperative plan is available by which guests can work to pay for their room and board and still get the same privileges as cash-paying participants. The idea is to make the program available for as many people as possible, rather than just to "soak up the money along with the sunshine."

Shangri-La aims to teach both the ill and the well the way to live a healthy and happily structured life, conforming to and using the laws of nature. It provides clean air, clean water, and clean food in a serene atmosphere. It can be a resort, an educational institute, a retreat, a sanctuary, or all of the above. —R.J.

Shangri-La
Bonita Springs, FL 33923

Meanwhile, Back at the Ranch

Here's one ranch where you won't be saddled with bronc-busting, cattle branding, or early morning chores.

What you will find at Esser's Hygienic Rest Ranch in Lake Worth, Florida, is a place for rest, repose, and a return to good health.

Under the personal management of William L. Esser, this health farm is based on the idea that the normal state of the body is health—anything below normal is disease.

To help you achieve your "normal" state of well-being, the Ranch is designed to place you under healthful influences. With the aid of fasting, nutritious foods, sunlight, pure air, pure water, exercise, and regenerative relaxation and sleep, you'll be galloping back along the trail to the healthy exuberance of youth.

The Ranch is equipped with a variety of private and semi-private rooms and is near the beaches of Lake Worth and Palm Beach.

Rates are from $24 to $66 per day depending upon accommodations. Accommodations are limited at the Ranch—many applicants must be turned away simply because there isn't enough room. So only contact the Ranch if you are really serious about going. —P.T.

Esser's Hygienic Rest Ranch
P.O. Box 161
Lake Worth, FL 33460

Day-Tripping to Health

If you're a spa-shopper, you already know that most of these places simply demand a week or so of your time to bother with you. Not so at Glen Ivy Hot Springs. They're ready to welcome you any day (or part of any day)—except Mondays.

The area has been known for its therapeutic mineral springs since the time of the Luiseno Indians a couple of hundred years ago. Then in the late 1800s, the current spate of spas began to develop. Glen Ivy continues in this tradition—and even displays their own photo collection of turn-of-the-century bathing costumes for your giggles.

The serious spa facilities at Glen Ivy are: springs (natural, HOT!, mineral), mud/clay pools, massage, and sauna. Their cafe offers wholesome and generous lunches and goodies.

The air is clean, and the location is surprisingly close to Los Angeles (they say it's an hour's drive). The combination of convenience and facilities make it an excellent way to invest a day in yourself.

Facilities are available for poolside parties for groups of 20 to 200. Catering is available for groups as well. Oh, one other thing: the cost. $3 per person (children under 15: $1.75). —J.A.

Glen Ivy Hot Springs
25000 Glen Ivy Rd.
Corona, CA 91720

Regain and Maintain

Say that you can cure a disease, and you're a fool or a knave. That's what Dr. H. M. Shelton claims, and, at his Health School, guests receive not cures but instruction in how to regain and maintain good health.

Natural laws are the key, says Shelton. At Dr. Shelton's Health School guests do what that name implies—learn to be healthy. Health cannot be bought, in Shelton's view—it can only be built.

Diet is this edifice's foundation. Added on are the "legitimate and proper" uses of the "ordinary elements"—food, air, water, sunshine, emotional poise, and the like.

Suffer from rheumatoid arthritis, for example? At the Health School you will fast in order to "rapidly eliminate the gastro-intestinal irritation which represents the starting point of all cases of rheumatoid arthritis." Then you'll learn to live properly, the Shelton way.

What's the cost of learning the Shelton way? Anywhere from $26 daily to $224 weekly, depending upon the type of accommodations selected. Instruction, supervision, use of the facilities, and meals for nonfasting guests are included in the package. —R.McG.

Dr. Shelton's Health School
Route 10, Box 174-E
San Antonio, TX 78216

Spartan Sanctuary

The Ashram is no ordinary spa. Located just outside Los Angeles—in a secluded Calabasas, California, valley surrounded by mountains and streams—the Ashram's antiflab campaign is heavy on yoga and natural foods. But the goal is not mere weight loss—it is "optimum health within and without."

Personal attention is the Ashram's forte, with no more than eight guests in residence at one time. Upon arrival, every guest is thoroughly checked by the Ashram's resident physician, and all therapeutic programs are individually planned.

All guests, upon arrival, are urged to sever ties to the outside world during their seven-day stay at the Ashram because "even a phone call has proven to be a disruptive influence to your daily routine." No wonder. Every moment is programmed, from the morning's 6:30 meditation through the 10:00 p.m. bedtime. In between, guests go for hikes, swim, jog, exercise to music, do yoga routines, hit the gym, and get massaged.

Three meals daily are provided, but they are hardly square. Raw foods predominate, and vegetarians are delighted. Some guests, however, are banished from the chow line, with therapeutic fasting prescribed instead.

Self-imposed discipline is the Ashram's way of life, and this regimen's developer is Dr. Anne Marie Bennstrom, a pioneer in the field of Preventive Health. Her assistants include Catharina Hedberg, "another Swedish dynamo," who "runs the Ashram with a firm but loving hand."

Life at the Ashram is spartan—there are no lavish fringes and guests are not treated to herbal wraps, facials, manicures, and the like. But every guest is fully schooled in Dr. Bennstrom's philosophy of exercise, and that has proven a powerful lure. Despite the $800 tariff for a week at the Ashram, guests flock to the Calabasas retreat.

Accommodations, food, and the Ashram attire (sweatshirt, T-shirts, robes, kaftans) are included in the fee. Guests are urged to bring only walking shoes and essential personal articles. But don't arrive with more than a few personal effects—the Ashram strongly discourages the practice, and for good reason. With that tight daily schedule, guests will be lucky to find even a few free minutes. But that is the Ashram's way. —R.McG.

The Ashram
P.O. Box 8
Calabasas, CA 91302

Un-Fat Au Naturel

In your heart of hearts you know what the best way to lose weight is—stop eating. At the Berkshire Health Manor, you may be able to accomplish that goal with a vengeance.

When Dr. Rune Schylander says what you ought to do is stop eating, you might say he's a man of his word. Berkshire's preferred program is called a "water diet." That's what you get—water—for a week. Virtually a guaranteed weight loser.

While you're purifying your system of fat (and, incidentally, elevating your mind through the ordeal), Berkshire will make you as comfortable as possible under the circumstances. All manner of recreational possibilities abound, including a solar reflector which will give you a winter tan.

For those who are not up to the water diet (sissies), there's a nutritional juices/salad combo which assuages those pains of foodlonging somewhat.

Berkshire is emphatically not a hospital, convalescent home, or nursing home. No medical advice is given. As a matter of fact, they suggest you OK yourself for the regimen with your own physician.

Then go starve yourself thin. That gorgeous skinny person is waiting there inside you. —J.A.

Berkshire Health Manor
Copake, NY 12516

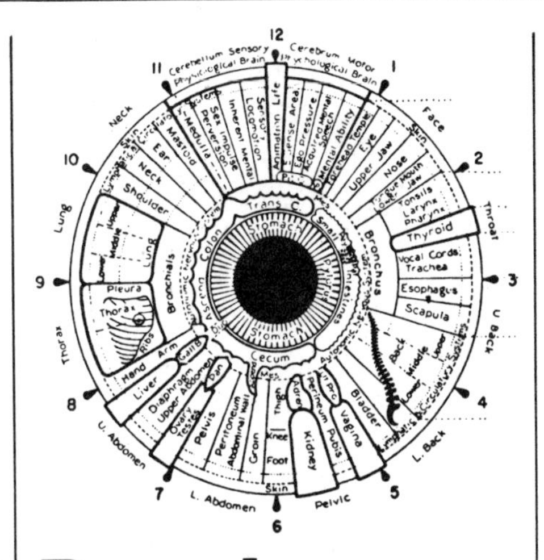

Down in the Valley

Extra! Extra! Read all about it! Dr. Jensen initiates new series of rejuvenation weeks! Classes start immediately for those who want "to learn to live correctly"!

Dr. Bernard Jensen, D.C., has recently announced that he is initiating a new series of rejuvenation weeks to be held at his House of the Seventh Happiness in Escondido, California.

Dr. Jensen believes that the informed person should keep himself well, and to achieve this goal he will work with each patient individually on a program of "elimination, transition, and building."

The first day Dr. Jensen will perform an iris analysis on each patient, and from this he will determine the patient's inherent strengths and weaknesses, health level, and chemical type.

The first three days will be devoted to cleansing, purifying, detoxification, and elimination.

On the second day self-acceptance and the capacity of self will be discussed. The third day the discussion will focus on transition from the old to the new and on harmony with relatives and family.

On the fourth and fifth days there is a transition to solid foods. The sixth day Dr. Jensen will discuss harmony with the female and male principles, and the last day there will be a feast and a final iris analysis.

Program fee for the entire week is $400. —E.H.

Rejuvenation Weeks
Hidden Valley Health Resort
Route 1, Box 52
Escondido, CA 92025

Less Is More

Based on the simple idea that anyone who stops eating will lose weight, the Pawling Health Manor in Hyde Park, New York, has been successfully starving its guests for 18 years.

Among the best-known of the nation's health retreats, the Pawling Manor states its methods as simply "sunshine, fresh air, exercise, natural foods, and rational fasting." Guests pay to exist on well water for days; toward the end of the week they can greedily attack salt-free vegetables, fruits, and salads, while indulging in mild exercise. Smokers are not allowed through the door.

The program is restful—perhaps the most exciting activity is a lecture series on weight control given by a biochemist and nutritionist. Pawling devotees insist that the combination of fasting and rest dispels nervous tension and brings about a cleansing of mind and body.

Pawling says that it offers no medical treatments and suggests that clients check with their doctor before participating. Once enrolled, guests must stay at least a week. Weekly rates run $161 and up for room and very little board. —J.W.

Pawling Health Manor
Box 401
Hyde Park, NY 12538

It's the Water

Rio Caliente proves that health spas aren't merely for the rich. Well off the beaten track in a mile-high forest outside Guadalajara, Mexico, the 28-room ranch offers the joys and services of an expensive spa at a price most anyone can afford—$16 a day single occupancy, $14.25 each for a double room.

Customary delights such as massage rooms, pools, and a beauty shop are available, but you can fill your days as you choose. Though you could easily pack your stay with workshops, swimming, yoga, hiking, and horseback riding, you might just choose to spend the time kicking back in the lithium-rich, naturally heated river that flows through the ranch.

A national park with a bizarre botanical mix of pine trees and tropical and desert plants surrounds the site. Complementing the quiet is a healthy offering of vegetarian cuisine, including tropical fruits, garden vegetables, grains, and juices. Much of the food is grown at the ranch.

Accommodations are in cozy rooms

or bungalows, each with its own fireplace and wood supply. Many of them are just a splash away from the three naturally heated swimming pools. Workshops by visiting group leaders in the areas of psychology, education, nutrition and health, esoteric studies, music, and dance are also available. —G.D.

Rio Caliente
Apdo. Postal 1-1187
Guadalajara
Jalisco, Mexico

Life would be infinitely happier if we could only be born at the age of eighty and gradually approach eighteen.
MARK TWAIN

Flower Power

Rock rose, star of Bethlehem, impatiens, clematis, and cherry plum—so runs the recipe for Dr. Edward Bach's rescue remedy, antidote for fear, shock, irritability, weakness, and loss of equilibrium. A prominent Harley Street physician working in vaccines and immunology, Dr. Bach concluded his career in the 1930s with the discovery and development of flower essence healing. His earliest remedies he called the 12 healers, to which he subsequently added 26 more.

Most people find it difficult to determine the appropriate flower essences for themselves without the aid of an experienced practitioner. Richard Katz has used flower essences for nearly three years in self-healing, counseling, and teaching. He brings to his work over ten years' experience in healing and psychospiritual growth and has studied with Claudio Naranjo; Tarthang Tulku, Rinpoche; Jack Schwartz; Rob Menzies; O Shinnah Fast Wolf; and Leonard Orr. Katz has taught in healing centers throughout Northern California and is available for counseling, introductory classes, and professional workshops.

Flower essence healing is natural and benign, and combines well with any form of healing or therapy. The goal is for you to discover your inner divinity and learn to express it creatively in the world. —M.W.

Richard Katz
P.O. Box 586
Nevada City, CA 95959

Viva la Spa!

We're sure you don't have any of these problems:
—overweight
—irritability
—insomnia
—lack of sex drive
—depression
—headaches
—digestive disturbances
But maybe a friend of yours is troubled in one or more of these areas. If so, tell him about Villa Vegetarina, a health spa in Cuernavaca, Mexico. For only $150 to $250 per person per week, he can fast or enjoy the organic vegetarian menu; he can benefit from pressure-point massages; and he can learn to speak Spanish. Also available are classes in yoga, fasting, and exercise; and there are evening lectures on nutrition and diet. The facilities include a swimming pool, outdoor gymnasium, handball court, volleyball court, bicycle paths, and hammock havens.

This is not a plush health spa but rather a homey, adults-only spa where everyone is on a first-name basis. That should help make your friend feel more at ease.

All rooms have private baths and some have solariums for nude sunbathing.

So tell your friend. —E.H.

Villa Vegetarina Health Spa
P.O. Box 1228
Cuernavaca, Mexico

Luxury's Lap

Splendor Inn

If money is no object and if the object is to lose weight in an atmosphere of unsurpassed splendor, then the Golden Door could be the resort for you.

Nestled in the softly rounded hills of Southern California, the Golden Door knows no boundaries in its quest to offer a place for repose and a return to a healthier, slimmer outlook on life.

As you enter the Golden Door you cross a 141-foot footbridge that spans a camellia-banked stream. Behind you is the hustle of calorie-laden modern life, and before you, past the brass and gem-studded "golden door" that greets you in a sleek wooden building, is an Oriental oasis of healthy eating combined with a program of exercise to revitalize the mind and body.

The complex, built at a cost of nearly $4 million, is an exquisite re-creation of a Japanese *honjin* inn. You'll find yourself surrounded by lush gardens, delicate wooden walkways, and small Japanese-style houses, each decorated with centuries-old Oriental art objects.

Deborah Mazzanti, the owner and creator of the Golden Door, explains why she chose a Japanese inn as the theme and motif for her resort: "I wanted to avoid the commonplace and the conventional—to offer my guests a new serenity, a new experience unlike anything they could find elsewhere."

The food at the Golden Door is fresh, much of it grown on the premises. An average of 800 calories makes up a day's diet. Belgian-born Michel Stroot is the Golden Door's chef, and while no dish takes more than a half-hour to prepare, the cooking is timed to finish just as you sit down to dinner. Everything is served in diminutive lacquered bowls from Japan that only hold a cup and a half of liquid but are designed to give an illusion of a much larger portion.

The Golden Door's day begins at sunrise. You start your day with a prebreakfast walk/jog that's designed to waken both your body and your mind.

The day's schedule blends active and passive activities. After the morning jog it's breakfast in bed, then aerobic exercises in the gym. Fresh gazpacho and juice cure hunger pangs, while the rest of the morning is spent in a herbal wrap and in an invigorating game of water volleyball. Lunch at poolside, a soak in the sun, and then an afternoon of yoga, tennis, Japanese spin walks, a Swiss shower, and pore-by-pore attention to your skin.

Dinner is served at seven preceded by nonalcoholic cocktails. Following dinner is a quick walk and a visit to the bathhouse for sauna, steam, Jacuzzi bath, and massage—then to sleep.

Certainly not your typical nine-to-five.

The Golden Door is primarily a woman's domain, but eight weeks are scheduled for men only, and two weeks are set aside for couples. And they've recently added mother-daughter and father-son weeks.

The cost for a week's stay at the Golden Door is $1575. —P.T.

The Golden Door
Box 1567
Escondido, CA 92025

The Spa That Refreshes

Treat yourself to one of the hottest fads now sweeping America—good health. Whether you have several weeks or only a weekend to devote to fixing up the body you live in, Rancho La Puerta, in Tecate, Mexico, has a program for you.

The spa uses natural food diets geared for sensible weight loss, combined with exercise programs that range from the vigorous to the relaxed. If you are the athletic type, you can hike, jog, swim, and play tennis and volleyball. If you are somewhere between jogging and slogging, you can work out in the mechanical gym or do ballet. And if your fastest sport is backgammon, you can put yourself in the hands of the masseuses, cosmeticians, and herbal wrappers.

More economical than most of its competitors, Rancho La Puerta is well worth a try and has served as the model for many other, better-known spas in the West. Weekends start at $130 per person; weekly programs are as low as $315 per person, with reduced rates for couples. It is a fitness vacation fit for everyone. —R.J.

Rancho La Puerta
Tecate, CA 92080

Melt the Too, Too Solid Flesh

Imagine breakfast delivered prettily on a tray as you lie propped among rosy sheets. No matter that your meal totals only 150 calories and your stomach still growls afterward.

Your tray bears a card listing your activities for the day. No decisions about whether to tackle the kitchen floor or attend the PTA meeting. This schedule includes an hour at the Charles of the Ritz Center to make your face look younger, some exercise followed by a soothing massage, and a formal dinner where even the carrot sticks are expertly curled.

You are at the Greenhouse, Neiman-Marcus's one-upmanship version of the health and beauty spa. NM advertises its retreat as a "gently disciplined program that rejuvenates both mind and body," with a staff of 100 to pamper and prod no more than 36 guests.

An oasis on the barren prairie outside Dallas, the Greenhouse boasts more scenery inside than out. The NM brochure discreetly avoids mention of prices. Apparently, if you have to ask you can't afford it. —J.W.

Neiman-Marcus's The Greenhouse
P.O. Box 1144
Arlington, TX 76010

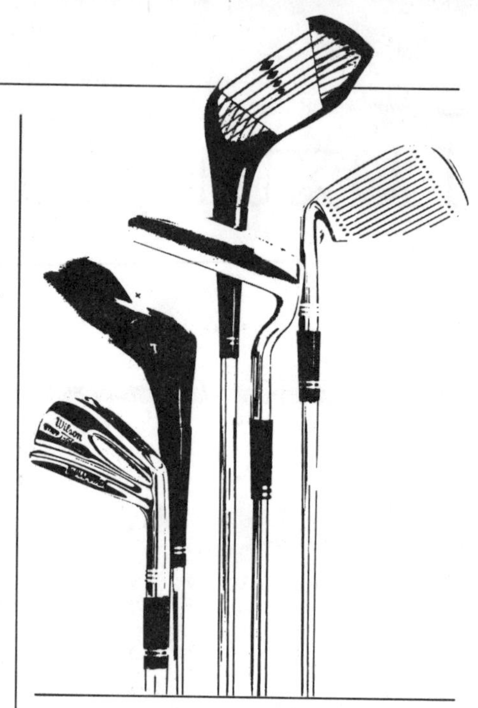

Pound of Flesh Reducers, gainers, and the flabby, take note. The Pala Mesa Resort in Southern California has programs at its Spa that might interest you. They have three- or seven-day programs that include exercise, diet, massage, and foot and hand reflexology. The cost is from $345 to $795.

The Spa at Pala Mesa Resort
2001 South Hwy 395
Fallbrook, CA 92028

Portly? "The North Shore of Long Island is fortunate to have a new 'fat farm' equipped for both men and women of all ages, to not only lose weight, but to maintain their weight after they have reached their goal." So states the brochure of the Port Washington Manor. Their supervised program is based on a protein-sparing modified fast, and they also aid "in correcting improper dietary habits." The price is from $175 to $260 per person per week.

Port Washington Manor, Inc.
372 Main St.
Port Washington, NY 11050

By the Sea, By the Sea "No one is ever a 'number' here," at the Harbor Island Spa. "You're treated as an individual with individual needs whether that may be to lose or gain weight." And the people at the Spa take their nutrition, health, and fitness programs seriously—"even our waiters and waitresses are trained in proper nutritional guidance." The Spa and its prices are luxurious—from $40 to $122 per person per day depending on the season.

Harbor Island Spa
On the Ocean
West End, NJ 07740

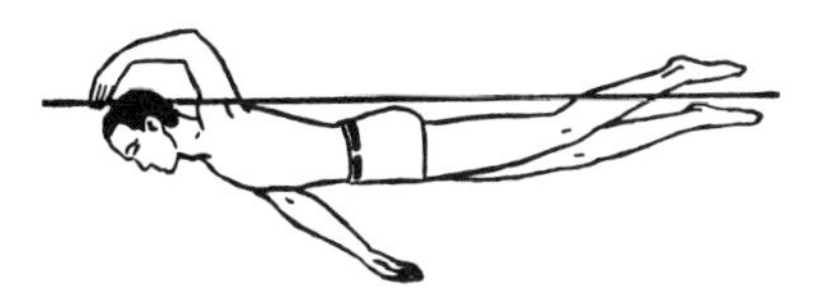

Outstanding Figures We provide "an ideal environment for men and women wishing to lose weight, stop smoking, or simply relax and restore that sparkle in their eyes and the spring to their steps," say the people at Hubbardsville Manor Health Spa. They do this by controlled fasting and nutritious, low-calorie diets. "There are no gadgets or magic formulas, but gratifying results are achieved with the program when followed seriously." The cost is $125 per person per week.

Hubbardsville Manor Health Spa
Hubbardsville, NY 13355

In Hot Water The Jacumba Hot Springs Health Spa "offers you a chance to live again." It offers supervised exercise; clean, dry air; wholesome foods; and pure, spring water—mineral water to be exact. They're not fancy and make no claim to be. Instead, they emphasize their casual, relaxed, and healthy atmosphere. Rates are $85 to $195 per week.

Jacumba Hot Springs Health Spa
Box 466
Jacumba, CA 92034

For Ladies Only Your stay at the Englewood Cliffs Spa will, they say, "make you look and feel ten years younger." Their weight control program is medically supervised and directed, and "is one that you will be able to continue on a daily basis after your departure from the Spa." Their program includes exercise classes, daily walks, massage, and jogging. One important item, however: this spa is for women only.

Englewood Cliffs Spa
619 Palisades Ave.
Englewood Cliffs, NJ 07632

Here's Your Chance

Sunday
Dear Diary,

I'm finally here! It seems that I've wanted to come to Maine Chance for as long as I can remember. Somehow the expense of a beauty spa always seemed so frivolous. But then Jim handed me the ticket to Phoenix and the $1300 check made out to Maine Chance. He said he'd manage without me for a week.

Monday

Well, Diary, I'm having the time of my life. No diapers, no dog to feed, no meals to fix. Today started with breakfast in bed. What a treat! My first 30-minute exercise class was at 9:00. Then I went into the steam cabinet. After that I had a massage and 30 more minutes of exercise. At 11:30 I had a one-hour face treatment. That's more time than I spend on my face in a week at home. At 12:30 I had a scalp treatment and at 1:00 had lunch. (They serve the most delicious 900 calories a day here.) At 2:30 I went to a make-up class, and at 3:30 I had another 30 minutes of exercise. It's fun exercising here because it's done to music. Tonight I played bridge with two ladies from the East Coast and one woman from London. (We didn't discuss toilet training once.) —E.H.

The Maine Chance
Phoenix, AZ 84018

Building the Body Beautiful

Herbal wraps are not for chickens. They are for people—and, at La Costa's spa, the upshot is not a tasty baked dish. It's a more-knowledge-able-about-your-health, better-feeling you.

Sign up for La Costa's Spa Plan and you'll get—besides that promised herbal wrap—bodily delights such as massages, facials, skin analysis, manicures, pedicures, and oil treatment. That's for men as well as women, although women do get *two* herbal wraps to the men's one.

When your body's not being catered to, it will be enjoying "aqua-thin-ics," dance, yoga, and "Costa curves." And, for women only, there are makeup classes and hair treatments.

There are also, for both sexes, lavish meals (diet meals can be had, too) and forays into all that Greater San Diego has to offer. Or, just skip the spa and enjoy La Costa's luxuries—because exercise is not mandatory here.

Cost of La Costa's Spa Plan—including use of spa facilities, accommodations, and food—is $250 per couple daily. Go alone and the tariff is $150. Skip the spa plan and costs are lower still—with spa facilities available on an a la carte basis. —R.McG.

La Costa Hotel and Spa
Costa Del Mar Rd.
Carlsbad, CA 92008

Probably nothing in the world arouses more false hopes than the first four hours of a diet.
DAN BENNETT

Designs for Living

Weighty Problems

You are what you eat may be the slogan of the natural fooders, but for the thousands of members of Overeaters Anonymous it is not what you eat that matters—it's how and how much. Because O.A. members are self-confessed compulsive overeaters.

Founded in 1960, O.A. describes itself as a "fellowship of men and women who meet to share their experience, strength, and hope with one another in order that they may solve their common problem." Basing its program upon the proven principles of Alcoholics Anonymous, O.A. stresses mutual member assistance and its Twelve Steps—with the first, maybe the biggest, step being admission of "powerlessness over food." The remaining steps take members down the path of recovery and conclude with a call to members "to carry this message to compulsive overeaters."

But O.A. is not a diet club. It does suggest a diet plan, but members are urged to consult their personal physicians before embarking on any diet. Besides, says O.A., while diets are an important step toward correcting members' *physical* problems, there remains the spiritual realm to consider—and remedy. Because it is in that realm that the compulsion to overeat arises. Members, accordingly, are asked to recognize that "a Power greater than ourselves could restore us to sanity." But O.A. imposes no set definition on the nature of this Power and some members, says O.A., see the group itself as fully embodying this Power.

Is O.A. for you? Nobody but you, O.A. says, can answer that question. The only membership requirement is the desire to stop eating compulsively, and no fees or dues are charged. O.A. is fully self-supporting, however, and members are requested to contribute whatever they can to help meet the group's expenses.

Sporting over 3000 chapters in 16 countries, O.A.'s supporters are legion. So are success stories, and reports of 50 or 100 lost pounds are common. But poundage dropped, insists O.A., is not the key. Coming to grips with one's desires to eat is what really matters. —R.McG.

Overeaters Anonymous
World Service Office
2190 190th St.
Torrance, CA 90504

The Diet Is Cast

Dieting has long since replaced baseball as the national pastime. Subscribers to the many different reducing philosophies, from Weight Watchers to the Calories Don't Count clan, are fanatical about their "system."

Weight Counselling Services in Massachusetts doesn't have a weight-control plan. "Each person puts on weight for different reasons, and each person takes off weight differently," says the director. There are no contracts or guarantees.

The institute is staffed by registered nurses and clinical social workers. Everyone who comes in for help must have a complete physical exam before the first private diet consultation. After that, the service suggests a minimum of six weekly half-hour private sessions, for individual diet planning, moral support, handling emotional problems, and general self-growth.

The staff works with the dieter's family and physician, and there is a telephone hotline to prevent trips to the refrigerator.

Frequently counselors suggest shopping among local diet clubs for one that will add momentum to the effort, or they recommend community or hospital services. The group is unique in that they expend more effort helping clients than luring them in.

The cost for the first session is $15; the fee for half-hour sessions is $10. —J.W.

Weight Counselling Services
424 Newtonville Ave.
Newtonville, MA 02160

Whoa, There

It has been estimated that nearly half of all American adults are either on a diet, thinking about going on a diet, or presently cheating on a diet. From the midst of the great fray have come three front-line soldiers—former "heavies" who won their fight—with a weight-losing plan that seems simple, sensible, and best of all effective over a long period. They are three New Jersey housewives who have taken an idea patterned on the successful Weight Watchers program and turned it into Diet Control Centers, Inc., a franchise operation that claims 250,000 members.

Disdaining the many fad diets that have come and gone in recent years, the DCC program instead allows its members to eat most anything they want, as long as they do it in a sensible fashion. "Controlled portions," they call it, and they supplement their nutritional ideas with a series of exercises and a comprehensive program of behavior modification.

Members attend weekly classes at any of the company's 29 outlets, where they receive instruction and encouragement by trained professionals. There is also a bimonthly newspaper full of testimonials to the positive results of the program. —C.McB.

Diet Control Centers, Inc.
1021 Stuyvesant Ave.
Union, NJ 07083

Guinevere's Camps

Camelot . . . a fairy-tale place populated by handsome young knights and willowy young damsels. And now there's another Camelot, one designed for young women between 18 and 29 who are seeking that willowy look of yore. Camelot is a group of camps, located at six major college campuses across the country, where young women can lose an average of 30 pounds over the summer. And they can do so while having fun and developing the proper eating and life-style habits to keep the extra pounds off in the future.

Camelot begins with the understanding that overweight women are sensitive about their problem. The program provides a helpful and supportive atmosphere in which young women can develop desirable eating habits using behavior modification techniques. The menus are varied and nutritious and have only 1200 calories. Some of the many activities offered are belly dancing, swimming, backgammon, tennis, and yoga.

The camps are located at colleges in New York, Pennsylvania, Colorado, Michigan, North Carolina, and California, and the facilities of the schools are available for the campers' use. Camelot also offers camps for teens. —P.T.

Camelot Centers, Inc.
949 Northfield Rd.
Woodmere, NY 11598

Lean Line Your head is the smartest place to start a diet according to Lean Line, Inc., a weight reduction company with classes in eight states. They offer "a sensible, well balanced, and nutritionally stable weight reduction program." Even such foods as spaghetti, bagels, and lox are allowed. Fees are from $3 to $7.

Lean Line, Inc.
1600 Park Ave.
South Plainfield, NJ 07080

Do or Diet The Private Diagnostic Clinic of the Duke University Medical Center in North Carolina doesn't fool around. It takes severely obese men and women (average weight: 250 lbs.), and in a matter of one year helps these people lose an average of 130 lbs. each. Patients follow Dr. Walter Kempner's Rice/Reduction Diet Program and are monitored *every* day by Dr. Kempner and his staff. The cost is from $185 to $220 per week.

Rice/Reduction Diet Program
Medical Private Diagnostic Clinic
Duke University Medical Center
Durham, NC 27710

Behavior Mod for Your Bod

Riddle #1: What is shapely, wears a big smile, and lives in Wisconsin?

Answer: A successful Weight Loser.

Riddle #2: What is a Weight Loser?

Answer: A Weight Loser is a member of Weight Losers International, a Wisconsin-based organization devoted to helping people lose weight. Their approach to the problem of weight loss is behavior modification. They try to take the attention off the scale and onto eating behavior. Weight Losers attend classes where planned techniques and procedures are used to pinpoint and modify individual eating problem areas. Each of the 16 weekly classes costs $2.50, and there is an additional registration fee of $3.50. A "Weight Loss Wonder" (a student who reaches goal weight) receives full maintenance instructions plus free lifetime membership and benefits. Some of the benefits of membership in Weight Losers International are: a proven, completely nutritious and interesting food program; weekly recipes to make eating more enjoyable; membership in their Globe Trotters travel group; delicious flavor extracts to perk up your meals; and the help of others who understand weight problems. —E.H.

Weight Losers International
4962 N. Hopkins St.
Milwaukee, WI 53209

Masters of Flesh

If you're fat in or near Philadelphia, you have a friend at Weight Masters of America. Trained counselors man the phones until midnight seven days a week to make sure you have someone to talk to when you're faced with a food crisis.

The 16-week Weight Masters program is designed to re-educate your eating habits, probably even improving your self-image in the process. No medicines, calisthenics, or mimeographed diets are used, and you can even drink (in controlled moderation).

Your own personal counselor comes to your home or office for your once-a-week sessions which cover Controlled Food Intake (you'll be calling it CFI), mental programming and behavioral reconstruction, and, during the fifteenth and sixteenth sessions, maintenance (or how to keep it off).

Weight Masters promises you'll lose weight *and* keep it off. And they'll refund all fees if, after following their instructions for four weeks, you decide the program is not for you. —D.P.

Weight Masters of America
1405 Locust St.
Suite 411
Philadelphia, PA 19102

Where Losing Is Winning

If you're a woman who's really serious about losing weight—but who doesn't want to be grim about it—why not do it for college credit or for the sake of liking yourself better? At Green Mountain, in Poultney, Vermont, women between the ages of 18 and 55 can use a scientifically designed nutritional and behavioral approach to weight loss for college credit or just for its health value. The nutritional education gives lifelong learning, and that's worth a few months, a few dollars, and some college credit along the way.

Green Mountain is different from the wealth of camps and spas that intermingle diets with mudpacks and stretching exercises with suntans. While weight loss is the end product of the course, it's only one result of a program emphasizing body awareness and aimed at making a woman an expert in the theory and practice of keeping herself trim and healthy.

Instruction is given to participants in eating techniques, physiology, and "fat cell theory." Personal and career guidance is also offered for the woman who is working at getting ahead. Both summer and winter sessions are scheduled, stressing participation in a structured and supervised eating and exercise program monitored to make certain weight loss is occurring at the right pace for each individual. And every effort is made to give each woman a program she can follow for the rest of her life.

Thus, even if a woman has only a pound or two to lose but wants to learn the good habits she can depend on the rest of her life, she will benefit richly from this program.

Thelma J. Wayler, a dietician and nutritionist with impeccable credentials, is director of the weight control program. She has long been concerned with metabolic disorders and has developed a weight maintenance program over many years of experience.

Exercise programs are geared to each participant's needs and desires, and sports instruction is available in case there's something a woman always wanted to learn about, but never did. Depending on the season of the year, she can swim, jog, play tennis or golf, dance, bicycle, ski, skate, snowshoe, and learn what each sport provides in muscle conditioning as well as in calorie burning. Many other sports and types of conditioning—for example, downhill or cross-country skiing—are also provided.

Because it takes time to destroy old habits and replace them with new ones, Green Mountain requires participants to enroll for at least four weeks, at a cost of $1400. Many, however, stay for eight-, twelve-, or sixteen-week sessions. Part of the attraction of Green Mountain is not only that the community works, or that it provides an education that can be removed from the setting of the community yet still operate well, but that it emphasizes building self-confidence and self-esteem in each participant. —R.J.

Green Mountain
230-10 64th Ave.
Bayside, NY 11364

For some of us are out of breath,
And all of us are fat!
LEWIS CARROLL

Watch It! Being overweight can be miserable in a thin-workshipping world—ask any chubby adult. Better yet, ask an overweight teenager or child. Extra poundage is as bad or worse for them. Weight Watchers offers a summer of fun, friendship, learning, and—oh yes—weight loss—at one of its Camps for both boys and girls.

Weight Watchers Camps
183 Madison Ave.
New York, NY 10016

The Tell-Tale Heart Next to our brain, our heart is the most important organ of the body. We should treat it kindly but we often don't. "Heartbeat" Workshops in vegetarian cooking, stress management, coronary risk screening, and others are held yearly in Pennsylvania. Cost ranges from free to $45.

"Heartbeat" Workshops
Bucks County Seventh-Day
Adventist Church
Green and County Line Rds.
Warminster, PA 18974

One Is Company Learn how to relax and care for yourself. Become aware of your body; become one with yourself. Learn Rolfing, acupressure, foot reflexology. Learn it cheaply: $5 to $45.

Riley Educational Association
1150 Lunaanela St.
Kailua, HI 96734

Ay, There's the Rub Yes, we know. Think of a masseuse and you think of sexual encounters. But the graduates of the Massage Institute are serious men and women, interested in massage as a health career. At the Institute they have studied anatomy, kinesiology, physiology, ethics, hygiene, and other related areas. Tuition is $510 or $590.

The Massage Institute
3119 Clement St.
San Francisco, CA 94121

His ideas of first-aid stopped short at squirting soda-water.
P.G. WODEHOUSE

Dis-Stress

Situation: You live in the Philadelphia area. You are under a lot of stress. You are currently handling your stress in one of several harmful ways: smoking, overeating, drinking. You have $15 and would like to spend it on a six-week stress management seminar, but don't know how to find one.

Solution: Contact the Better Living Center. They can help you gain control over harmful stress. Their seminars employ relaxation exercises, films, slide shows, talks by doctors and health educators, small-group work, charts for keeping track of personal growth, and guided practice in setting and reaching life goals. You will hear a doctor's explanation of what happens to the body when a person is suffering from stress, you will learn eight basic health guidelines for restoring inner calm, and you will hear of proven ways that aid in adjusting to major life changes. —E.H.

Better Living Center
155 Bethlehem Pike
Philadelphia, PA 19118

Eastern Wisdom for Western Health

It has been said East is East, and West is West, and never the twain shall meet. However, irrespective of the fact that you can buy a Big Mac in downtown Tokyo, East has met West in Boston, Massachusetts.

The East West Foundation is an ambitious organization that seeks to bring the wisdom of the East to bear on the health problems of the West.

The Foundation offers classes in isokinetic therapy, a combination of yoga, acupuncture, and diet therapy that defines where energy blocks are located in the body. The course is taught by David Carmos, one of the most respected teachers in the field.

In an effort to approach the problem of starvation in the world and to produce food that is reasonably priced and free of chemicals, the Foundation is seeking to purchase a tract of land in New Hampshire.

In addition, the East West Foundation, which puts out a newsletter and various periodicals, offers intensive six-day seminars in macrobiotic healing and serves as headquarters for the World Macrobiotic Society. —P.T.

East West Foundation
359 Boylston St.
Boston, MA 02116

Ashes to Ashes

We've all seen or heard of them—the men and women who try to give up smoking. We hear of some of them trying to quit "cold turkey." We hear how they become excessively irritable and how they use food as a replacement for their cigarettes. We see how some others try to ease out of their habit and take up needlework to give their hands something to do and how they start to chew gum to give their jaws something to do.

Some of these men and women succeed—they quit smoking. But most others fail—the smoking habit is too hard to break.

But the Better Living Center in Philadelphia says its Five-Day Smoker's Plan "is designed to help even the *heaviest* smoker 'kick the habit' with an absolute minimum of discomfort" in five days. The Center claims an 80 percent success rate by using a "mix of personal and group therapy, multi-media techniques, and special diet," all under direct medical supervision.

The cost is $20. —J.S.H.

The Five-Day Smoker's Plan
155 Bethlehem Pike
Philadelphia, PA 19118

***When a Forsyte died—
but no Forsyte had as yet died;
death being contrary to their principles,
they took precautions against it.***
JOHN GALSWORTHY

Give Yourself the Business

Is physical fitness a key to a successful career? That's the claim of the Women's Sports Foundation, and, this group asserts, today's businesswomen who lack background in sports are handicapping their career development.

A busy career is no excuse for neglecting fitness—in fact, says the Foundation, the more pressured the career, the more imperative fitness becomes. That's because "sports and fitness act as mental and physical stimulants to make participants more productive as individuals and as women in business."

To bring this message to women, the Foundation offers seminars nationwide. Offering two basic formats—a two-hour presentation, and a one-day comprehensive program—the Foundation encourages corporations and groups to sponsor programs for their members. Seminars open to unaffiliated women are also available. Although the organization's chief thrust is women in business, programs geared to other groups are also offered. Costs vary with each program's exact nature. —R.McG.

Women's Sports Foundation
1660 S. Amphlett Blvd.
Suite 266
San Mateo, CA 94402

Born at Home

Where do you want your baby to be born?

Traditionally, American babies are born in hospitals, but there is a growing number of people who'd like to change that.

ACHI is the Association for Childbirth at Home, International. They give classes for prospective parents aimed at making childbirth at home a viable choice for healthy women in every community. Their stated goals are: "to bring the choices, responsibilities, and experiences of childbearing back to the woman and her family, where they belong," and "to improve the quality of the experience of childbearing for the baby, the mother, and the family—thereby improving the quality of life on this planet."

The ACHI Home Birth Series is offered throughout the United States and Canada. They also offer courses in becoming a certified childbirth educator and in advanced leader training.

ACHI is a nonprofit and "independent international organization supporting homebirth and dedicated to parents' right to decide where and with whom they will give birth." —E.H.

Association for Childbirth at Home, International
Box 1219
Cerritos, CA 90701

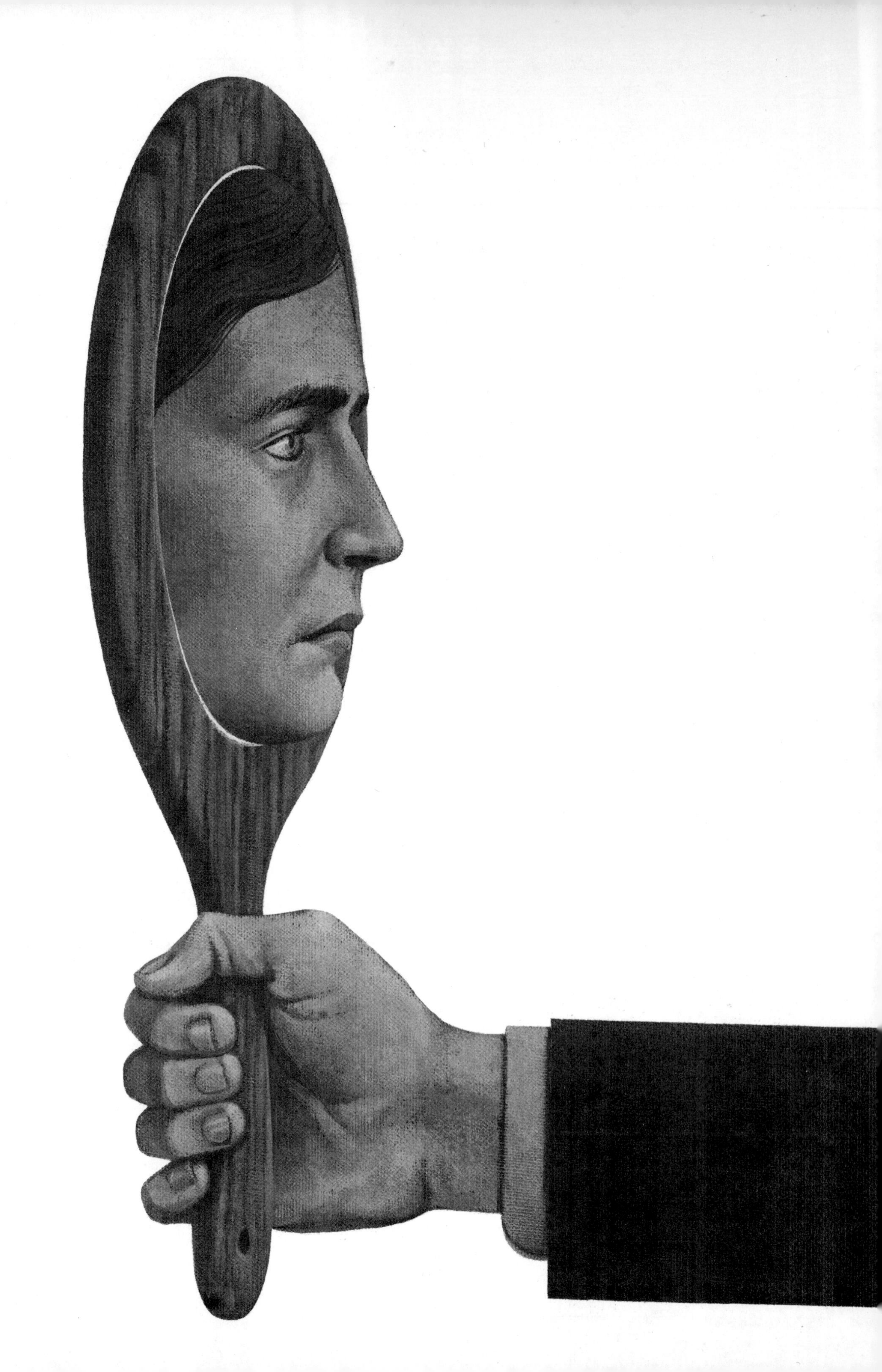

When mind soars in pursuit of
the things conceived in space,
it pursues emptiness.
But when man dives deep within himself
he experiences the fullness
of his existence.
MEHER BABA

Looking Within

Somewhere this side of the rainbow, four zany figures danced their ways toward a radiant city the color of hope, ruled by a powerful Wizard.

And as they followed their yellow-brick road, those four zanies typified some very real searches in the lives of very real people. The Tin Woodsman wanted a heart. The Cowardly Lion wanted courage. The Scarecrow wanted a brain. And sprightly little Dorothy wanted a ticket back home. Those four quests (courage, emotion, intellect, home) account for some of the important things in life. And it's with just such quests that this chapter is concerned.

Without a mind and soul at peace, a human being is no more than an eternal voyager, forever seeking a way to serenity. That way may lie in "workaholism," in obsession, or in everyday, garden-variety neurosis. Everyone knows, however, that the search for self ends only with honest self-discovery.

"Looking Within" is a compilation of programs to help you do just that. We've made no attempt to choose a path for you to follow—just to let you know some of the paths there are to choose from.

If you want to explore your psyche and achieve better self-understanding, we have programs in hypnosis, personal growth, assertiveness training, and stress management. For your body we have holistic programs, body manipulation, and physical challenges.

We've catalogued the famous and the shy here: from the outward-thrusting Esalen Institute to the unearthly quietude of the Abbey of Regina Laudis.

If you've always wondered whether yoga would help, here's your chance to find out. We've yoga of more varieties than anyone could ever need. We've listened closely to the music that wafts in on the "Breezes from the East" and can offer you programs in shiatsu, tai chi, and Zen.

Within the pages of this chapter you may find meditation techniques from around the world: Judaeo-Christian, Ananda, Zen. You'll find programs designed especially for women who want to raise their feminist consciousness. You'll even find help for men who want to raise their feminist consciousness. And right alongside the most traditional, you'll read about California's Elysium Institute (one of the country's foremost "clothing optional" retreats).

We can't recommend any of these programs to any individual—because each individual has different needs and different styles. Where one needs courage, another needs brains. Where one needs a loving heart, another wants nothing more in all the world than simply to get back to Kansas. We hope that you, like Dorothy, can find a happy ending here.

Illustration by Tom Gould

Helping Yourself

Light Up Your Life

When was the last time you measured the development of your psyche? Has it reached its fullest potential? You may not have the appropriate tools in your own workshop to make the necessary measurements. But Arica's workshops are staffed with teachers who would like to measure your development in detail. Using a scientific approach, Arica will teach you how to achieve self-realization in a remarkably short period of time.

Arica's goal is to teach individuals to become happier and better human beings through self-understanding and self-awareness. Courses range in length from a 320-hour program to a 15-hour program. Home-study materials are also available.

The 320-hour course, titled The 40 Day Training, will teach you the two sources of all internal conflict: the physical condition of your body, and the mental conditioning acquired from past experience. If you've got any repressed emotions, this course is sure to drag them out! Arica has developed over 1000 questions that will evoke memories of past events. You will come to understand who you are, your relationship with your parents, your role in the world, your ambitions for power, the need to be loved, how to express yourself, your sexuality, your internal being, and your spiritual life. Once you've mastered these areas, you should be able to approach any life situation free from the burdens of your past.

If all that seems too much for you, you could try Three Days to Kensho. This course promises you a full understanding of yourself as a human being. It outlines the laws of consciousness and the structure of the psyche. The workshop lasts three days, meeting 10½ hours per day. Between lectures, each of which lasts about an hour, simple meditation and relaxation exercises are performed.

Or how about a little chuak'a? That is, deep body massage. Learn to release tension and increase vitality in your body and brain by massaging the appropriate muscles and vortex points.

Other Arica courses cover the following topics: understanding human behavior; achieving satori; new ways for couples to discover a more rewarding relationship; psychocalisthenics; and recognizing change as a challenge.

Course materials as well as books, tarot cards, clothing for meditation and exercise, health food products, lecture cassettes, jewelry, and a monthly newspaper can be purchased separately. Yantras—designs that use color and shape to convey information to the inner self without the use of written or spoken words—are available in the form of posters, greeting cards, paintings, silkscreens, and tapestries.

Arica programs are conducted throughout the United States, Europe, Canada, and South America. Schedules and tuitions vary. All programs are available in detailed instructional manuals with teaching aids. Interested participants are welcome to teach their own courses. The only requirement is that you purchase or rent the materials from Arica. —B.H.

Arica Institute
235 Park Ave. South
New York, NY 10003

Beginning Anew at Lands End

Feeling at loose ends? No wonder, says Lands End. It's tough out there and, because it is, many of us lose ourselves in the fight to survive. Playing the game is paramount, but the playing sometimes destroys the players.

But all is not gloom. Lands End—an 18-acre retreat adjacent to the Adirondack Forest Preserve—offers surcease. Its specialty is programs in human relations, ones that are "theologically, spiritually, and psychologically valid for the growth and education of individuals and groups."

Lands End is an educational, not a therapeutic, experience. Its program is packed with courses in personal development, assertiveness training, creative movement/sensory experience, and group development. Learning is relaxed but professional at Lands End, as participants are immersed in a learning-by-doing atmosphere.

Cost of most offerings ranges between $100 and $200; most courses are slated to run five days and are offered periodically throughout the year. Lands End is affiliated with the Northeast Synod of the United Presbyterian Church, but all programs are open to nonmembers of the church. —R.McG.

Lands End
Star Route 109, Box 5
Saranac Lake, NY 12983

Busibodies

Changing oneself, you might be thinking, is an expensive undertaking. But it ain't so. Just drop by any of the People's Center workshops and see.

The *most* expensive People's Center offering is the 18-hour marathon personal growth workshop, where participants explore communications, support, feedback, and other techniques of self-improvement. The cost? Twenty dollars.

But the bulk of the People's Center offerings are priced at $5 weekly and run for eight weeks. Interested in self-hypnosis as a possible key to weight loss or as a way to stop smoking? Eight nights, spread over two months, sets participants back a mere $40.

The same goes for workshops in Family Communications, Stop Smoking, Sex Education, Study Skills, Assertion Training, and Total Image. And every workshop is conducted by a qualified professional, one who is certified and licensed.

Conducted by National Busibody Services, the People's Center is committed to keeping its fees within reach of all. Scholarships are available to those unable to pay.

This, in short, is one busibody who is not a nuisance. —R.McG.

National Busibody Services, Inc.
6343 S. Eastern Ave., Suite B
Bell Gardens, CA 90201

See the Light What are we? What is the meaning of life? What is the world? What is time? What is space? These are a few of the time-honored questions you will be exploring if you join the Order of Wholemind. For your membership fee of $10 and monthly dues of $5 you will receive two segments each month of the Intuitive Research Program. This program provides studies and experiments designed to help you understand the workings of your mind and reach true Enlightenment. And you can do it all in the privacy of your own home.

Wholemind Institute of Intuitive Research
P.O. Box 639
Indian Hills, CO 80454

Happy Talk You can learn to be happy. At least that's what the people at Happiness Pursuits believe. And they've developed a one-year correspondence course to prove it. You pay $20 a month for the course, which begins with a "Happiness Pursuits Survey." After that you receive regular monthly learning assignments. Perhaps money *can* buy happiness.

Happiness Pursuits
P.O. Box 12
Port Washington, NY 11050

Sounds Interesting What'sa matter, Bunky? You say you've got problems? You say you've tried therapy, yoga, massage, meditation, primal scream—and nothing seems to work? Well, all is not lost. Light and Sound has an unusual approach to problem solving that may just work for you. You will focus on your problem as you listen to a cassette tape of sound frequencies while color patterns are projected onto your body. It's $25 for the tape and color slides, plus instructions. Smile, Bunky.

Light and Sound Headquarters
1170 Gunn Hall Dr.
Virginia Beach, VA 23454

Insight Information Within you are hundreds of wonderful ideas waiting to be born. How do you get to those ideas, and what do you do with them once you've got them? Find out how to tap your resources by attending one of the Creative Problem Solving Institutes offered in major cities throughout the year. Write for dates, places, and fees.

Creative Education Foundation
State University College at Buffalo
Chase Hall
1300 Elmwood Ave.
Buffalo, NY 14222

Alpha Bet The American life style is active, competitive, and full of tension and stress. Many are finding that the key to survival in this busy world is knowing how to relax. Science tells us that the relaxed brain emits alpha brain waves, so learning how to produce alpha waves is one way to achieve relaxation. Life Dynamic Fellowship offers a cassette course called "Alphanetics" to increase alpha wave production. To take the course you need to become a member of the Fellowship by making a $99 donation to this nonprofit organization.

Life Dynamics Fellowship
P.O. Box 418
Laguna Beach, CA 92652

Stress but No Strain Prolonged stress contributes to more than half of all diseases contracted by Americans today. Learning how to control stress is thus a high priority for our health and well-being. Psychologist Gerald H. Stephenson has developed a stress management system that utilizes rational behavior training, biofeedback, and relaxation training to help people cope with stress and gain inner peace. Write for information on this cassette tape program.

Human Development Systems
825 N. Bishop
Dallas, TX 75208

Change Your Program Want to become wealthy and successful? Improve your memory? Stop smoking? Lose weight? Develop self-confidence? Improve your sex life? It's within you to do all these things. Through self-hypnosis you can overcome your subconscious programming that prevents you from doing what you really want to do, and you can reprogram yourself for success. The Covina Center for Hypnosis provides cassette programs in a number of different areas. Write for their catalog.

Covina Center for Hypnosis
312-G North Citrus
Covina, CA 91723

The true profession of man is to find his way to himself.
HERMAN HESSE

Red Alert

Communications are breaking down and your distress signal is flashing. No, you aren't stranded on a highway in a snowstorm. You're in your own home, surrounded by your family. What's wrong? It could be anything from a threat to your crops to a fight with your spouse.

We all face pressure in our daily lives—pressure that can cause emotional and physical damage if not handled properly. The West Central Minnesota Workshop for Rural People is designed to help members of the agricultural community learn to live and cope with such stress.

The workshop's main objectives are to explain the relationship between emotional stress and physical health, to identify the warning signals of possible physical and mental breakdowns, to release tension, and to provide suggestions for expert help if needed. Causes of poor family relationships are discussed, and suggestions for improving husband-wife and parent-child relationships are offered. The workshop lasts one day and the fee is $20 per person, or $30 if both husband and wife attend.

Another one-day workshop is called Living Together, Working Together. It emphasizes improving the quality of family life (father-son relationships, a farm wife's perception of herself), as well as managing the family farm. —B.H.

Continuing Education
and Regional Programs
University of Minnesota
226 Community Services Building
Morris, MN 56267

You Are Getting Sleepy

Mildred James was once a chain-smoking housewife. Now she's an authority on how to quit smoking through hypnosis. Mildred kicked her smoking habit in 1962 through hypnosis, and she and her associates have helped many others do the same since then.

"Self-improvement through relaxation" is how James describes her technique, which she says will help you quit smoking, lose weight, and even improve your golf game.

The trick, she says, is to use hypnosis to free your mind of the clutter and self-defeating attitudes that keep you stuck in the same old rut.

A business that began in Mildred's living room has since expanded to the point where she and several associates work out of a studio and give group sessions to as many as 350 people at a time.

If you can't make it to her studio outside Seattle, Ms. James offers a cassette tape series that covers topics as diverse as concentration, self-confidence, sleep, golf improvement, fear of flying, bedwetting, alcoholism, weight gain, and breast development. —G.D.

Mildred H. James, Inc.
P.O. Box 5203
Kent, WA 98031

Trying to define yourself is like trying to bite your own tongue.
ALAN WATTS

Meditate on This

According to Gurudev Shree Chitrabhanu, founder of the Jain Meditation International Center, words are sharper than a knife, and not easily forgotten. By watching our words we can protect other people and not add to the burden of our own souls. This is one way that Gurudev encourages individuals to use their energies for the benefit of all. The Jain Center further proposes that salvation comes when you put yourself in the place of all living beings.

The programs at the Jain Center focus on expanding awareness primarily through meditation. Some of the courses include: The Seven Centers of Energy; Thursday Night Talks; Mastering the Mind; Introduction to Meditation; and Transforming Emotions. Lectures are also available on cassette tapes.

Friday evenings are devoted to sound, song, and music. This includes poetry, talk, and sitar music. Tai chi and yoga classes are also available at the center, as well as special weekend meditation retreats. Regular course fees range from $2 to $25. —B.H.

Jain Meditation International Center
120 E. 86th St., 2nd Floor
New York, NY 10028

The Sound of Music

"Music," Congreve wrote in one of the most misquoted lines ever, "has charms to soothe a savage breast." Be it beast or breast, the folks at ICM Training Seminars are devout believers in music's charms.

ICM's core is GIM—Guided Imagery and Music—a technique that involves listening to carefully selected music while in a deeply relaxed state and "making use of the imagery, symbols, and deep feelings which arise from the inner self to initiate creativity, self-understanding, therapeutic intervention, and religious experience."

Lectures, workshops, training programs, and casual "drop-in evenings" are ICM's tools for advancing the GIM approach to well-being. The curious are cordially invited to try a "drop-in evening" (second Friday of every month except October), where an introduction to GIM is provided for a $4 donation. Day-long workshops provide further instruction at a cost of $30 and, for the committed, there is a five-day intensive workshop ($400, including room and board) and a five-week training session ($650, lodging excluded). ICM also stocks monographs, tapes, and books. —R.McG.

ICM Training Seminars
204 S. Athol Ave.
Baltimore, MD 21229

Winning at the College Game Whether you're just out of high school and planning to go to college or you're going back to college in later life, you need to mentally prepare yourself for the college experience. Yakima Valley College offers an intensive five-day seminar, "Winning at the College Game," that covers reading improvement, effective listening and studying, and goal setting. Offered just before school starts in the fall, the course costs $61 (applicable toward Yakima Valley College tuition fees).

Continuing Education
Yakima Valley College
P.O. Box 1647
Yakima, WA 98907

Stars in Your Eyes Tired of relying on the newspaper for your horoscope each day? Want to cast your own horoscope and understand what astrology is really all about? Then sign up for Dr. James T. Hayes' home study astrology course. You'll get 12 lessons at $6 each, and you can proceed at your own pace. You'll learn about the planets of the solar system, the signs of the zodiac, and the methods for casting and reading a horoscope. And when you've passed the final exam, you'll get a diploma in professional astrology from the Kentucky Academy of Astrology. The universe awaits.

James T. Hayes
1604 Belmonte Dr.
Murray, KY 42071

You Must Remember This There are lots of memory systems on the market today, from sleep learning to word association methods. But the instant memory approach offered by the Institute of Advanced Thinking is definitely different. IAT claims that everyone has a photographic memory—we record everything going on at all times. Instead of trying to train our memories, we should be trying to *release* them, and that's what the instant memory course is designed to do. For $10 you get the complete course (in the form of a booklet), which shows you how to improve your memory, your creativity, and even your personality.

Institute of Advanced Thinking
845 Via de la Paz
Pacific Palisades, CA 90272

I celebrate myself, and sing myself.
WALT WHITMAN

Integrating Body & Mind

Dionysus Revisited

Personal liberation through sensual celebration—that's the Elysium experience. Clothing's optional at this lush refuge from the environs of metropolitan Los Angeles, and the many workshops have a strong flavor of Southern California hedonism about them.

To the ancient Greeks, Elysium was a paradise for the dead. But at the Elysium Institute the emphasis is very much on living—and paradise, too.

The eight acres of tree-shaded lawns, swimming and Jacuzzi pools, and other recreational facilities provide a stimulating setting for courses that bring groups together for physical pleasures and individual growth.

The place offers everything from simple socializing and "airbathing" on the lawn to a special massage session for lovers only. In between, there are special groups for singles (including those over 45), workshops combining mind and body games, and even a course on nude photography.

In addition to several regular weekly workshops (perhaps better described as playshops), the Institute features special offerings throughout the year, led by experienced instructors. Among them: Female Sexuality (For Men Only); Music with Feeling; How to Enhance Your Open Relationship; The Tactile Celebration; Cleaning Your Body Inside and Out.

Many of the courses are designed to help singles get to know other singles. Workshops focus on social and sexual skills for singles, how to feel good about being single, and nurturing ways to make new friends. Other events include a Friendship Celebration Day, and for those over 45, dances, parties, potluck suppers, and a seminar discussing relationships and sexuality among older folks.

Though most of the courses are designed to increase your sexual awareness while getting you free of hang-ups, sexual activities aren't an official part of the program. A supportive, nonthreatening environment is always maintained, but apprehensive single women are encouraged to bring along a female friend.

Sex at Elysium is considered a private matter between consenting adults, with privacy provided in the form of several meditation rooms, should the spirit move you.

While the car-free grounds aren't open to the public, workshops at varying but reasonable fees are open to nonmembers who preregister. Participating membership entitles you and your guests to the joys of the grounds six days a week. —G.D.

Elysium Institute
814 Robinson Rd.
Topanga, CA 90290

Everything in excess! To enjoy the flavor of life, take big bites. Moderation is for monks.
ROBERT A. HEINLEIN

Healthy, Happy, and Holy

This organization can offer you anything from yogic therapy to natural food restaurants, from landscaping services to their own line of shoes.

The 3HO Foundation (Healthy, Happy, Holy Organization) is a nonprofit corporation, dedicated to the advancement of the individual through education, science, and religion. Its programs range from a "transitional medicine" course, which is registered with the California Board of Medical Quality Assurance, to a ladies' training camp that will teach you to "enter your husband's sphere with swan-like grace, and support him throughout the life in his growth to infinity."

Other courses offered include: Tantric Yoga—a way for men and women to relate to each other beyond the physical and emotional planes; Inside the Real Man—a look at the power of masculinity; Holistic Healing—nutrition, kinesiology, acupressure, meditation, breathing, and aura strengthening; Summer Solstice—uniting the individual consciousness with the infinite; and meditation.

Tuitions, lengths, and locations of courses vary. 3HO's international headquarters is in Los Angeles. It has branches throughout the United States, Canada, and other parts of the world. —B.H.

3HO Foundation
P.O. Box 35906
Los Angeles, CA 90035

Bound for Glory

Get ready for this one. Jog around the block and do your push-ups. Pretty soon you'll be tracing the course of swift-flowing streams in thickly forested valleys, traversing glaciers that glisten in the sun, and climbing 10,000-foot peaks that tower above the surrounding wilderness.

Outward Bound is the kind of adventure that most people only read or dream about. Its challenges aren't easy, but they're within anyone's capabilities. The central purpose of Outward Bound is to help you discover personal characteristics that will make it easier for you to "survive" in every-day life. Utilizing the challenges of outdoor adventure, the program concentrates on developing the self-confidence, self-awareness, and compassion for others that will give you the inner strength to take care of yourself in even the roughest of life's situations.

Northwest Outward Bound's courses take place in the snowcapped mountains and vast forests of the Pacific Northwest. Depending on the time of year, you will learn rock climbing, first aid, route-finding, snow and glacier travel, campcraft, cross-country skiing, and the construction of igloos and other shelters.

A full-length course lasts 24 days and costs $600. No special equipment or previous wilderness experience is required. —B.H.

Northwest Outward Bound School
0110 S.W. Bancroft
Portland, OR 97201

Thanks, I Needed That

Wake up, you sleepy heads. Odds are you've been fast asleep and didn't know it. The folks at the Dharma Self-Help and Analytical Center will gladly provide your wake-up service.

Specializing in experiential learning, Dharma offers courses in a variety of Eastern approaches to self-awareness. Polarity therapy, yoga, massage, posture, and astrology dot the syllabus. But self-help, rather than dependence on therapists, is Dharma's principal theme. Therapy is not the goal—learning is.

Curious? Try the one-day seminar Self-Awareness as Re-Evaluation, a course that takes off from the question "Who am I?" and concludes wherever you wish. One needn't change as a result, Dharma notes, but participants invariably find themselves on voyages of self-discovery.

Founded by Anna and John Koehne, Dharma finds its roots in the belief that "as each journey begins with one step so also changing the world begins with changing oneself." Dharma is the Koehnes' laboratory for positive change.

Costs are low and often contingent upon one's personal income. Rarely do costs exceed $80 daily, and room and board are included in every package. Membership in the Dharma Center, which puts one on the mailing list and nets a 10 percent discount on all activities, is available at $10 yearly. —R.McG.

Dharma Self-Help
and Analytical Center
RFD #1, Box 113-AA
Shipman, VA 22971

If the Spirit Moves You

Interested in working toward your doctorate in spiritual healing? Scan this course listing for the subject matter you'll need to master: Reincarnation and Laws of Karma, Methods of Divination, Techniques of Astral Projection, Aura and Color Healing, Secrets of Numerology, and New Age Prophecy. You'll also need to study the teachings of Don Juan, dream interpretation, astrology, and radionic healing.

This series of courses is offered by the Atlantis Rising Educational Center (AREC) in Portland, Oregon, but you don't need to be in Portland to take them—they are all taught by mail. Upon completion of the twelve spiritual healing courses, you can take a comprehensive exam leading to a degree of Doctor of Natural Healing (as recognized by the Alternative Medical Association, a creation of the founder of AREC).

AREC also has a twelve-part home-study course in natural healing that covers herbalism, nutrition, physiology, body manipulation, iridology, acupuncture, massage, medical astrology, and first aid.

If you're in the Portland area, you can drop in for free individual holistic health counseling (by appointment only), you can take classes in natural and spiritual health (with an emphasis on herbology), and you can buy herbs, oils, and books in AREC's retail outlet. —J.E.

Atlantis Rising Educational Center
7909/7915 S.E. Stark St.
Portland, OR 97215

The self is not something one finds: it is something one creates.
THOMAS SZASZ

Mind Your Body

How does this sound: ten days on an isolated beach in Baja California, exploring your physical awareness with several other adults and children? You practice body manipulation techniques, meditation, psychodrama, role playing, and other approaches designed to put your mind in touch with your body.

Or how about a camping trip in Death Valley with an emphasis on Reichian training, massage, group dynamics, and movement training—with disco dancing no less?

These programs are two of the many special workshops that have been offered by The Centering Association, a group dedicated to the study of physical awareness. In addition to special workshops, Centering provides regular weekly and weekend seminars in acupuncture, deep muscle work, dance, polarity balancing, herbology, hatha yoga, tai chi, and other body awareness topics.

Centering's trained professional staff also offers individual body therapy of all types, including Rolfing, structural awareness, postural integration, kinestrics, and energenesis.

Costs of the workshops and seminars vary (the Baja trip was $100 plus a nominal transportation fee; the Death Valley workshop was $375). You can find out about Centering's future programs by sending $2 to be on their mailing list.—J.E.

The Centering Association
2650 30th St.
Santa Monica, CA 90405

Rub-a-Dub-Dub

If you thought that the "laying on of hands" was just something for oldtime faith healers, there's a surprise awaiting you at the Institute for Holistic Studies.

Dedicated to the delightful task of teaching people how to rub others—and themselves—the right way, the Institute offers courses in massage and self-hypnosis that will teach you an approach to good health you'll never hear from your family doctor.

The Institute's faculty feels that health is the result of both spiritual and physical balance. One way to reach that balance—and it happens to be the Institute's specialty—is through massage and self-hypnosis.

Courses in the "laying on of hands" are taught using the widely known techniques of Swedish massage, as well as the Eastern approach of shiatsu massage. Using acupressure points, shiatsu is designed to break up somatic congestion and thereby free energy "frozen" in the body.

Self-hypnosis is taught as a means of entering the subconscious and reprograming it—to break bad habits or simply to bring oneself into balance.

Six classes in massage and self-hypnosis are available to laypersons, at a cost ranging from $10 to $20 a session. The Institute also offers an extensive program of professional education. —G.D.

Institute for Holistic Studies
4827 Loma Vista
Ventura, CA 93003

Desert Dance

Try a little vertical yoga and you'll soon be dancing with the universe—rappelling, traversing, and zipping over 300-foot pour-offs.

Desert Dance offers 28-day climbing "expeditions for the spirit" that take you into the beautiful and remote water-carved canyons of the Mexican Chihuahuan Desert. The purpose of these adventures is to explore the wealth of creative potential contained in your own body, mind, and spirit.

The philosophy of Desert Dance is that fear can greatly limit your potential. Most people share a basic fear of heights. On a "dance," be prepared to leave that fear and others behind in the desert canyons of Mexico. Securely attached to a system of ropes and other safety equipment, you will confront your fear of heights and learn to "dance" beyond it.

You will also learn to recognize the control you have over the quality of your own experience. This exercise in spirit revitalization is accompanied by incredible scenery, food, people, and good times. Above all, it makes you strong inside—strong enough so that your whole life can be a "dance."

Each expedition consists of four men and four women, plus two instructors. Experience is unnecessary, and the cost is $960. —B.H.

Desert Dance
Box 77
Terlingua, TX 79852

You'll Bend but Not Break

An exercise it is not. A discipline it is—that's yoga, which its followers say means "to make whole, to bring together."

Feeling a bit fragmented yourself? Yoga may be for you. Originating thousands of years ago in India, yoga remains popular today, and for good reason. Its goal is a full understanding of the body. No easy feat, but that's where students at the Center for Yoga are heading.

Hatha yoga classes are the Center's core, with programs available for both beginners and advanced students. For those seeking an introduction to yoga and its way, classes—in which basic positions are stressed—are available at about $4.50 per session.

Students who've mastered the postures graduate to Y.E.S.—The Yoga Educational Seminar in which Ganga White, Director of the Center, explores yoga's many aspects. Philosophy, medication, and diet are all included. The Center also offers seminars and workshops in meditation, herbology, nutrition, polarity, acupressure, and like pursuits. —R.McG.

Center for Yoga
230½ N. Larchmont Blvd.
Los Angeles, CA 90004

Let It Out Would you like to be able to express yourself spontaneously, without inhibitions or fears? Would you like to improve your interactions with others and resolve your emotional problems? Perhaps what you need is selbstdarstellungs (SD). This approach to self-expression was developed by an organization called AAO, a communal group based in Friedrichshof, Austria. SD programs are offered in cities throughout the world, including Boston in the US. It's only $2 to attend a guest evening and find out what it's all about.

AAE Boston
59 Munroe St.
Sommerville, MA 02143

Breaking Through Very few of us tap the wealth of potential that exists within ourselves. We live our lives of "quiet desperation," not daring to long for something different. But it need not be so. Give yourself a chance to explore your inner strengths by trying "Breaking Through," a program designed to blend the "inner game" with the "outer journey." Through white-water rafting, rock climbing, and mountaineering experiences you can see what stuff you're made of. A seven-day program runs about $275.

Outdoor Leadership Training Seminars
2220 Birch St.
Denver, CO 80207

Get Your Act Together Tired of talking about your problems? Want to *do* something about them? Acting out your problems—psychodrama—may help you to understand the central issues of your life and to deal with them. "The realizations that can take place in the psychodramatic experience can be so immediate, so vivid and intense, as to make a lasting impact," say the people at the Moreno Institute. Psychodrama takes place in a group setting, and one can often learn as much from other people's experience as one's own. Write to the Institute about group sessions, residential weekends, and costs.

Moreno Institute
259 Wolcott Ave.
Beacon, NY 12508

A sound mind in a sound body is a short but full description of a happy state in the world.
JOHN LOCKE

Breezes from the East

East Meets West

During the Camp David talks, Menachem Begin and Anwar Sadat were reportedly flown by helicopter to the Maryland center of the East West Foundation for a special weekend program to help restore their physical, mental, and spiritual resources.

The East West Foundation is a federally approved, nonprofit educational and cultural institution founded in 1972 by Michio and Aveline Kushi to spread the macrobiotic way of life. There are offices in Boston (the national headquarters), Baltimore, Philadelphia, Washington, DC, and Miami, as well as affiliates in most major world cities.

The agenda of the Begin-Sadat talks was secret, but the topics discussed probably included: cosmology of yin/yang and the order of the Sinai Desert; the dualistic monism that created the Suez Canal; principles of macrobiotic cooking in the new settlements; woman-man relationships and family development in the Gaza Strip; Oriental medicine; shiatsu; moxabustion; massage; folk remedies; diets; ancient world cultures; great teachers and scriptures; history according to yin/yang and logarithmic spirals; and consoling spirits.

The visitors from the Middle East were intrigued by accounts of the East West Foundation's model natural-agriculture facility near Ashburnham, Massachusetts. It was thought that the organic farming methods for cultivation of high-quality grains, beans, and vegetables might possibly be transferable to the Negev, Sinai, and Gaza strip. As a gesture of their appreciation, Messrs. Sadat and Begin promised to send seed stock for date palms and fig trees to the Foundation's farm.

Visitors are treated to Noh dramas, tea ceremonies, flower arranging, Indian dance, aikido, tai chi, and martial arts—all part of the Foundation's extensive cultural exchange program.

Publications of the Foundation include *The Order of the Universe* and *Case History Report* (both quarterlies), *A Dietary Approach to Cancer According to the Principles of Macrobiotics*, and *A Nutritional Approach to Cancer*. Michio Kushi has also written *Macrobiotic Approach to Major Illnesses* and *Oriental Diagnosis*.

Last summer the Foundation conducted a concentrated one-week program at Amherst College in Massachusetts, titled 'One Peaceful World Through the Recovery of Humanity.

Beginning at 5 a.m. participants spent an hour in meditation and chanting, followed at 6 by either Zen yoga or BKS Iyengar yoga. At 8, students chose among tai chi, macrobiotic and natural food cooking, and shiatsu massage. Since each class was repeated four times (at the same time each day), the student could eventually partake of every class.

Each day there were also two-hour seminars by founder Michio Kushi: one on macrobiotics and Oriental medicine and another on society and civilization.

A special four-hour event, a Conference on a Nutritional Approach to Cancer and Major Illnesses, was held one afternoon midway through the week. —L.S.

East West Foundation
6209 Park Heights Ave.
Baltimore, MD 21215

We are most asleep when awake.
PAUL REPS

Tranquillity in an Envelope

If you'd like to learn meditation in the comfort and privacy of your own home, there's a new correspondence course just for you. Shree Gurudev Ashram in San Jose, California, has developed a six-month basic home-study course in siddha meditation that is designed to help you meditate deeply and easily.

Siddha meditation is one of many types of meditation being practiced today. According to SGA, siddha meditation "is the perfect form of meditation because it is not something you have to work at, but something that happens automatically once you know how to get started. It is different from other forms of meditation, for in essence it is not a technique at all, but rather a vehicle."

The siddha meditation methods taught by SGA are based on the principles and teachings of Swami Muktananda Paramahansa ("Baba"), whom *Time* magazine described as "the Perfect Guru of the West."

The correspondence course comes in the form of weekly Siddha Meditation Guides and costs $29.95 for three months, $49.95 for six months. The guides are written in simple language to facilitate understanding and ease your way quickly to constructive meditation experiences. Advanced lessons are also available for interested students. —J.E.

Shree Gurudev Ashram
1121 Rollingdell Ct.
San Jose, CA 95129

Eat Your Way to Heaven

Eat your way to a new you. But don't stuff yourself silly with French pastry—become the new you the macrobiotic way at the Kushi Institute.

The macrobiotic way of life is *the* way at the Kushi Institute, founded and operated by Michio and Aveline Kushi. The goal here is to develop the whole personality, and a smorgasbord of courses is offered to that end. Included are: The Philosophy of Macrobiotics, Fundamental Macrobiotic Cooking, Shiatsu Massage, Spiritual Practices, and Intensive Looks into Yin-Yang Theories.

Attendance at the Kushi Institute is not casual—a firm commitment to macrobiotics is required and applications are carefully screened. Every student must first be admitted as a member of the Institute ($25 annual fee) before full-time participation ($275 monthly) is allowed. For those with less intense interests, supporting memberships are available at $10 yearly. Supporting members are welcome to attend special studies and discussions at the Institute (admission fees are additional). —R.McG.

Kushi Institute
P.O. Box 1100
Brookline Village
Boston, MA 02147

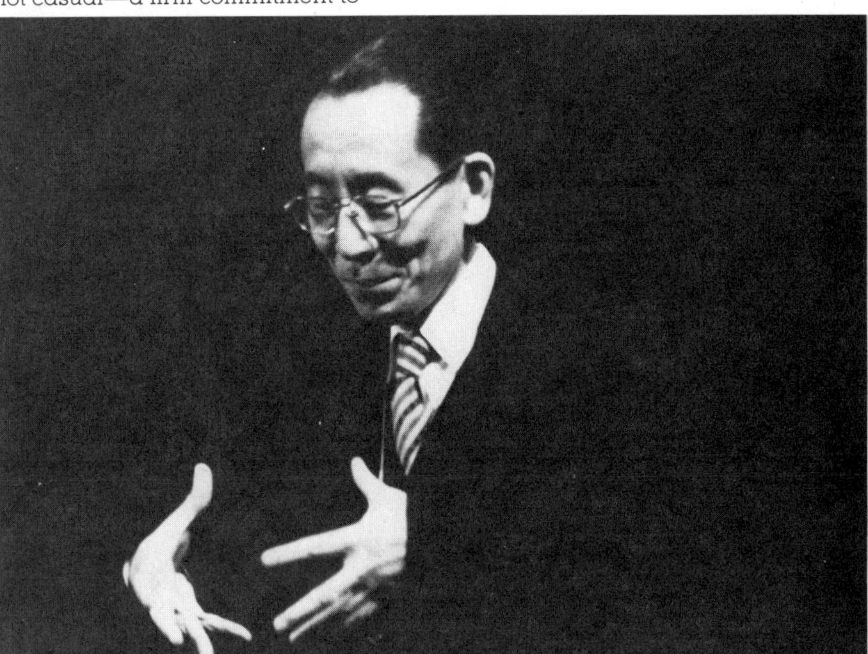

Prime Meridians

We sent our eager editor, Victoria Voyeur, to New York to report on the sex therapy course at the Shiatsu Education Center. We handed Victoria our miniature camera. "Clean photos!" we warned.

Three days later she phoned. "I've enrolled in Ohashiatsu for Daily Life. I'm learning acupressure. The body has 14 channels of energy and 361 pressure points. I'm studying self-shiatsu and Makko-ho exercises; I'm learning to stretch energy channels in my back, front, sides, head, and shoulders. I need $185 tuition."

"What about sex therapy?" we inquired.

"Later. Next week we take up shiatsu-in-a-chair."

The following month Victoria called again. "I'm now taking the Intermediate Course and expanding my knowledge of meridians, tonification, sedati, and yin/yang. I'm improving my utilization of body gravity so I can give more effective shiatsu! I need $195."

"Did you get some sex therapy photos?"

"Mr. Wataru Ohashi, the Director, wants me to take the Advanced Course next."

Another month went by. "I'm taking anatomy for bodywork," she said. "I'm learning about skeletal, muscular, and nervous systems."

"When will you get into sex therapy?"

"I don't need to. Mr. Ohashi says I already know almost enough to teach it. I sold the camera." —L.S.

Shiatsu Education Center
52 W. 55th St.
New York, NY 10019

Bold, Boulder, Boldest

The East is getting less and less mysterious all the time. Rudyard Kipling thought that East and West—that famous twain—could never meet. Western intellectual traditions have long stood in opposition to the more intuitive Eastern schools of thought, as embodied in Buddhist teaching and practices. What could bridge the gap between these two historically distinct paths to knowledge?

The Naropa Institute's curriculum aims to do just that. In fact, the entire ambiance of the Institute suggests the fusion of intellectual and artistic study with the practice of awareness. Classes in dance and martial arts teach awareness of the environment and how one's body occupies space. Classes in Buddhism and psychology open the mind's awareness to how the meditative and scholarly can be integrated. Classes in music, poetics, and theater open the senses' awareness to rhythm and color. Almost everyone at the Institute stops briefly at certain times during the day for meditation.

Founded by Chogyam Trungpa, Rinpoche, a Tibetan Buddhist scholar and meditation master, the Institute offers year-round classes open to everyone and summer sessions with expansive and varied programs. The Institute features a complete range of Buddhist studies, and both undergraduate and graduate degrees can be obtained in this field. Tuition charges are computed on the basis of cost per credit hour: $33 per hour for those who do not wish to acquire academic credits and $45 for those who take courses for credit.

The Institute is located in Boulder, Colorado, a mile above sea level in the Rocky Mountains. Besides the beauty of its mountains—and their usefulness for skiers—Boulder has theaters, a symphony orchestra, and good night spots. The University of Colorado is also located there.

Students at the Institute participate in the community life of Boulder and invite the community to become involved with the Institute. And there is no sharp hierarchical distinction between students and faculty. There are many spirited discussions between them, which sometimes go on into the night.

A sample of the class listings shows how Eastern and Western traditions are melded. *Dance:* Modern Dance, primarily the Merce Cunningham technique; Bugaku, a Japanese dance form. *Martial Arts:* Tai Chi Chuan; Aikido; Tai Chi Sword. *Psychology:* Maitri, Awareness of Psychological Space; Discovery of the Unconscious, Freud's *Interpretation of Dreams. Theater:* Kite Tail Mime, a Balinese art. *Poetics:* Known and Unknown US Poets, taught by Allen Ginsberg.

If East and West ever do come to fully understand each other and achieve a meeting of minds, some credit will have to go to this bold institute at Boulder. —A.L.

Naropa Institute
1111 Pearl St.
Boulder, CO 80302

I do not know whether I was then a man dreaming I was a butterfly, or whether I am now a butterfly dreaming I am a man.
CHUANG TZU

Gleaning the Golden Thread

The search for ultimate truth has been a preoccupation of the human animal throughout the ages. At Kayavarohana (near St. Helena, California), that search continues.

With an exceedingly ecumenical approach, the Sanatana Dharma Foundation dedicates itself to "discerning that golden thread and living accordingly." Models are provided from cultures as diverse as European Christian (St. Francis of Assisi and St. Thomas Aquinas), Moslem (Mevlanna Jalalu'ddin Rumi, founder of the Whirling Dervishes), Hasidic (Baal Shem Tov), and—of course—Hindu (Shiva).

Kayavarohana is a religious community that practices meditation and restraint. They welcome visitors, and they welcome new permanent inhabitants. But you don't have to trek to northern California to partake of their peace. They have a cassette tape catalog that is extremely comprehensive.

Priced at approximately $6 per hour, the tapes are largely composed of the sayings and teachings of the resident Guru, Yogeshwar Muni. They deal with all forms of yoga, with Sanskrit scripture, and with widely applicable techniques of personal improvement. Visitors to Kayavarohana pay a nominal $80 per week. —J.A.

Sanatana Dharma Foundation
3100 White Sulphur Springs Rd.
St. Helena, CA 94574

Sesshin Sessions

When the hurly-burly of daily life finally gets to be too much, try visiting a Zen Buddhist monastery high in the Catskill Mountains, 140 miles northwest of New York City. The monastery's Zen master, Abbot Eido Shimano Roshi, provides opportunities for lay people of any faith to participate in the Zen way of life. There are also programs for serious Zen students. The monastery lies peacefully surrounded by forest and also has a lake within its boundaries.

You can go for a three-month stay—a Kessei—for $600 ($400 for a repeat Kessei). Or you can sign up for a Sesshin, which runs from two days to three weeks, with cost depending on the length of the stay. The one-week Holy Days Sesshin, for example, which coincides with Buddha's birthday, Passover, and Easter, costs from $110 to $150, depending on your status as a student of Zen.

The monastery runs its own transportation between the New York City center and the Catskill site.

If you are unable to tear yourself away from the hurly, or find yourself too deeply enmeshed in the burly, there are also workshops and meetings held at the Zen center in New York City. —A.L.

The Zen Studies Society
223 E. 67th St.
New York, NY 10021

Oriental Expression From the Ancient East comes a 1000-year-old art that can make you feel younger today. Tai chi is an exercise method that emphasizes slow, even, balanced movement. The emphasis is on calmness and ease, leading to physical and mental relaxation and tranquillity. Noted dance teacher Sophia Delza studied tai chi in China and now conducts courses in New York City. Write for schedule and costs.

School of T'ai-Chi Ch'uan
Studio 607
Carnegie Hall
881 Seventh Ave.
New York, NY 10019

The Way of the World Eastern philosophy and religion have an ageless appeal. They ask us to shake off the bonds of our highly technological life style and seek the tranquillity that a simple life of contemplation can offer. At the Son Zen Lotus Society in Toronto, people practice Mahayana Buddhism, with an emphasis on Zen. Stop in at one of their evening classes for beginners or one of their Sunday afternoon services to find out if this is the Way you've been looking for.

Son Zen Lotus Society
378 Markham St.
Toronto, Ontario M6G 2K9
Canada

Leap Like a Tiger There are many Zen centers in the United States that offer meditation, chanting, and other Zen practices. What makes the Providence Center a bit different is its seven-day intensive training periods in Zen practice called "yong maeng jong jin," or "to leap like a tiger while sitting." The "intensive" involves full days of sitting, chanting, bowing, and work periods, as well as private interviews with Zen Master Seung Sahn (Soen Sa Nim). The intensives are open to everyone but reservations are required.

Providence Zen Center
48 Hope St.
Providence, RI 02903

The way is like an empty vessel
That yet may be drawn from
Without ever needing to be filled.
LAO-TZU

Getting Away from It All

And the Soul Shall Sing

The Abbey of Regina Laudis was founded by two French nuns who witnessed the American liberation of Paris from the Nazis and wanted to find a way to thank the United States. Without money or extensive contacts, they came to New England in the aftermath of World War II and founded a monastery with gifts from people they had convinced to help them.

Set on 300 acres extending toward the foothills of the Berkshire Mountains in northwestern Connecticut, Regina Laudis ("the Queen of Praise") is the only totally enclosed Benedictine monastery for nuns in the United States. Since an enclosed order is one in which the nuns vowed to the house never to occupy the same space as the guests or retreatants, a set of wooden grills divides the church, the refectory, and the parlors. The Abbey grows its own food, keeps bees, raises sheep and cows, and holds to the Roman Catholicism of "Primitive Observance."

The monastery is very much a natural and peaceful world of its own. All its buildings (with the exception of the Abbey itself, which is presently under construction) are original prewar structures (the nuns' dormitory, for example, is a converted factory). The church, paneled in pine, is a reverent blend of Old World shapes and New World materials. The beauty of the natural setting completely surrounds the retreatant. Manual work is encouraged for those who want to contribute some part of their retreat to the upkeep of the monastery. There is also a gift shop, featuring honey, herbs, religious products, and craft goods made by the nuns—some spun and woven from the wool of the Abbey's sheep.

Regina Laudis possesses a fine library of art and patristic studies, and some of their books are made available for research purposes. As a result, the Abbey has a reputation for nurturing artists—painters, musicians, filmmakers. Its peace and beauty are truly inspirational to the creative spirit.

Reservations for the limited accommodations (separate for men and women, with some provision made for married couples) are required. All reservations must be made by mail, in advance. —R.J.

Guest Mistress
Abbey of Regina Laudis
Bethlehem, CT 06751

One of the great necessities in America is to discover creative solitude.
CARL SANDBURG

Apprenticeship in Joy

Some years back, the Ananda Apprentice Program in Nevada City was a bit more woodsy than it is now. You'd have begun by pitching a tent under a tree at the meditation retreat site; every morning you'd have bounced six miles to the communal garden in the back of a pickup truck. These days, the program is geared much more closely to intensive meditation.

"If you could only get within your own Self," writes Swami Kriyananda, "you would see that Joy is You!" The Apprentice Program prepares you for just that ineffable experience.

The Ananda community was born out of Swamiji's dream of bringing men and women once more to the consciousness of joy as their divine birthright. While an apprentice, you'll practice cooperative living as you meditate and work with Ananda residents and fellow apprentices. You'll participate in a disciplined group sadhana ("spiritual practice"), and you'll practice karma yoga ("selfless service").

While a novice, you'll also learn a particular aspect of day-to-day operations (such as dairy operations, vegetarian cooking, or publications). The necessary time investment is quite considerable; cost is $40 per week, with children paying slightly more. —J.A.

Ananda
900 Alleghany Star Route
Nevada City, CA 95959

White Clouds and Sylvan Lining

The woods are enticing. The setting, serene. And the food is scrupulously natural at White Cloud, the Pocono Mountains retreat and natural food inn.

Meatless meals are the specialty of the house, and, for the strictest vegetarians, entrees are available that exclude egg and milk products. But, important as the food is at White Cloud, there is far more to this 20-room inn's approach to natural living.

Fifty acres of unsullied woods and fields, for example. And five acres of lawns and gardens. Guests are invited to explore both.

Explore the library, too, if you wish. The stock is rich with metaphysical, philosophical, and religious titles. If you've a yen for more physical pursuits, try the tennis courts, swimming pool, shuffleboard, or the game room's ping pong or pool tables. Winter months see White Cloud guests gamboling off to nearby ski slopes, and hiking is a sport for all seasons here.

Founded as a retreat for members of the Self-Realization Fellowship, White Cloud's facilities are open to all with a taste for life's quieter side. And costs are kept low—about $25 daily, including all the natural food you can eat. —R.McG.

White Cloud Sylvan Retreat
RD 1, Box 215
Newfoundland, PA 18445

Group Sloop "Explore your own inner self while sailing over a tropical sea" reads the brochure about Passages, Inc.'s recreational marathons. The idea is to spend a week at sea with a group of like-minded people and a psychiatrist, alternating group sessions with recreation. Groups are based on specific interests—child-rearing, coping with divorce, communication and closeness—so you can join the marathon of your choice. Write for dates and prices.

Passages
P.O. Box 12132
St. Petersburg, FL 33733

A Summer Place Here's a summer camp unlike any other you'll ever encounter. On a farm in Central Missouri you can spend a few weeks learning macrobiotic philosophy, Oriental medicine, natural agriculture, shiatsu massage, survival living, and the like. Or, if you just happen to be in the area at other times of the year and want to drop in, you can stay for $3 a day if you want to help around the place or $6 a day if you want to take it easy.

Spiral Inn East/West Center
Route 3, Box 114
Bowling Green, MO 63334

Retreat Yourself "Transforming the self, and the world, means truly knowing the self and gaining mastery over one's duality." With this philosophy at its core, 3HO Foundation offers a special ten-day sadhana (spiritual discipline) in which participants camp out in New Mexico studying meditation, defense techniques, and Tantric yoga. The 1978 sadhana was $150 for singles and $250 for married couples, with lower rates for children. Write for info on future sadhanas.

Summer Solstice Sadhana
1620 Preuss Rd.
Los Angeles, CA 90035

If you don't like what you're doing, you can always pick up your needle and move to another groove.
TIMOTHY LEARY

Becoming Whole

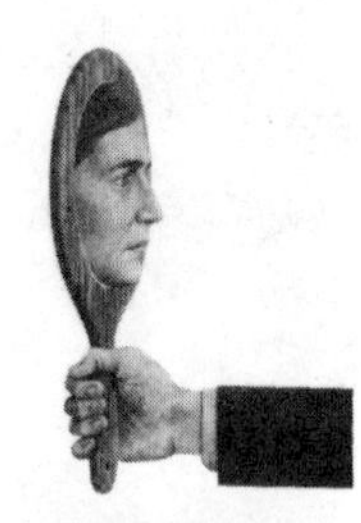

Growing, Growing, Gone

Do you need a tune-up? A little body work? If the answer is yes, consider checking into Cambridge House for some Gestalt and shiatsu. These are only two of the many areas of study this growth center offers to help you get in touch with your own vitality.

Cambridge House is a nonprofit, educational organization located in Milwaukee, Wisconsin. It originated in 1956 when several women, aware of their need for change, created a place to search for meaning in their lives. Over the years Cambridge House has expanded to include all the major areas of instruction and training in the modes of achieving greater self-awareness.

Its facilities consist of two old houses, one a Victorian mansion built over 100 years ago. A staff member lives in each house, and both are filled with comfortable pieces of antique furniture. For groups staying more than one day, bedrooms accommodate 24 people and meals are served in a spacious dining room.

Cambridge House is *not* a mental health clinic, a social club, a religion, a cult, or a mystical experience. It is a program for responsible people who are looking for a way to improve the quality of their life. Participants range in age from 18 to 80. The Cambridge philosophy is that anyone who wants to learn, can. You're never too old to grow by their standards.

Gestalt, psychodrama, and bioenergetics provide the basis for many of their courses. Some of these include: Body-Mind Workshop—healing or eliminating the body/mind split; Gestalt and Body Awareness—your relationship to yourself as a prerequisite to your relationship with your environment; Self-Acceptance Training—achieving an inner sense of being alive and real; The Energy Experience—discharging blocked energy and achieving a stable, more centered consciousness; Gestalt Approach to Self-Appreciation—exploring the hidden values in your style of behavior.

If you'd rather give your mind a break and work on your body instead, try relaxing the shiatsu or Feldenkrais way. Shiatsu is a Japanese system of acupressure that reduces muscular stiffness and fatigue and enhances the body's self-curative abilities. It uses pressure applied by the thumbs to specific points of the body and develops acute sensitivity in the hands. The Feldenkrais method releases chronic movement patterns and muscular tension through a series of gentle and effortless exercises.

Or have you ever wondered what your chicken-scrawl says about your personality? Try the Handwriting Analysis Course. Active participation is invited, so, if you're bold, some of your writing might be used for demonstration purposes.

Courses at Cambridge House are ongoing, and are available in weekly, weekend, and one-day sessions. Some courses are specifically designed for professionals, but most are for anyone interested. If you're in the area, you're invited to drop in on Monday nights to talk or on Friday nights for the Social Encounter for Singles. —B.H.

Cambridge House
1900 N. Cambridge Ave.
Milwaukee, WI 53202

May the Circle Be Unbroken

The *I Ching*, when asked to provide a name, responded with the hexagram *Gathering Together*, and that's how this group came to be tagged. That hexagram was a good omen, because it foresaw the collective piety which the folks at Gathering Together have harnessed to meet the challenges of the day.

Calmness is Gathering Together's leitmotif and, within that calmness, there is strength to heal and to rejoice, say the members. Healing circles, accordingly, are a regular group activity—as are classes in tai chi, Taoist yoga, and Tibetan Buddhist meditation. Sunday evenings, for example, are a time for group meditation—consisting of visualizations, chanting, and sitting practices—followed by a Dharma talk. All are invited to share in Gathering Together's "pujas" (a $1 contribution is requested).

Intensive exposure to the way of Gathering Together is available in its three-month training program, one that will "inspire and nourish personal transformation." Healing—the self and others—remains the focus as one explores a variety of Eastern techniques. Cost is $525 (housing included).

More casual courses are also available, and Gathering Together publishes a newsletter ($4 subscription), too. —R.McG.

Gathering Together
Box 1193
Ashland, OR 97520

Color Your World

Are you into aura and Bach flowers? Here's a clue—they are *not* new psychedelics. Still curious? The man to see for an explanation is Barry Taylor, a friendly doctor of naturopathic medicine and the founder of Getting Free & Letting Go workshops.

Getting Free's aim is ambitious—to achieve "health, holistic natural healing, celebration, joy, truth, peace, and love." The tools are many. Aura (color vibrations), Bach flowers (essence of flowers), homeopathy ("like cures like"), transactional analysis, and music and color are all called into play. Put all the tools together and, in the process, one gains in awareness and responsibility as the consciousness is gradually clarified.

Sponsored by The Healing Center of Lavina, Montana, and staffed by experts in aura reading, healing arts, and humanistic psychology, Getting Free & Letting Go seminars are held throughout the nation. Recent workshop sites included Eureka Springs, Maui, and Portland. Wherever there is sufficient interest, a workshop will be held—and inquiries from potential sponsors or attendees are strongly invited. —R.McG.

Getting Free & Letting Go
The Healing Center
South Route, Box 12
Lavina, MT 59046

Who need be afraid of the merge?
WALT WHITMAN

To Sur with Love

The next time you start to yell about what your doctor, lawyer, spouse, or teacher did to you, stop and think: "Take responsibility for your every thought, your every feeling, your every action."

These words of wisdom come from Fritz Perls, father of Gestalt therapy. Abandon your personal faculties of discernment, of evaluation, of self-reference, and you lose your integrity. These thoughts form the basis of Esalen's philosophy. For more than two generations Esalen has been helping people take responsibility for their life situation. It advocates the development of self-awareness and self-responsibility.

Esalen considers itself an educational laboratory, and its professors and guest lecturers are highly recognized in their fields. Techniques used in the various workshops include Gestalt, role playing, fantasy, breathing, music, massage, exercise, bioenergetics, and encounter techniques. Some of the workshops offered are: Awakening the Magician Within; God, Sexual Energy and Your Body; Inner Love; Personal Integrity; The Language of Dreams; Fear, Panic and Vulnerability to Crisis; and The Many Faces of the Self.

Esalen is located in Big Sur, majestically overlooking the Pacific Ocean. Tuition covers food and lodging and varies depending on the workshop you choose. Scholarships and work-study programs are available. —B.H.

Esalen Institute
Big Sur, CA 93920

Inner Visions

There are schools and there are schools. And then there are places like the Whole Life Learning Center.

You won't find any help with your reading, writing, or arithmetic at the Denver headquarters of this nonprofit organization, but you *may* discover a new outlook on life, a method for dealing with inner aches and pains, or perhaps just renewed strength to cope with tomorrow. And just to show you that their heads aren't in the clouds all the time, they'll also teach you how to make a wicked egg foo yung.

Defining itself, the WLLC states: "The Center is a non-denominational, interdisciplinary, wholly independent organization whose purpose is to seek ways to be of assistance to individuals of every race, creed and religious persuasion or personal philosophy in the development of their human and spiritual potential."

To do this, the Center offers classes, workshops, and individual counseling in the areas of personal growth and healing, focusing on the integration of mind, body, and spirit. Among the subject areas covered are massage, psychic development, dream exploration, alternative healing, tai chi, Feldenkrais, neo-Reichian work, and nutrition.

WLLC operates by charging modest fees for classes, workshops, and services, as well as through occasional individual contributions. It has a regular staff and a branch location in Colorado Springs. Recently the Center found a mountain retreat two hours outside of Denver that it hopes to purchase. Its A-frame lodge, 39 motel units, and 28 acres of land bordered by national forest will provide a beautiful setting for retreats and intensive growth programs.

Here's a sampling of some of the diverse courses now presented at the Center: Vitalistic Massage; Rebirthing; Psychocalisthenics; Ritual Celebrations; Depth Dynamics; Controlled Relaxation; Your Lives: Past & Future; Tai Chi for Senior Citizens; Tarot Cards and Exploring Life; Full Moon Ritual; Better Vision Without Glasses: A Cooperative Approach; and Perceiving the World of Children.

Besides its regular sessions, the WLLC offers counseling services on an individual basis; specially designed programs for groups using methods like simulations, dialoguing, fantasy, drama, healing techniques, body work, and meditation; innovative weddings and special ritual ceremonies; developmental meditation cassette tapes; and a personal development program for those who seek more intensive training in the school's various fields.

Additionally, the WLLC sponsors an annual symposium on Parapsychology, Transpersonal Psychology, and Psychic Phenomena in both the Denver and Colorado Springs locations. —C.McB.

Whole Life Learning Center
1730 Franklin
Denver, CO 80218

Mountain Mystique

Cold Mountain was a wild and crazy kind of guy, legend has it. A poet-hermit during China's T'ang Dynasty, Cold Mountain took his name from the mountain where he lived. His singular quest in those remote surroundings was to understand himself and his role in the universe.

Cold Mountain Institute, with centers in Vancouver and Cortes Island, takes its name from that ancient seer and his search for meaning. Its goal is his— the learning and development of the whole person within the context of his or her society. Most people who come to Cold Mountain, says its staff, share a dissatisfaction and uneasiness about their quality of life. Cold Mountain's aim is to put those feelings into perspective and perhaps to resolve them.

Offering a wide variety of programs—from one-day discussions and seminars to degree-oriented course work in conjunction with Antioch College—Cold Mountain's syllabus runs the gamut from "A New Image of Aging" and "Toward an Independent Self" through "Sexuality Seminars" and "Loneliness." Fees vary with program length, but a typical weekend course costs about $75; five-day workshops cost about $250; continuous Sunday evening get-togethers are tagged at $4. —R.McG.

Cold Mountain Institute
Granville Island
Vancouver, BC V6H 3M5
Canada

The Foundation of Truth

"Religion can only take man to a limited realization of the truth, because of the formal limitations inherent in all doctrinal teaching. The complete attainment of spiritual truth [requires going] beyond God in order to become identified with the Universal Reality."

Does this idea—that there is something larger than organized religion—correspond with your own thinking? Would you like to have a structured situation in which you could pursue this idea, guided by others who have undergone years of spiritual training? Then you should look into the Beshara Foundation, which has centers in England, Canada, Australia, and Berkeley, California.

The philosophy of the Beshara Foundation is not based on any particular religion or tradition and is not preached by a particular guru. Its goal is disseminating knowledge to people interested in the idea of unity in all existence. To achieve this goal, four main activities are emphasized: study, meditation, service, and zikr (remembrance).

Beshara's Sherborne House center in England offers an eight-month intensive course with instruction in these four activities, as well as the writings of Ibn 'Arabi. Although this course is not available in the US, the Berkeley center does offer a one-week course based on the Sherborne House model. The Berkeley center also provides regular study and meditation sessions and is open daily for private study and research. You can write them for the details. —J.E.

Beshara Foundation
2448 Prospect St.
Berkeley, CA 94704

What a Way to Grow Here's a self-exploration center that offers a wide variety of seminars and workshops for professionals and laypersons interested in personal growth. Among course offerings are interpersonal competence, stress management, death and dying, holistic health, smoking control, hatha yoga, couple's communication, psychosynthesis, and overeating control. The Center also has a sensory isolation tank, biofeedback equipment, and private Rolfing.

Center for the Development
of Consciousness and
Personal Growth
501 Wallace Rd.
Wexford, PA 15090

Another Time, Another Place Grab your sleeping bag and towel and head for central New Hampshire and one of the many fascinating conferences held at Another Place. They've got everything from weekend writers' conferences to four-day winter solstice celebrations. Or how about a weekend for lovers, where you can learn Esalen massage, polarity balancing, and other ways of sharing experiences with someone you love? Another Place conferences are community experiences, so expect to help in the cleaning, cooking, and child care.

Another Place
Route 123
Greenville, NH 03048

That's the Spirit Interested in learning how to recognize and strengthen your psychic senses of knowing, seeing, and hearing, and healing your higher self? Courses designed to do just that are available at the Fourth Center. In addition to classes in psychic awareness and spiritual healing, the Center teaches self-expression through music, writing, and visual art. Eight-week courses run $60. You can also stop in and have a clairvoyant reading done, for a nominal fee.

The Fourth Center
P.O. Box 30
Kings Beach, CA 95719

There can be no progress except in the individual and by the individual himself.
CHARLES BAUDELAIRE

Feminist Perspectives

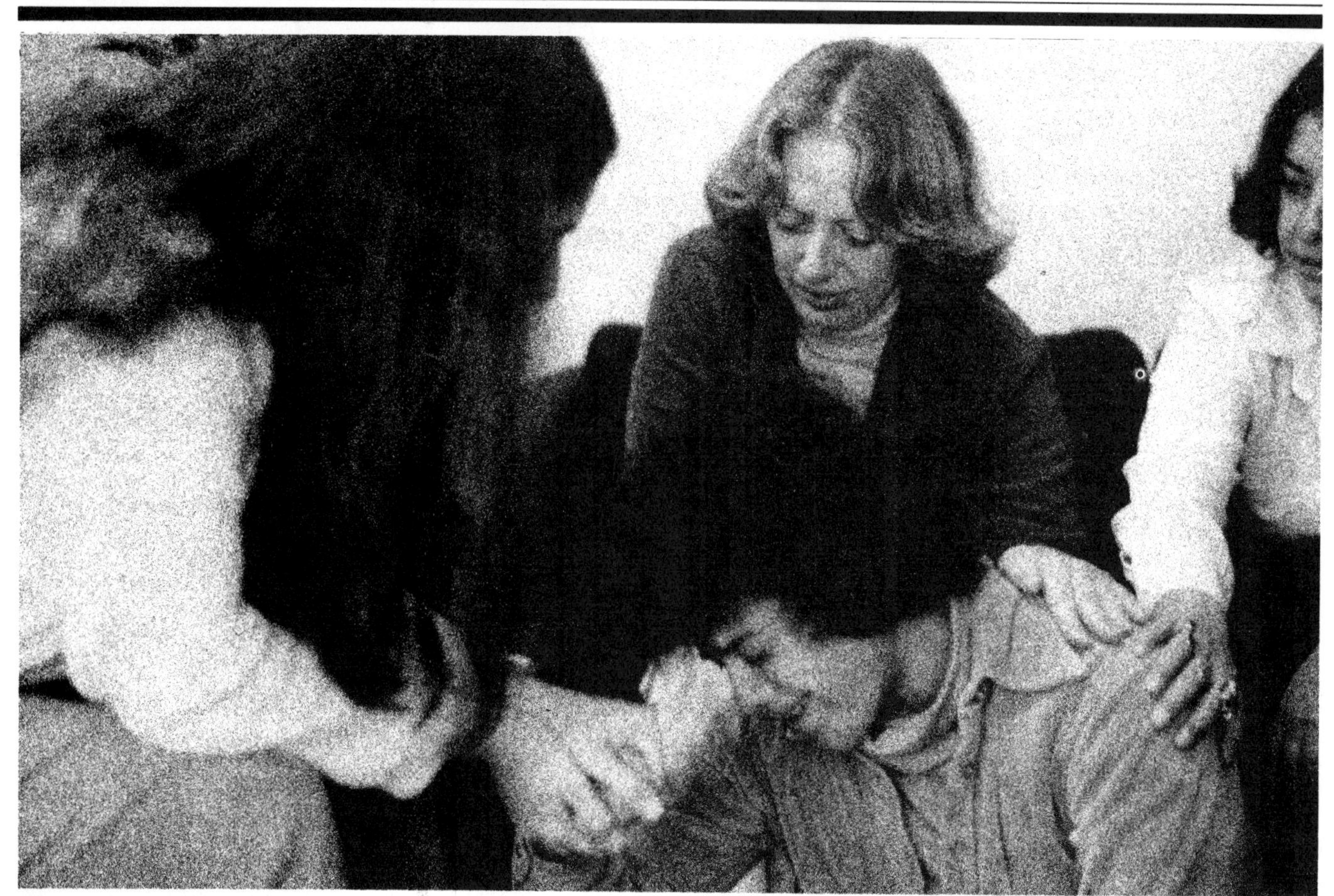

Breaking Through

Even when it's summertime, living just ain't easy anymore. We're in a time of great social and cultural change, and the changes seem especially dramatic for women. To help both women and men sort out the implications of these changes, the Center for Feminist Therapy operates a number of classes, workshops, and ongoing groups. It also offers individual therapy and counseling.

Even though the Center uses the word "feminist" in its name, its point of view is nonsexist. Its goal in all of its programs is to encourage individual women *and* men to explore and discover their uniqueness. This kind of self-awareness can only be achieved when a person recognizes that part of his or her outlook and behavior stems from society's expectations about "appropriate" sex roles.

Many of the Center's workshops are one-day, all-day get-togethers, costing $25 or $35 per person. The range of subjects is wide. One workshop tackles the whole idea of sex roles and suggests strategies for breaking out of stereotypes. Another deals with women's experience of stress and offers techniques for stress reduction. There's also an experiential workshop exploring issues of aging.

Workshops for men and women together deal with intimate relationships between friends, lovers, and/or spouses, as well as with styles of being a parent.

There's a Neo-Reichian workshop, employing techniques to help men and women get rid of "body armor," the barrier that keeps feeling and being, mind and body, separate in so many people in the modern world.

A Workshop called "Before Words, Images Were: Seeing with the Mind's Eye" helps participants to go beyond the verbal to the realities of innermost needs. Its aim is to provide an experience that will allow each individual to create her or his personalized space.

Among the ongoing groups, which generally meet once a week for two hours, are a growth group for women between 40 and 60 and a feminist growth group. These groups cost between $50 and $60 a month.

Stereotypes are hard to break. They're just as tough when the stereotypes are ones we hold about ourselves. Many women—and men—need help in examining these attitudes, so they can know and value their individual selves. This kind of self-knowledge can make living a lot easier, all year round. —A.L.

Center for Feminist Therapy
1640 Fifth St., Suite 220
Santa Monica, CA 90401

Enchanted Sisterhood

Reach inside yourself—way down inside your feminine psyche—and retrieve that whole, valuable person awaiting you there. The message of the Khalsa Women's Training Camp seems to be, "Women of the world, rejoice! Unite!"

Held in Espanola, New Mexico (the Land of Enchantment), Khalsa offers women an experience of challenge and growth under the guidance of Siri Singh Sahib Bhai Sahib Harbhajan Singh Khalsa Yogiji. The core of the program is learning what the master terms "the ancient arts of being a woman."

But in addition to the ancient arts, there are modern arts and techniques hiding in the tent city at Khalsa. Women participants attend classes in self-defense and rape prevention. Group activities include volleyball, tennis, rope climbing, music, and swimming.

The diet is vegetarian, and all participants draw KP regularly, which is one of the benefits: you learn to cook delicious vegetarian foods. You also learn the arts of self-healing, massage, and child care.

The living conditions are rough and simple, and your time will be spent under the glorious blue skies of Espanola in "the most beautiful sisterhood ever to be imagined." Cost is $365. —J.A.

3HO Foundation
1620 Preuss Rd.
Los Angeles, CA 90035

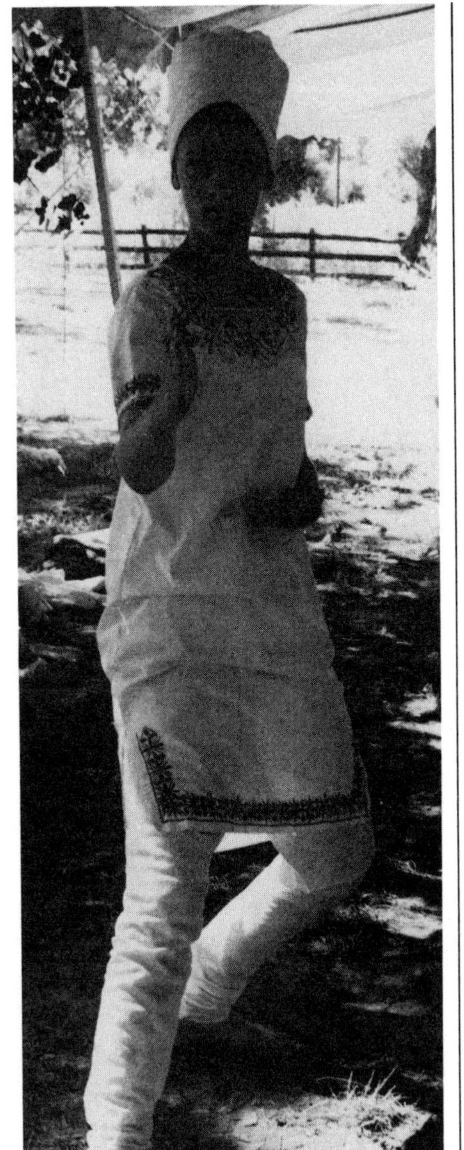

Power Play

The top floor office of a Manhattan skyscraper may not be your idea of success, but whatever your career aspirations, the USC seminar on Power Management for Women will help you realize them.

The folks behind the Power Management program seem to be suggesting that women stop griping about the male power structure, the isolation, the discrimination, the exploitation, and really get down to business. This weekend course will help you create a supportive career environment and take control of your interpersonal relations. In short, you will be schooled in the art of being a successful woman.

Leading psychologists and business administrators will help you understand the motivations and needs of your co-workers. You will learn which "power tactics" to employ and which ones to submit to. Using lectures and group exercises, instructors provide techniques for managing the work environment and its invisible web of personal power structures.

The price of such achievement seems small indeed. The $135 fee for this two-day seminar includes lunch, refreshments, all materials, and parking. And as an expense for education to improve professional skills, it may be tax deductible! —C.G.

College of Continuing Education
University of Southern California
CES
Los Angeles, CA 90007

To the extent that women gain economic self-control and enhance the social significance of their daily activities, and to that extent alone, they will become men's equals—and superiors.
THOMAS SZASZ

Looking Out for No. 1 Whether you're a man or a woman, you can benefit from the women's courses offered by Purdue University's continuing education program. Among course offerings are assertiveness training, the psychology of love and anger, and several career and management seminars. Courses range from one-day seminars to eight weekly two-hour sessions, and prices go from $25 to $70.

Institute for Continuing Education
Purdue University
Hammond, IN 46323

The Best Defense Your high heels click against the quiet sidewalk as you hurry down the dark city street. Suddenly, a man looms before you, knife in hand. What do you do? Don't rely on your instincts or on your mother's advice. Be prepared for an attack by taking a course in self-defense for women. The University of West Florida offers a one-day lecture and clinic to teach you basic principles for defending yourself. Fee is $15.

Division of Continuing Education
University of West Florida
Pensacola, FL 32504

Women's Tuition In olden days, courses for women were invariably given in home economics departments and consisted primarily of cooking and sewing. Now women can sign up for specially designed courses in financial planning, marketing and management, public speaking, writing skills, and loads of other fun areas. UCLA Extension offers all these courses and more, including a special "creative living" course for the mature woman. Write for schedule and fees.

UCLA Extension
P.O. Box 24902
Los Angeles, CA 90024

Equal Writes Woman as writer and communicator receives special emphasis in NYU's continuing education program. Course topics include women and the media (with guest lecturers from broadcasting, publishing, advertising, and public relations), women writers and criticism, and beginning and advanced writing workshops. Also of interest are business and assertiveness courses. Write for NYU's catalog.

School of Continuing Education
New York University
2 University Place, Room 21
New York, NY 10003

I love the idea of there being two sexes, don't you?
JAMES THURBER

The primary purpose of a liberal education is to make one's mind a pleasant place in which to spend one's leisure.
SYDNEY J. HARRIS

Leisure Learning

It was the loudmouthed Queen of Hearts who roared at tiny Alice that it takes all the running you can do to stay in the same place. "If you want to get somewhere else," she bellowed, swinging her croquet mallet, "you must run at least twice as fast as that!"

Children giggle delightedly at such patent nonsense. Adults don't giggle; they groan. Why? Because it's so painfully true. It does take all the running you can do—and then some. Between time and inflation and technology, we're all on the road to being obsolete before we have a chance to turn around.

And even with all the running (and panting) you can do, you may still fall behind. Some whippersnapper comes along with a new technique you've never heard of—someone who went to school after you did and knows the more recent technology. And it may turn out that what was hot stuff when you were a sophomore is now just lukewarm.

Doctors, teachers, lawyers, and dentists have it easy; their continuing education is mapped out for them by rules and by strong professional associations. In many school districts, for instance, a teacher's salary is increased each time he or she completes an additional graduate course. That's a sufficient incentive for any wage-earner.

But what about the rest of us—the ones who finished school and went to work? or had children? or just commenced living in the real world? We've neither the time nor the inclination to go back to school, at least not school the way we remember it.

But now you can.

You can join the Queen of Hearts in her regal solution—but without the running. You can pick up your family, your wits, and your croquet mallet and trot off in pursuit of knowledge.

We've poked around the campuses of the United States, and we've found some interesting things happening. It seems that even the institutions themselves are beginning to realize that education doesn't end at graduation.

Here are introductions to a variety of ways to approach the situation. There are family learning vacations: take the kids with you, and feel secure that there'll be plenty for them to do while you hit the books.

There are farm visits: you can stick a straw between your teeth, and show your kids how to catch catfish with a bamboo pole—or how to milk a cow. They won't ever have to know you're not an old hand at it yourself.

There are retreats where you and your family can pause from the daily routine to get to know each other once more. And while you do it, you can learn something about our heritage, our history, or our natural resources.

If you need other inducements, consider learning French while you live in a cozy Gallic village. Or cogitate on Buddhism and the martial arts on a peak in the Rocky Mountains.

And if your memories of school are less than enchanting, we promise you something extraordinary: no boredom, no drudgery, no more teachers' dirty looks. When you enroll in these learning vacations, you enroll for an educational experience that is both enjoyable and informative.

So haul out your pencil box, your lunchpail, and your spiral notebook—and get a move on!

Construction by John Odam

Learning Together

Get Piqued!

If yours is a do-it-together family, Indiana University has a summer program on its Bloomington campus that may excite all hands, from two-year-old tots to eighty-year-old grandmas.

Billed as an "educational vacation," IU's "mini-university" offers—in one five-day period—everything from picnics and bridge to classes on Tibetan life, Lizzie Borden, and *le jazz hot*. There are no exams or supplies to buy for the 60 or so scheduled classes, each taught by a university professor.

"A wonderful, affordable vacation," said an Illinois attorney who attended with his wife and two kids. "It's a great chance to immerse yourself, again, in university life. I wanted our kids to get the 'feel' of a great campus."

Families live and have meals in campus dormitories. and while the oldsters attend classes (high school age children may also attend, no extra charge), preschoolers enjoy themselves in a licensed nursery. Kids from eight to sixteen enroll in a recreational camp run by IU's physical education department and may select from a gamut of activities including horseback riding, swimming, tennis, archery, and group events.

Indiana University, a pioneer in the "learning vacation" field, has been widely imitated by other institutions offering similar programs throughout the nation. Its "mini-university" was organized to serve people who believe that education *begins*, not *ends*, with the sheepskin ceremony. "There are no prerequisites," an official explains, "and anyone interested in feeding his mind is invited to participate."

Among the mind-food items on the educational menu in one recent program were the following:

—A Writer Reads His Poetry for and About Children
—Finding Your Roots
—Recent Advances in Genetic Engineering
—Communication Between Man and Animal
—How the Life Insurance Buyer Can Avoid Being Taken
—Egypt Today
—Positive Parenting

And for those who would rather play hookey, there are such round-the-clock diversions as golf, tennis, bowling, bridge, and movies.

Registration fees are modest and housing costs (including three meals a day) are so low that one can scarcely afford to stay home. Example from one recent program: two adults and two kids under six—$174, or about $35 a day.

"An exciting experience," said the Illinois lawyer's wife. "The courses piqued us to do more reading. We'll go back!" —D.H.

Indiana University Alumni Association
Indiana Memorial Union
Bloomington, IN 47401

The purpose of learning is growth, and our minds, unlike our bodies, can continue growing as we continue to live.
MORTIMER ADLER

Summer Means Fun

Your day begins with an early morning "surprise" exercise program. Straightaway, you know this is no ordinary summer school.

The University of Oregon's Family Vacation College is held but once a year—usually in July—and it promises seven days of intellectual and physical stimulation for every family member.

The course of study is appropriately limited to the family. Lectures by distinguished University of Oregon faculty focus on the issues selected for that session, and open discussions enable participants to directly explore these concerns.

But all is not work here. There's a wealth of recreational activities to choose from, and children, in particular, are lured by swimming, hiking, arts and crafts, and like pursuits. Adults needn't be shy about joining in, although that morning exercise period *is* optional.

Housing is provided in university dormitories, with one dorm for children and another for adults. Cost, including meals and housing, is $145 for adults, $55 for children ($25 for kids under five). —R.McG.

Summer Session
University of Oregon
Eugene, OR 97403

In America there are two classes of travel—first class and with children.
ROBERT BENCHLEY

Canadian Sunburn

Take a vacation and what do you get? "A sunburn and a handful of souvenirs," says the University of Guelph. But if that's not enough for you, the University may have just what you do want.

Try their Summer Campus, where dozens of one-week courses are offered. The session runs for two weeks, and participants are free to stay for all or part of that time. Courses are not repeated from session to session.

Offerings include agriculture, plants, beekeeping, personal finance, French, wine-making, drawing, writing, personal growth, and parapsychology. Guelph also provides a raft of organized activities to occupy children of all ages while parents are off studying.

Courses consist of 20 hours of instruction and discussion, plus at-home study as required, but afternoons and evenings are free for students to take advantage of the University's recreational facilities. Yes, you just may take home a sunburn, too.

Cost is $60 per course, and the tab for children is $30 weekly. Accommodations are available at about $100 per week (with two meals included daily) for each person. The family rate for two adults and two children is $250. —R.McG.

Office of Continuing Education
University of Guelph
Guelph, Ontario N16 2W1
Canada

Vive la Difference! The Alumni College at Dartmouth (the oldest in the country, by the way) dedicates itself to refreshment. Not refreshment like eats, but refreshment like spiritual rejuvenation. Each year a unique vacation experience awaits you at the Hanover campus. As an example of the provocative topics, one recent summer was spent on the proposition: Men & Women: What's the Difference?

Dartmouth Alumni College
201 Crosby Hall
Hanover, NH 03755

There Is Nothing Like Notre Dame Although she may be better known for football than for summer school, the grand lady of South Bend offers a most intriguing program in her summer alumni college. The July programs at Notre Dame are theme-oriented and vary from year to year. Recent topics have included "Contemporary Music: New Noise or Liberal Art" and "The Church and the Quality of Life."

Alumni College
Center for Continuing Education
Box W
Notre Dame, IN 46556

MIT Fine And then there's the MIT Summer College, which sometimes is in Cambridge (where MIT almost always is), and sometimes not. In previous summers, for instance, it's been in Hawaii and at Aspen, Colorado. Topics are very MIT: "The Coastal Zone: Engineering Its Development and Preservation" and "Molecular Genetics," for example.

MIT Alumni Summer College
77 Massachusetts Ave.
Cambridge, MA 02139

Summertime in Vermont If you've an urge to get back to Lake Champlain, but still don't feel like spending your whole vacation playing golf, there's a program waiting for you at the University of Vermont in Burlington. Classes and lectures abound, but plenty of provision is made for the multitudinous summer activities the lake provides.

Continuing Education
University of Vermont
Grasse Mount
Burlington, VT 05401

The purpose of a higher education is to make men aware of what was and what is; to incite them to probe into what may be.
OTTO KLEPPNER

Lead a Cloistered Life

Harken ye all to a rare medieval holiday at The Cloisters, a branch of the Metropolitan Museum of Art in New York.

In a building complete with Romanesque chapel and apse and Gothic doorways (some dating as far back as the 12th century), The Cloisters has been devoted to the arts of the Middle Ages for more than 40 years. Rich selections of finely woven tapestries, hand-tooled ivory, precisely executed illuminated manuscripts, stained glass, and panel paintings are but a small part of the Cloisters experience.

Situated in Fort Tryon Park overlooking the expansive Hudson River, the museum boasts a variety of medieval gardens, among them a herb garden containing more than 200 species of plants that grew during the Middle Ages.

Public tours of the magnificent collection are conducted every Wednesday at 3 p.m. Guided tours of the entire complex for groups of all ages and interests are available by appointment. Groups that specify particular interests will be accompanied by tour guides especially qualified in those areas.

In addition, The Cloisters maintains ongoing educational programs for grade school children, high schoolers, and adults. The programs for the younger set are carefully planned to fit the ages and interests of each group. For the older students and adults, The Cloisters conducts workshops in a selection of medieval crafts. The courses, which run for three to ten weeks, cover the fine art of stained glass, the skills of tapestry weaving, and the delicate techniques of manuscript illumination.

Summer at The Cloisters is a marvelous experience, beginning with apprentice and journeyman workshops geared toward The Cloisters' annual Festival. Apprentices (grades 5 through 8) learn to make costumes, banners, and other decorative materials. Apprentices should apply before June.

Journeymen are strictly volunteers. They assist the workshop craftsmen in teaching the apprentices and preparing for the Festival. Applications should be submitted before the end of April.

Then comes the Festival, where knights joust on mighty steeds, troubadours woo the hearts of fair maidens, and feasts of delight fill the fancies of all. Here a duel bursts to the fore, there a juggler captivates the crowd. Dancers and musicians tempt audiences to a stage where players perform a period farce. Along the streets, craftsmen make and sell their wares, while clowns and puppets, kings and serfs decorate the celebration with their costumes and personalities.

What better way to top off your visit than by romping in the revelry of a medieval festival?

The Festival is The Cloisters come to life, a walk through a painting where the subjects sing, dance, and lighten your heart. By all means, bring your own costume. The more, the merrier! —M.C.W.

The Cloisters
The Metropolitan Museum of Art
New York, NY 10040

Family Fare

Don't hit the beach this summer. Hit the books instead, and learn while you relax at Penn State's Alumni College.

It's a family affair at Penn State, with probing courses to entertain adults and a plethora of lures—from swimming through spelunking—for their children. Formal courses change yearly. In 1978 participants devoted a week to a meandering through "Evolution—Change Through Time." Starting with ancient creativity as exemplified by the Egyptians, the course rapidly took students up to today's world and our current complexities. In the second week, "Revelations—Contemporary Fare" served as the basis for discussion.

The 1979 program focuses on "The Nature of Man" (human relationships and the search-for-self phenomenon) and on "Man and Nature" (mankind and its physical, intellectual, and aesthetic environment).

Participation is open to all, and one is welcome to attend one or both courses. Tuition, room, and board costs about $150 for adults, less for children. Tuition alone is $90 weekly. —R.McG.

The Penn State Alumni Association
104 Old Main
University Park, PA 16802

Cornell Knowledge

It's the get-more-out-of-your-summer summer, says Cornell University, and it's up to you what you'll get. The program is Cornell's Alumni University, although participants needn't be Cornell alumni to be eligible. Interest alone suffices.

There's lots to be interested in. How about Chinese cooking? Darkroom techniques? Natural history of the Finger Lakes? Backyard birding? Literature of the holocaust?

And there are many more to choose among. Most courses last for one week and, throughout the summer session, each week features a new slate of offerings.

For children, there's a lot to keep busy with, too. While parents are off perusing Moliere, the kids can go horseback riding, swim, learn photography, tinker with creative arts, or—for teens —try their hand at computer programming. Babysitters are available for infants.

Cost per adult—including housing, meals, and course materials—is $215 weekly. For children, the bill is $125 weekly. Nonresident rates are available, too. —R.McG.

Alumni University
Cornell University
626B Thurston Ave.
Ithaca, NY 14853

Virginia Whispers

Tube the Smith and feel
your senses tense
when white-water whips
or laze a slow
easy
pace
through calm still shallows.
Ride on horseback
with the rhythms of the trail
where woods spread
mountain spirits tall and one
deep breath is nature set
on Blue Ridge grandeur
lined with hiking trails
and the scents of dreams.
Take a plunge
in the indoor pool
or take to the courts
or to the classroom.
Evening seminars abound
while not far off
the night life shines.
Sample the stage
or the finest cuisine.
Or relax where you are
with a mountainous meal.
For the time of your life
for the life of your time.
For fun
for families
for less than you'd expect
($142 per double per week). —M.C.W.

Summer Programs
Ferrum College
Ferrum, VA 24088

Great Getaway At Concordia College, summer school isn't the lock-in; it's the "Great Getaway." Why? Because it offers everything for everyone in the family. The junior program begins with five-year-olds, and the adult program reaches into extreme elderhood. And there are tickets to the Guthrie Theater, a soccer game, and the Minnesota Zoological Gardens. What more can one ask from a getaway?

Alumni College
Concordia College
Hamline and Marshall
St. Paul, MN 55104

Brush Your Mind at Colgate
Here's an idea for some profitable time spent in upstate New York. Try the Family Summer Program at Colgate University. For the adults, there are stimulating weekday morning seminars with faculty members. For the children, there are organized activities, sports, and trips. Topics under consideration might include: "Einstein and Freud in 20th Century Art," "Jazz: Yesterday, Today, and Tomorrow," "Thomas Mann's *Magic Mountain*," and "Experimental Biology." Now that's what you call a wide range of subject matter.

Family Summer Program
Colgate University
Hamilton, NY 13346

The Family that Plays Together
A typical day at the Danebod Family Recreation Camp includes singing, dancing, children's games, and a discussion period. There are crafts aplenty, and swimming. There are nature hikes. And there's a nine-hole golf course. There are nighttime communal campfires and—best of all—babysitters galore.

The Danebod Folk School
Tyler, MN 56178

To bring up a child in the way he should go, travel that way yourself once in a while.
JOSH BILLINGS

D.C. ABC's

Ever thought about taking the family to college for a vacation? Well, you can at the American University's Vacation College, a variety of one-week sessions combining leisure and learning in the political heart of America—Washington, DC.

Get the inside story about government from Congressmen, executive branch representatives, and special-interest groups—energy, education, health insurance.

Or explore your own career development: Find out where you could be going and how to get there. This seven-day program focuses on occupational satisfaction, nontraditional job hunting techniques, and practical tips such as resume uses and abuses, interview survival, and making and keeping inside contacts.

You could look inside Washington media, see the news machine in action, and get a chance to talk to some of the capital's oldest newshounds.

There's even a special children's program (meals included) of supervised recreation and exciting field trips.

Attend classes in the morning, then spend your afternoons and weekends sightseeing or enjoying the University's recreational facilities. In the evenings, receptions and reduced rates to Kennedy Center and Wolf Trap performances are all part of the fun.

Fees for tuition and housing are adults, $180; children 7-12, $100. —M.C.W.

Summer Vacation College
American University
Washington, DC 20016

Do It Up Brown

Brown isn't a reporter from the *Baltimore Sun*, it's an Ivy League university and, if you've a hankering for a bit of that old school charm, Brown is hankering for you. That's because every summer the university opens its doors to adults looking for a little learning, and not just frivolity, on their vacations.

Each summer features a one-week course on a set theme. This past year, for example, participants explored Transitions: The Life Cycle from Childhood to Maturity, and lecturers included Erik Erikson as well as Brown faculty members. The year before the topic was Explorations in Time and Space, with lecturers including Isaac Asimov. That's the way you'll spend your mornings.

Come the afternoons, you're invited to attend your choice of creative workshops. Writing, art, film, music, and the like are all included.

Fret not. You've time aplenty. There is no homework, and ample opportunity is provided for individual explorations.

Children, too, are welcome at Brown. A special roster of activities is provided.

Cost, including most meals and an on-campus room, is about $210. Children are accommodated for about half the adult rate. —R.McG.

Brown University Continuing College
Box 1920
Providence, RI 02912

American Beginnings

Roots and Offshoots

The flavor of mountain folk culture is alive and well in Cosby, Tennessee, at the Folk Life Center of the Smokies. Thanks to the founders and co-directors, Jean and Lee Schilling, the folks in these parts have come to know their roots and offshoots, too.

The Folk Life Center is built on land once used for moonshinin'. Today, what's being bottled up is the cultural heritage of these Appalachian mountains. So if you hanker for a taste of American folk life, you've found the right place.

Life in the Appalachians was never easy. The folks made what they needed or they did without. And it seems that music and beauty were necessities. At the Folk Life Center even the smallest bits and scraps contain in them sufficient magic to create a spark of beauty.

Don't be surprised to find yourself spinning wool with a spindle made from a potato and a pencil. Or fashioning buttons from scraps left behind by the woodcarving class.

The whys and wherefores of blacksmithing, lathe turning, and weaving are preserved in year-round workshops. Shucks, there's even corn husking.

Cloth is not the only thing you can learn to weave. The high art of story-telling comes alive in the presence of Aunt Ella Costner. Tall tales, folklore, and hair-raising stories rekindle the spirit of American traditions.

Add to this, inkle-loom weaving, vegetable dyeing, troutfishing, pottery, and herb gathering (this class is "Wild Eatins" by Bill Hooks), and you begin to get the picture of the bountiful harvest of mountain folkways contained in the Folk Life Center of the Smokies.

An annual folk festival is sponsored by the Center and features both local and far-fetched talents for a weekend gathering of friends of old-time music. Toe-tapping jam sessions, special workshops for children, and stage concerts highlight this family event.

There's the Great Smoky Mountain National Park just up the road a piece with trails and creeks and such. How 'bout a morning hike to Hen Waller Falls? Primitive camping sites are to be found at the Center, while lodging and meals are available at nearby Sunset Gap. Admission to the Festival, which is $10, includes a camping space; five days of workshops runs about $100 per person.

The Schillings' Folk Life Center is proof that music and art have only to be sung and lived to survive. —C.G.

Folk Life Center of the Smokies
P.O. Box 8
Cosby, TN 37722

Since we cannot know all
that is to be known of everything,
we ought to know
a little about everything.
BLAISE PASCAL

A Soil Rich and Pure

Weave a bee skep
from ryestraw and hickory.
Whittle with a master
(and keep the knife).
A century and a half
of culture and craft
to sample and share,
to learn.
The Pennsylvania Farm Museum
of Landis Valley
rich with the history
of European settlers
ripe with heritage
of rural tradition.
Throughout the year
programs and workshops
lectures and seminars
from Harvest Days
to courses in crafts
display and demonstrate
and teach this fine past—
the life of the canaller,
traditional tinsmithing,
a robust family-style German feast
(complete with polka),
pottery, pleating, vegetable dyeing,
wool dyeing, blacksmithing,
soap making,
beekeeping, bean snapping,
saddlery.
From toleware painting
to pump boring tools
the knowledge and skills
of Pennsylvania generations
flourishes amid this time-stopping
agricultural museum.
A four-day workshop
is usually $50 per person.
Museum admission is $2 per adult,
children free. —M.C.W.

Pennsylvania Farm Museum
of Landis Valley
2451 Kissel Hill Rd.
Lancaster, PA 17601

An American will tinker with anything he can get his hands on.
LELAND STOW

A Just Settlement

There is still a place where life smiles simply, where the blather of modern living doesn't invade nature's serenity, where people work together with each other and the environment in the stewardship of the earth, in the stewardship of themselves. That place is Pine Mountain Settlement School, 800 acres of forest and farmland located amid the mountains and coalfields of Harlan County, Kentucky.

Rich in Appalachian tradition, Pine Mountain is devoted to encouraging human kinship through the understanding and appreciation of the environment. The school offers environmental education programs for groups and individuals, including workshops in wildlife habitat and medicinal plants. Food and lodging are provided on campus, and guests share in all school duties. Length of stay may vary from one day to several weeks.

The Settlement School also sponsors annual events, such as the Spring Wildflower Weekend (April) and the College Term in Appalachian Culture and Environment (December through January), which are open to individuals and groups alike.

Alcoholic beverages are prohibited, and cigarettes, soft drinks, and public television are not available on campus. Maximum cost for the programs is $5.00 per person per night (lodging) and $6.50 per day for meals. —M.C.W.

Pine Mountain Settlement School
Pine Mountain, KY 40810

Where Have All the Folkies Gone?

Education is entertaining, say the folks at Blackpoint Camp, and it's all the more so there because the focus is music—folk music, to be exact. Under the sponsorship of The Living History Center (and with a National Endowment for the Arts grant), Blackpoint Camp's roster of distinguished folkies is ever ready to help you strum and pick your way to good times.

Beginners and the more experienced alike are both invited to enroll in the week-long music camp. There are ample folk-life and music seminars and workshops, many sing-alongs, and lots of fun. And, for accomplished folkies, master classes under the instruction of professionals are available.

Campsite is Blackpoint Farm, 240 acres of rolling hills, oak forests, rustic barns, and sunny glades. Better still, at seminar's end there's the Blackpoint Old-Time Music Festival Concert—two days of drop-in workshops and non-stop music.

Attendance at the camp costs $150, inclusive of meals. Rooms are available at about $100 for the week, and college credit can be arranged. For those wishing to attend only the festival, admission is $5 per day. —R.McG.

The Living History Center
P.O. Box B
Novato, CA 94947

Go for Folk

Chances are the ladderback chair you sit in during Homer Ledford's dulcimer class will be handmade. Just about everything around the John C. Campbell Folk School in Brasstown, North Carolina, speaks for the preservation of the mountain culture found in Appalachia.

The Folk School was founded way back in the 1920s with the enthusiastic support of local citizens. Volunteers built cabins and donated furniture and land. They wanted a school that would do more than make "teachers and preachers."

This special sense of community still exists. A thriving cottage industry known as the Brasstown Carvers is a visible sign of the local dedication to the American folk heritage. And there's the Sunday "get-acquainted supper," which is sure to make you feel at home.

Instructors at the John C. Campbell Folk School range from PhD's from nearby universities to native mountain folk like Homer Ledford, who will fill your ears with the history and legends of the Appalachian Mountains.

For about $135 a week you can participate in a living museum of American crafts and culture with classes in blacksmithing, basketry, pottery, weaving, quilting, spinning, vegetable dyeing, and wood-carving. The Family Folk School accommodates families with children for two-week sessions, and weekend workshops and individual craft courses abound. —C.G.

The John C. Campbell Folk School
Brasstown, NC 28902

Razorback Lore

Grab your dulcimer and head for the hills—the Ozarks, that is. This summer Arkansas College is offering two fascinating programs on the culture of the Ozarks.

The one-week Ozark Folklore Workshop focuses on the music of the early Ozark settlers. Studies of British ballads and American folksong, selections from the Wolf tape library, and live performances by area musicians are enhanced by an introduction to Ozark folk tales, superstitions, and cures. Craft workshops are conducted daily at the Ozark Folk Center, and field trips (including an evening at the Arkansaw Traveller Theatre) further complement the program.

The summer course in Ozark Folklore is a month-long exploration of Ozark geography, history, and culture. Morning seminars in music, crafts, folklore, and architecture are followed by visits to traditional Ozark homes. Evenings sparkle with the excitement of authentic folk music and dance. Individual exploring and discovering can be done on weekends.

Lodging is available at nearby motels, camping facilities, and the Folk Center Lodge (reservations necessary). Cost for the workshop is $60. The summer course is $180, plus a $10 nonrefundable application fee. College credit is available. —M.C.W.

Ozark Folklore Workshops
Continuing Education
Arkansas College
Batesville, AR 72501

Old Homestead Week

Looking for more than another button to push? A homesteading week is a natural alternative.

The Homesteading Center, a 70-acre hilltop of rich woods and velvety meadows, is a small working/teaching homestead. In an atmosphere fresh with sweet clean air, pure sunshine, and the life's-breath sensation of rural community, the Center provides a variety of intensive working courses in the basics of homesteading.

From Basic Homesteading Week (prerequisite to other weeks), where beginners learn the fundamentals (wild foods, basic hand tools, medicinal herbs, and plowing, to name a few), to the more advanced Work-Horse Week (which includes a Farrier's certification upon completion), the courses teach the essentials of natural living.

But there's more than just the satisfaction of working with the earth. Center activities also include archery, leathercraft, poetry reading, true "folk" music, and writing for a community newspaper. You can even learn about midwifery, or take a two-week course in the art of building a log cabin (maybe your own!).

A Homesteading Festival (held yearly on Memorial Day and Labor Day weekends) is a great way to get acquainted with the Center and its people. Classes, folk craft, song, and friendship are all part of the biannual festivities. Cost is $15 per person or family. Bring your own tent and food, and camp out under the sky by a crackling fire. —M.C.W.

The Homesteading Center
Oxford, NY 13830

Leisure is the most challenging responsibility a man can be offered.
WILLIAM RUSSELL

Historic Occasion The Fort Armstrong Folk Festival offers you and your family a trip on a Pennsylvania time machine. The history of the region dates back to a conflict between Colonel John Armstrong and the Pennsylvania Indian Confederacy in 1756. Today many of the lost skills of that frontier age are still alive and well in Armstrong County. The early-August festival offers exhibits in such arts as soap making, pewter casting, glass blowing, quilting, funnel cakes, chair caning, and sheep shearing, to name only a few.

Fort Armstrong Folk Festival
P.O. Box 590
Kittanning, PA 16201

Folklore Galore Founded in Wheeling, West Virginia, 35 years ago, the Folklore Village Farm may be found today in Dodgeville, Wisconsin. The reason for the move is complex, but interesting; ask Mrs. Farwell when you're there. The Village offers summer programs in Norwegian rosemaling, French quilling, candle-making, folk dancing, weaving, ceramics, puppetry, wild foods, and recorder playing. There are activities for the whole family, and the visit is played against the backdrop of a real family farm that still functions right there in America's Dairyland.

Folklore Village Farm
Route 3
Dodgeville, WI 53533

Colonial Craftwork If your tastes run to something in days of yore, Sturbridge Village may be your ticket. The Village is a nonprofit educational institution whose long-term growth is supported by memberships and grants. Their "Crafts at Close Range" programs and "mini-programs" offer an unparalleled opportunity to peek into the past—at revolutionary-era blacksmiths, chandlers, and farmers.

Secretary for Special Events
Old Sturbridge Village
Sturbridge, MA 01566

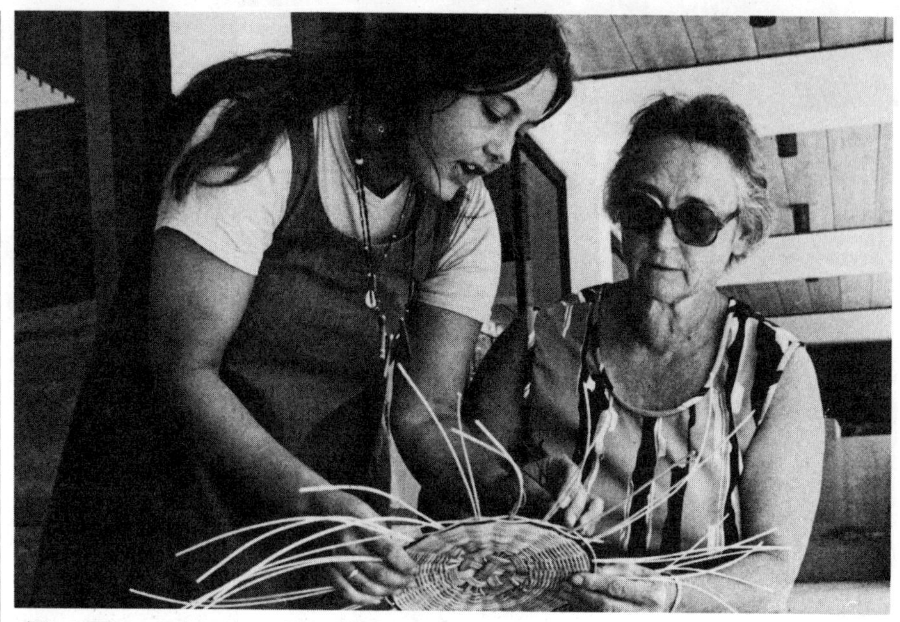

A-Tisket, A-Tasket

A week at the Augusta Heritage Arts Workshop is sure to soothe the savage breast of any hardcore city-slicker. A community-sponsored project of Randolph County in West Virginia, the Workshop provides a total-immersion summer program designed to introduce you to the proud mountain heritage of America's Appalachias.

Instruction in white oak basketry starts with the splitting of the log and ends with a finished basket. Those enrolled in the class in herbs of the Appalachian region spend half a day foraging and the other half preparing traditional ointments and scents.

Chairbottoming, china painting, woodcarving, quilting, spinning, and weaving—all were once crafts of necessity in these hills.

If the hammered mountain dulcimer sounds like music to your ears, you might want to learn to build one. Or learn to play the fiddle. Back in Californy, the five-string banjo on your knee might be one of your own design and construction. Whatever your calling, the good ole mountain air is sure to fetch you back to Augusta year after year.

The cost of most of the one- to five-week classes runs about $45 per week for West Virginia residents, and slightly higher for nonresidents. —C.G.

Augusta Heritage Arts Workshop
P.O. Box 1725
Elkins, WV 26241

Evocations of the Past

Is your grandmother's teapot an antique—or just old? Find out what distinguishes an object as "antique" by attending "An Introduction to Antiques," a learning weekend (Thursday through Sunday) at Colonial Williamsburg in Virginia.

In an atmosphere of one of the world's greatest collections of 18th century furnishings, you traverse the world of antiques through slide show presentations, lectures, tours, and workshops.

On your first day, after a hearty reception, you learn what exactly constitutes an antique from Wendell D. Garrett, editor and publisher of *Antiques*. Consider the elements of beauty, age, craftsmanship, and the supreme individualizing quality—history.

On subsequent days you will be lead through a cornucopia of provocative sessions with staff curators and craftsmen. Artistry in furniture, ceramics, textiles, and silver are just a few of the exciting subjects you'll enjoy. After morning lessons, exhibit and workshop tours will bring to life the facts about the art of antiques.

Per person rates start as low as $145 and include lodging, most meals, talks and tours, and a free ticket to the exhibition buildings and craft shops. And on your last night, feast on a fabulous Groaning Board Dinner.

"An Introduction to Antiques" can be your key to understanding antiques and the past they represent. —M.C.W.

The Colonial Williamsburg
Foundation
Williamsburg, VA 23185

City Slickers & Hayseed

Fertile Fields

It's "over the hills to grandma's" the year round at Drumlin Farm, 220 acres of real live, working farmland in Lincoln, Massachusetts.

Drumlin is one of the few farms left in Middlesex County, says farm director Daniel L. Hart. The Massachusetts Audubon Society, which sponsors Drumlin, keeps it operating so that grownups and kids alike can enjoy "the crowing of roosters, the sweet smell of hay, and the joys of harvesting" in a nation where such simple pleasures are fast becoming mere memories.

Children as young as three may enjoy "hand-in-hand" visits to Drumlin's animal residents and trips to field, pond, or barn. Other courses are available for youngsters of all ages through the ninth grade. Special programs can be arranged for groups of senior citizens to explore the farm by vehicle.

Saturdays are "family adventure" days, when parents and kids share outdoor experiences. Typical Saturday programs include helping a farmer harvest crops, pressing your own apple cider, and digging for artifacts at the site of an old blacksmith shop on the farm. Families may also try their hands at milking a cow and churning their own butter or ice cream.

Birdwatching and natural history courses figure strongly in the adult programs. Beginning naturalists are invited "to come prepared to get dirty" while learning about creatures living in the pond or while studying New England animals from woodchucks and chickadees down to the tiniest invertebrates.

There is also an intriguing morning session for "backyard farmers." "Before the day of the supermarket," says Mr. Hart, "the farmer and his family had to provide their own necessities. This 'how-to' class lets people watch and try their hand at such things as making soap and candles, drop-spinning, tanning leather, and other early-day farm activities."

You may also learn how to "raise sheep for fun and profit," raise your own backyard chicken flock, or keep a milk goat. Drumlin Farm's remarkably varied offerings also include courses on beekeeping, herb culture, baking breads "plain and fancy," and identifying, gathering, and cooking wild edible plants. For the conservation-minded, there is instruction in solar heating and heating with wood.

If you want your kids to gain an appreciation of agriculture and the natural world, we can think of no better activity than a family visit to Drumlin Farm. There you will find the agricultural and conservation ethics not just preached, but lived. A Drumlin Farm experience will change your perspective—we guarantee it. —D.H.

Drumlin Farm
Massachusetts Audubon Society
South Great Rd.
Lincoln, MA 01773

Arizona Biways Where the desert meets the mountains, that's how they describe Kay El Bar Guest Ranch. It's right there on the Hassayampa River, just a bit under a mile high, and a mite north of Phoenix. What you can plan on at Kay El Bar is a good rest, with a good measure of passive cowboying as you see fit. Accommodations are just like home.

Kay El Bar Guest Ranch
P.O. Box 98
Wickenburg, AZ 85358

Home on the Range Hidden Valley Ranch out yonder in Cody, Wyoming, is a working cattle and horse ranch. But there's a difference at HVR—they accept a few guests each summer. Cabins are modern and comfortable, and each guest has his own horse. Riding lessons are included. If you get there in the spring, you can go bear hunting, but in the summer you must content yourself with small game and a wealth of fishing. And there's 4,000 acres of range for you to explore.

Hidden Valley Ranch
Southfork
Cody, WY 82414

Dude It The Greenhorn Creek Ranch offers dude-ranching in the California High Sierra. For some, it will be nostalgia time (hayrides, square dancing); others will call it "fishing heaven"; still others will find out what clean air is all about. And it's an education in high living for all. In case you hanker for a bit of action, Reno's a stone's throw away.

Greenhorn Creek Guest Ranch
P.O. Box 11
Spring Garden, CA 95971

Grin and Bear It You're hiding behind a tree on the bank of the McNeil River in Alaska. The sound of the water rushing over the nearby falls obliterates the constant clicking of your camera. And there at river's edge is the world's largest meat-eating animal: 1500 pounds of brown bear, calmly fishing salmon out of the river for his dinner. Mike McBride's Kamishak Bay Brown Bear Camp is a paradise for wildlife photographers. Bears are not the only targets; you'll also shoot musk ox, walrus, moose, and mountain goats. In case that's not enough, try a hike up to the local active volcano.

Brown Bear Camp
Kachemak Bay Wilderness Lodge
China Poot Bay
Homer, AK 99603

The Real McCoy

Old MacDonald's farm, this ain't. These are the farms of James Dougherty, John Altvater, Robert Shanks, Mrs. Richard N. Jackson, and a couple of dozen others. But forget old MacDonald—that's the stuff of nursery rhymes and fairy tales.

Yes, Virginia, there still are farms—hundreds of them—and lots are in Maryland. Forget the rural life as we might, farmers never do, and so we're provided with daily crops of vegetables, dairy products, beef, and eggs for our tables. But none of this is magic and, delicate as the processes are, today's farm is a business. These farms are the real McCoy—working farms—and you're invited for a visit.

City slickers, suburbanites, and the just plain curious are all invited to tour dozens of Maryland farms on Farm Visitation Day, an event sponsored each summer by the University of Maryland. Participating farms are scattered throughout the state and produce a variety of crops. Even a goldfish farm, a vineyard, and a breeder of Arabian horses were numbered among recent participants.

Best of all, attendance is free and open to all. —R.McG.

Cooperative Extension Service
University of Maryland
College Park, MD 20742

Here a Pig, There a Pig

Agriculture is still the biggest single sector in the US economy, even though less than 4 percent of the labor force is needed to keep it functioning. Today's industrial farms bear little semblance to the rustic barnyards shown in children's picture books.

City kids can go through life these days thinking that the farms and farm animals they see in their books are no more real than the Munchkins of Oz or Dr. Seuss's fantastic creatures. Cows and pigs and lambs become mythical beasts.

The Suits-Us Farm, nestled snugly in the Catskill mountains, houses a full complement of farm animals and offers lots of opportunities for learning about country life. You and the kids can ride the horses, milk the cows, feed the pigs, pet the rabbits, gambol with the goats, and love the lambs. No huge agribusiness here. There's even a brook and a pond, with fish and frogs and ducks.

You can stay at the farm for a couple of days or a couple of weeks. With all meals—and good country snacks—the rates run about $23 a day for adults ($115 a week) and $12 to $19 for children, depending on their age ($60 to $95 a week). —A.L.

Suits-Us Farm
Bovina Center, NY 13740

The Source

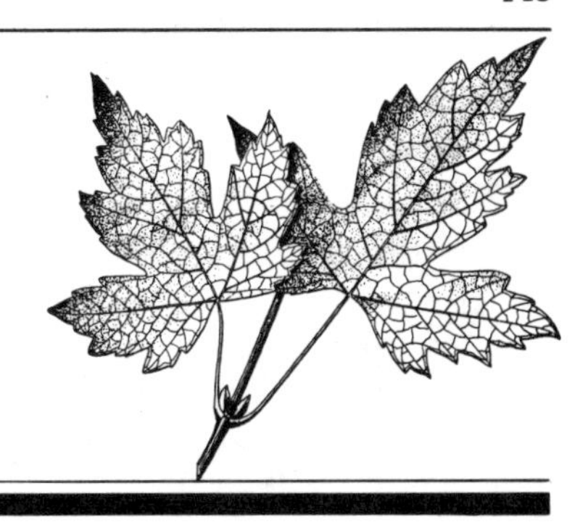

Room at the Top

You've heard of summit meetings: SALT summits, economic summits, peace summits. Well, here we have a Conservation Summit—on a summit. That is to say, we have here a family learning experience on the peaks of the Blue Ridge Mountains in North Carolina. It's sponsored by the be-all and end-all of conservation, the National Wildlife Federation.

By registering for this exciting and refreshing adventure, you sign up for a better understanding of the interrelationships between man and the natural world. And you sign up for a heightened awareness of the earth's resources. All this takes place near Asheville, on Black Mountain.

There are programs for singles, for couples, and for families. There is a mini-summit for mini-people, where children can experience some highly provocative sensory activities: crawling through a hardwood forest, feeling mud ooze between their toes, walking in a cold mountain stream. More sophisticated programs are available for teenagers. Study for young people concentrates on ecology, pollution, mapping, and flora/fauna.

For adults, the horizons are even wider and include a university credit program, arranged with San Francisco State University. The university facet of the Summit is conducted by Dr. William Hammerman, professor of education at San Francisco State.

But whether or not you apply for university credit, the Summit in the Blue Ridge is an enriching, invaluable experience. The classes offered fall into four major categories: pollution control, ecology, arts, and wilderness survival. Within those areas, the breadth of coverage is impressive.

You'll learn Challenging Your Local Electric Utility and Strategies for Citizen Action. You'll be offered courses in creative environmental teaching: awareness, concepts, values, and strategies.

You'll get to know birds, bison, and beavers. You'll learn to identify fungi (edible vs. inedible mushrooms). You'll have a chance to choose between a Nature Walk and a Nature Creep. You'll learn tree and wildflower identification.

For relaxation, you'll be able to choose courses in folk arts, folk history (tales and tales and tales), and folk music ("I was born in East Virginny, North Carolina I did roam . . .").

Then you can elect nonschool topics like trail cookery, wilderness medicine, and flycasting. There are even courses in basic and advanced nature photography.

The faculty is distinguished in every sense, and the vacation will be one you'll not soon forget. It's a chance not only to learn about the historic wilderness that has been the strength of America; it's a chance for a family to learn more about being together.

Each Summit lasts six days and accommodates 550 persons. Free child care is available. You supply the gear.

Costs were not available as we went to press. —J.A.

Conservation Summits
National Wildlife Federation
1412 16th St., NW
Washington, DC 20036

High on the Hog

Sixty miles northeast of Portland, Maine, is Hog Island, a jewel of natural beauty a quarter of a mile offshore at the head of Muscongus Bay. It is the home of the Maine Camp of the National Audubon Society, the 333-acre Todd Wildlife Sanctuary.

Established in 1936 as the first Audubon Camp, the purpose of Hog Island is to introduce adults to the ecology of the legendarily beautiful Maine seacoast. While there, you'll visit meadows, spruce woods as sweet-smelling as those that greeted Leif Erikson, limpid forest ponds, and teeming tidal pools. Every day will bring unexpected thrills.

You'll share the brilliant blaze of the cardinal flower and the smell of salt air. You'll photograph harbor seals sunning themselves on rocky ledges. You'll marvel in stunned silence at the mystery and magic of a colony of great blue herons, and listen to the musical song of the winter wren.

And the fish you'll eat—family style, New England style—will be an experience your mouth will never forget.

College credit can be arranged with the University of Maine, and the total fee for the two-week stint is $395. —J.A.

Maine Camp Program
National Audubon Society
950 Third Ave.
New York, NY 10022

On the Rocks

These rocks are not those of a prison yard. They are part of this nation's heritage of wide open spaces—part of Rocky Mountain National Park. But you needn't be on your own on these rocks. Rocky Mountain Nature Associations will gladly show you around and, in the process, provide you with ample opportunity for intensive summer study of the Rocky environment.

The classroom is the spacious Rocky Mountains, of course. After an initial orientation, students and their instructors set out on intensive and extensive explorations of the area. Past summer courses (all ran one week) included bird, insect, and alpine ecology, mountain geology, and developing awareness through drawing. Courses are conducted consecutively, from early through late summer, and students may sign up for one or all of the offerings.

The fee per course is $60. Pay an additional $25, complete an individual project, and you'll gain college credit, too.

Meals and lodging are arranged by each participant, but inexpensive park campsites are available. For those with a taste for more elegant living, there are also motels in the vicinity. —R.McG.

National Park Service
Rocky Mountain National Park
Estes Park, CO 80517

Camper College

Get lost . . . in North Carolina's Great Smoky Mountains.

Western Carolina University hopes you will lose yourself in a series of summer adventures they have dubbed "Camper College." The program is designed for singles and families who want more out of their vacation than a succession of motel stops.

"All outdoors is our campus," says a Camper College staffer. "We'll show you how to catch a trout, make it on your own in the wilds, backpack in the Smokies or capture wildlife and flowers on film."

If woodcarving's your thing, you can learn the art from a full-blooded Cherokee. Another expert on the Cherokee will recount fascinating legends about plants and animals and will demonstrate how Cherokees use wild plants for herbs and medicines.

"We hope you'll get lost with us," says the staffer. "You are sure to find some things you didn't know about mountains and Indians—and maybe even about yourself."

Courses last two days. Tuition is $25 per course, with special rates for families. —D.H.

Division of Continuing Education
Western Carolina University
Cullowee, NC 28723

Risk! Risk anything! Care no more for the opinions of others, for those voices. Do the hardest thing on earth for you. Act for yourself and face the truth.
KATHERINE MANSFIELD

Water Tigers and Felsenmere

Not, it's not a fairy tale. It's the Ecology Camp run by the National Audubon Society at Devil's Lake in northern Minnesota. Its purpose is to familiarize participants with the fascinating array of natural habitats that abound in this still-wild place.

You will have an opportunity to canoe in wild scenic areas. You will be able to study limnology from a floating classroom (the *Potamogeton*). You'll walk on a felsenmere and snorkel in a glacial lake. You'll prospect to find wild orchids in their natural settings (yes, orchids, in Minnesota!).

You'll listen for the cry of the loon on a wilderness lake and watch with sympathetic pride the soaring spirals of bald eagles and ospreys as they forage for food. You'll trek in the darkness to encounter owls in their night hunting. And, wonder of wonders, you'll meet a water tiger.

All these experiences—and dozens more—await you at the Ecology Camp. And while you're absorbing the wonders of the wilderness, you'll be taught by expert instructors in geology, plant and animal ecology, ornithology, canoeing, and environmental problems.

College credit is available. Total weekly enrollment fee is $210. —J.A.

Minnesota Ecology Camp
National Audubon Society
950 Third Ave.
New York, NY 10022

Tip-Top

You and your family can go to the top for a week-long program that is both instructive and fun-filled.

Conservation Summits, run by the National Wildlife Federation, are conducted in the Adirondacks in New York State.

The Summit program is designed to help people understand the vital interrelationships between human beings and the natural world.

Each Summit program offers a whole spectrum of classes for adults, giving instruction in natural phenomena from algae and fungi to birds and bugs to stars and planets. All classes are taught by experts in the field. There are also practical, "how-to-do-it" courses—in backpacking, nature photography, and map and compass use. If at some time you choose not to take classes, there are various kinds of sports and recreation available.

Special programs are conducted for children between 5 and 15, under the expert supervision of trained youth leaders. The programs not only teach, they let young people experience the outdoors with all their senses and absorb its various moods.

Costs of a week at the Summit, including meals, run from $89 to $212 for adults. Costs for children run from $44 to $85. A small price to pay for a peak experience. —A.L.

Conservation Summits
National Wildlife Federation
1412 16th St., NW
Washington, DC 20036

Summit Conferences

How about a summer vacation spent under the tutelage of the Head Creeps? No, Stan and Dodie Mulaik are not executioners or tormentors. They're an instruction team at the National Wildlife Federation's summer conservation summit in the Colorado Rockies.

Sign up for the Mulaiks' workshop and you'll get a quick but thorough introduction to the life that's visible through a 10-power hand lens. If creepy-crawlies aren't your thing, there are also classes in birding, backpacking, outdoor cooking, wildflower identification, and other ecological pursuits.

For the kids, there are programs galore, too. The Summit Youth Program introduces children to the world of nature through age-coordinated activities such as scavenger hunts, sports, and "blind walks" where the goal is to identify natural objects by touch alone.

All summits run for one week. Sites for the coming summer include Black Mountain, North Carolina; Estes Park, Colorado; and Silver Bay, New York. Complete information on costs and a full roster of activities are available from NWF. —R.McG.

Conservation Summits
National Wildlife Federation
1412 16th St., NW
Washington, DC 20036

The growth of the human mind is still high adventure, in many ways the highest adventure on earth.
NORMAN COUSINS

Lodger Domain

So there you are, sitting in front of the TV. There's a nature documentary on. Or maybe you're watching "Grizzly Adams" or reruns of "Bonanza." You think to yourself how beautiful it'd be to get out there in that beauty and just live.

But a body can only get excited about so much backpacking, right? Even a real nature enthusiast would like to think there's more to the wilderness than just hiking and sleeping bags.

At Strathcona, there's an endless stream of that "more." There, you may be able to locate what it was you were yearning for: not just wilderness, but a different way of life . . . a feeling of knowing that—city slicker and all—you can cope sanely and safely with the great outdoors.

How is it all accomplished? First of all there's the location. Strathcona is located on 40 acres of land bordering a three-mile lake. Beyond that lake lie the snowcapped splendors of Canada's rugged Rockies. The air is clean, the water is clean, the land is clean (no pop-tops, no beer cans, no sandwich bags from yesterday's picnic).

Add to the superb natural setting a staff that is surprising both for its high degree of professionalism and its sheer size. The 1979 Strathcona catalog lists 30 full-time instructors and Lodge personnel, with expertise in fields like kayaking, ornithology, communication, mountaineering, folk music, and exercise physiology. In fact, to look at the credentials, you might get the impression that Strathcona is an institution of formalized higher learning.

The learning you'll get at Strathcona is higher, all right, but Strathcona's no college. In fact, the atmosphere is more like a 19th-century homesteading village than a college campus. There are courses in canoeing and log-building, for starters.

There are mountains and glaciers to be conquered in intensive outdoor workshops and treks. The Comox Glacier Rock, Snow, and Ice School, for instance, offers a basic grounding in such skills as snow camping, ice axe use, crevasse rescue, snow climbing, and belay techniques.

And there's a world of native culture to be absorbed that most outsiders have never been aware of. It is a way of life in harmony with nature: the way of the Nootka, Kwakiutl, and Salish people. There are petroglyphs to be examined and myths to be heard over roaring campfires. If you're primarily interested in native cultures, you can take a boat trip to Friendly Cove (the land of Chief Maquinna and Captain Cook) and to places where the Nootka hunted whales in canoes.

Ah, and there's more! There's a course called West Coast Gourmet, to delight the tired palates of restaurant-weary city-dwellers. You'll feast on salmon, mussels, and cod. And you'll taste the delights of fresh (fresh!) huckleberries right off the bush—all foods prepared in the manner of the native dwellers of the area.

If you're getting the idea that Strathcona is a sort of museum, you're close to correct. Strathcona is the ideal sort of museum—where the skills and ideals of the past endure. It's a bastion of the free soul, a home for the soaring eagles that hide dormant in the breasts of us all. —J.A.

Strathcona Programs
Strathcona Park Lodge
Box 2160
Campbell River, BC V9W 5C9
Canada

The Tides of Kachemak

If Thoreau were still around, he would probably head for Kachemak Bay Wilderness Lodge. Old Henry would cherish the opportunity to kick an ice-blue glacier, stalk a brown bear (world's largest carnivore), or smell a whale's breath!

Mike McBride and his wife Diane own and run the lodge. Listen to Mike: "Kachemak Bay has been statistically documented as one of the richest bodies of water in the world in tons of marine life per cubic acre. Our bay, China Poot—where we are the only residents—is Kachemak's prime estuarine bay, and with the world's second-largest tides may be the richest such bay in the world."

This family-operated lodge is truly one-of-a-kind, geared to families or singles who love nature and solitude. The McBrides—both former teachers—think of their lodge (which is also their home) as primarily a learning experience. "Whatever the guest's interests," says Mike, "we try to help the person to grow in his or her chosen field. We share in every way."

Stays at the Lodge are timed to correspond with the natural rhythms of the bay—spring runs of king salmon, extreme low tides for tidepool exploration, early summer activity at a nearby bird rookery, or concentrations of brown bear on the salmon streams.

Five-day visits are recommended. Kachemak Bay Lodge sits at the tip of Alaska's Kenai Peninsula, 100 air miles southwest of Anchorage. Access is via car or airline to the small fishing village of Homer, where the McBrides will meet you and whisk you away to their arctic Shangri-la. —D.H.

Kachemak Bay Wilderness Lodge
China Poot Bay
Homer, AK 99603

Trees Company

Trees fascinated Joyce Kilmer and, if they intrigue you, too, then the National Audubon Society's Ecology Workshop in Connecticut is for you. But trees aren't the only subject for investigation. Forests, ponds, animals, people, and nonliving elements of the environment are delicately woven into the fabric that is our ecosystem, and, as important as that weave is, an understanding of that fabric is often hard to come by. Audubon's Ecology Workshop is the answer.

Participants spend their week in the workshop learning by exploring. Field trips are held twice daily, with one scheduled each morning and afternoon. Weather, geology, identification techniques, and use of equipment such as binoculars and other tools of the ecological trade are explored.

Instructors are classroom teachers drawn from high schools and colleges, and academic credit is available. Ample free time for relaxation or individual adventures is also provided in the busy schedule.

Cost for the week is $210, inclusive of meals, housing, and instruction. Participants must be 18 or older, and workshops are held throughout the summer months. —R.McG.

Connecticut Ecology Workshop
National Aububon Society
950 Third Ave.
New York, NY 10022

Roughing It Camp Denali is a wilderness vacation retreat on the north boundary of Mt. McKinley National Park. It is designed for those seeking the sincere, informal hospitality of the bush country, where nature—not man—dominates. Beauty and wildlife abound, but there is no plumbing, electricity, or central heating. You win a few, you lose a few.

Camp Denali
McKinley Park, AK 99755

Trapp Trip Want to wake up in the morning to a view of the Worcester Mountains, painted vivid in the sunrise? Then you're ready for a visit to Stowe, Vermont, where the Trapp Family Lodge awaits you. The pace is slow at TFL, and the atmosphere is a mite lazy. But there's plenty to do, and there's always a Trapp on duty, to regale you with stories of this and that. And they say the hills are alive with the sound of music.

Trapp Family Lodge
Stowe, VT 05672

A-Hunting You Will Go Are you the last of the big game hunters? Do you imagine yourself sitting in a den surrounded by heads, antlers, and umbrella-stand feet? If that's your fantasy, and you'd like to make it all come true, then Ray McNutt is your kind of guy. Trek with Ray and you can shoot grizzly bears, polar bears, glacier bears, brown bears, or black bears. You can kill elk, goats, moose, walrus, and bison. And just think how much fun it will be to skin and dress the meat for your freezer.

Ray McNutt
Registered Guide & Outfitter
Sterling, AK 99672

A school should not be a preparation for life. A school should be life.
ELBERT HUBBARD

Returning with a Purpose

Exploring Mann and Nature

More than three-quarters of a century ago Abner Stanton Mann acquired title to what he called "Linda Loma," or beautiful land. His dream was to establish a ranch in the high pasture and timber lands between Redwood Valley and Cape Mendocino.

Today, Mann Ranch, 3500 acres of natural wonder, still operates as a working ranch. It is also home of the famous Mann Ranch Seminars.

Founded in 1970 by Larry T. Thomas, grandson of A. S. Mann, the seminars are dedicated to the exploration of human existence, human culture, and the physical context of nature.

The main house, built originally as the family home, is now the seminar center. The high, open-beamed ceilings, magnificent stone fireplaces, and oversized plate glass windows combine with antique furnishings to stimulate the seminars' informal and intimate tone.

The seminars cover a broad range of topics—philosophy, psychology, fine arts, music, mythology, even King Arthur—but focus on knowledge and the individual. Amid the majesty of woods and grasslands, the two-day sessions approach adult learning from the personal side. The lectures, discussions, and workshops are designed to encourage leisure activities, which are believed to be an essential part of the complete learning process. All meals are prepared at the Center, leaving guests free to walk, swim, bask in natural splendor, or visit with seminar leaders, fellow guests, and staff.

Prominent seminar leaders have included Joseph Campbell, Daniel Ellsberg, Rollo May, Bruno Bettelheim, Moshe Feldenkrais, and Marie Louise von Franz, plus a host of other renowned experts from a multitude of disciplines.

In addition to the ranch seminars, special study tours are scheduled from time to time. This year the flavor and feeling of the Mann Ranch Seminars will be carried to France for a study of Celtic origins and French mythology, with particular emphasis on the history and legends of Brittany. This study tour will pursue a leisurely itinerary of education, exploration, and entertainment, guided by a Mann Ranch seminar leader and several native experts who will join the tour along the way.

The journey, which includes round-trip air travel, first-class accommodations, meals, and even a Paris banquet, will pass through Vitre (a well-preserved medieval town) on the way to Brittany's southern coast. There you will see thousands of megaliths more than 30 centuries old, as well as the famous Forest of Paimpont, witness to King Arthur's search for the Holy Grail. Toward the end of the adventure, guests will have almost a full week of free, unguided time for individual discovery and exploration. For current prices and details, write or phone the Mann Ranch.

The Mann Ranch has no facilities for children, and because it is a real ranch, absolutely no dogs are allowed. Smoking is discouraged during the seminars and is prohibited in the main room.

Costs of the two-day seminars, including all meals and lodging, range from $135 to $325. Camping and nearby motel accommodations are also available. —M.C.W.

Mann Ranch Seminars
P.O. Box 570
Ukiah, CA 95482

He who wonders discovers that this is in itself a wonder.
M. C. ESCHER

Sand Castles

Some call it a remnant of the counterculture. But to architect/philosopher Paolo Soleri's followers, the vertical town being constructed in the desert north of Phoenix is the 21st century happening today.

It's called Arcosanti, and it's being built by a cadre of permanent residents and "workshoppers," who pay $500 for six weeks of living, working, and studying at the construction site. That includes a weekly session with Soleri or visiting scholars.

Stunning in its conception, Arcosanti is a prototype for Soleri's answer to our ecological and urban ills. He contends that only by building upward and in harmony with nature can we adequately solve our contemporary environmental problems.

Workshoppers rough it in small bunkhouses and communal facilities. But the high desert is stunning, the intellectual vibrations are supercharged, and the food is fine in a down-home way.

A four-day public festival each October draws some of the nation's finest avant-garde musicians, artists, and thinkers to the site. Slowly growing cottage industries are providing windbells, pottery, and a year-round cafe. —G.D.

Cosanti Foundation
6433 Doubletree Rd.
Scottsdale, AZ 85023

Ferme Offer

Go to France without knowing French and you just may be a stranger in a strange land. But you can beat that feeling. Go to France to vacation *and* to learn French—with La Ferme, a family vacation-learning program.

Located in La Petite Eguille, a tiny village near the South Atlantic coast, La Ferme marries education and recreation. The course of instruction is flexible, but thorough. Participants devote about three hours a day to classes and a like amount of time to conversation. Finish the program, says La Ferme, and you've gained the equivalent of at least one year's formal instruction in French.

But you've also had time to explore another culture. The South Atlantic coast, with its sandy beaches, awaits you. So do forests, oyster beds, monuments of French and Roman history, and rustic villages.

La Ferme's program is open to all seeking to learn or to improve their French. Cost for two weeks—including instruction, room, and two meals daily—is about 2700 francs. For three weeks, the tab is about 4000 francs. —R.McG.

La Ferme
La Petite Eguille
17600 Saujon
France

Run Away to School

Your kids will be jealous. One week of school, only in the mornings. In the afternoons, you choose from a whole buffet of recreations or just curl up with a book in the warm sun, surrounded by the beautiful Oregon woods.

Vacation College's week-long program begins every day with a hearty breakfast and exercise regimen. The lectures are presented from 9 a.m. till noon, with breaks for coffee and discussion. Everyone, including the faculty, dines together. In the afternoon there are organized activities for those who want to participate—visits to museums, libraries, laboratories, or local points of interest. If you prefer, you can swim, hike, or play tennis and golf. Or do a lot of serious nothing. In the evenings, there is entertainment—plays, concerts, games.

The week's lectures are organized around a particular topic, presented from several points of view. For example, the topic "Paradoxes and Perspectives of the Mind" is addressed by professors of psychology, philosophy, biology, and literature.

The program is for adults but may include sons or daughters of high school age. The fee of $230 pays for everything—room, board, tuition, theater tickets, sporting activities, and maid service at the nearby University Inn. —A.L.

Vacation College
Summer Session Office
University of Oregon
Eugene, OR 97403

The man who has ceased to learn ought not be allowed to wander around loose in these dangerous days.
M. M. COADY

Summer Prime At the College of Wooster, summertime is no light matter. It's a time for serious learning for alumni and for the family and friends of alumni. You might even be able to sneak in if you never attended Wooster—space permitting. The program is full day and night. Topics of lectures and classes might include "American Civil Religion," "The Gospel According to NBC," "Copper Enameling," or "The Shakespearean Revolution." In addition, there are concerts and an evening at the Great Lakes Shakespeare Festival.

The College of Wooster
Wooster, OH 44691

You Slept Here When you go back to school at George Washington University, you do it in style. Alumni College classes are held at Airlie House, a converted estate designed as a conference center with tennis, swimming, hiking, riding, and fishing. The subject matter is sober but fascinating: "Augustine," "The Enigma of Man Destined for Good yet Inclined Toward Evil," or "Thucydides on Athens." There are no accommodations for young children at Airlie House.

General Alumni Association
George Washington University
Alumni House
Washington, DC 20052

Rhode to Knowledge Rhode Island may be a teen-tiny state, but the University of Rhode Island's Vacation College is no little thing. It's an expansive and thoroughly attractive program, with components ranging from European Cake Decorating through Oriental Rug Making to Subliminal Advertising and Introduction to Graphology. Cooking classes abound, and some languages are offered. The Vacation College is geared to mesh well with a summer music series, excellent summer theaters, and a couple of award-winning summer film series. There are daytime and evening versions, so inquire for full details.

URI Vacation College
204 Green Hall
University of Rhode Island
Kingston, RI 02881

A liberal education . . . frees a man from the prison-house of his class, race, time, place, background, family, and even his nation.
ROBERT MAYNARD HUTCHINS

Suddenly—There's the Clearing

The Clearing is a place where one feels "the beginning, and the true importance, of nature and of life." Simple as that statement seems, it profoundly sums up the philosophy of the late Jens Jensen, a noted architect and founder of The Clearing—a vacation school for adults.

Now sponsored by the Wisconsin Farm Bureau—a private coalition of farming families—The Clearing beckons to all adults, regardless of age. "Happiness and full self-expression," Jensen thought, "can only be found by spreading one's roots in the soil." The Clearing is a place where one can do exactly that.

Situated on 128 acres of forested land on the tip of the Wisconsin peninsula, The Clearing offers a rich menu of one-week courses running from late spring through fall. You can study spring birds, French, religion and society, chamber music, or even Mother Goose nursery rhymes. All are investigated at The Clearing.

Weekly classes begin with Sunday supper and end with Saturday breakfast. All vacationers are in residence at The Clearing, where meals are served family style and enrollment is limited to 28 members per week. Cost of one week is about $150—including tuition, room, and board—and visitors who wish to "peek" at the program are invited to drop in any Sunday afternoon. —R.McG.

The Clearing
Ellison Bay, WI 54210

Intellectual Feast

Hors d'Oeuvres: films, drama, musical comedy, choral and folksong concerts for the mind. Swimming, golf, and tennis for the body.

First Course: an excursion into the history of New England. Visit the haunts of Ethan Allen, Harriet Beecher Stowe, and Mark Twain. A ferry ride to a flagstone castle built by the famous Sherlock Holmes thespian, William Gillette.

Entree: take an intellectual odyssey from your personal island of dullness to the campus of Wesleyan University and discover the patterns emerging from the seas of seeming chaos. Freud may douse you in discontent, or Faust may drive you toward redemption. Marx and Engels may prophesy your destiny, or Buckminster Fuller may whisper of doomsday.

But fear not these ill tidings: Euclid and Euripides, Shakespeare and Sterne will also be your companions at Wesleyan's summer seminar. The faculty, in concert with these illustrious figures, will help you find your way to intellectual rejuvenation.

Dessert: crafts and music performance. "Drumming" will teach you basic rhythmic patterns of Ghana; "Drawing" will start from the beginning for bashful amateurs.

Children's programs abound as well, and prices are reasonable (about $100 for a full week, including room and tuition). —J.A.

Office of Alumni Relations
Wesleyan University
Middletown, CT 06457

New Beginnings

Road Scholars

Phaedra Phoxy has an unusual plastic surgery problem. She's visited dozens of surgeons. They all laugh and send her away; they refuse to have anything to do with her case.

She has no double chin, and her face is wrinkle-free. Her bust doesn't sag, and she has no visible scars. In fact, she is only in her mid-twenties. So what's the problem?

Phaedra Phoxy has her heart set on joining the Elderhostel movement, a national program that combines the best of education and hosteling traditions. The catch is that you have to be at least 60 to take part. Phaedra wants to be able to spend a week at different campuses during the summer, attending noncredit liberal arts courses. She loves the idea of no grades, no exams, and no homework.

You might wonder why she doesn't simply keep her 25-year-old identity and audit regular college courses. Ah, she says, it isn't the same thing at all! Phaedra craves the exchange of ideas that's possible only with people who have experienced 60 or more years of living in the world.

Elderhostel is a network of over 200 colleges in 30 states that offer low-cost, one-week residential academic programs for older citizens during the summer months. Each session is limited to 30-40 elders. They start on Sunday evening and end on Saturday night (or later).

At each campus hostelers choose from at least three informal courses, all taught by regular faculty members. No previous knowledge is necessary, though some hostelers have MA or PhD degrees. Many have little or no formal education.

In 1979 the maximum charge is $115/week, covering room, board, tuition, and extracurricular activities (like panty or pantry raids). Some public agencies have offered subsidies.

Program administrators are amazed at the stamina of senior citizens. They quickly adjust to the minor inconveniences of dormitory life: sharing bathrooms, doing without elevators. They tramp across campuses without complaining.

Courses do *not* include the standard gerontological repertory ("Making Retirement Work," etc.). Older people really don't want courses on aging.

The program was begun by Martin Knowlton and David Bianco in 1975 at the University of New Hampshire, with 220 students at five nearby colleges. By the summer of 1978 the total national enrollment had increased to over 10,000.

Of each $105 fee, $9 goes to the regional office and $1 to the national office. The rest goes to cover tuition, board, and room. There is no fat bureaucracy.

Phaedra Phoxy has not given up. There *is* one exception to the minimum age restriction: if she were to marry a 60-year-old hosteler, then she *could* take part. All you single oldsters had better watch out! —L.S.

Elderhostel
55 Chapel St.
Newton, MA 02160

Go to the Head of the Class

How would you like to be teacher *and* star pupil for a day? If you're a recently retired professional or executive, you can have your day at the head of the class.

The New School's Institute for Retired Professionals is a unique opportunity in adult education. The program was developed in 1962 by retirees themselves, with the help and encouragement of the University.

This do-it-yourself teaching/learning program provides the intellectual stimulation and creative atmosphere that is necessary to a continued learning and growing process. At the Institute for Retired Professionals, you once again become an initiator, a doer, a learner, and a teacher.

Volunteers from the membership devise the curriculum for the 80 courses or "groups" currently meeting and arrange the recruitment of lecturers from the membership. At each session a different member presents a research paper, making him or her teacher for the day.

The many courses offered fall into these general categories: the Current Scene, Language Studies, Literature, The Arts, Science and Math, Workshops (guitar, drama, yoga, etc.), and the Social Sciences.

The yearly membership fee is $265 and also entitles students to take one course per semester at the New School. —B.H.

Institute for Retired Professionals
New School for Social Research
66 W. 12th St.
New York, NY 10011

Second Wind

Over 40 years ago you traipsed down the auditorium aisle to grab that long-awaited high school diploma. No more pencils, no more books, no more teachers' dirty looks. But that was over 40 years ago, and now you're ready to learn some more about yourself and the world around you.

If you're hesitant about going back to school after a hiatus of 40 years or so, the College at 60 Program could be what you're looking for. This special opportunity for students 50 years old and up was founded in 1973. At that time it offered one seminar, "Major Philosophies of Life," and was attended by 14 students. Today there are over 20 seminars available and more than 200 students enrolled.

A sampling of the courses offered includes: Ancient Egypt and Israel; The 20th Century Novel; The Art of Film; Psychology of Adulthood; Maturing and Aging; New Look at Economics and Politics; Understanding Music; Math and the Computer; and Our Changing Environment.

The program is open to anyone capable of undertaking college level work. Tuition is charged. Upon successful completion of four seminars, students may enter Fordham's College of Liberal Arts without having to meet any additional admission requirements. —B.H.

College at 60 Program
Fordham University
113 W. 60th St.
New York, NY 10023

All that I know
I learned after I was thirty.
GEORGES CLEMENCEAU

Finishing School

Perhaps the most valuable resource America has is the deep well of talent and ability that exists—largely untapped—in our senior citizens. Twenty colleges and universities in Minnesota are trying hard to cultivate that resource.

As an extension of the nationwide Elderhostel movement, a program for persons over 60, Minnesota's institutions of higher education have put together a dazzling array of college-type courses for seniors, totaling 28 weeks of instruction throughout the summer.

The cost is low ($75 per week, including room and board), and the quality exceedingly high. Courses are well designed for maximum appeal and learning. It is folly to try to list them all, but a sampling yields the flavor: Dream Journey to Germany (no travel, just mental voyaging), The Faust Tradition, Hatha Yoga, Children's Literature, The Making of Modern America, Detective Fiction, and Exploring Music in Our Environment.

The scope is as wide as the traditional college curriculum, and the course material is not watered down. It is taught by regular members of college faculties. Elderhostel says it is for "any older person who has not finished learning." We heartily concur. —J.A.

Minnesota Elderhostel
201 Westbrook Hall
77 Pleasant St., SE
Minneapolis, MN 55455

Indian Summer

For those of you 60 or over who still have an urge to discover, consider exploring the 1979 Pacific Northwest Elderhostels program. Last year the Northwest Region offered courses in astronomy, local history, American literature, Russian literature, and roadside geology, to name only a few.

In 1977 the University of Montana became the first school in the West to offer Elderhostel. It became the Pacific Northwest regional headquarters for the program in 1978 and now directs colleges and universities in Montana, Oregon, Idaho, and Washington.

Courses are supplemented with field trips and recommended readings and are conducted at an academic level comparable to that of the regular offerings at each institution.

One hosteler from last year's program remarked, "You get sick and tired . . . with most senior citizens' programs . . . the mind is ageless." Tim Welsh, director of the Pacific Northwest Region, says that hostelers "don't hesitate to smoke out the best and worst instructors on the first day." Hundreds of older men and women will flock to the participating Northwest schools this summer, hungry for classroom experience and relief from patronizing social service programs. Join them if you can. —B.Hu.

Northwest Region Elderhostel
University of Montana
Main Hall 107
Missoula, MT 59812

In the midst of winter,
I finally learned that there was in me
an invincible summer.
ALBERT CAMUS

For Those Who Think Young

Beauty, says the philosopher, starts in the eye. And adventure, says Pace University's Active Retirement Center begins in the *mind*. Think "dull," and the world will be drab. Think "exciting," and new vistas will open all around you.

To help "active retirees" think "exciting" Pace offers special programs on its three campuses: New York City, White Plains, and Pleasantville. Its Active Retirement Center (PARC) helps members (men and women 55 and older) stretch their intellectual horizons. Membership is a mere $25 a year (plus a pledge to enroll in at least one course per year). But there is one more requirement: members must bring with them, from past experience, something of value to share with others. The indifferent are not welcome.

As a PARC member you may audit or enroll for credit in an astonishing array of disciplines, among them art and music, drama, economics, education, English, foreign languages, psychology, history, marketing and management, speech, and many more.

The Center also operates a Job Placement Service for members interested in full-time, part-time, volunteer, or even "once-in-a-while" jobs, some of them within the University.

PARC is dedicated to the proposition that great events take place—first—in the mind. They are there to help such events happen. —D.H.

Active Retirement Center
School of Continuing Education
Pace University
New York, NY 10038

Hostel Environment If you're over 60 and have a hankering to go back to college—but only for a little while—the Elderhostel program is right up your alley. You stay on the campus of one of the sponsoring colleges, taking up to three courses while you live in the dorms and eat in the college dining hall. Among courses offered by Florida Elderhostel are mental gymnastics, poetry and fiction writing, music history, world religions, personal development, and theater arts. Cost is $115 for your one-week stay.

Florida Elderhostel
Eckherd College
P.O. Box 12560
St. Petersburg, FL 33733

Boola Boola College Days for Retired Persons is a program held each summer at Auburn University. Educational workshops cover such wide-ranging topics as first aid for choking and weatherizing the home. Recreational activities run the gamut from pine straw weaving to fishing and golf. Fees are modest enough to fit the tight budget of any retired person. Write for information on this summer's program.

Auburn University
Office of Continuing Education
208 Samford Hall
Auburn, AL 36830

Grand Hostel Elderhostel is in North Carolina, too. Among courses offered in the 1978 program were television production, Appalachian music and dance, the literature of Thomas Wolfe, nutrition, and Afro-American music. Elderhostel also offers a number of social and recreational activities for participants, depending on which campus facilities are available.

Continuing Education
204 Abernathy Hall 002-A
University of North Carolina
Chapel Hill, NC 27514

Anyone who stops learning is old,
whether at 20 or 80.
Anyone who keeps on learning stays young.
The greatest thing in life
is to keep your mind young.
HENRY FORD

Remember that the most beautiful things in the world are the most useless, peacocks and lilies for instance.
JOHN RUSKIN

The Call of the Wild

As we go about our citified lives—our jobs, our homes, our schools and supermarkets—occasionally we pause and hear it: a sweet, silvery, earthly song wafting out of the mountains and forests.

It echoes off the rocky cliffs of the Grand Tetons and the icy splendors of Alaska's untouched wilderness. It drifts gracefully past the Spanish moss and up the lazy rivers of the Everglades. It rides the wind of seacoasts, and carries with it the enchantment of trackless places. It is the siren song of the wilderness.

In these pages we've tuned into that special sound. We've found—for you—unmatched experiences in the wildernesses of the world. Some of them are one-to-one treks into the wild; others are less demanding physically but are no less rewarding.

You'll find rugged courses in outdoor survival and winter living. Right beside them, you'll find opportunities for learning basic backpacking skills while seeing the splendors of Banff, Yosemite, or the historic Blue Ridge Mountains.

There is no perfection like nature's perfection. And urban creatures that we are, we are drawn back to the world that nature created. Jack London termed it "the call of the wild" and we are at a loss for a better description.

What we've tried to gather in this chapter is a dual approach to the wild: a set of chances to experience it in a safe, responsible way, and a set of programs whose purpose is to keep some of the wild, wild.

So we've included backpacking forest treks and schools of glacier climbing. We've got birdwatching programs and seminars whose classroom is the habitat of nature's animal wonders.

But we also present some people who have organized to save the wilderness as we experience and study it. You'll meet the Sierra Club and the National Audubon Society here. You'll be able to choose wildlife and ecology programs worldwide, ranging from "Life in Suffolk Churchyards" to tropical studies in Hawaii; from African safaris guided by biologists to Yosemite birding treks.

Prick up your ears and listen. The harmony of nature sings a song of incredible perfection. And if you want to listen more closely, these pages will help.

Sand, Mountain, & Shore

Southwest Safaris

The small plane dipped down and back—back into time itself. Back to the days of the cowboy and his horse. Back to the time of the Indian and his civilization. Back further still, to an era of ancient inland seas, of volcanoes and tiny cracks in the ground that widened into gullies, then gorges, and finally, into great canyons . . .

The campers sipped their coffee and made small talk, as the sun faded well below the vast horizon. All afternoon they had jeeped through a maze of buttes and spires, down through the heart of the deep gorge. Their day of natural history gave way to a night sky clustered with more stars than any of them had ever seen. The fire crackled, as a distant coyote sang his song . . .

They reined their horses, and began the climb to the Indian cliff dwellings that were carved into the great wall above them. Their guide pointed to the Indian pictographs and the unusual geologic formations. He told them of the Chaco Indians, who had built multi-storied apartment complexes, paved highways, and developed irrigation systems. He told them of their religion based on sophisticated astronomical observations. The Chacos had accomplished these things in this area several centuries before the birth of Christ . . .

Rubber rafts bumped and slid through the river waters, splashing the occupants with chilly, white foam. The rapids passed quickly, and they soon meandered through a long stretch of calm beauty. The passengers eased slowly to the shore, in order to investigate nature's touches firsthand. Dinner that night was a barbecue, and the camp was an ancient Indian ceremonial ground . . .

The American Southwest does not necessarily roll off the lips when great tour spots of the world are mentioned. Many people forget that the Grand Canyon, Monument Valley, the Petrified Forest, the San Juan Goosenecks, the Painted Desert, Los Alamos, the Colorado River, Mesa Verde, the Rio Grande, and the Rocky Mountains are among the sites that can be found in this corner of the world.

They call it the "Four Corners" region, the one place in the United States where four states come together and kiss at right angles. Utah and Colorado are on top; Arizona and New Mexico below. Contrasts run deep in this land. Cloud-capped mountains, deep purple canyons, endless deserts, roaring rivers, and the great plains all coexist here. The opportunities for the study of natural environments are enormous.

Southwest Safaris will show you the Southwest by plane, jeep, horse, and raft—a perspective that goes well beyond the typical nature tour. Their pilots/guides/experts will lecture on the natural history, geology, archaeology, and culture of the region, en route. Their deluxe holiday is a six-day air/land/river expedition covering the Four Corners region. It is scheduled from April to October at a cost of $659. One-day air/land adventures to selected locations are also featured, as well as two- to three-day natural history treks and winter expeditions. —C.McB.

Southwest Safaris
P.O. Box 945
Santa Fe, NM 87501

And Please Don't Feed the Bears

You can't go to Yosemite without becoming convinced that Mother Nature has absolutely no restraint. From the floor of the Yosemite Valley to the heights of the Sierras, she displays her prodigality like a Medici courtesan, wearing all her most dazzling jewels at once.

Can there be a better natural laboratory than Yosemite? Its hundreds of waterfalls, its snowcapped mountains, its abundance of animal and floral variety, make it the ideal location for a group called The Yosemite Institute.

The Yosemite Institute is a nonprofit teaching group whose Board members include industrialists, publishers, lawyers, writers, and politicians—as well as conservationists. The teaching programs offered by the Institute are centered largely on their installation at Crane Flat, a breathtaking site 6200 feet above sea level. Learning experiences include nature hikes, lectures, snowshoe treks, studies of Indian lore and artifacts, and close encounters with the plants and animals. The program's components are in eight major areas: botany, zoology, history, aesthetics, philosophy, geology, the politics of land use—and a wonderfully romantic capper—winter survival.

If you want to find out the facts about using virgin redwood as lumber, about the relationship between black bears and man, about the land and its creatures, the Yosemite Institute should be high on your list of preferred alternatives. —J.A.

Field Trips Program
Yosemite Institute
P.O. Box 487
Yosemite, CA 95389

The Hawaii Experience

Ah, yes! you say. The Hawaii Experience. Leis over the head, as you step off the plane. Being whisked to your high-rise, beach-view hotel. Rum drinks full of fruit, flower-shirted night life, shopping.

Ah, no! we say. The Hawaii Experience is hikes through steaming volcanoes and dense bamboo forests. It is camping on remote beaches, and snorkeling among reefs teeming with tropical fish. It is exploring ancient Hawaiian temples.

If you go for the first scenario, then check with any travel agent. But, if the second catches your fancy, Sea Trek Hawaii is the only way to go.

This 18-day educational tour of Hawaii is an award-winning program designed for the adventurous and inquisitive. Through lectures, films, and on-sight inspections, you'll find the heart and soul of these sunny islands, the Hawaii most tourists never begin to see. The emphasis is on learning in one of the most beautiful classrooms in the world.

The tour is open to groups of 15 to 30. The $675 price covers all expenses. There is also an 11-day tour available at a cost of $450. —C.McB.

The Hawaii Experience
Sea Trek Hawaii
47-696-1 Hui Kelu St.
Kaneohe, HI 96744

On Sea-Fari

Unspoiled Baja California is a mosaic of ecological islands—rocky sea coast, mangrove swamp, desert, alpine meadow—and is one of the finest natural laboratories in the world. On the islands off the coast live bizarre, sometimes unique plants and animals. You can now place yourself in this scene by joining a Sea-Fari Natural History Adventure to Baja.

Travel on a Coast Guard-approved ship, complete with a naturalist's library and an onboard video system, to several remote islands and coastal destinations. Visit the San Ignacio Lagoon, where the California gray whale ends its stately migratory parade to breed and raise young. What you do at the stops is up to you—you can choose between leisurely exploration or vigorous activity. Naturalists are on hand to answer questions and offer talk and slide shows on board ship in the evenings.

Trips range in length from four days to a little over a week. Prices—from $290 to $550—include all meals and accommodations. Special charters for groups are available. College credit may be arranged in advance through several universities. —A.E.

Sea-Fari Natural History Expeditions
H & M Landing
2803 Emerson St.
San Diego, CA 92106

Old Geysers of New Zealand

There are those who swear that New Zealand dropped into the Pacific one day and is not, in fact, part of the earth at all. Their evidence? Strange vegetation and unique animal life—like, for example, the flightless kiwi. The truth is that New Zealand was separated fom other land masses for almost 200 millions years, so its flora and fauna evolved in isolation. Without predatory land animals, even flightless birds could survive. It's a fascinating land of volcanoes and geysers, of geological fireworks that result from its location on the "Ring of Fire," an active tectonic zone. New Zealand Natural History Discovery offers two 23-day tours, which leave Los Angeles in early February, when it's summer in New Zealand. If you're interested in studying natural history while you travel, these tours may just be for you.

Highlight: a five-day safari—led by Maoris—through Urewera National Park, the ancestral Maori lands. The park, like much of New Zealand, is largely unspoiled. The base for the safari is Rotorua, the center of an intense geothermal zone, where the air smells of sulphur and lakes are known to boil. Highlight: Fox Glacier, and the beaches of the Tasman Sea, where sea birds line the cliffs, and fur seals bask in the sun. Highlight: A four-day field trip through the remote wilderness of Mt. Aspiring and Fiordland National Parks, where you'll hike through virgin rain forests, frolic in alpine meadows, and explore glacial lakes. And more: three days in Tongariro National Park, where you can climb a volcano, see a fumarole, take a white-water rafting trip, and explore remote sections of the park on horseback. A visit to the Waitomo Caves, and an underground boat ride in Glowworm Grotto, where you can find yourself under a shimmering canopy of more than a million glowworms.

Accommodations are in hotels and lodges, as well as in huts and tents. Transportation is by air, bus, and train. When you hike, you carry only a small daypack and travel over moderate trails at a rate of no more than ten miles a day. The cost: $2475 round trip from Los Angeles includes everything, except a few lunches. College credit is obtainable from the University of California, Santa Barbara—$40 for three postgraduate units. —A.E.

New Zealand Natural History Discovery
Pacific Exploration Company
Box 3042
Santa Barbara, CA 93105

Mountains are the beginning and the end of all natural scenery.
JOHN RUSKIN

Highland Haven

You've been through the 50 states and, fun as birding is, you despair at ever seeing a new species. Or maybe it's just time for a change of scene—time perhaps to explore the Scottish Highlands, Aigas Field Centre's turf.

Wildlife and field study holidays are the emphasis, but with a Highland twist. Bird residents, for example, include puffins, ptarmigans, and Slavonian grebes. Bog cotton, sundew, and gray seals number among the other flora and fauna.

Since natural treats are the Aigas specialty, the programs are structured to include fall, spring, and summer flora and fauna. Come in April and your visit will differ—totally—from last year's August experience.

Sessions last for six days, and cost ranges from $200 to $400. Beginners and experienced naturalists are both welcome—one need bring only a "waterproof, a stout pair of walking shoes or boots, a knapsack, binoculars, and an ever-inquiring mind." —R.McG.

Highland Wildlife Enterprises
Aigas Field Centre
Beauly, Inverness-shire IV4 7AD
Scotland, UK

Hut Two, Three, Four...

For most hikers, the appeal of a mountain trip is settling down to a hot meal by a warm fire at the end of a day. On extended trips, however, this bit of relaxation is preceded by setting up a new camp before sunset. For folks who prefer to enjoy the scenery without worrying about where to make camp each night, the Appalachian Mountain Club's Friendly Huts are made to order.

The AMC, under a special permit from the U.S. Forest Service, maintains eight huts spaced a day's hike apart in the White Mountains of New Hampshire.

The hut system provides an extensive trail network through some of New England's highest peaks. Hikers can enjoy their travel without the burden of a heavy backpack. Trails vary in elevation from 2000 to 4000 feet and wander through forests, tundra, and alpine areas. It's in these locations that hikers are treated to mountain views of up to 100 miles. The huts are an especially welcome accommodation by the end of an active day.

The huts are equipped with bedding and bunks, and visitors can obtain both supper and breakfast. Hikers should bring trail food, personal items, and clothing appropriate for the changing mountain weather. Daily rates range from $10 to $14. Some huts are open on a limited basis throughout the year, while others operate only in the spring and summer. —G.R.

The Friendly Huts
Guided Overnight Hikes
Appalachian Mountain Club
Pinkham Notch Camp
Gorham, NH 03581

Okefenokee and All That Swamp

Some of the great untouched outdoor spaces that manage to survive in these United States are located in the states of the Old South. And it is to just those places that Wilderness Southeast addresses itself—and you.

There are high country adventures near Slickrock Creek in North Carolina, replete with trout streams that flow through waterfall-y gorges. There's the Cattooga River and the Great Okefenokee Swamp, with its endangered alligators.

There's a guided expedition through the Smoky Mountains in search of seldom-seen flora and fauna. There's backpacking in Appalachia at the peak season for flowering shrubs, with unending vistas of color. There are snorkeling tours of the Coral Reefs in the Florida Keys.

And there are riches in the Sea Islands of Georgia—the Catfish Row of song and story.

Programs are geared to short time periods (weekends, three days, four days), and the prices vary from $52 to $75 per person. Longer programs are available, with prices commensurately higher. —J.A.

Wilderness Southeast
Route 3
Box 619 Whitfield
Savannah, GA 31406

I know a bank whereon
the wild thyme blows,
Where oxlips and
the nodding violet grows
Quite over-canopied
with luscious woodbine
With sweet musk-roses
and with eglantine.
WILLIAM SHAKESPEARE

Hotsprings in Iceland Iceland has something for everyone. For geologists, there are hotsprings and glaciers. For botanists, there are bogs and marshes. For birders, there are 241 species of winged friends . . . Florida—an equally rich environment with the Everglades, scrublands, and wildlife refuges. Consider these field trips: Iceland, two weeks, $1300. Florida, in February, $500.

Field Trips Program
Maine Audubon Society
118 Old US Route 1
Falmouth, ME 04105

All Come to Look for America The social and natural ecology of America is explored with the assistance of over 100 specialists in Expedition Institute programs. Maine tidepool inhabitants, Smithsonian fossil studies, and Pennsylvania Amish community relations serve as both textbooks and classrooms. Courses run on a year-round ($4900), semester ($3300), intersession ($480), and summer-term basis ($160).

Expedition Institute
National Audubon Society
950 Third Ave.
New York, NY 10022

Baja Bound See nature as it has been, with a visit to Baja. Cruise on a vessel complete with a natural history library. Head to the Sea of Cortez (eight days, $695), or explore the cave paintings of the "Great Mural" region (two weeks, $495). Trips run year-round.

Baja Expeditions, Inc.
P.O. Box 3725
San Diego, CA 92103

There's More Than Dust in the Desert "Outdoor interpretation" and the scientific stories behind the wonders of Utah's canyons are the focus here. Examine the forces that carve canyons, and look for Indian inscriptions. Three-day sessions run from April to September. Cost: $15 per session. Families are invited to attend.

Desert Ecology/Nature Workshops
Canyonlands Environmental
Education Center
Box 177
Moab, UT 84532

Wild Classrooms

You'll never be the same again. That's the likely result if you take a wilderness university course from the University of California Extension, Santa Cruz.

Be forewarned—these backpacking trips are strenuous. Ranging in length from a week to a school quarter, Wilderness Studies trips emphasize particular environments of the American West. Example: The Rocky Mountains, a 15-unit, spring-quarter course, is a trek following the migration of big horn sheep. Example: The Grand Canyon, a two-unit, one-week course, is a backpacking trip down the north rim to the Colorado River to do field study of canyon evolution and plant and animal ecosystems. Example: Natural History Field Quarter in Hawaii, a 16-unit, one-quarter course offering a personalized field program in earth history and ecology in the magnificent Hawaiian back-country.

Individual studies are encouraged, and plenty of time for solitude is allowed. Costs, which range from $50 to $320, depending on the number of credits, cover instruction only. You are responsible for your own transportation and must supply equipment. A certificate of health is also required. —A.E.

Wilderness Studies Program
University of California
Extension Office
Santa Cruz, CA 95064

Rated: Exotic

As you sit around the campfire in the African evening, the Director of the Los Angeles Zoo will present his talk on the animals that you saw that day. Or, as you float down the Amazon on a riverboat, your botany professor will identify the flora in the tropical rain forests along the way. In the company of scholar/guides and in the setting of the exotic, you can acquaint yourself with the richness of unfamiliar environments by joining a Natural History/Tropical Ecology Tour offered by the University of California, Los Angeles.

In the midst of the botanical paradise of Costa Rica, you can study tropical horticulture for two full weeks. In the living laboratory of evolution, the Galapagos Islands, you can learn about ecology in the field for 13 days. You can witness the behavior of animals in the wild and study their environment on a 24-day excursion to Zambia and Botswana. Or you can live on remote islands in the Sea of Cortez, attending lectures and guided natural history hikes by day and camping out by night.

College credit is available through the University of California. Cost of instruction and tuition varies with the individual trip. Travel arrangements to the natural history destinations must be made through a travel agent. —A.E.

Natural History/Tropical
Ecology Expeditions
Dept. of Biological & Physical Sciences
P.O. Box 24902
University of California
Los Angeles, CA 90024

Behold the Birds & the Beasts

Unearthly Earthly Locations

This world of ours—the one we keep getting told has no frontiers—is a globe full of surprises. There are still plenty of unearthly earthly locations, and two of these are featured in Society Expeditions' treks to Galapagos and Antarctica.

Nearly 150 years ago, the young British scientist Charles Darwin saw the sights you'll see in the Galapagos Islands. His voyage became one of the most storied expeditions of all time. Why? Well, in Galapagos, you'll see modern-day descendents of dinosaurs and dragons, creeping with scaly paws over lands untouched since prehistory. The fearsome land iguana looks like St. George's opponent with its four-footed, four-foot-long body and its armor of red and orange.

But Galapagos has inhabitants other than modern-day dragons. The skies of Galapagos resound to the cries of seabirds rare and legendary: frigate birds, with wingspans of nearly eight feet; boobies, albatross, hawks, penguins (yes, penguins), and cormorants. The waters frolic with porpoise and whales, and the nearly extinct fur seal is slowly rebuilding his population within this isolated environ.

If you prefer the snow, there's always the South Pole and the stretches of Antarctica. There is no destination more remote or more unspoiled by the encroachments of civilization. You'll travel along the Patagonian Coast of Argentina, and onward to the ice mountains and spectacular vistas of the Antarctic Peninsula. For those travelers with an interest in wildlife, you'll marvel at the tame behavior of Antarctica's residents. You'll walk right up to tuxedo-suited penguins, and snap a super closeup. Your party will be witness to the earth-shattering mating calls of nearby sea elephants. Your boat will be accompanied by whales spouting alongside.

A staff of naturalists accompany both the Antarctic and Galapagos cruises, and lectures are given regularly on such topics as marine biology, wildlife, ornithology, and geology. Your three-week Galapagos jaunt—including Quito, Ecuador, as your jumping-off spot for the Islands—will cost about $2200, plus air fare. Your Antarctic expedition will also not be cheap, but prices will vary depending on the accommodations you choose. —J.A.

Project Galapagos/Project Antarctica
Society Expeditions
P.O. Box 5088
University Station
Seattle, WA 98105

A wonderful bird is the pelican,
His bill will hold more
than his belican.
He can take in his beak
Food enough for a week,
But I'm damned if I see
how the helican.

DIXON LANIER MERRITT

Gorillas Galore Forest-dwelling gorillas rarely have visitors, but you can be one of that select lot when you join a gorilla safari. Gorillas, we hear, are shy, reclusive creatures who are "rather curious of large primates such as ourselves." Adventures run for 16 days in July. Cost is $2415. Kenya safaris are also available.

Wildlife & Gorilla Safaris
Adventures International
4421 Albert St.
Oakland, CA 94619

Where the Deer & the Antelope Play The Africa you read about can now become a reality. Bongo, kudu, cheetah, and gazelle can all become more than mere names on a Kenya Adventure that includes in-field lectures and seminars by wildlife experts. The tour in February is $2567 for 18 days and includes all expenses.

Kenya Adventure
Smithsonian Associates
A & I Room 1278
Smithsonian Institution
Washington, DC 20560

We hope that, when the insects take over the world, they will remember with gratitude how we took them along on all our picnics.
BILL VAUGHAN

Night of the Iguana The Enchanted Isles are not merely found in fairy tales and legends but are the name given to the Galapagos Islands by Nature Expeditions International. You can be introduced to short-eared owls, American oystercatchers, and marine iguanas in this greatest natural laboratory on earth. Slide lectures and informal discussions are a nightly feature. Trip length: 20 days. Cost: $1390.

Expedition to the Galapagos Islands
Nature Expeditions International
599 College Ave.
Palo Alto, CA 94306

Do Monkeys Really Eat Bananas?

It is one thing to read books about animals, and still another to observe them in controlled environments, like zoos. Monkeys in the Caribbean, fish in Hawaii, insects in Ecuador—here are animals climbing, swimming, and buzzing in their natural habitats. And here is a dimension that allows us to comprehend the mysteries of who they really are.

Through the University Research Expeditions Program, you can be where the animals are and aid, as well, in serious research related to their behavior and environment. The program unites scientists and laymen, allowing each to draw from the other's presence. Scientist-layman teams have studied the population and ecology of the vervet monkey on St. Kitts Island in the Caribbean. Underwater collections of tropical fish in Hawaii's Kaneohe Bay have been undertaken. The jungles of Ecuador have been the site for the examination of plant/insect relationships.

Field projects vary from year to year, with most running for a period of three weeks. Laymen are expected to contribute between $400 and $1400 (depending on the project) to cover expenses. Laymen need only show a keen interest and serious desire to participate. —C.McB.

University Research Expeditions Program
University of California
Berkeley, CA 94720

Conservationist Safaris

A hundred years ago, "safari" meant a great, gory killing expedition. The successful safari-goer had, as trophies, the tusks of elephants, the heads of tigers, and the feet of rhinoceroses. Such predation is not the forte of the Conservationist Safaris, as you might already tell from their name.

Abercrombie and Kent sponsor worldwide safaris, but it is their conservationist trips that have an outstanding educational component. You'll be taken to Kenya, India, and Nepal, where you'll track wildlife on foot, accompanied by experienced guides. You'll watch hippos wallowing in river pools, crocodiles coming for bait, and experienced tribal dancers in their villages. The trips take advantage of newly created National Parks and wildlife preserves in their host countries—such as Dudwa and Karnali Parks in Nepal, and Aberdare and Mt. Kenya National Parks in Kenya.

If you have a yen to travel to vanishing wildlife wildernesses, the Conservationist Safaris may be just the ticket you want. Accommodations are luxurious, and prices match the accommodations. This could be the wildlife vacation of a lifetime. —J.A.

The Conservationist Safaris
Abercrombie & Kent International, Inc.
1000 Oak Brook Rd.
Oak Brook, IL 60521

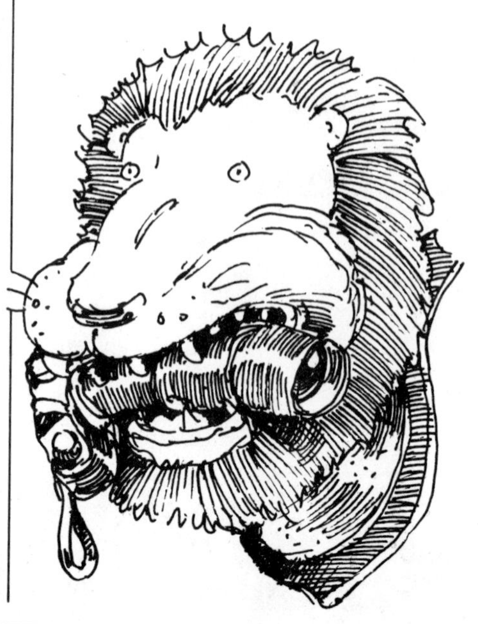

Birding in Your Own Back Yard

We promise not to tell you that this program is for the birds. We promise, too, not to say that you shouldn't duck it.

Ornithology, of course, is the study of birds—birds of all sizes, shapes, and kinds. Through scientific and educational activities, the Cornell University Laboratory of Ornithology helps to expand our knowledge and appreciation of these flying creatures. One of the ways in which the laboratory does this is through a nine-lesson home study course in bird biology that is written and graded by its expert staff members. The lessons, which are beautifully illustrated and cost $13 each, cover the evolution of birds, their behavior and nesting, the growth of their young, and migration.

The laboratory also serves as a world center for the study of birds. It sponsors summer field seminars for both beginner and advanced bird enthusiasts. The week-long seminars consist of lectures and field trips to various bird habitats in the Ithaca area. Costs vary from $140 to $240, depending upon housing arrangements.

We promise not to say that a wise old owl told us so. —C.McB.

Bird Biology Home Study Course
Laboratory of Ornithology
Cornell University
159 Sapsucker Woods Rd.
Ithaca, NY 14853

Birds in the Bush

Rachel Carson's pioneering book on ecology, *Silent Spring*, pictured what a world would be like without birds. What would a town be like without the familiar calls of winged neighbors? The picture was eerie.

Jornee Unlimited has the opposite picture—birds of all kinds in all kinds of places. They offer birding and wildlife expeditions to Senegal, Hawaii, Nepal, Trinidad, Polynesia, Israel, Peru, and Tanzania—to mention just a few.

Each tour is led by a naturalist with good academic credentials, and regular programs on ornithology and zoology are included in the schedules. Proper attention is paid to the irresistible impulse to take pictures. And what pictures you will take!

You'll see birds like the long-tailed cuckoo, the kaka, and the pied tit. You'll see glowworms and Inca ruins. You'll see van-tailed manakins and tropical rain forests. You'll marvel at African fishhawks soaring high over elephant herds. In fact, if you can name a place famous for its abundant bird life, Jornee Unlimited most probably goes there. Prices vary with destinations. —J.A.

Worldwide Birdwatching Experiences
Jornee Unlimited, Inc.
40 Hungerford St.
Suite 300
Hartford, CT 06106

Close Encounters of the Bird Kind If the only birds you ever get to see are seagulls by the shore or pigeons by the bench, then it's about time for a change. A tropical change, that is, to Panama or Costa Rica, where bird buffs unite in ornithology workshops. Over 760 species are awaiting your binoculars. Bored with parakeets and canaries? This might just be the tour for you.

Tropical Ornithology Workshops
Holbrook Travel, Inc.
3520 N.W. 13th St.
Gainesville, FL 32601

Let the Coyotes Point It Out One fine day, you might just find yourself in the "Mexican Mountains" of southeastern Arizona. And if you do, the Coyote Birdguide Service has a host of trained guides to keep you thoroughly entertained. How many sulphur-bellied flycatchers or coppery-tailed trogons do you encounter in your daily routine? Half-day (four-hour) rates are $20/person; full days (eight hours) are $30/person. Rates are halved for additional participants.

Coyote Birdguide Service of
Southeastern Arizona
P.O. Box 861
Patagonia, AZ 85624

Birds of the World, Unite! Twenty-six select tours to the richest birding areas on the face of the globe—from Tucson to Madagascar to the Yucatan—are available for bird buffs. These tours attend to human comforts, with an eye out for comfortable lodgings, fine restaurants, and a relaxed pace. Now you can learn how bird songs are really "the poetry of the earth."

Victor Emanuel Nature Tours, Inc.
P.O. Box 5789
Austin, TX 78763

Feathers in Florida Most people think of Florida as the land of hotels and transplanted Northeasterners. Not so! Remote wildlife area tours can be yours for the viewing in Glades County, the best representative of Florida's wilderness. Tours given by research biologists can be tailored in the direction of birds, vegetation, or ecology. One-day tours: $75/person. Wild turkeys await you.

Lykes Wildlife Wilderness Tours
Attn: Tour Consultant
4005 S. Main St.
Gainesville, FL 32601

Sweet Tweets

Birds are basically good folks.

They're clean, they're family types, they stick to their own kind, and they're often good singers. Oh, there's the occasional evil vulture and screaming blue jay, but every group has its few rotten apples. Mostly, though, birds have a good rep, as they like to say on Mad Ave.

Birds are also smart enough to go south in the winter, to work outdoors, to feather their nests, and not to smoke—which might help to explain why birdwatching has become more popular than people-watching of late.

If you are into birding, or think you'd like to give it a try, may we recommend the birding seminars held each spring and fall in California's lovely Yosemite National Park. Conducted by the Yosemite Natural History Association among the lakes, waterfalls, and redwoods of the Sierra Nevada, these outings appear to be a treat for both the beginner and the experienced watcher.

Three courses are offered to all interested, for three- and five-day periods. The prices are most reasonable: the three-day courses are $40, and the five-day course is $50. Participants are expected to provide their own camping gear and food and to be in good enough physical condition to engage in moderate hiking.

The basic Yosemite course is titled "Birds of Yosemite National Park: Their Populations and Breeding Ecology." It is conducted entirely in the field and delves into the flight, molt, migration, reproduction, and population dynamics of birds, as well as their identification by plumage and song.

The five-day course, "Birds of the Yosemite Sierra: Their Natural History and Breeding Ecology," offers similar instruction with an additional two days of identification techniques and avian diversity in the Yosemite Sierra. Five two-hour lectures and 30 hours of field laboratory work are included in this session.

The third offering is "Bird Migration in Yosemite: A Bird-Banding Workshop." Students gain actual field experience in bird-banding, record keeping, and data analysis. The course consists of 12 hours of lectures and 19 hours of field work.

Seminars are taught by avian experts, and college credits are available. —C.McB.

Birding Field Seminars
Yosemite Natural History Association
P.O. Box 545
Yosemite National Park, CA 95389

Seals & Bears on the Icepack

Hanns Ebensten Wildlife Adventures have a real touch of the wild to them. In March, for example, six-day expeditions head out to the frozen icepacks of Canada's Gulf of St. Lawrence to witness the migration and childbearing rituals of the harp seals. With the aid of helicopters, tour members enter into the midst of the seal herds for an intimate look at these gregarious mammals and their newborn white pups.

On the other hand, why not join a five-day venture to the vast Hudson Bay in northern Manitoba for a close-up view of the great white polar bear migration? The team's base, this time around, is in the town of Churchill, just 600 miles below the Arctic Circle. Land vehicles and helicopters will enable participants to watch these lumbering giants as they head for the bay's iceflows, their hunting grounds in winter.

A 17-day air/land/sea journey to see the ecology and wildlife of the Galapagos Islands is also available.

Tours are accompanied by specialists who provide expert briefings to travelers. Costs are: seals—$1085; polar bears—$1475; Galapagos—$1625; Hudson Bay—$1850. —C.McB.

Wildlife Adventures
Hanns Ebensten Travel, Inc.
55 West 42nd St.
New York, NY 10036

The Taming of the Vole—er—Shrew

Natural history has never been a subject that paled for lack of attention in Britain. There have been times in British history, in fact, when it seemed the animals were getting a better shake than the population at large.

Carrying the flame today is the Field Studies Council, which operates ten field centres throughout the UK. It appears to be the goal of FSC to offer courses in absolutely every aspect of nature and animal life. And as their latest catalogs reveal, they are well on the way.

You can study relatively commonplace topics, like the ecology of seabirds, insect behavior, mountain weather, and British mammals in the field. Or you can go for the abstruse: voles and shrews, the world of spiders, the life of polecats, ferrets, and their relatives, even "Wildlife in Suffolk Churchyards."

The field centres themselves are worth visiting, and give the feeling of stately (or at least once-stately) British homes. The curriculum is nothing short of fascinating. Most courses are one week in length. The standard fee is £52/week. —J.A.

Field Studies Council
Wildlife Programmes
Attn: The Information Office
Preston Montford
Montford Bridge
Shrewsbury, SY4 1HW
England, UK

Bagpipes & Badgers

Well now, laddie, did you hear the one about the Scotsman who got two birds with one scone? OK, we'll spare you our kilt jokes and get right back to the birds. Birdwatching, that is, in the land of bagpipes and Loch Ness monsters.

We refer to Scotland, of course, and to the Scottish Wildlife Holidays that are offered by the Caledonian Wildlife Services in Inverness.

These week-long holidays are conducted through the Scottish Highlands, a diverse terrain that allows for an amazing variety of animal habitats: rugged mountains with deer, eagle, and raven; lochs and streams with osprey, divers, goosander, and salmon; wild moors with golden plover, grouse, wild flowers; gentle woods with roe deer, badger, and songbirds; mudflats and gravel beaches with shelduck and scoters.

The tours, limited to ten people at a time, are based at the Tigh a' Mhuilinn (Gaelic for "House of the Mill") in Inverness. Day trips offer hiking from April to October. You are accompanied by local experts, and the reasonable week's cost (approximately $190 to $235 depending on the season) includes all amenities right down to binoculars. —C.McB.

Scottish Wildlife Holidays
Caledonian Wildlife Services
2 Kingsmills Gardens
Inverness, IV2 3LU
Scotland, UK

Tropical Trills

What a delight—a tropical delight—for bird fanciers, nature lovers, and plain old vacation seekers. We speak of the Trinidad and Tobago bird life study program run by Wonder Bird Tours of New York.

Serious birders may find their hearts taking wing at the thought of hundreds of color-splashed species to be found on these two Caribbean jewels. We're told it is not unusual for even experienced watchers to add 120 to 150 sightings to their "life-list" during the 15-day stay.

(Imagine an explosion in a paint factory as we give you a quick sampler of the island's winged natives: lilac-tailed parrotlets, green hermits, violaceous trogons, streaked xenops, purple honeycreepers, yellow-breasted flycatchers, and turquoise tanagers.)

The tour includes 12 field trips with local birding experts in attendance. In addition, summer trip-takers may participate in tropical ecology, entomology, nature photography, and ornithology seminars.

Travelers stay four nights at the Arnos Vale Hotel in Tobago (called a "Shangri-La" by the prestigious Fielding's Guide) and ten nights at the Asa Wright Nature Centre in Trinidad. Double-occupancy cost for the package, which includes air fare from New York, is $843 per person. —C.McB.

Trinidad & Tobago Bird Life Study
Wonder Bird Tours
500 Fifth Ave.
New York, NY 10036

British Words on the Birds

Some activities are done in private, and birdwatching may be one of them. But if you've grown lonely for company, you can join some of Britain's most respected ornithologists, and voyage to the Greek isle of Crete, Istanbul, or India.

Go for one week to Istanbul on the "Birds over the Bosphorous" tour, and take in the sight of thousands of eagles making their migration south. You'll be accompanied by Dr. Jim Flegg, director of the British Trust for Ornithology, whose commentaries could add an extraordinary dimension to your tour. Or go for two weeks on a springtime holiday to Crete, and catch an eyeful of feathered species within a hundred yards of your hotel. If India, however, is your dream, you can make your way there instead, and "scan the waters anxiously for the first glimpse of Siberian Crane," as the brochure states. Eric Hosking, noted bird photographer and ornithologist, could then be your escort.

Eagles, alpine swifts, and lammergeiers all await you. Here's to birdwatching with the best of them. —S.C.

Birds, Sites & Wildlife Holidays
Town and Gown Travel
40/41 South Parade
Summertown, Oxford OX2 7JP
England, UK

The eider ducks have arrived to breed about the shore and the islands; they bring with them that most evocative and haunting of all sounds.
GAVIN MAXWELL

Meeting on Their Turf

W. F. & R. K. Swan Ltd. offers a time machine—a glimpse at animal life which remains largely unchanged from a century ago. Swan's safaris to Kenya, Tanzania, Zambia, and the Seychelles include unbarred views of rhinoceros, giraffe, ostrich, and elephant, the animals any Tarzan would equate with Africa.

Now in its fourteenth season, Swan's tours travel through national parks and conservation areas, assisted by specialists in science. Guest lecturers from fields such as zoology, animal behavior, ecology, ornithology, botany, and photography accompany each safari and enhance the understanding of the bushbuck and the white-tailed mongoose. Each tour member receives, as well, a suggested list of books to help with "pre-safari" studies.

Safaris have ranged in cost from $2173 to $2879 (excluding air fare to London, but including English breakfasts). The program is offered in 19- and 24-day packages.

Photographs of amboseli and crested barbet and memories of the centuries-old nomadic life of the Masai are timeless. The experience of a Swan safari is much more durable than a leopard coat. —J.H.

On Safari
Esplanade Tours
Gen. Sales Agents for
Swan (Hellenic) Ltd.
38 Newbury St.
Boston, MA 02116

Bound Beyond an Outing

Take Care, Out There

Be warned right off: if you're an "oh, let's get mellow in the mountains" person, you would probably do well to look elsewhere in this book for a program more in tune with your needs.

It's not that the people at the National Outdoor Leadership School are opposed to those ideas, it's just that they believe that what they're doing—namely teaching outdoor leadership and skills—comes first. While mellowness and self-discovery can occur on a NOLS program, these are not their chief concerns. Learning to take care of yourself in the wilderness is, however.

NOLS has organized a core curriculum composed of six basic areas of outdoor expertise. These components are: (1) Minimum Impact Camping, (2) Travel Techniques, (3) Outdoor Living Skills, (4) Environmental Awareness, (5) Mountaineering, and (6) Expedition Dynamics. Each expedition offered is broken down along the lines of the core curriculum. In the area of travel techniques, for instance, participants learn packing and carrying, energy conservation, map reading and compass use, time control plans, off-trail route finding, navigation, river crossing, and hazard evaluation.

The classrooms for these courses are in Wyoming, Colorado, Utah, Montana, South Dakota, Washington, Alaska, Mexico, and Africa. Yes, we said Africa. Though NOLS is headquartered in Wyoming, it also has year-round branch schools in Naro Moru, Kenya, as well as seasonal branch schools in Anchorage, Alaska, and Mexico's Baja California.

The school lists dozens of courses with few limitations as to age, sex, or experience. Their shortest program is two weeks in duration; their longest is 14 weeks. Class sizes range from a low of seven students and two instructors to a high of 17 students and three instructors. Prices vary from $300 at a minimum to $2200 at the top. All classes offer university credit.

Among the school's most ambitious projects are what they call "semester" courses. Their African course, which lasts 70 days and costs $1800, covers Kenya from Mt. Kenya to the Indian Ocean, from coral reefs to snow zones, from African history to bargaining procedures in Swahili food markets. The Alaskan course, lasting 75 days at a cost of $2100, takes in whales, icebergs, glacier treks, and Arctic tundra. The Rockies program, costing $2200 and covering 14 weeks, crosses four states and passes through environments ranging from river to desert to forest to mountain to subterranean cavern. Up to 14 college credit hours are available for "semester" programs.

When it comes to learning outdoor leadership and skills, NOLS is a demanding, difficult, and relatively expensive way to go. It may, however, also be the best. —C.McB.

National Outdoor Leadership School
Box AA
Lander, WY 82520

Canadian Bush Lands

Living in the wild provides you with a deep feeling of well-being and an awareness of your physical and spiritual strengths. In the bush, you are totally alive. And it's to the bush that Headwaters will take you.

Headwaters' home area is the Temagami Region of Northern Ontario, in the midst of the Canadian midcontinental wilderness. Lakes and rivers abound, legacies of the most recent Ice Age. You'll travel these sparkling waterways by canoe in summer, and by snowshoe in winter.

With an eye to history, participants read explorers' journals, accounts of earlier travelers, and atmospheric wilderness heritage pieces that are uniquely Canadian. You'll become aware of the balance of nature and man's position in that delicate cycle. These expeditions are not assaults on the wild; they are opportunities to reach a fuller understanding with the land and its rhythms.

Programs are reasonably priced, and run between two weeks and a month in length. —J.A.

Wilderness Travel in the Canadian North
Headwaters
P.O. Box 288
Temagami, Ontario P0H 2H0
Canada

Mountain Macrobiotics

For most folks, a backpacking expedition is a nice, healthy escape. But for Willy Berliner, a backpacking expedition is an escape to health itself.

Berliner is the man behind Macro Polo Travel, an outdoor expedition outfit with a wholesome difference. His hiking and camping trips cover all the "standard procedures" associated with the great outdoors, but they also go into a wilderness approach to macrobiotics, massage, and chanting, which certainly isn't your normal run-of-the-woods stuff.

Included in the program (entitled Macrobiotics in the Mountains) are basic skills like backpacking, camping, cooking, fishing, plant and animal identification, orienteering with map and compass, and finding and making shelter. But, in addition, participants learn macrobiotic philosophy, wild food foraging, first aid (both Western and Eastern), chanting for clarity and endurance, Do-In self-massage, shiatsu massage, acupressure, and foot reflexology.

Macro Polo forays have been held in the New England area, the Rocky Mountains, and British Columbia. They last from several days to several weeks, at costs between $100 and $676. New expeditions are always on the drawing boards. —C.McB.

Macrobiotics in the Mountains
Macro Polo Travel
Round Island
Portsmouth, NH 03801

Tracking the Winter Lynx

Lynx Track Winter Travel School is out to prove that winter is not just something from which to flee indoors, but rather a reflective, educational experience. To this end, Lynx Track offers instruction in cross-country skiing, snowshoeing, igloo building, and dogsledding. Dogsledding?

Dogsledding. The Minnesota school also teaches winter camping, map reading and compass skills, ice safety, first aid, and survival techniques. In fact, whatever most concerns non-motorized travel is taught during Lynx Track's standard (seven-day) and advanced (eight-day) seminars and weekend mini-courses.

Aside from technique training, Lynx Track offers an opportunity to experience the feeling of the winter wilderness through star gazing, winter nature lore, and a one-day solo outing. Additional two- and three-day family adventures emphasize snow games and animal tracks for young children.

Lynx Track programs begin December 27 and continue through April 14. Costs range from $225 for an eight-day expedition (including meals, accommodations, and major equipment) to $56 for a weekend trip.

Mush! —J.H.

Winter Travel Program
Lynx Track
4375 Eureka Rd.
Excelsior, MN 55331

Thank Goddard!

No matter how strongly the public *feels* about keeping wild places wild, nothing really matters without the knowledge of how that task is to be accomplished. Wilderness has a fragility about it; it is so perfectly in balance that the slightest disturbance can start it on the road to destruction.

The Summer Program in Outdoor Education sponsored by Goddard College combines the investigation of biology and botany with actual wilderness experience and the examination of environmental issues. The program serves students of the natural sciences, youth group leaders, and just plain old nature enthusiasts.

Courses carry no-nonsense names and are made up of no-nonsense components. A sampling of the program yields courses in wildlife management, wilderness survival, summer flora, and field biology. Other offerings include such fascinating topics as wild foods, natural medicines, and harvesting game.

There are several program options, with the primary emphasis on the full 12-week summer program. Those wishing to continue their studies in outdoor education may apply to the Program in Integral Education, an alternative BA experience combining summer residencies with nine-month internships and independent study.

Courses in outdoor education run from early June through late August, and the cost of $2250 is comprehensive: food, room, and classes. —J.A.

Summer Program in
Outdoor Education
Goddard College
Summer Programs Office
Box J-2
Plainfield, VT 05667

Ride 'em High The "Cowboy King of Good Times" outfitter can take you to the Superstition Mountains in Arizona and introduce you to the legends of the desert. Or, you can partake in a six-day experience to the "Switzerland of America"—the San Juan Mountains in southwestern Colorado. Learn some basic horsemanship, as well as camping and conservation skills. Get your butt in gear for riding. And write for the costs.

American Wilderness Experience, Inc.
753 Paragon Drive
Boulder, CO 80303

Wilderness, Where Art Thou? Where to begin, oh where to begin—that is the novice's question. And now for the answer: outdoor education and growth seminars in Colorado are calling for outdoorsmen with the desire to learn, and learn properly. Camping is more than just an overnight visit to the wild; it is a personal approach to expedition planning, emergency and safety care, navigation, and group management. Intensive workshops and extended internships are available.

Outdoor Skills & Leadership
Training Seminars
P.O. Box 20281
Denver, CO 80220

Life with Mother

Mother Nature can be mean when you don't respect her and nasty when you mistreat her. Wolfcreek Wilderness is on good, respectful terms with nature, however, for they emphasize outdoor living skills in the trips and courses they offer.

Adventures take place in the mountainous back-country of Georgia. Programs include: (1) A Wilderness Experience, ten-day trips at $295, focusing on discovery and safety in the outdoors; (2) Women in the Wilderness, eight-day trips at $240, bringing women of various backgrounds together in the wild; (3) Wilderness Emergency Medical Aid, a two-day course at $65, teaching emergency measures, evacuation techniques, and psychology of the injured; (4) Leadership Instruction, 14 days at $330, balancing outdoor skills with training in group management; and (5) Winter Leadership, five days at $150 in the South Carolina mountains, dealing with outdoor skills for the winter wilderness.

College credit is available through Georgia State University. Prices include food, accommodations, equipment, and local transportation. —A.E.

Wolfcreek Wilderness
P.O. Box 596
Blairsville, GA 30512

Back to Basics What would you plan to eat in the wilderness that's tasty enough to look forward to at the end of a long hiking day? And what materials do you think would safely start a fire on a cold, dark night? Six to ten days of backpacking and survival courses can teach you the general principles of outdoor living. College credit is available. And you thought you knew it all!

Outdoor Recreation Courses
Health, Physical Education, &
Recreation Dept.
University of Idaho
Moscow, ID 83843

The Man in the Gray Flannel Sleeping Bag

O come all ye corporate presidents! Doctors! Lawyers! Architects and engineers! Put aside your briefcases and your stresses, your blood pressure gauges and calculators. Let your Boards and VPs fend for themselves for a while, and restore yourselves to wholeness at the Banff Centre Wilderness Seminar for Executives.

A Wilderness Seminar for Executives? Yessir; right, sir. And at issue here will be the fundamental question of the twentieth century: what is a fair environmental/economic/psychological balance of trade-offs and compensations?

When you stop to think about it, it's a perfect idea. All these shakers-and-movers shed their flannels, and become just plain folks for ten days in the wild. Within this environment, no one can be the biggest cheese of them all. That way, on an equal footing, such topics can be discussed as "Stress and the Reduction of Stress Levels," "Physical Fitness in a World of Technology and Sedentary Work," and "Man's Responsibility to the Environment."

The organizers of the Wilderness Seminar have designed an integrated experience that includes living in a remote valley of the Canadian Rockies, sharing the adventure of alpine mountaineering, and elaborating on the experience through lectures and discussions.

This is no plush trip, mind you. Those who join really rough it. The seminar is an experience in "holistic education"—the intersection of mind, body, spirit, and environment. It is an opportunity to develop physical fitness, increase energy levels, and learn techniques for health maintenance. It assists the executive in facing social change and developing a sense of responsibility to the environment.

Participants must be in good physical condition. Home base will be Skoki Lodge in Banff National Park, accessible only by an arduous seven-mile hike up a 1400-foot incline. The complete seminar fee is $1350 (Canadian), exclusive of hotel accommodation in Calgary. Travel from your home base is not included. The fee includes all meals and accommodations at Skoki Lodge, your tuition, and specialized mountaineering equipment.

Enrollment is severely limited, and seminars fill up right fast. Face the grandeur of the Canadian Rockies, and the chance to go unnoticed in civvies for a few days. Corporate presidents are, after all, just plain folks like the rest of us. —J.A.

Wilderness Seminar
The Banff Centre
School of the Environment
Box 1020
Banff, Alberta T0L 0C0
Canada

The adventurer gambles with life
to heighten sensation,
to make it glow for a moment.
JACK LONDON

Outdoorsmen Extraordinaire

It's unlikely that even the most seasoned backpacker has experienced camping atop an Alaskan glacier, or gazing down a Mexican volcano, or living in a snow cave while exploring the Montana Rockies in winter.

For outdoor enthusiasts who are serious about backpacking and mountaineering, Hondo Rast & Co. of Laramie, Wyoming, offers these experiences and more.

Hondo Rast, named for a legendary western woodsman and staffed by a group of professional outdoorsmen, conducts six different expeditions. The trips focus on instruction that includes climbing, plant and wildlife identification, and expedition planning. Prior climbing experience is not necessary, but the staff does advise that applicants be in good physical condition.

Four of the trips head for Alaska where the terrain permits instruction in all types of outdoor skills. Expeditions focus on Glacier Bay, the Brooks Mountains above the Arctic Circle, and the massive glaciers of the Chugach Range.

Hondo Rast also offers trips to the volcanoes of Mexico, featuring climbs to the third, fifth, and seventh highest peaks in North America.

The Alaskan expeditions are 30-day trips, while Montana and Mexican adventures run about two weeks. Costs range from $330 to $995, not including transportation. Hondo Rast will provide all of your equipment. —G.R.

Hondo Rast & Co.
P.O. Box 231
Hamilton, MT 59840

The Island Above the Border

North and west of Seattle, up and above the Canadian border, sits a great stretch of land called Vancouver Island. As one runs up its 300-mile length, the island evolves back to a state of natural splendor. Only scattered logging and mining towns on the coast interrupt great pine trees and trails, thick brush and mountains, and clear lakes and streams. It is here that you find Strathcona.

Strathcona is a school that teaches the outdoors in the outdoors, from its base camp at Strathcona Park Lodge. It has gathered to it a staff of outdoor experts who present programs ranging from weekend snowshoeing to three-month residency courses.

A sampling of offerings would include A Gentle Introduction to Trail Living, which covers hiking from step one on up; Survival for Winter Snow Travelers, a course on winter camping, emergency shelter building, winter route selection, and avalanche safety; and Wilderness First Aid and Rescue, which deals with the "unexpected" in the wilderness such as search and evacuation procedures.

Most of Strathcona's courses last from 6 to 11 days at prices that run in the $200 to $400 range. —C.McB.

Outdoor Education Society
Strathcona Park Lodge
Box 2160
Campbell River, BC V9W 5C9
Canada

Readings for the Road

Big pictures are seen by everyone, but their subtle shades are usually visible only to those who understand the experience of painting.

This is the idea behind the Adirondack Institute: students read literature dealing with the wild, then they venture out into the wilderness itself. The insights gained go far beyond the normal classroom or, for that matter, nature experience.

Three separate programs are conducted each summer: in the Adirondack Mountains in upstate New York, in the San Juan Range of the Colorado Rockies, and in the woods of North Ontario, Canada. In each case, students take off from ten days to two weeks for a real taste of what they have read. Outdoor skills from map reading to river fording, and from rapelling to bush medicine are taught as well. Activity periods are followed by reflective time, with daily journals being kept as part of the course. College credit is available, if desired.

The program is limited to 10 students in both Colorado and Ontario, and 12 in New York. The cost for the New York and Colorado course is $325. The Canadian program is $425. —C.McB.

Adirondack Institute
Skidmore College
Saratoga Springs, NY 12866

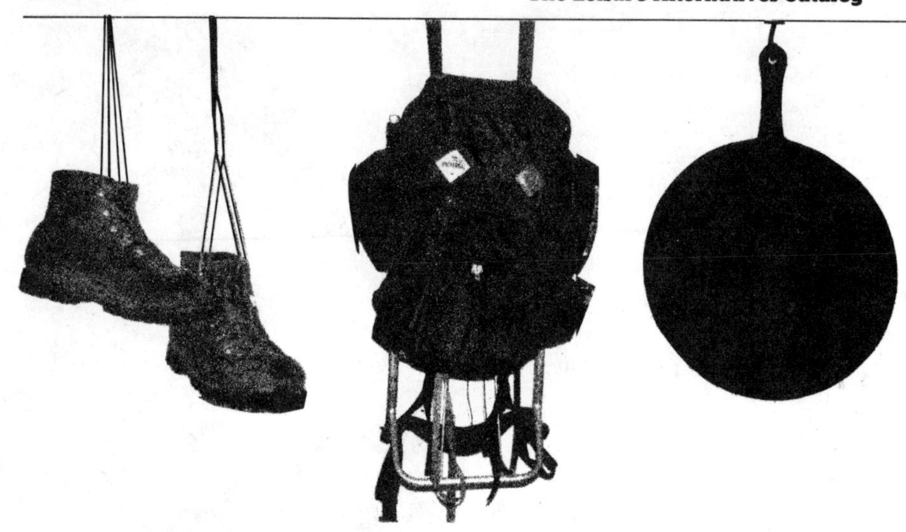

Brrr-ing the Winter There are ways to deal with winter's snows other than shoveling your driveway. Now you can learn to live—and to love—winter by enrolling in fundamental cold weather instruction courses. Build survival shelters, learn to treat winter injuries, cross-country ski, and become versed in the art of route finding. The seven-day Colorado experience is $195. Write for info on their British Columbia course.

Winter Survival Course/
Basic Snow & Ice Course
Iowa Mountaineers
P.O. Box 163
Iowa City, IA 52240

Over the Hump Camel's Hump and the Northern Presidentials may sound like make-believe places to you, but Killington Adventures assures us they are the real-life sites of backpacking expeditions for adults. Two days of training introduce the novice to the hiking experience and provide the knowledge you'll need to arrange your own trips with friends. Week-long sessions in July and August are $170.

Adult Programs
Killington Wilderness Adventure
Killington, VT 05751

The Shape of Things to Come
What, as Americans, have we done, are we doing, and should we be doing with our natural resources? To find out about the real shape of our future, you can take a BA or BS in Natural Heritage Studies. Here is a needed, but long-neglected offering on the nation's campuses in which you can *constructively* study man's relationship to his natural environment.

Natural Heritage Studies Program
Western Montana College
Montana University System
Dillon, MT 59725

Doorway to the West

To pass through the Western Door, according to Indian legend, is to enter another world at death and to leave the familiar behind. The Western Door Wilderness School promises, along similar lines, to take you away from your usual pace, and to place you in the world of the wild.

Try, for instance, a course in mountaineering that guarantees you will discover "as much about yourself and the mountains as is possible in 24 days." Learn geology and meteorology, and take time out for baking and fishing. But be prepared to sweat.

Western Door offers 12- and 24-day courses in the Utah wilderness that include natural science, plant identification, soil and water analyses, and observation of animal life zones.

Or, if that isn't enough, Western Door penetrates the Utah desert—the Canyonlands—at a time of year when its wildlife is visible. Instruction is given for 12 or 18 days in basic hiking and camping skills and desert climatology. Ancient Indian ruins are also explored.

The prices: 12-day courses are $245; 24-day courses are $475. You may feel like rejoicing before you're through. —S.C.

Western Door Wilderness School
172 N St.
Salt Lake City, UT 84103

Tepees in Vermont

Vermont—beaver ponds, abandoned roads, wild back-country. How do you want to explore it—on snowshoes, on foot with backpack, on foot without backpack, on a bike, or in a canoe? How do you want to spend your nights there—in an inn, a cabin, a sleeping bag out in the open, or even an Indian tepee? Hike-Skitour Vermont has something for everybody—a potpourri of hiking, snowshoeing, and backpacking trips that last from two to five days.

Ranging from plush and adventurous to stark and adventurous, the trips are priced accordingly—from $79 for a weekend in a tent to $398 for a five-day "inn-to-inn ramble."

Weekend courses in basic winter outdoor skills and in backpacking introduce the neophyte to ways of dealing with the forest—from learning how to bushwhack to emergency first aid. The "tepee tour," a weekend snowshoe trip, culminates in a tepee evening in which meals are cooked over open fires. What about summer and fall? Well, there's a "multi-media" (bicycle, canoe, horseback, shank's mare) tour of Vermont, and there are inn-to-inn rambles, led by guides who will help you identify animal tracks and plants along the way—goosefoot maples and hobble bushes, for instance. —A.E.

Hike-Skitour Vermont
R.F.D. 1
Chester, VT 05143

I frequently tramped eight or ten miles through the deepest snow to keep an appointment with a beechtree, or a yellow birch . . .
HENRY DAVID THOREAU

Bound for Glory

"Outward Bound" is *not* an oblique description of a tightly cinched but expanding waistline. Just the opposite. It's a physical and a natural challenge—from scaling a mountain glacier through spending day after day at sea.

Above all, Outward Bound is a chance to discover nature, limits of endurance, and yourself. Joy is mixed with hardship in the Outward Bound program, as every participant finds himself or herself thrust out of everyday routines and into a voyage of self-awareness.

Nature is the classroom in this program, which was founded during World War II as a training school for British seamen. It worked for them and, the Outward Bound staff believes, it will work for you. So far, 50,000 people are numbered among Outward Bound's US graduates.

A year-round learning experience, Outward Bound is geared to offering participants a range of challenges. Climatic conditions are those *you* choose—from bitter cold to desert heat.

There are seven Outward Bound centers offering courses and challenges appropriate to each region. Skiing and mountaineering, for example, are the staples in Colorado. In the Southwest, it's desert living and ecology.

The courses are never "snaps," however. Take the Northwest's standard course—a three-week mountaineering program in which participants quickly master towering mountains. And if you can't put in three weeks, there's no excuse—there's an eight-day short course, too, one offering many of the 21-day trek's challenges.

Sound scary so far? It isn't. Every Outward Bound expedition is guided by experienced instructors trained in outdoor living.

Is Outward Bound for you? Few prerequisites—other than good health—are required. Minimum age varies from course to course, but many are open only to those who are 16 and above. There is no maximum age.

What *is* required, Outward Bound says, is "determination to put out everything you have." That's all, but it's a lot because, as the staff insists, most of us quickly discover our self-imposed limits. Our capabilities, however, are far greater than what we think.

Most courses start with the basics—safety, first aid, route finding, and the like—and gradually ease participants into more demanding situations. But it's the "final exam" that requires your endurance—a concluding journey undertaken with minimal instructor supervision. You're not totally on your own in the wild, but you're pretty close to it.

Cost varies with the program, but most standard courses—the three-week sagas—run about $650. Short courses—eight days—cost around $300. Fees include instruction, equipment use, and food. Financial aid is available, as is college credit in some instances. —R.McG.

Colorado Outward Bound School
945 Pennsylvania St.
Denver, CO 80203

Dartmouth Outward Bound Center
P.O. Box 50
Hanover, NH 03755

Hurricane Island Outward Bound School
P.O. Box 429
Rockland, ME 04841

Minnesota Outward Bound School
308 Walker Ave. S.
Wayzata, MN 55391

North Carolina Outward Bound School
P.O. Box 817
Morganton, NC 28655

Northwest Outward Bound School
0110 S.W. Bancroft St.
Portland, OR 97201

Southwest Outward Bound School
P.O. Box 2840
Santa Fe, NM 87501

She deserves a rest—backpacker Carolyn Hoffman at the completion of a seven-month, 3,246-mile trek across the US sponsored by IBA.

Backpack Facts

Whatever you do, don't bring your car. Forsake the world of motorized motion, says the International Backpackers Association, and learn to walk—and to enjoy it.

Easier said than done, right? IBA knows that, too. That's why they annually schedule several installments of their School of Outdoor Skills. Enroll for five days, and you'll rapidly be immersed in the intricacies of camping, hiking, using maps and compasses, assembling a pack, outdoor safety, and selecting equipment.

Seeking a bigger challenge? Try IBA's five-day hike along the Appalachian Trail. A learning-by-doing experience, this trek is geared to more advanced hikers, ones seeking a more strenuous—and rewarding—outing.

All IBA courses stress environmental awareness and the need to preserve our dwindling wilderness. Enrollment is open to all adults, and children under 15 are accepted in special family sessions.

Good as all that is, the best part may be the cost—$50—and that includes food, hot showers, shelter, and like needs. For non-IBA members, a $12 membership fee is tacked on. —R.McG.

School of Outdoor Skills
The International Backpackers Association, Inc.
P.O. Box 85
Lincoln Center, ME 04458

Up Those Slopes

When you come to grips with nature, you come to an understanding with yourself. The Wilderness Institute gives you the opportunity to do just that, with journeys into the wild lands of North America.

Trips combine adventure with environmental education—backpacking and canoeing are flavored with wilderness survival and mountaineering instruction. Most trips are limited to people between the ages of 15 and 55, and some family outings are included.

Adventures are led by experienced members of the Institute's instructor/guide staff. The Wilderness Survival and Mountaineering School provides the fundamentals for both navigation and camping activities. You will tackle mountains, descend faces of cliffs, backpack in some of the most beautiful country in the American West, and finally test your endurance in a solo survival outing.

Cost for two weeks: about $295 for everything. —A.E.

The Wilderness Institute
Wilderness Survival & Mountaineering School
P.O. Box 338
Bonners Ferry, ID 83805

So You Want to Learn How to Camp...

There are no fancy slogans, catchy tunes, or high-flown promises that come with the leadership courses of the American Camping Association's Outdoor Living Skills Program. These people get right down to the nub of it: they will teach you skills adaptable to outdoor and camping environments, and they will do it with experts on a professional level.

The ACA uses a three-step approach in their teaching, beginning with what they call a Campcrafter course designed for those with little outdoor experience. The basic skills that are taught at this level include pocket knife use, simple knots, gear and shelter, health and safety, compass reading, basic map skills, conservation, campsite selection, firecraft, outdoor cooking, and expedition planning.

From this level, campers move on to Advanced Campcrafter and finally Tripcrafter courses in which skills and abilities are greatly expanded. These courses, which include practical field application, produce confident and mature outdoor leaders and guides.

The ACA is a nationwide organization headquartered in Indiana. Its Outdoor Living Skills Program is being offered by its outlets in several geographic regions across the country. Costs vary according to the particular course and location. —C.McB.

Outdoor Living Skills Program
American Camping Association
National Headquarters
Bradford Woods
Martinsville, IN 46151

Wilderness: An Endangered Species

Politics of Protection

In this all-too-civilized world of ours, the opportunities to experience absolutely wild terrain are few. Wilderness areas are disappearing, vanishing into recreational sites, natural resources for industry, even towns and cities.

But there are places—still—where the call of the timber wolf pierces the night, where the clash of horned elk echoes off rocky precipices. The American Wilderness Alliance has two aims for these unspoiled, magical places: to preserve them, and to share them with others.

The Wilderness Is the Baseline program is designed to expand individual awareness of such ecological systems, to acquaint participants with the value of wilderness areas, and to explore the tools and techniques which can aid in the preservation of the wild.

The courses are realistic and romantic at the same time, and they range from rugged wilderness treks to the straightforward Wilderness Politics course. The latter employs seminars, field lectures, interviews with land management officers, and discussions of public participation in decision-making procedures. It includes a six-day backpack trip into the heart of the Holy Cross wilderness area in Colorado, and it leaves from Vail. If you participate, you'll see soaring peaks, spruce-fir forests, remote lakes, and cascading streams.

The difference between AWA programs and its imitators is both spiritual and educational. The knowledge you'll gain here is more than simple, experiential knowhow. Yes, you'll see the unearthly blues of mountain skies. Yes, you'll sneak up on mountain beaver dams and see the world at your feet. But you'll also get more. You'll get a real, practical knowledge of how the balance of nature is forever being affected by the incursions of man—and government—and industry.

Wilderness is an important part of the American heritage. It has shaped and sustained the growth of this nation. Viewed with awe and apprehension by early settlers, the American wilderness has been woven into our country's folklore, history, art, and literature. Even today, these magnificent expanses of wild country continue to shape the national character.

If you decide to let AWA help shape your own character, you can virtually pick a wilderness and AWA will be there. Programs are very, very small—limited to five persons per group. And groups are led by knowledgeable and experienced naturalists.

Programs are geared to the duration of a week, and prices are extremely reasonable. Typical costs (you get to the base camp on your own) are: Black Range Wilderness, $215; Absaroka Horseback Adventure, $150; Wilderness Politics, $395.

The times you spend can't be priced or valued. They will, however, be magical. —J.A.

Wilderness Is the Baseline Program
American Wilderness Alliance
4260 East Evans Ave.
Denver, CO 80222

Timber-r-r!

Can loggers and wildlife survive in the same forest? Can a range that is the home for 2000 elk be restored after it has been decimated by timber clear-cutting?

For outdoor enthusiasts who want to learn more about modern forestland management, the University of Idaho offers a learning vacation that focuses on these resources. And it's billed by these folks as "a nontechnical course for people who enjoy and care about forests."

The six-day class, conducted in northern Idaho's Clearwater National Forest, explores the logging industry and its coexistence with wildlife and other forest inhabitants. Students can examine, firsthand, the environmental impact of the logging industry, as well as the effect of recreational activities (hunting, camping, and backpacking) on the natural environment.

Instructors are professionals from the University's College of Forestry, the US Forest Service, and the Idaho Fish and Game Commission. Students are taken to different sites each day to view forest management techniques, but plenty of time is also reserved for hiking, fishing, or just relaxing in some of the West's most stunning mountain and forest scenery.

Participants camp at primitive forest sites that are accessible by road. You bring your food and camping equipment, as well as your tent. Cost is $30 per person, and the class is open to anyone over eight years old in good physical condition. —G.R.

Forestland Resource Management Program
University of Idaho
Office of Continuing Education
Moscow, ID 83843

Open Spaces Equal Wild Places

We are a world that seeks information. Good information, when used properly, can lead to a desired end.

The Colorado Open Space Council's purpose is to provide up-to-date and on-the-mark information about the wilderness areas remaining in that state. Such material is compiled into organized reports for the Forest Service and local and state governments and is then used to advocate the preservation of Colorado's qualified wilderness areas.

The COSC Wilderness Workshops are, in effect, both summer backpacking experiences and fact-finding tours. Parties of ten spend several days hiking throughout the state, taking notes and photographs, reviewing maps, and generally evaluating natural and man-made influences on the environment. Trip findings and recommendations can—and have—led to positive changes in laws and attitudes associated with these regions. This is a chance to go well beyond the mere "lip service" that most individuals seem to pay to the environment.

The trips, which range through some of the West's most spectacular scenery, cost $195. Participants are expected to provide their own hiking equipment. —C.McB.

COSC Wilderness Workshops
Trailhead Ventures
P.O. Box CC
Buena Vista, CO 81211

Stash the Trash—Elsewhere

"Ask not what the wilderness can do for you; ask what you can do for the wilderness." The Sierra Club's 6- to 12-day Service Trips offer the chance to build a close relationship with the American environment—a relationship based on mutual giving. You can plan to work hard and use your free days to explore the areas you are working to preserve.

Now in their twentieth year, the Sierra Club Service Trips work with forest and park services across America. You might find yourself rebuilding a stream habitat in the Lewis and Clark Forest in Montana. You could be restoring vegetation to a winding road 500 feet from the summit of Colorado's 14,418-foot Mt. Massive. Other trips have focused on the Teton Wilderness in Wyoming, Two Mouth Lake in Idaho, Cranberry Backcountry in West Virginia, and Railroad Creek in Washington.

If you are over 16 and are up to a strenuous hiking vacation with 15 to 25 other volunteers, there's valuable experiences in them thar' hills. —J.H.

Service Trips
Sierra Club
530 Bush St.
San Francisco, CA 94108

Walking Holidays

Silk Sheets or Forest Floors

You know as well as we do that there are wildlife expeditions and there are wildlife expeditions. One person's idea of roughing it may be sleeping in a queen-sized bed overlooking the bush. Another person's concept is a truly scientific, forest-floor trek through places where no man's foot has trod.

There's no reason why you should have to sleep on pine needles, if you want to sleep in a bed. But there's no reason why—if you're up to it—you shouldn't don your helmet and hack your way through the bloody bush to your heart's content. Well, Nature Expeditions International recognizes all of these needs.

What NEI does is grade its expeditions A-B-C-D, with A being a bit hoity-toity and silk-sheetsy, and D being exceedingly woodsy and whiffy. Each has its place, don't you think?

The locales for these trips are worldwide, though a good deal of emphasis is placed on the Western Hemisphere. Destinations include the Galapagos Islands, the peaks of the Andes, the tribal carpet from Asia to Iran, the Mayan territory in Central America, and Pinnacles National Monument in the USA.

There are wildlife expeditions—such as the natural history and photography safari in East Africa. There are island-hopping jaunts in the South Pacific, and river-running trips everywhere. There are romantic explorations of Scottish islands like St. Kilda and Rhum, as well as mountain-climbing journeys to the mysterious Himalayas.

Whether posh or minimal, NEI expeditions are all led by folks with impressive credentials. The Mountain Walking Safari to East Africa (you'll climb Mt. Kenya, among others) is led, for example, by a professor of biology at Merced College, a PhD candidate at the University of Nairobi, and a Cambridge-educated naturalist.

One of our favorite NEI expeditions is a 24-day walking expedition focusing on the cultures, people, wildlife, and natural history of the Kingdom of Nepal—with emphasis on the regions of Katmandu, Pokhara-Jomosom, the Annapurna Range, and the Royal Chitwan National Park. The entire expedition is conducted below the 10,000-foot level, but there are options to climb to Himalayan heights.

Because of the wide variety of trips that are available, it is difficult to quote prices. If you're healthy, though—and adventurous—you can take a D-level trip and really experience forest-floor places. That's an option not many tours can offer. On the other hand, if you're relatively well-heeled, you can have your glass of Pinch ready for you on a silver platter wherever you go.

Whatever you choose, NEI will show you both a good time and a good slice of knowledge. —J.A.

Nature Expeditions International
599 College Ave.
Palo Alto, CA 94306

Hungry for the Himalayas?

You've seen Paris so many times, you say, that the thought of going again is almost boring. You've done the Orient and boated the Rhine, all without any great excitement. You wish that someone would come up with something really different in the way of a trip. You want an adventure.

How does a trek through Nepal's spectacular Kali Gandaki river gorge between the soaring peaks of Annapurna and Dhaulagiri sound? Or a visit to that country's most isolated province, Mustang, where the inhabitants still believe the world is flat and do not use the wheel?

An outfit that runs such unusual tours is International Treks and Travel, based in Knoxville, Tennessee. Participants in the trek experience learn about some of the world's most remote places and cultures, relying, in most cases, on old-fashioned foot power.

Aspiring trekkers will become familiar with trail situations such as weather conditions, route finding, and first aid. And on some of the trips, members may buy fresh vegetables and barter for animals to slaughter in small villages along the way.

The price tags attached to these unusual excursions may seem on the high side (from $1400 to $2275, not including air fare). But then, if adventure is your wish, you may consider the tab a bargain, indeed. —C.McB.

The Mayana Trek Experience
International Treks & Travel
1005 Maplehurst
Apt. 2
Knoxville, TN 37915

These beautiful days . . . saturate themselves into every part of the body and live always.
JOHN MUIR

Mountain Magic

During those few days when spring is giving way to summer in the meadows of New Hampshire's White Mountains, nature puts on its annual spectacle, and hikers are treated to a dazzling array of mountain wildflowers.

It's at this time that the Appalachian Mountain Club conducts its weekend workshops aptly entitled "Celebrating the Mountains."

The AMC, founded in 1876, is the oldest club of its kind in the United States, and through its summer workshop program, the club tries to pass along its conservation heritage.

The workshops offer hikers the opportunity to learn more about the New England environment and to improve outdoor skills. The workshops, which run from two days to a week, range from basic backpacking to bushwhacking. Seminars are taught by professional naturalists and are held in the mountain ranges of northern New England, primarily New Hampshire, Massachusetts, and Maine. The club also offers special excursions/hikes in Canada, the Japanese Alps, and Nepal's Himalayas.

For most workshops and hikes, the Club will provide lodging and meals, and participants will have the option to camp. Costs vary. —G.R.

Appalachian Mountain Club
5 Joy St.
Boston, MA 02108

Walk on the Wild Side

A walk in the woods for fun and a touch of adventure—that's the speciality of the Wilderness Institute.

Oh, true enough, there are ample opportunities for learning many of the facets of the great outdoors through their Wilderness Survival and Mountaineering School but, at the root of it, these folks are into taking you backpacking through some of the most beautiful wilderness areas of the West. That is their meat and potatoes, and it makes for a hearty meal.

From June through August, some two dozen backpacking trips are conducted. They'll lead you through the lush alpine meadows of the West Elk Wilderness in Colorado; down the glacier-carved valleys of the Gallatin Range in Montana; past the moose, elk, and deer herds of the Teton Mountains in Wyoming; along the deserted beaches and cliffs of Washington's Olympic National Park; through the ruins of Indian villages in British Columbia's Coastal Range; and into the snowfields surrounding America's highest peak, Mt. McKinley, in Alaska.

Most of the trips are ten days in length. The cost for most hikes is $235, though some are priced higher. There is also a 10 percent discount to backpackers who provide their own hiking and camping equipment. —C.McB.

Backpacking Trips
The Wilderness Institute
333 Fairfax St.
Denver, CO 80220

Rambling Soles & Walking Sticks

Some European holiday tours resemble assembly lines more than vacations: people are crammed into jets and flown to Europe, where they spend their vacation jumping on and off trains and checking in and out of hotels. If you would rather spend a European vacation walking leisurely through some of the continent's most beautiful countryside, check out Ramblers' Walking Holidays.

Ramblers has conducted walking holidays throughout Europe for the past 30 years, and offers more than 50 different trips, most of them to hills and mountains.

Walkers may select from seven trip categories of varying degrees of hiking difficulty. Easy walks of five or less hours per day to strenuous nine-hour hikes above the timber-line are offered. The two-week tours usually include several rest days for exploring some of the most scenic and out-of-the-way spots. Walkers stay in huts and mountain hotels along the way, many of which are several hundred years old.

Trips are offered in most European countries, with an especially wide selection in Italian, French, and Austrian mountain ranges.

Prices vary for each trip, but include round-trip air fare from Britain to tour starting points, accommodations, and meals. —G.R.

Ramblers' Walking Holidays
The Ramblers Association
1-4 Crawford Mews
York St.
London, W1H 1PT
England, UK

Backwoods Smorgasbord

There is a little something for everyone in this sampling of wilderness stew.

"Eclectic" might be the best word to describe the range of outdoor trips and adventures offered by The University of the Wilderness. They'll take you to St. Vincent Island, Florida, for some sun, sand, and nature; or they'll lead you on an elk-spotting hike in the roadless Du Noir region in Wyoming. They'll help you explore unnamed sand reefs in Mexico or the wilds of the Canadian northwest.

The U of W likes to emphasize that their field trips (canoe, backpack, ski, or snowshoe) are conducted leisurely and with little structure. They operate with the belief that wilderness learning occurs when people are having fun.

Courses are open to anyone in good physical condition (children below 16 must be accompanied by an adult). The five- to eight-day trips cost between $160 and $295, and participants are expected to provide their own camping gear. —C.McB.

Field Trips Program
The University of the Wilderness
29952 Dorothy Rd.
Evergreen, CO 80439

Peaked Alaska Moose ranges and wolverine-populated expanses are strange blends of environments that characterize the Brooks Range. Endless panoramas of snow, mountains piercing the horizon, and miles of flower-decked tundra all confirm Alaska as an entity all its own. Only the experienced guide can promise the very fullest of experiences in this primitive land. Contact Eugene, and let him be the one to assist you.

Wilderness Wildlife Camps
Attn: Eugene Witt, Guide & Outfitter
El Rancho Motel
SR 60328
Fairbanks, AK 99701

Follow the Yellowstone Road
"Taste the bite of a mountain spring in the morning and feel the night tacked above your head by stars almost within your reach." Yellowstone Guides will show you what mountains are *really* all about in well-planned expeditions to the high country. Designed for beginners to hardened veterans, the trips are four days to two weeks in length. Prices vary.

Backpacking & Mountaineering Trips
Yellowstone Wilderness Guides
Red Lodge, MT 59068

Partners in Pursuit The Outdoor Program in Oregon is a unique opportunity for those in pursuit of the wilderness, for all trips are initiated by volunteers and all costs are shared equally. Since its creation in the late 1960s, the program has served as a model for others across the nation. Between 400 and 500 trips are offered each year, as well as extended world expeditions.

Outdoor Program
University of Oregon
Erb Memorial Union
Eugene, OR 97403

Hike, Hike & Away A walk in your neighborhood park may refresh your spirits temporarily, but nothing can "cleanse the system" like an invigorating hike in the woods. Feeling a bit hesitant? Take a combination horseback/backpack trip. Feeling more ambitious? Indulge in a 10- or 15-day hiking adventure. Never been to Montana in July or August? Now is a good time to start, for backpacking can offer you a new freedom. Check out those prices.

Backpacking with Barrow
Attn: Shirley M. Barrow, Outfitter
P.O. Box 183
Whitefish, MT 59937

Rocky Mountain High Experience the wonders of Rocky Mountain backpacking through some of the most breathtaking terrain in America. Five- and ten-day trips ($190 and $295) are offered to those with little or no experience. A 12-day in-depth mountaineering course is also available for true adventure seekers.

Back of Beyond Wilderness Excursions
Rocky Mountain Writers Guild, Inc.
2969 Baseline Rd.
Boulder, CO 80303

Outdoor Odysseys The American wilderness is woven into our folklore, history, and arts. It has served the scenic, scientific, and recreational needs of the American people. What about *your* needs—to vacation, to get back in shape, or simply to escape? Pick a spot and AWA programs go there. Trips do vary in length and cost, but then walking has never been better.

American Wilderness Alliance
4260 East Evans Ave.
Denver, CO 80222

I could scrape the colours from the petals, like spilt dye from a rock.
HILDA DOOLITTLE

Knapsack on Back

"Knapsacking" is a term which suggests wrapping your lunch on the end of a fishing pole, and heading down to the mill pond for the rest of the day.

The Sierra Club's Knapsack Outings are, however, a bit more invigorating than that. They have "clung to the term knapsacking for a long time, and prefer it," but backpacking is really what they do.

Nearly 300 backpacking trips are offered in the United States and Canada. The outings offer the hiker a choice of altitude, climbing difficulty, and type of ground to be covered. Trips fall into one of five categories that range from "leisure" (25–35 miles of fairly easy hiking per week) to "strenuous" (trekking through rougher terrain, usually at higher elevations).

National parks, forests, and wilderness areas are the bases for Knapsack Outings. Experienced Sierra Club members act as leaders, and the trips are limited to small groups only. Hikers bring their own backpack, sleeping bag, tent, and personal items; the club provides the food and cooking gear.

Trips are run in a cooperative manner, with everyone pitching in on cooking and camping chores. Outings range from four days to two weeks, and costs from $100 to $200. —G.R.

Knapsack Outings
Sierra Club
530 Bush St.
San Francisco, CA 94108

Wolverines on the Frontier

The majestic Brooks Range rises skyward from the plains of northern Alaska—like a Great Wall separating the Arctic Circle from the rest of the world. It is an ecosystem in danger of heavy-handed tampering since the completion of the Trans-Alaska Pipeline from Prudhoe Bay to Valdez.

Alaska Wilderness Unlimited offers guided learning journeys through this last great American frontier. The mode is backpacking with a 40-50 pound pack. Although the exertion is great, the rewards are enormous.

Photographic opportunities never quite end here, as they are among the finest available on earth. You'll visit Kaktovik, an Eskimo village whose main occupation is subsistence hunting, fishing, and trapping. You'll see caribou, grizzly bear, and Dall's sheep, wolverines, foxes, and polar bears.

The peak of this voyage will be a bush plane flight to some of the finest untouched wilderness in the Brooks Range, where vertical elevations of 7000 staggering feet can be seen.

Alaska is a wilderness unlimited, and this, quite simply, is a trek not to be missed. —J.A.

Alaska Wilderness Unlimited
Drawer 8-M
Anchorage, AK 99508

Packer's Peaks

Brrrrrrr. It gets cold at 11,000 feet in a Colorado winter. Make a mistake and it may be your last. What would you do were you stranded?

A fine first step is to enroll in Iowa Mountaineer's eight-day winter survival course. Taught in the Collegiate Range, the course stresses survival in the outdoors. Cross-country skiing forays are provided as well. And cold as it gets up there, you'll very likely remain warm. Special tents and equipment are provided to allow for comfortable living. Survivors receive a certificate upon completion, and no previous experience is required.

But that's not all Iowa Mountaineering offers. There are month-long climbs in Europe's Alps, lengthy New Zealand expeditions, a month in Alaska, and ten days of hiking and climbing in Colorado's San Juan camp. All courses emphasize education—academic credit is available in some instances through the University of Iowa—and, for beginners, there are introductory backpacking and rock climbing courses.

Costs are reasonable, but participation requires membership in Iowa Mountaineering ($7). Other than that, only a love of nature and good health are prerequisites for most expeditions. —R.McG.

Iowa Mountaineers
P.O. Box 163
Iowa City, IA 52240

Our Brethren Above the Border

About the oddest thing Canadians will do is to end their sentences with the inquisitive "eh?" though that's hardly worse than the American closer "you know?" The fact is, though, you'd have a hard time distinguishing a Canadian from an American. They speak the same language, wear the same clothes, and drink the same whiskey.

When it comes to putting on nature tours, Canadians and Americans, again, have much in common. Canadians know, just as Americans do, that unless you are part polar bear, your best bet is to head south in the winter. That's why the folks at Canadian Nature Tours schedule nature trips to places like the Bahamas and its 700 sunny islands during times of snowfall.

And Canadians, like their brethren below the border, know that people just love the seashore in the summer. So CNT lines up July and August expeditions to wave-lapped locations like the Gulf of St. Lawrence Islands, Newfoundland, and the Queen Charlotte Islands.

The emphasis in these trips is on the pleasure of journeying. Participants range in age from 18 to 70 (and there are lots of the latter, we're told). Costs differ according to the trip, but range anywhere from $100 to $1000. —C.McB.

Canadian Nature Tours
355 Lesmill Rd.
Don Mills, Ontario M3B 2W7
Canada

You in Utah Grand Gulch and Paria Canyon are examples of the scenic and the wild, but they are also the sites for backpacking adventures sponsored by an organization called, naturally enough, Wild and Scenic. Directors Susan and Patrick will accompany each six- and seven-day trip through Utah's primitive areas. Prices: $280-$315/person. Trips run April through June.

Wilderness Backpacking Trips
Wild & Scenic, Inc.
P.O. Box 2123
Marble Canyon, AZ 86036

On Top of Old Baldy Fish in Idaho canyon streams, ascend Big Baldy Mountain, revitalize at Pistol Creek Hotsprings, and enjoy the splendor of meadows as you backpack through Idaho's picturesque wilds. Six-day ($210), ten-day ($330), and fifteen-day ($450) trips are available.

Wilderness Trails
P.O. Box 9252
Moscow, ID 83843

Inner Explorations Ah, a new you. Push yourself to your limits, and discover your capabilities. Hike, canoe, ski, sail, and kayak through the wilderness environments of North America. Trips vary in length from 8 days of Idaho ski touring ($390) to 35 days in the Yukon wilderness ($1570).

The Infinite Odyssey
57 Grant St.
Waltham, MA 02154

The wild places are where we began. When they end, so do we.
DAVID BROWER

Work consists of whatever a body is obliged to do.
Play consists of whatever a body is not obliged to do.
MARK TWAIN

OK, Sports Fans

The spirit of competition and the personal rewards of achieving goals—these are two of the biggest reasons why Americans have always been strong on sports.

A clean mind in a sound body, or a sound mind in a clean body—that's another reason. Sports bring age-defeating, youth-retaining fitness. A flat tummy, good wind, and a remarkable bicep. Alternately, a flat tummy, good wind, and legs that would stop traffic.

But really, most sports are played for the good of the soul. If you interviewed the teams that scale Everest and Annapurna, you'd probably find out that they hate driving snow just as much as the next guy. But their spirits yearn to see the view from the pinnacle of the world.

Athletes don't love the pain of sports. They're there for the game and the action. And when you define sports, there's no way around that word: *action*. And have we got a potpourri of action and thrills for you in this chapter!

We've found sailboats and snorkeling and waterskiing. We've found mountains to climb and high-performance race cars to drive. We've a spiffy array of tennis programs—and a wealth of golf holidays to boot.

We've hockey and running and jogging and martial arts. We've fitness programs and swimming and soaring and hang gliding. We've parachuting and plain old airplane flying. We've navigation and scuba and fishing and windsurfing and kayaking and canoeing.

As a matter of fact, there are precious few individual sports we've missed. We haven't devoted much time and space to the more popular team sports. Our focus here is on personal excellence, personal achievement, and personal experience.

If you elect to take advantage of these programs, you may get to know the great silences of the upper atmosphere as you ride in a soundless glider or hot-air balloon. You may thrill to the feeling of the wind whipping by you as you skydive or ski or bicycle down a summer alp.

You'll feel the salt spray of the sea from a yacht, and stare from behind goggles at an astonishing variety of tropical fish as you snorkel the clear waters of vacationlands.

You'll dream your way into bliss on a lazy fishing trip, or crash through bubbling white rapids on a long-distance kayak trek. You'll scale sheer cliffs and noble mountains.

Whatever your preference, we've tried to include something *you* can enjoy. There are programs here for beginners and programs for the incredibly advanced. Most will accept anyone with a need to have fun and a good sense of humor. After all, one of the most important by-products of good sportsmanship is the saving ability to laugh at yourself.

Enjoy!

On Your Own

The Summer Snows

It's been said that no matter what you do, it's more fun to do it with your clothes off. But if what you like to do is ski, you don't get much of a chance to combine outdoor sun-on-your-skin with your slaloms and schusses. If skin and skiing are what you're looking for, Toni Sailer's Summer Ski Camp is bound to delight you.

In Whistler Mountain's huge north-west bowl, near Vancouver, British Columbia, the 11-year-old camp operates for six weeks each summer, offering intensive training to both adults and juniors (ages 10-18).

A teaching camp is only as good as its teachers, and this camp has some of the finest staff available anywhere.

For racing: The advanced program is directed by Toni Sailer, who has also been a director of the camp program since just after it was founded. He brings to the task a background with three Olympic gold medals (1956), three World Championship golds (1958), and four years as head coach of the Austrian ski team. Nancy Greene Raine, director of novice and intermediate racing and a director of the camp since 1969, is probably Canada's greatest woman skier, with six Canadian and three American titles, two World Cups, and two Olympic medals (1968). The racing program emphasizes the improvement of individual skiing combined with lots of slalom practice and instruction geared to each student.

For freestyle: Wayne Wong is section director and one of the best freestyle skiers in the world. He's been a European and Japanese champion, and he leads a team of skilled teachers who can bring hotdoggers all the way from apprentice to advanced, stressing safety while they build assurance and ability. Those students who want to get into aerials—in addition to ballet and moguls—will be head-over-heels into the supervised trampoline instruction before they try any such maneuvers out on the slopes.

For recreational: Wayne Booth has been with the camp for over a decade. As director of Canada's largest ski school (on Mt. Seymour), he runs an instructional program consisting of 100,000 lessons a year and is thus uniquely qualified to teach skiers ranging in skill all the way from "a couple of trips down the beginners' slopes (and I do mean, trips)" to "maybe next year at the Winter Olympics."

The camp fee of $360-$395 per person per week includes accommodations, meals, tows and lifts, coaching, and activities such as sailing, canoeing, and swimming. Nonskiers (at $250) are welcome, so if you're a compulsive skier paired with someone who thinks all skis should be broken up for kindling, there will be plenty to keep your partner occupied. —R.J.

Toni Sailer Summer Ski Camp
#205-1111 W. Georgia St.
Vancouver, BC V6E 3G7
Canada

Come Ski with Me

You don't have to be an international jet-setter, a celebrity, or a daredevil to enjoy the excitement of skiing. The Jackson Hole Ski Corp in Grand Teton National Park offers all kinds of ski instruction, beginning or expert, private or group, cross-country or downhill, slalom racing or giant slalom racing.

Just fancy gliding down the lower slopes of one of the most picturesque mountain ranges in the world, surrounded by white-capped peaks that span the sky to 14,000 feet, and imagine the sensation of being part of this natural glory—just you, the snow-covered slopes, the wind, the trail, your skis, and your new skiing skill.

Two special racing camps in December and May deliver an intensive training experience, with videotape evaluation, lectures, and movies. The six-day camp in December prepares recreational skiers for the race season. Its $245 cost includes lifts, coaching, room, lectures, and videotape evaluation; youngsters ten and older are accepted, as well as adults. The May camp ($360) offers eight days of instruction for adults 19 and older and includes meals and additional activities—tennis, skydiving, and soaring—along with the other features of the December camp. —R.P.

Jackson Hole Ski Camps
Jackson Hole Ski School
P.O. Box 269
Teton Village, WY 83025

Men. Who Needs 'Em?

A woman's touch, it has been said, is gentler than a man's. At least that's what Elissa Slanger's charges claim. Every year, hundreds of women come to her for instruction in the mystery and mastery of steep ski slopes. But a woman's approach to skiing differs from a man's, Slanger stresses. It's fun and exhilaration women seek on the slopes, not competition. Her Woman's Way Ski Seminars accordingly offer a five-day program of on-the-slopes instruction geared to providing participants "a cooperative environment" in which they set their own pace and goals. Beginners as well as the more polished are welcome.

Founded by Slanger three years ago in California's Squaw Valley, Woman's Way Ski Seminars are now found in winter resorts across the country. Explaining the program's rapid expansion, Slanger says, "It's a relief to women to have their frustrations, fear and stress replaced with fun and self-confidence."

Cost varies with seminar location, but the average is $175. —R.McG.

Woman's Way Ski Seminars
P.O. Box 1182
Tahoe City, CA 95730

Solving a Ski Problem with Maria The hills are alive with the sounds of swooshing. The Trapp Family Ski-Touring Center offers ski-touring lessons to anyone who wishes to learn—kids and adults, beginners through advanced. A two-hour course is $8; five days of instruction is $50.

Trapp Family Ski-Touring Center
Trapp Family Lodge
Stowe, VT 05672

The Bestes in Estes "Learn ski touring in Rocky Mountain National Park with the experts," says the brochure of Rocky Mountain Ski Tours. They have private and group ski-touring instruction for beginners through advanced. They also have courses for seniors. Prices are from $10 to $42 for the one- to five-day courses.

Rocky Mountain Ski Tours
Box 413
Estes Park, CO 80517

Ski Borealis Northern Lights Alpine Recreation offers a guided ski-touring program where the levels of physical and technical difficulty can be arranged to suit your skill. Each night you will sleep in the Delphine Lodge, and during the day you will ski along various nearby trails. The cost is from $100 to $350 for the two- to seven-day packages.

Ski Touring
Northern Lights Alpine Recreation
Box 399
Invermere, BC V0A 1K0
Canada

Schuss Svensk Scandinavian skiing has come to Colorado. The Scandinavian Lodge holds ski-touring schools and clinics for persons who already know how to ski. Tuition for the three- to seven-day programs ranges from $55 to $179.

Ski Touring
Scandinavian Lodge
Mt. Werner Training Center
P.O. Box 5040
Steamboat Village, CO 80499

Royal Canadian Mountaineering

In Alberta and British Columbia, the summers are snowy and the spaces are—well, spacious. The mountaineering and rock-climbing all year round are unsurpassed.

Northern Lights Alpine Recreation programs, since 1970 under the direction of Arnor Larson, offers mountaineering camps for basic, intermediate, and advanced levels of students—indeed, for anyone who wants to develop wilderness skills or just to escape from day-to-day weariness in a glacial paradise.

Offered in both winter and summer, the camps are widely varied depending on the need and taste of the individual client. In fact, so specialized are some of the sessions that they can be planned by and geared for the participants themselves. These special sessions can include (though they're by no means limited to): snow and ice work (emphasizing glacial travel, crevasse rescue, and high-angle ice); alpine rock-climbing, scaling solid but steep 3000-meter peaks (with a maximum of only two participants); and first ascents, which concentrate on new routes to peaks. Other sessions, all with only a few participants, can be arranged to emphasize different aspects of technique or terrain, depending on individual interests.

More structured experiences are available for those who wish them. The Arctic Expeditionary Mountaineering Seminar is for the experienced mountaineer and features glacier camping, igloo and snow cave construction, navigation and route finding, itinerary planning, and many more skills necessary for getting away from it all or to the poles, whichever you desire. Skiing for cross-country and cross-glaciers is also taught.

Also available in winter is a program designed for the harried working person who wishes to "get away from it all." The Hermitage is a small cabin set in the mountains, completely surrounded by opportunities for different kinds of mountain adventures. No matter what sort of mountaineering you devote yourself to during the day, night brings a return to the warmth and companionship available in the cabin setting. For those who prefer to glide into solitude rather than climb, and who have considerable skiing as well as mountaineering expertise, there is an alpine ski route to the cabin also.

Participants in all camps are required to provide their own equipment, though some rental equipment is available. During the winter, some sessions may be taken by the day, instead of by the week. Prices range from $13 to $30 per day, depending on the scope of the camp and the amount of equipment the camper supplies or rents. Costs for special sessions may vary more widely. —R.J.

Northern Lights Alpine Recreation
Box 399
Invermere, BC V0A 1K0
Canada

Mountain Maneuvers

Wild as big-city streets may have become, they are tame compared to the thrills of the natural wilderness of the Sierra Nevada Mountains—a wilderness the Mountain People School knows well.

Founded in 1974, the School offers a variety of courses geared to exciting both the novice and the more experienced in mountain living. Of particular interest to beginners is the two-day course in basic rock climbing ($35). Knots, rope handling, belaying, rappelling, anchors, *and* the good judgment necessary for making every climb a safe one are stressed in this brief introductory adventure.

For those seeking intensive exposure to the joys of steep cliffs, the School offers one- and two-week expeditions as well as a two-day winter climb-and-contract course tailored to the desires of participants. —R.McG.

Mountain People School
157 Oak Spring Dr.
San Anselmo, CA 94960

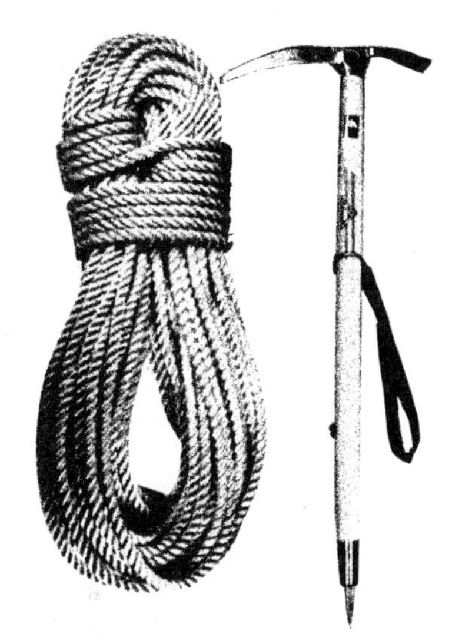

Sun Rising on the Mountain

Some people think there's a lot to be said for being caught between a rock and a hard place. They do it deliberately and happily on ropes, pitons, and the open rock face. If you want to learn to do the same, the EE-DA-HOW (Sun Rising on the Mountain) Mountaineering Guide Service in the Sawtooth National Recreation Area in central Idaho may be the place for you.

EE-DA-HOW offers 6- and 12-day climbing courses, including snow and ice experience, and 21-day mountaineering leadership seminars. Each course is offered regularly from mid-June through early September and can be combined with wilderness backpacking for those who desire.

Each course begins, after gear is packed, with a hike to base camp, which six-day climbers use for the entire course of instruction. Climbing is taught first in practice areas and then on progressively more difficult slopes.

The leadership seminar also emphasizes actions to take in case of injury, the carrying out of rescue operations, and dealing with fear. Protection of the environment is constantly stressed. —R.J.

EE-DA-HOW Mountaineering
P.O. Box 207
Ucon, ID 83454

High Jinks

If the thought of scaling a wall of ice or negotiating a path up a vertical mountain face sounds as appealing to you as opening a bottle of Sancerre Chavignol '76 does to a wine aficionado, then the place to turn to is Lute Jerstad Adventures. Based in Portland, Oregon, Lute Jerstad Adventures has led mountain trips all over the world in addition to offering courses in ice climbing, rock climbing, and mountaineering.

The ice-climbing seminars are held on the Eliot Glacier on Mt. Hood. The seminars last five days and usually operate with a student-guide ratio of four to one. The beginner course teaches the basic skills and then finishes with an actual climb up a sheer face using modern ice climbing techniques. The advanced course involves learning how to climb frozen waterfalls and navigate long alpine ascents.

The three-day mountaineering seminars for experienced climbers take place in moving camps in the Washington Cascades to give experience in high mountain travel, including route selection, rope fixing, and expedition logistics. Jerstad also offers basic and advanced rock climbing seminars.

Fees for the courses, which usually include all meals and equipment, range from $250 for three days of advanced mountaineering to $285 for a one-week climbing course. —P.T.

Lute Jerstad Adventures
P.O. Box 19527
Portland, OR 97219

And high the mountain-tops,
in cloudy air,
The mountain-tops where
is the throne of Truth.
MATTHEW ARNOLD

Challenge/ Discovery

"Sing in me Muse, and through me tell the tale of that man skilled in all ways of contending."

Odysseus, of course, had Athena's help when he met challenges on his voyage of self-discovery, but even if you don't have divine guidance, you are welcome at Challenge/ Discovery—so long as you want to learn how to contend through wilderness experience.

The school believes "education is a journey, not a destination" and that wilderness means self-discovery and adventure.

They provide all the equipment; you provide the desire. Beginners are welcome. You can take rock-climbing classes for 1 day or 23. You'll learn basic skills, safety techniques, and route planning. Or you can take classes that work up to 14,000-foot climbs and that teach woodcraft, emergency skills, rappelling, navigation, medical aid, and snow and ice training.

River-skills courses are also offered, such as kayaking on white water. All courses are sponsored by Antioch College.

Teachers' courses, designed for educators and administrators, are also given. The bottom age is 16, though some classes have a higher limit. The 23-day classes are under $600. A $100 deposit is required. —J.S.

Challenge/Discovery
Box 229
Crested Butte, CO 81224

Climb Every Mountain

You'll likely wind up with sore muscles and a bouquet of blisters, so straightaway you know this isn't an ordinary vacation jaunt. It's mountain climbing—learned safely under the watchful guides of Heather Mountaineering School, in Washington State.

But, popular as it's becoming, mountain climbing is not for everyone. The sport is rugged, and safety first is a critical rule of thumb, not a tired old saw. That's why safety is Heather Mountaineering's first rule—and every climber's best friend.

Offering a six-week instructional course (involving three evening lectures and six weekend climbs), Heather thoroughly equips participants with the knowledge that means power over the threatening cliffs. Basic techniques and more advanced topics are covered and the cost is $150. Individually tailored instruction and climbs are also available. —R.McG.

Heather Mountaineering
4721 Belvedere
Everett, WA 98203

From the Ground Up

Get high. But do it climbing mountains with the expert instruction offered by Yellowstone Wilderness Guides, long-time explorers of Wyoming and Montana's North Central Rockies.

Offering an array of year-round programs geared to participants' skills and experience, Yellowstone Wilderness Guides promises mountaineering adventures that will excite both the novice and the seasoned climber. Of special interest to the beginner is the Mountaineering/Alpine Instruction Camp, a program carefully designed to rapidly take you from the ground up. Participants advance from the rudiments to artfully scaling the towering mountains of the Beartooth Range. The cost for this seven-day package (including food and necessary gear) is $325.

Custom arrangements, advanced courses, and programs for teenagers are also available. Cost ranges from $150 to $450 for programs ranging from 4 to 14 days. —R.McG.

Yellowstone Wilderness Guides
Red Lodge, MT 59068

To the Top

"Cramponing techniques, French pointing, rappelling, belaying, arrests, prusik systems"—here we go again, another cryptic memo from that boss of mine. That man hasn't been the same since he attended that Mt. Adams Wilderness Institute on his vacation

last month. His whole personality seems to have changed and he keeps scribbling these strange memos. Sometimes I wonder what he was doing on that mountain!

He claims he climbed to the summit of Mount Adams (12,276 feet) as part of an eight-day mountaineering class he attended. I've never even seen him climb the stairs around here. He says it was possible because of their "intensive, individualized instruction."

He sure seems to have learned a lot, considering I happen to know the eight days only cost him $325, including food, equipment, leadership, and transportation to and from the Portland airport.

I wouldn't have thought he was in good enough shape to do it, and maybe he wouldn't have been if they hadn't sent him a physical conditioning program last spring. He says the other nine people in his session were really good companions and that that was half the fun of it—which explains that phone call last week . . . —E.H.

Mt. Adams Wilderness Institute
Flying L Ranch
Glenwood, WA 98619

We've done the bugger!
SHERPA TENSING (on climbing Everest)

Up the Down Rockface

The tougher the going, the more people want to go. Palisade School of Mountaineering has a waiting list each year of students who aspire to scale the Sierra Nevadas with ropes chafing their backs and rocks under their fingernails.

PSOM offers the widest spectrum of mountain climbs and classes in the United States, including a mountain medicine seminar for ascending doctors and expedition leaders. Participants in that session can opt for comfort at lower-altitude lectures or join the rock climbers above.

Basic and advanced classes are conducted in wilderness skiing during the winter, and in rock climbing and mountaineering in the summer.

The California school for mountain masochists demands that its students be in top physical condition. Everyone carries a share of the community backpacks. No one under 16 or over 80 is allowed along.

Classes are usually limited to no more than nine students. Prices average $295. —J.W.

Palisade School of Mountaineering
P.O. Box 694
Bishop, CA 93514

Pitons Away! Grab a piece of that rock! The Bob Culp Climbing School teaches such skills as basic rock climbing, advanced rock climbing, and ice climbing. Prices range from $25 to $140.

Bob Culp Climbing School
1329 Broadway
Boulder, CO 80302

Blue Ridge Rockers You folks in the South can learn rock climbing, too. The Nantahala Outdoor Center offers weekend lessons in this sport. The price is $85.

Rock Climbing
Nantahala Outdoor Center
Star Route, Box 68
Bryson City, NC 28713

The Top of Banff High Horizons can teach you and your child how to climb a rock—each in your own separate course. The prices range between $200 and $550.

High Horizons
P.O. Box 1166
Banff, Alberta T0L 0C0
Canada

The only thing on the level is mountain climbing.
EDDIE QUINN

High Performance Varoom

Varoom! Step on that gas pedal, shift those gears, and zoom on over to Bob Bondurant's to find out everything you just did wrong.

Driving is hard; safe driving, harder still. Hardest of all is fast and safe driving. That's Bondurant's specialty.

A former Formula I racer, Bondurant is no longer active on the professional circuit but his zest for performance driving lives on—in him and in his thousands of students. Offering a complete range of courses year-round, Bondurant's School of High Performance Driving is not just for aspiring A. J. Foyt's. It's for everyone with a bit of the varoom.

Take Bondurant's course in high performance driving, for example. Not a training ground for future professionals, this course's goal is to make that daily freeway commute a bit safer and pleasanter. Cornering, handling, downshifting, heel-and-toeing, and automotive suspensions are all explored in this two- to three-day program. Supplemented by classroom probings of driving's finer points, on-the-track practice is provided in ample doses as students move closer to complete car control.

Fearful of kidnapping? Bondurant can help here, too. There's his four-day program for corporate chauffeurs that is open to all who are interested in learning evasive driving techniques. But the stress is on the realities of terrorism and ways to escape—miles before capture. Along the way, students are trained to control *all* threatening driving situations—and track practice makes certain that the lessons are learned.

But do visions of Grand Prix trophies line your imagination? The solution is the Grand Prix course. Mixing classroom time with track practice in sedans, sports cars, and Formula I racers, Bondurant stresses learning-by-doing as students master steering, braking, skids, and the cornering techniques of entry, apex, and exit. A five-day course, this program thoroughly covers the nature—and excitement—of racing. Successful graduates are rewarded with full IMSA certification and a half-credit toward the SCAA (Sports Car Club of America) training requirement, two required steps on the way to racing's big time.

Bondurant's program provides courses and advanced instruction in all aspects of driving. Cost varies with each course, but averages about $175 daily or $1000 for a week. Meals and lodging are not included in most packages. —R.McG.

Bob Bondurant School of High Performance Driving
Sears Point International Raceway
Hwys 37 & 121
Sonoma, CA 95476

Drive, He Said

You're speeding down the highway at 60 miles per hour and the driver immediately ahead of you slams on his brakes. What *do* you do? Skip Barber has the answer.

Barber, a retired professional automobile racer, knows the pitfalls of racetrack and street driving alike. And his skills are available for hire at the Skip Barber School of Performance Driving.

For drivers seeking safety on the highways, Barber's one-day street driving course may be the ticket to safety *and* more enjoyable driving. The aim, explains Barber, is to instruct street drivers in the race-derived skills required for safety. Only the most important techniques are taught and ample on-the-track practice is included. Cost is $175.

And for aspiring Mario Andretti's, Barber's three-day racing school provides instruction in all skills "needed to race successfully," including the fine automotive arts of heel-and-toeing, downshifting, and double-clutching. The course, with all the driving time "you can stand," costs $650. A one-day short course—minus the intensive practice sessions—is $175. —R.McG.

Skip Barber School of
High Performance Driving
1000 Massachusetts Ave.
Boxboro, MA 01719

The New Centaurs

In classical mythology there existed a race of powerful creatures who were half man, half horse. The centaurs. The modern equivalent of these swift, powerful combinations of man and beast is probably the racing driver and his car. Strapped into the driver's seat, roaring along the track, the racer seems to be one with the car.

The kind of skill a driver needs to be in total control of all that power and speed doesn't usually come naturally. It has to be learned. And the Precision School of Racing is there to teach it. The School offers several phases of instruction.

Phase I, a two-day session, is for those drivers who have not yet competed. The student gets at least 170 miles of actual in-car training, plus classroom sessions showing films of how great drivers like Andretti and Revson do it. The School uses Lola Formula B cars for beginners. Satisfactory completion of this course will qualify the student for an IMSA (International Motor Sports Association) license. Tuition is $750.

Phases II and III are for more advanced drivers. They prepare you for sprint or endurance racing, help you with setting up your car, and show you how to organize your crew. These are also two-day sessions; Phase II costs $995, and the cost of Phase III depends on the expense of renting the track, hiring mechanics, etc.

The School is located in Tampa, Florida, and makes use of the Florida International Raceway at Lakeland and the Gainesville International Raceway.

Gentlemen, start your engines. —A.L.

Precision School of Racing
P.O. Box 18083
Tampa, FL 33609

A Well-Rounded Education

If you've never climbed a mountain because you felt foolishly ignorant of how to go about it, or if you've stayed off the ski slopes and tennis courts for the same reason, take heart. You can become a dilettante in all these skills at one school in Vermont.

The folks at Killington teach not only novices but intermediates and pros as well. The programs are called "learning vacations," and although there is some classwork, most of the time is spent "doing." The school has developed accelerated methods of teaching tennis, backpacking, freestyle skiing, and ski patrolling or racing.

In the tennis program you get a crash weekend course or a five-day midweek session, with personalized instruction and video playback of your actions.

Adventure camps teach mountain climbing, canoeing, and wilderness existence.

The Killington Freestyle School for skiing has a national reputation for its fall, spring, and summer camps. The school for ski instructors promises its top graduates teaching positions.

Prices range from $125 to $345 for the two- to five-day courses. —J.W.

Schools of Killington
723 Killington Rd.
Killington, VT 04751

Sports of All Sorts

You've heard of some of the great educational institutions in Colorado, such as the University of Denver and the University of Colorado. But near Denver is an educational institution you probably haven't heard of: Copper Mountain Institute, a camp whose students truly pursue a peak experience.

Copper Mountain offers a unique combination of sports and personal exploration and growth at a village in the Rocky Mountains. This is the heart of Colorado's famous ski country, so it's natural that there would be a winter emphasis on skiing.

A series of five four-day seminars for skiers of more than average ability is offered throughout the winter. The seminars give students the opportunity to improve techniques at tasks such as moguls, deep powder, racing, and cross-country, but they also emphasize nutrition and body conditioning. Sessions are demanding, but the skier emerges from them at new ability levels and ready for new challenges. Off the slopes, lectures provide theory and insight into the sport. The fee for four days (exclusive of lodging) is $175 ($75 deposit), fully refundable up to ten days prior to each seminar.

In addition to those skiing seminars, a special five-day seminar is directed at the problems of women. The "Woman's Way Ski Seminar" offers ski techniques and physical training specifically for the female skier and emphasizes fun while learning with other women of comparable ability.

In line with a program of separate women's studies, Copper Mountain offers a three-day summer "Emerging Woman Seminar," which is geared to exploring woman's role in the modern world. Distinguished faculty members lecture on such topics as career planning, single living, attaining success, and maintaining relationships.

Also offered during the summer are a cycling camp and a running camp. Each one week long, the camps emphasize fitness and training. The cycling camp also provides lectures on massage, nutrition, and tactics. As in all other seminars at Copper Mountain, videotapes are used to provide feedback on form and technique.

A short but exciting seminar offering college credit, and especially aimed at teachers and coaches of young sports participants, is the "Children in Sport Seminar" given in the fall. This two-day course, including films, lectures, and practice, considers such questions as the advantages/disadvantages of organized vs. spontaneous play; the value of competition, and how much may be too much; special problems of the young athlete; and the impact of sports on children. The seminar fee (exclusive of accommodations) is $75 ($25 deposit).

All Copper Mountain seminars have a strictly limited enrollment, so early registration is stressed. You can easily see that Copper Mountain is one place offering all-around sports and self-improvement programs for a better, more skillful you. —R.J.

Copper Mountain Institute
P.O. Box 1
Copper Mountain, CO 80443

The Sword of Tai Chi

"An evocation of the martial spirit which recognizes the unity of opposites—*yin* and *yang*—and the unity of all things."—The Naropa Institute

Ready, class? Relax and exercise. At the same time.

To Western ears this may sound contradictory. But in fact this unity of opposites forms the theme of the Naropa Institute's martial arts program. This program emphasizes that a calm mind and relaxed body will lead to precise control and balance of the body.

Extensive classes are offered in tai chi ch'uan, an ancient system of Chinese exercise. Levels range from beginning to advanced, and additional courses are offered in tai chi sword and teacher training. Courses are taught by Bataan and Jane Faigao, who have studied under Grand Master Cheng Man-ch'ing.

Aikido, a Japanese martial art, is also offered. Like tai chi, aikido is both a physical and a spiritual discipline. By continuous practice, one learns to use an attacker's movement and energy to one's own advantage.

Classes range in price from $50 to $135. —M.J.

Martial Arts
Naropa Institute
1111 Pearl St.
Boulder, CO 80302

Wheeling Through

The recent emphasis on fitness, nature, and free time has found an all-encompassing outlet in Vermont Bicycle Touring, a company that opened its doors in 1972 and has been wheeling merrily along since.

Quite simply, the idea is that you come to Vermont and bicycle through its beauty during the day, then spend evenings in its lovely country inns at night. VBT handles the details, from maps and tour leaders to meals and inn reservations, and they even provide a truck that follows along carrying your luggage and spare bicycle parts.

There are 17 different tours available covering all the districts in the state. They run anywhere from a weekend up to 28 days and from 10 miles per day on level roads to 75 miles per day over mountains. Most trips are conducted at a leisurely pace, allowing time for rests, swims, antique browsing, and visits to historic sites.

Additionally, VBT holds a five-day bicycle repair clinic and a bicycle tour planning service, which helps individuals and groups plan their own tours.

Tour rates go from $77 for a weekend up to $257 for seven days. Special prices are available for children and for tours of more than nine days. —C.McB.

Vermont Bicycle Touring
R.D. 2
Bristol, VT 05443

Two-Wheel Dreams

"Know thyself," Socrates said, but most people are in the dark about how to go about it.

One popular self-study method is to tour new places; another is to challenge yourself.

Bike Dream Tours offers you both.

Each year they offer a few informal jaunts in North America and Europe. The terrain and routes are carefully selected for interest and challenge. The tours are as educational as you make them.

One 1978 tour covered Oregon in 14 days from the Columbia Gorge to Mt. Hood—from Indian reservations to the coast. The most elaborate tour, and most expensive package, costs $585 for 14 nights, 14 breakfasts, 15 dinners, tips, taxes, mapbook, sagwagon, and hosts. You are on your own for getting to the start, for repairs, and for personal items.

The meals are big, but rooms are shared. Good health, a ten-speed bike, safety knowledge, and some riding and repair skills (no beginners) are required.

Children are welcome (with parents)—ages range up to 80 and include all kinds of people. Ride at your own speed; you'll always have company. Biking is the purpose of the trip, but you're free to wander. —J.S.

Bike Dream Tours
P.O. Box 20653
Houston, TX 77025

Up, Up, and Away

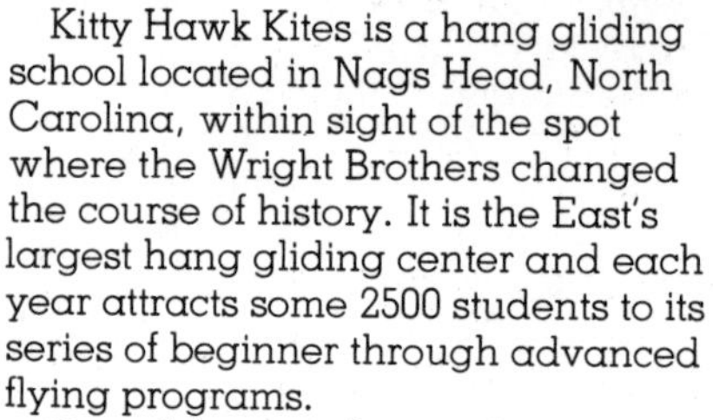

Hang in There

We took a flight of fancy yesterday morning and imagined that the Wright Brothers stood by our side. Orville nodded and Wilbur asked kindly: "Please, show us around." We did, watching their reactions as we went.

At LAX and O'Hare and Kennedy their eyes bulged and their heads shook in amazement. When the pilot of their 747 came back and shook their hands and told them how honored he was to meet them, they modestly insisted that the honor was theirs.

The Blue Angels, the precision jet flying team, drew their applause; an aircraft carrier landing earned their admiration; and a tour through the control room at NASA in Houston provoked a reaction somewhere between awe and bewilderment.

Finally, we took them down to Kitty Hawk in North Carolina, right where it had begun for them and for all of us. They puttered around a bit, stopping to reflect and reach down and touch the dirt. Then we pointed out a hill just off in the distance where men were soaring in the sky beneath the wings of kites. "Hang gliding," we told them, and they looked at each other and smiled smiles full and wide. "We know," they both said at once.

Kitty Hawk Kites is a hang gliding school located in Nags Head, North Carolina, within sight of the spot where the Wright Brothers changed the course of history. It is the East's largest hang gliding center and each year attracts some 2500 students to its series of beginner through advanced flying programs.

One of the nice things about the school is that there isn't a lot of fiddle-faddle time spent learning theory in the schoolhouse. Your first lesson, which lasts about three hours, takes you from the classroom to the nearby sand dunes and to the air, soaring on Atlantic breezes.

Expect your initial taste of flying to be a quick one: most first flights cover 200 feet at about 10 feet off the ground. But things move onward and upward from there. Someday you may find yourself challenging hang gliding records that include a drop from 23,000 feet, a flight up to Mt. McKinley (21,000 feet), staying airborne for nine hours, or covering over 100 ground miles.

For those who wish only to sample the thrill of flight, the beginner's course is available at a cost of only $29. For the more earnest, the school offers a beginning package of three courses and a chance for a Hang I test rating (through the United States Hang Gliding Association) for $54, and a fledgling package of six courses and a Hang II test rating for $114.

Courses are conducted seven days per week throughout the summer and six days per week during the other three seasons. A shirt, long pants, and tennis shoes are the only equipment required. Kitty Hawk Kites provides the helmets and gliders.

Additionally, the school offers opportunities to learn and participate in power gliding, tow gliding, mountain flying, and parasailing. There is also an aero tours service available through the school. Visitors may select a 25-minute look-see flight around the area in a Cessna 172 or choose an all-day special that includes a sailing trip, village tours, and a champagne lunch. —C.McB.

Kitty Hawk Kites
P.O. Box 386
Nags Head, NC 27959

Flying Leaps

When next you're told to take a flying leap, consider doing it with a hang glider. Not only is it safer, it's more fun.

Old as this sport is—its roots go back to the Greek myths of Icarus and earlier—hang gliding is finding renewed popularity. And nothing comes closer to a bird's flight as the hang glider enthusiast—strapped to a giant wing—effortlessly moves amidst the clouds.

Sound like fun? It's all the more fun when learned from professionals. At Windhaven Hang Gliding Schools, where classes are offered weekly, that breathtaking first flight (with ample instruction included) costs $35. Once you've earned your initial wings, Windhaven offers more advanced lessons and also makes available a complete line of everything a hang glider could crave—from parachutes to handbooks. Gliders, starting at about $1000, are for sale. But rental gliders, at nominal charges, are also found at Windhaven. —R.McG.

Windhaven Hang Gliding Schools, Inc.
12437 San Fernando Rd.
Sylmar, CA 91342

Soar Spot

Flying free as a bird in a motorless airplane! Dangerous and farfetched as that sounds, it's not, says the Schweizer Soaring School, one of the nation's leading advocates of skysailing. What skysailing *is*, says Schweizer, is a natural high, where the individual uses his skills and those built into a carefully engineered sailplane to mesh with nature's own atmospheric energy.

Better still, soaring is safe, exciting, and an economical entree to the full range of aviation art and science—and it's open to everyone, 14 years and older. Few thrills match those of the pilot who succeeds in guiding a motorless glider smoothly and silently along a rising air column, nearly defying the earth's gravity.

For those with an itch to taste soaring, Schweizer offers an introductory course ($65) as well as a complete private course ($895), and more specialized instruction for advanced students. Schweizer Schools are found across the nation, and a full line of soaring books and equipment is also available. —R.McG.

Schweizer Soaring School
County Airport, Box 147
Elmira, NY 14902

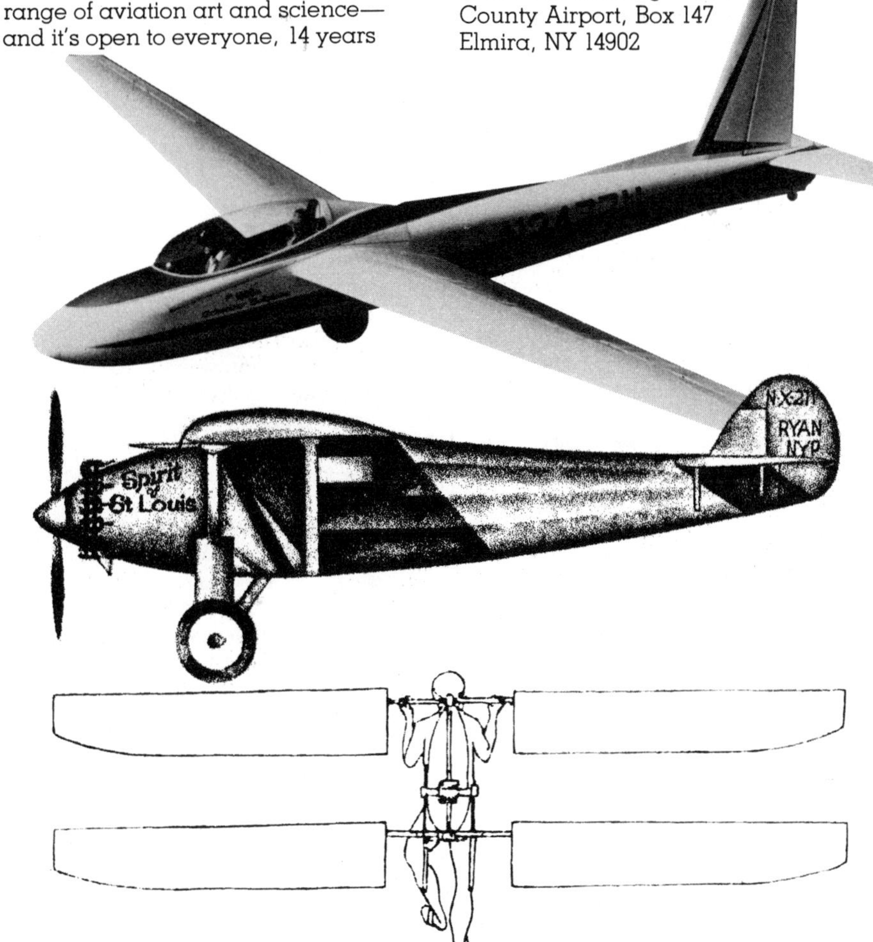

Geronimo!

It's true that a rose is a rose is a rose, but that maxim fails when we're speaking of doors. There is a world of difference and more between skipping out the front door of your house and taking that last, short step out the door of a soaring airplane—"the ultimate high," says the Southern Cross Parachute Center.

Ultimate high or not, inadequately prepared novice skydivers are risking the ultimate low—and that's why Southern Cross offers its one-day instructional course for beginners. Work begins on the ground where, for a half-day, the technicalities and rules of skydiving are fully explored. Then it's up aboard that soaring plane where students, equipped with sophisticated military parachutes and reserve chutes, step into that old wild blue yonder at 3200 feet. Fear not. Parachutes are automatically deployed and all jumps are made under the supervision of a fully licensed Sport Parachutist Jump Master. Full cost, including use of necessary equipment, is $49. —R.McG.

Southern Cross Parachute Center
P.O. Box 366
Williamsport, MD 21795

Fly and you will catch the swallow.
JAMES HOWELL

Deep in the Sky of Texas Birds soar and so can you. Southwest Soaring, in Texas, offers a basic soaring course for persons with no previous flying experience. Upon completion of the course you will be a licensed student pilot with authorization to fly solo in the type of sailplane used for training. The cost is $395.

Southwest Soaring
Box 460
Caddo Mills, TX 75005

Icarus Fulfilled The people at the Kutztown Soaring School say that "you can fulfill a dream that has sparked the imagination of man for thousands of years!" They offer complete basic soaring lessons that will qualify you for an FAA private pilot's license. They also offer introductory flights and lessons.

Kutztown Soaring School
Kutztown Aviation Service, Inc.
R.D. 1, Box 1
Kutztown Airport, PA 19530

But How Do I Land? Soar like a bird! There's no need to flap your wings—Sky Sailors, Inc. offers private soaring lessons for anyone over 16 years of age. Instruction is $14 per hour.

Sky Sailors, Inc.
Brookhaven Airport
222 Grand Ave.
Shirley, Long Island, NY 11967

Full of Hot Air

Do you like to get high? Would you willingly roll out of bed at five in the morning, drive several miles to a dew-covered field, climb into a small basket attached to a large bag of hot air, and go drifting off into the sunrise—only to be deposited in a cow pasture twenty miles away?

If the answer to both of these questions is yes, you may be a candidate for "Professor" Hall's Hot Air Balloon School of Higher Learning.

Thanks to modern technology, which gives us inexpensive liquefied propane, you no longer have to be the nephew or niece of a super-rich aunt to enjoy this elevating experience.

Modern ballooning has come a long way in the 200 years since Joseph and Etienne Montgolfier first filled their oversized paper sack with smoky heat from a damp straw fire and lifted the world's first aeronauts—a sheep, a duck and a rooster—off the ground.

"Professor" Hall's balloons are the type certified by the Federal Aviation Agency and his instructors are all FAA licensed pilots. It takes three to six months to complete the course and earn your lighter-than-air certificate. —E.H.

"Professor" Hall's Hot Air Balloon School of Higher Learning
1656 Massachusetts Ave.
Lexington, MA 02173

The empty, vast, and wandering air.
WILLIAM SHAKESPEARE

The Red Baron Soars Again

The only noise is the song of the wind. The snow-capped Grand Tetons rise majestically skywards and you're surrounded by a panorama of deep-blue sky, soft billowing clouds, and squared-off fields of rippling wheat and barley.

The sleek, long-winged glider hits a "lift," and instantly you're riding an invisible elevator to the clouds at 1000 feet per minute.

It's the closest you can come to man's timeless dream of flight—soaring. And if you want to learn this growing sport, an ideal place is the Red Baron Soaring School in Driggs, Idaho.

Classes for beginners and rated pilots are available. For beginners, a complete package course includes dual instruction, ground instruction, an instruction kit, and a solo flight leading to your private license. Cost is $588. Rated pilots can obtain their glider license in ten flights with no minimum air time or written exam. The School has an FAA designated examiner on full-time duty for your convenience. Complete cost is $345 and rated pilots can complete it in a weekend. —P.T.

Red Baron Soaring
Teton Peaks Airport
Driggs, ID 83422

Hotheads

Hot-air ballooning has to be just about the perfect NOW sport. It is simple, yet distinctive. It is nonaggressive. It does not endanger the environment or animals. There is a mild element of risk (hence exhilaration) involved. The mechanics are minimal. There are both actual and theoretical beauties involved. And, perhaps best of all, it is fun.

One of the most enthusiastic ballooning groups in the US is Golden Bear Enterprises of Glendale, California. They'll take you for a balloon ride if you wish, or they'll put you through an extensive training program to get you registered as a hot-air balloon pilot. They'll even sell you a balloon of your very own, should the bug really bite you.

If there is a drawback to ballooning, it would be its cost. A half-hour trip sets you back $40, while an hour for a couple runs $125. Should you wish to take pilot lessons, prepare to fork up $1200. And the price on that balloon of your own begins at $6000 and floats right on up. —C.McB.

Golden Bear Enterprises
P.O. Box 3682
Glendale, CA 91201

Bishop Wilkins prophesied that the time would come when gentlemen, when they were to go on a journey, would call for their wings as regularly as they call for their boots.
MARIA EDGEWORTH

High in the Sky

You'll learn to float on the whims of the wind on an ocean with no waves. It's hot-air ballooning, man's first experience with flight. It began over two centuries ago in France—120 years before Orville and Wilbur's historic flight at Kitty Hawk.

Most likely you will never make it around the world in eighty days or so, but after completion of the flying course by Balloon Excelsior of Oakland, California, you'll be eligible to receive your private pilot license after five to ten mornings of flying.

There's more than the traditional bottle of champagne and waving to the passers-by, and the Balloon Excelsior course involves the necessities of preflight preparation, inflation and mooring procedures, high-altitude flying, and landowner/agricultural landing considerations.

Excelsior's commercial license course involves a mere eight hours of flying.

The school does everything it can to help you along the route to whatever certfication you seek by issuing student certificates on the premises and providing you with study material and personal preparation for the FAA's pilot certification exam.

The fee is $900 for the private pilot course and $1500 for the commercial license course. —P.T.

Balloon Excelsior, Inc.
1241 High St.
Oakland, CA 94601

High at Noon This balloon won't pop—not the one you're riding in during your stay at the Balloon Ranch. The Ranch offers hot-air rides and ballooning lessons, besides resort activities such as tennis, swimming, skiing, and horseback riding. The complete ballooning course is $800; balloon rides are $45. These prices do not include the cost for staying at the Ranch itself.

Balloon Ranch
Star Route, Box 41
Del Norte, CO 81132

Phileas Fogg and You "Hot-air ballooning is a sport," says Thunder Pacific's brochure. "It can be a relaxing one, and for many there is nothing better than the ultimate escape from everyday business."

Thunder Pacific can teach you to fly one of those hot-air bags. The rate is $100 per hour. But the minimum FAA flight experience requirement for a private pilot balloon rating is ten hours. So be prepared to spend a good deal of money.

Thunder Pacific
114 Sandalwood Court
Santa Rosa, CA 95401

High Times It's a fact that hot air rises. You can rise with it with your new skill as a balloon pilot. The Life Cycle Balloon School offers balloon pilot instruction that will help you pass the FAA required exam. You will then be an FAA certified balloon pilot. The School also offers a two-day ground school for $25 that can help you on your way to becoming a balloon pilot.

Life Cycle Balloon School
1338 Fifteenth at Market
Denver, CO 80202

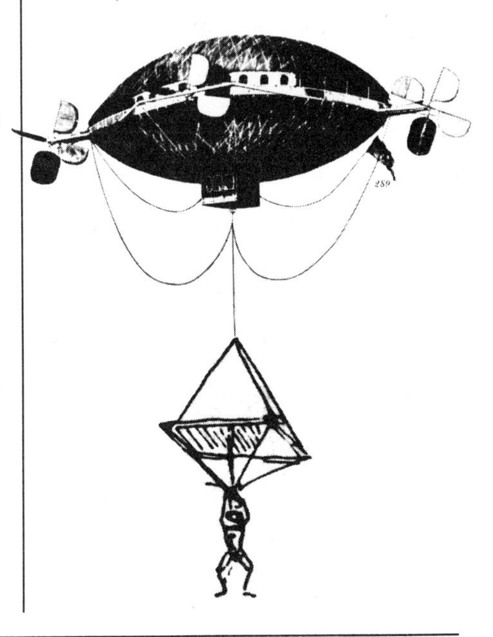

Water, Water Everywhere

In You Go

There's a whole other world down there.

A world free of rush-hour traffic, obtrusive mothers-in-law, and unbalanced check statements. A silent world, bursting with the infinite colors of the rainbow on fish who dart about in the crystal-clear Caribbean waters. A world of sunken Spanish galleons and of manta rays gliding above the ocean floor like prehistoric monsters in flight.

Whether you are an experienced scuba diver or just someone who has always yearned to explore the regions beneath the waves, the Underwater Explorers Society (UNEXSO) offers a series of classes and programs that will fit your needs.

UNEXSO is located in the Caribbean on Grand Bahama Island in the town of Freeport/Lucaya. Grand Bahama Island is internationally recognized as one of the diving capitals of the world. UNEXSO's headquarters offers a luxury hotel as well as diving facilities that *Skin Diver* magazine has called "one of the world's best."

The reefs surrounding UNEXSO range from a shallow area with depths varying from 4 to 15 feet, to where the continental shelf drops into a 2000-foot abyss.

For beginners, UNEXSO offers two methods for learning to scuba dive. The introductory course is a flexible, low-key approach for vacationers. Working with qualified instructors, you begin with an informal poolside session before learning the basic techniques essential for diving. From there it's practice in the 18-foot-deep training pool followed by an actual dive on a nearby shallow reef. You may be diving on a reef of 65 feet within a few days.

The other option for the beginner is a complete program leading to certification as a qualified scuba diver. This is an intense 30-hour class involving classroom, poolside, and open-water instruction, and is designed for the more serious enthusiast.

For the experienced diver there are daily boat trips to different diving locations and depths. The area's diving potential is so extensive you can dive for days without going back to the same dive site—yet each boat ride takes no more than 15 minutes. When conditions permit, there is night diving. On clear nights you can turn off the spotlights and let the moonlight be your guide.

UNEXSO is more than a recreational facility and offers a wide range of advanced programs as well. The experienced diver certification class offers divers the opportunity to get their "C-card," with classes taught on a one-to-one basis. The sport-diver course gives the diver a variety of scuba experiences. There is also a course to acquaint members of the medical profession with the problems of diving-related trauma.

Fees for the various courses range from $99 to $250 for UNEXSO members (membership costs $40 for an individual, $60 for a family) and is $125 to $280 for nonmembers. —P.T.

The International Underwater Explorers Society
P.O. Box 15933
W. Palm Beach, FL 33406

Diving the Ohio Ocean

Hundreds of miles from the sea, in Ohio, scuba diving has become the "in" sport. Collegians, housewives, factory workers, and bankers are lining up in full equipment to plunge into the clear waters of a swimming pool.

Through the Buckeye Diving School near Cleveland, students learn to handle the reefs of the far-off Pacific. The school, despite its location, runs one of the most comprehensive diving programs in the country, teaching care of equipment, diving physics, and decompression problems.

Divers who conquer the basic skills may wade into instructed adventures like ice diving, shipwreck diving, and night diving.

The advanced students are taken by Buckeye from local high school and YMCA pools to the greater depths of Ohio quarries, where they learn how to handle underwater emergencies.

The basic diving course is $60; the advanced is $40.

Buckeye also sponsors trips to the world's best diving lagoons. In past years groups from Cleveland have rippled the waters from Micronesia to Lake Erie's 200 buried shipwrecks. —J.W.

Buckeye Diving School
46 Warrensville Center Rd.
Bedford, OH 44146

Drop-Offs Unlimited

As you plunge downward into the warm azure water, you look up and see the hull of your diving ship receding away with the brilliant Caribbean sun behind it. A trail of bubbles is your only connection with the surface world. Here all is dreamlike.

Quixotic, wildly colored fish swim past you in shoals as you swim toward the Plancar Reef. A crusty sea turtle paddles gracefully and mindlessly past on one of its epic journeys. A startled ray darts from beneath you.

Where are you? You are diving off the island of Cozumel, 15 miles from the Yucatan. And your special mission on this dive is to gather lobster and conch for dinner. This diving expedition is one offered by See & Sea Diving Adventures—which claims to give you more dives for the dollar than any other outfitter.

Cozumel is the most popular destination, but it is by no means the only one. See & Sea offers a Great White Shark trip for the dauntless; it offers the placid waters of Sri Lanka or Fiji; and in a recent addition to its roster of voyages, it sails the Red Sea. Costs vary widely, depending on length of tour and destination. —J.A.

See & Sea Diving Adventures
680 Beach St., Suite 340, Wharfside
San Francisco, CA 94109

The Wet Set Get in deep. V. I. Divers, located in St. Croix, Virgin Islands, offers scuba "packages" for experienced divers (rates include diving, hotel, and breakfast) and a full scuba certification course for beginners. Prices range from $225 to $340 for the eight-day programs.

V. I. Divers, Ltd.
Pan Am Pavilion, Christiansted
St. Croix, US Virgin Islands 00820

Full Fathom Five The Virgin Islands are beautiful—above and below water. The Kilbride family offers underwater tours of these islands to experienced divers. Can't dive? The Kilbrides offer Professional Association of Diving Instructors approved scuba instruction. The cost is $50 to $75. Their tours cost between $40 and $285 per day depending on the season.

Kilbride's Underwater Tours
Box 40
Virgin Gorda
British Virgin Islands

Tiny Bubbles The people of the Pacific Sportdiving Company are honest. Their objective is to "operate a profitable business which provides recreational enjoyment for vacationing scuba divers." The Company takes divers and nondivers alike on diving cruises near Hawaii. While on board their cruise boat the *Spirit of Adventure* you can learn how to scuba if you don't already know how. The cost is from $119 to $900 per person.

Pacific Sportdiving Co., Inc.
4104 E. Anaheim St.
Long Beach, CA 90804

Immerse Yourself

People who grew up on *Sea Hunt* and later watched Jacques Cousteau's specials have always known that diving is exotic, unique, and exhilirating.

But those shows never gave a hint about how to get started at the sport under conditions that are unique enough to be truly interesting. Learning in murky water close to home just seems too much work. Many, I'm sure, also worry about the costs of learning at some more interesting spot.

Sea Life Discovery offers a way around these problems.

They offer courses and vacations at some of the most exotic locations possible and help you to get your feet wet. You learn with qualified teachers who also happen to be trained specialists in the ocean biome. You can learn at a not unreasonable price, or you can take a trip and just watch them do the diving, at a discount over the package tour.

They also offer an 11- or 12-day St. Croix Virgin Islands trip that teaches you to scuba dive if you don't know how and gets you certification. After your group's arrival, new divers will learn the ropes, while the experienced divers will see the "Cane Bay Dropoff" on their own (buddy system always in effect). The trip costs $895 for divers and $805 for snorkelers, including round-trip air fare from Miami.

Another tour, 11 days in the area around Grand Cayman Island, costs $935 for divers, $635 for snorkelers. It is led by Dr. Steve Webster, a Ph.D. in marine biology and an associate professor at San Jose State in California. He tours the prolific reefs and teaches divers about tropical reef biology as well, offering slides and discussions. A relaxed college-level course.

Diving is offered twice daily, but with a buddy you can dive more often. And there are excellent photo possibilities and a specialized camera store.

If you are a nondiver you are welcome on these trips at reduced rates. There are island tours, shopping, and beautiful beaches for walking and swimming. Skin divers are also welcome. Bikes, motorbikes, and cars can be rented at individual expense. Scheduled activities are designed for scuba divers, so nondivers should be somewhat self-sufficient.

The basic package also includes hotel expenses, meals, and biology instruction. You are on your own for excess baggage and equipment, insurance, immunization, medical costs, and personal expenses.

Custom-designed courses are also available. —J.S.

Sea Life Discovery
19915 Oakmont Dr.
Los Gatos, CA 95030

Make Your Trout Proud

If you were a trout, would you bite at a badly cast lure?

I bet you'd rather starve. Fish may be dumb, but they have pride. So show some respect and learn how to make your fishing hours count at the Montana School of Fly Fishing.

Their basic course is $395 for seven days and nights on Montana's Stillwater River. The price includes accommodations, maid service, three meals a day, all fly fishing tackle, and costs incidental to field trips.

School consists of 12 hours of classroom work, 12 hours of pond-casting instruction (forward casts, side-arm casts, and others), line control technique, and 24 hours of field-trip work including trips to other rivers.

The School teaches a variety of techniques, including assembly and selection of tackle. Flies will be discussed at length, including how to make them and use them, which ones to use under what conditions, and instruction on insect life and behavior as related to fishing. —J.S.

Montana School of Fly Fishing
Nye, MT 59061

Windsurf's Up!

Called by some the "ultimate free ride," the new sport of windsurfing calls on the inherent power and beauty of sea and air to provide its source of energy.

It's not surfing and it's not sailing; rather, it's a little of both combined to create a new and different sport.

And if you want to learn how to windsurf in a quarter of the time it would take you if you approached it on your own, lessons from Bay Surf Windsurfers in Menlo Park, California, are what you're looking for.

The windsurfer looks like a conventional surfboard but is twice as long and is considerably thicker. Resting on top of the board is a single sail that you control from a standing position as you glide along.

Bay Surf Windsurfers course for beginners consists of two three-hour lessons that begin on a dry-land trainer before moving out to the calm waters of the nearby lagoon. The school also offers advanced classes. Bay Surf supplies the windsurfer itself, a wet suit, hydrolic simulator, and special manual.

The two three-hour lessons cost $40, and advanced lessons are $30 per person for two hours. —P.T.

Bay Surf Windsurfers
940 Cotton St.
Menlo Park, CA 94025

Call of the Kayak

Dear Jill,

Remember when I told you I was thinking about taking kayaking lessons and you told me you thought I was nuts? Well, I went ahead and did it.

I spent nine days at the Sundance Kayak School on the Rogue River in Oregon. At first I was sorry I hadn't listened to you because, as I quickly learned, kayaking is no piece of cake. The first few nights I spent hours in the sauna trying to get my shoulders and arms to move again.

Eventually I got the hang of it and our group made an expedition together down the lower Rogue. My reaction was mixed—first humility as I was confronted by the power of the river, and then a tremendous sensation of achievement and control as I succeeded in maneuvering my way through the rapids. We all agreed it was as much a spiritual experience as a physical one.

I'd love for you to try it. Their All Women's Kayak School is coming up soon. I'll send you the information. —E.H.

Sundance Expeditions
14894 Galice Rd.
Merlin, OR 97532

The Other Annapolis

If you've always yearned to go to sea, but don't know a jib from a jab, why not learn from the oldest and the best? If you've wanted to enjoy the art and sport of sailing, and at the same time take a relaxing vacation for yourself or for your entire family, then the renowned Annapolis Sailing School deserves a closer look.

Not just another sailing school, Annapolis is the granddaddy of sailing schools. Founded over 20 years ago, it was the first school of its kind and has been credited with being a prime catalyst for the surge in popularity that sailing has experienced over the past two decades.

The cornerstone of the Annapolis Sailing School is its pioneering teaching method. The program is a two-part procedure that over 50,000 sailors, from landlubbing beginners to sea-worn veterans, have participated in. It's called the "Annapolis Way," and it begins with a broad selection of courses to accommodate the specific needs of students. The classes cover the fundamentals of sailing, followed by supervised practice on a fiberglass sloop specially designed and built for this program.

Before the ink has time to dry on your notebook it'll be time for the second half of the program. It's into the boats with your family and friends to enjoy the pleasure of gliding effortlessly over the water, powered by the whims of the wind.

The School bolsters its claim as the number one sailing school by pointing out that it alone is capable of organizing live-aboard cruise courses where students sail with their families or friends and learn the fundamentals of cruising.

The course offerings fall into three categories: basic, cruise, and advanced. All use the format of the "Annapolis Way."

There are three basic courses and they last from two to five days. The two-day course covers a weekend and is the most popular sailing course ever given. Other basic courses include a four-part class designed for persons within driving distance of the school, and a five-day vacationers course.

For the more experienced, the cruising courses offer the opportunity to spend two to five days sailing all day and harboring at night in secluded bays, while learning more advanced skills. In a cruising course you select the boat of your choice and live in the privacy of your own family (of two to seven persons), yet have the careful supervision of the school's instructors.

The advanced courses are for the serious sailor and involve material that ranges from celestial and coastal navigation to piloting and handling a cruising auxiliary.

The Annapolis Sailing School is headquartered in Annapolis, Maryland, on historic and picturesque Chesapeake Bay. It also has branches in Hull, Massachusetts; St. Petersburg, Florida; St. Thomas in the US Virgin Islands; Lake Geneva, Wisconsin; Puget Sound and Seattle, Washington; and San Diego, California.

Prices range from $110 per person for the weekend beginners course to $155 for advanced courses. —P.T.

Annapolis Sailing School
P.O. Box 3334
Annapolis, MD 21403

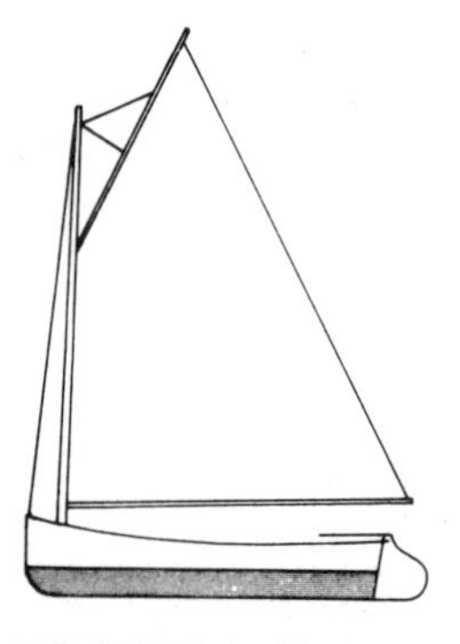
Gaff-rigged cat boat.

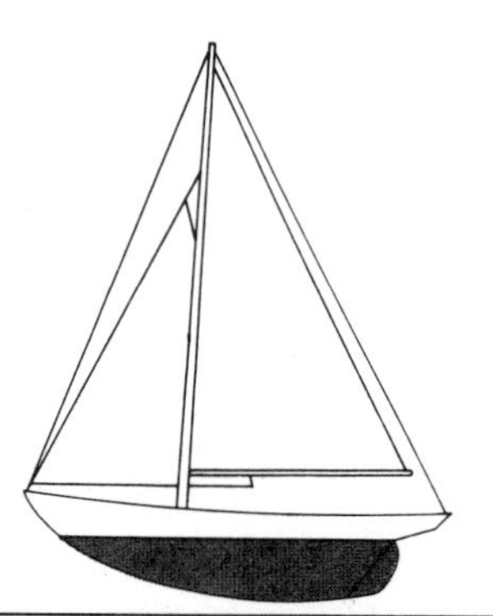
Marconi-rigged sloop.

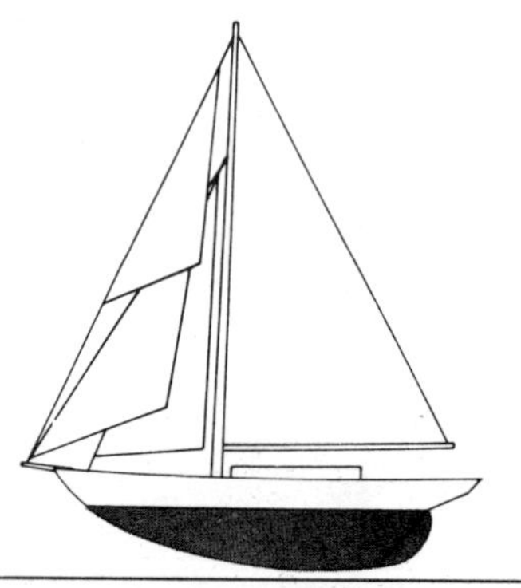
Marconi-rigged cutter.

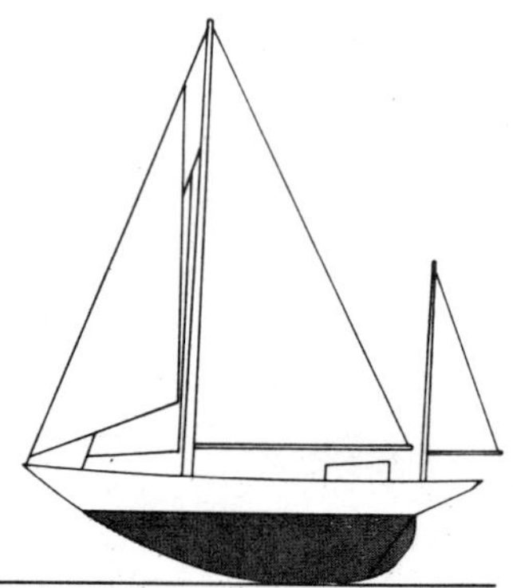
Marconi-rigged yawl.

Joy, Shipmate, Joy

Monday—I arrived in Barrington, Rhode Island, this morning and found my way over to the McVay Sailing School. I met Skipper McVay and his wife, Ruth. They are both veteran sailors and down-to-earth, friendly people. We boarded *Pizzazz*, a C&C 38 auxiliary sloop, and were assigned berths and indoctrinated in the correct use of the head.

Tuesday—A swim before breakfast (Ruth's a great cook), and we were under way for Dutch Island. We practiced reefing the mainsail, changing headsails under way, and man overboard drills.

Wednesday—There's really a lot to learn and Skipper McVay is determined we learn all of it. We secured in Mackeral Cove for lunch and a swim today. Enjoyed chatting with the other guests.

Thursday—Lessons today in tides, weather, safety at sea, and use of safety harnesses. I think I'm learning more because I'm participating in all aspects of the ship's handling.

Friday—Took full command of *Pizzazz* today as we sailed into Bristol Harbor. Wouldn't have believed at the start of the week that it would be possible. —E.H.

McVay Sailing School
64 Mason Rd.
Barrington, RI 02806

Hey, Sailor

Endless variety. That's what Oceanus, a nonprofit group of mariners, promises those who sign up for a hitch on their yachts.

Offering more than a dozen excursions yearly, Oceanus and its minifleet of 50- and 60-foot yachts explore the world's oceans, with the emphasis on imparting to passengers a sense of the spirit of adventure that all sailors share and of the excitement of the sea.

Each year's expedition itinerary is different, but recent months have seen Oceanus exploring the waters of Cuba, Haiti, the Bahamas, Guatemala. Along the way, passengers are invited to learn the basics of the maritime arts from the experienced crew and enjoy the ocean and its charms. The agenda, says Oceanus, is largely determined by the interest of the passengers.

Expeditions vary in length from a few days to two weeks. Cost ranges from about $300 to $1000, depending upon the trip's duration and destination. Meals and on-board sleeping quarters are included in the package. —R.McG.

Oceanus
Box 431
Ho-Ho-Kus, NJ 07423

Jib over Manhattan The people of RTY, Inc. want you to choose a sailing school carefully. And, naturally, they'd like you to choose theirs. They feel that you must learn the basics of sailing out on the water, in addition to learning them from a blackboard. Classes are small—three to four students. The cost for the basic sailing course is $175.

Basic Sailing Course
RTY, Inc.
225 Fordham St.
City Island
Bronx, NY 10464

Small Craft Advisories The United States Yacht Racing Union (USYRU) doesn't teach you how to sail. But they do have courses for advanced sailors, such as advanced racing clinics, instructors' seminars, Olympic Class training clinics, and others.

United States Yacht Racing Union
820 Davis St.
Evanston, IL 60201

I was born upon thy bank river
My blood flows in thy stream
And thou meanderist forever
At the bottom of my dreams.
HENRY DAVID THOREAU

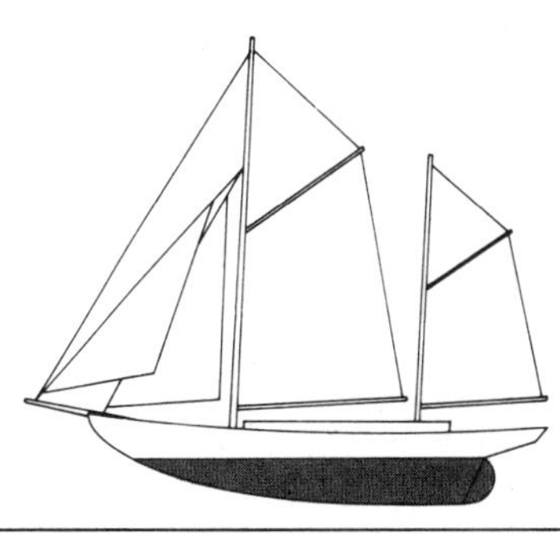

Gaff-rigged ketch.

Eye of the Hurricane

Outward Bound to Hurricane Island.

Well now, wouldn't that be a pip of a title for a swashbuckling sea adventure. Full of "avasts" and "ahoys" and high seas and pirates and all those other good things that send salt spray racing through the mind.

Fact is, though, it isn't a sea tale at all. But it is an adventure, one you can experience through the Outward Bound School on Hurricane Island up along the rugged coast of Maine.

Many are familiar with the Outward Bound schools by now. They're based on the idea of testing oneself against nature and the wilderness to learn more about oneself. It was a concept born in wartime Britain that has grown today into more than 30 schools on five continents. There are seven highly successful Outward Bound schools in the United States, with Hurricane Island being the only sea school.

Hurricane Island's speciality is a 26-day program that emphasizes seamanship—learned aboard a 30-foot open pulling/sailboat that soon becomes a second home for the eleven students and two instructors. The course, open to anyone age 16½ and up, is divided into several phases. Initially, the skills that will be used throughout the stay are taught: basic seamanship, sail theory, first aid, shelter building, navigation, and outdoor cooking.

Next comes what the Outward Bound folks call the "solo," a three-day stay on part of an uninhabited island, where the student uses his or her new knowledge to forage for food and keep dry and warm. It is a time of testing, of solitude, and of reflection.

The final phase is a five-day voyage charted by the students that may take them up to 100 miles along the coastline.

Students also spend two to three days learning the art of rock climbing on some of Maine's most beautiful granite cliffs, as well as taking part in group problem solving and community service. Total cost for the program is $825.

Additionally, the Hurricane Island school runs several other special courses. One is a 28-day session for teachers, educators, and youth workers that is similar to the 26-day course but that's shaped to emphasize the incorporation of experiential education into traditional teaching. It is open to educators 22 and up and costs $870. There are also five- and ten-day courses offered for those who cannot afford the time for the full sessions. Elements are similar to the longer courses, though greatly compressed due to the time involved. One of the ten-day courses stresses natural history and provides an opportunity to observe and study the unique flora and fauna of Maine's coastal islands. The ten-day courses cost $450, while the five-day sessions are $275.

Two other courses scheduled by the school are ten- and five-day winter camping expeditions in Maine ($450 and $275, respectively), and fourteen- and five-day sailing sessions in the Florida Keys and Everglades ($550 and $275).

The school also holds courses for other groups—juniors (14½ to 16½), men over 40, and women over 30. —C.McB.

Hurricane Island
Outward Bound School
Box 429
Rockland, ME 04841

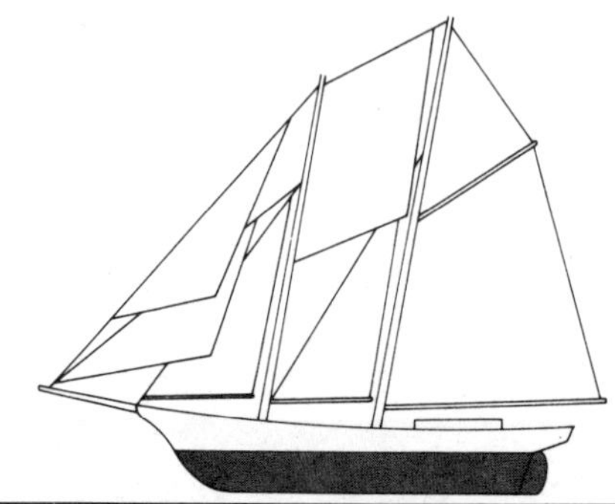

Gaff-rigged schooner.

Sail Away

You could be a novice who thinks that port is a red wine and that knots are what you get in tangled shoelaces. Or you could be an old pro familiar with mast bend, sail trim, and reading the wind.

Whatever your experience, if you've ever dreamed of mastering a sailboat, don't luff around. Plot a course to the nearest Offshore Sailing School with locations in South Carolina, Martha's Vineyard, the British Islands, Florida, Maryland, and New York. You could be on your way to one of the best week-long vacations you've ever had.

The School offers four levels of instruction: Learn to Sail, Learn to Cruise, Introductory Racing, and Advanced Racing. For each level a total of 20 hours of lessons is given on the fast and sophisticated 27′ Olympic Soling. And you won't have to compete for attention because there are never more than four students per boat.

Costs for the courses range from $129 to $249, depending on location and course level. Some locations have packaged costs, which include accommodations and some or all meals with the tuition. —B.H.

Offshore Sailing School, Ltd.
820 Second Ave.
New York, NY 10017

Stars as Roadsigns

What better way to learn the maritime arts than from a skilled sailor right in your home? But most of us, no matter how deep our interest in the sea, lack a personal mariner. And talk of the finer points of navigation, while exciting, just may leave us more confused than enlightened. The Audio Navigation Institute can help—no matter where you live.

Offering six mail-order courses in boating, the Institute's program covers both the basics—from selection of a power- or sailboat—through advanced sailing and racing techniques. Courses in coastwise, celestial, and electronic navigation are also available. Each course comes on an audio cassette and is taught by a recognized expert. And an advantage of learning by cassette, as the Institute points out, is that students are free to learn at their own rate and cassettes are always available for review of finer points—even during at-sea emergencies.

Cassettes range in price from $59.95 through $89.95. The Institute also retails a line of sophisticated navigational instruments. —R.McG.

Audio Navigation Institute
144 Pioneer Way
El Cajon, CA 92020

Seeing Through the Dark

Even though the Coast Navigation School is on the Pacific (in Santa Barbara, California), you don't have to find your way there in order to take classes. The School offers home-study courses in navigation.

Whether you're a new sailor or an old salt, one of their courses may be right for you. The School was founded by Captain Svend T. Simonsen, Master Mariner, to enable pleasure and professional boat owners to learn the arts of seafaring and navigation in their spare time at home.

There's a course in coastwise navigation, teaching basic skills like reading a chart and laying out a course; figuring time, speed, and distance of your passages on the water; using tide and current tables; and using navigators' instruments. The School supplies all text materials and charts plus instruction at a cost of $115. Navigational instruments are needed, and they may be purchased through the school.

There's also a course on celestial navigation, the classic technique used by sailors for centuries. It teaches how to use both sun and stars to locate your vessel's position and chart your course. Cost: $180.

Other home study courses—"Marine Meteorology," "Boating and Seamanship," "Introduction to the Art of Sailing," and "The World of Cruising"—are available. —A.L.

Coast Navigation School
22 North Milpas
Santa Barbara, CA 93102

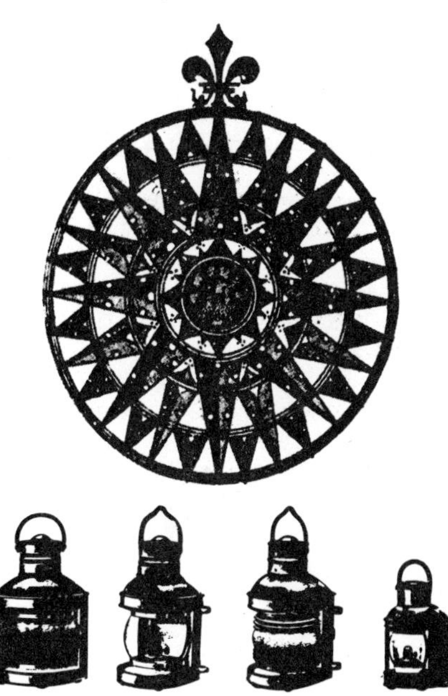

The Competitive Spirit

Love on the Court

You just know, deep inside, that with a little professional polishing you could demolish Jimmy Connors or Chris Evert on the tennis courts. And Bobby Riggs, you mutter, would be *lucky* to finish with love.

Here's your chance. The instruction at Stratton Mountain, Vermont, is catered by John Newcombe, one of the games greatest aces.

The basis of Newcombe's lessons is "Newk Plus"—a comprehensive view of the game and its ingredients. Tennis basics are stressed as students start at the ground and, over five days of lessons, work their way to levels they just might find incredible. Go through "Newk Plus" and Bobby Riggs might not be that hard to beat.

Can't believe it? Instruction is organized around a series of mini-clinics, each taught by a teaching professional. And, yes, Newcombe himself does teach here.

Master the basic elements of tennis, Newcombe thinks, and you're well on your way toward controlling the whole game. The mini-clinics make certain you are on the right track—the instruction is painstakingly detailed.

Everything from the rudiments—equipment, volley, elementary tips—through tennis esoterica—three zones of the court, groundstrokes, and backhand—is explored in the mini-clinics. Limited to four to six students per pro, mini-clinics are designed to give each student detailed personal attention and, in the process, every student is challenged to improve all aspects of his or her game.

In the doubles clinic, for example, students arrive at 2 p.m. to soak up "Tips on Tennis" and proceed to the two and one-half hour instruction clinic. Following the instruction, there's the two-hour round-robin doubles tournament, where students put into practice what their instructors preach.

Clinics are scheduled from 9:30 a.m. through 7 p.m. every day of the week. For students seeking the full Newcombe treatment, the five-day tennis program is suggested, where all aspects of the game are covered. Local residents, and others seeking to improve a single element of their game, are invited to sign up for mini-clinics on an a la carte basis.

Package plans are available that include room and board. And, worry not, you're sure to get ample court time. Besides eight Har-True courts, there are two indoor courts where play goes on round-the-clock. That's serious tennis playing, but *nobody* ever said Jimmy Connors isn't serious, right? —R.McG.

John Newcombe Tennis Center
Stratton Mountain
Stratton Mountain, VT 05155

Braden Knows Best

Are you having trouble with your balls? Do you need to work on your strokes? At the Vic Braden Tennis College they promise "Four strokes a day, 1900 balls a day, and a laugh a minute."

The College, located in Trabuco Canyon, California, offers two-, three-, and five-day courses that cost from $125 to $300 (not including food or lodging).

The Braden method of teaching tennis includes the use of films, videotapes, charts, diagrams, and take-home instruction booklets. All the coaches are personally trained by Braden himself, whose goal is for you to "laugh a little, learn a lot, and take home a good game that you can keep making better."

Braden is a tournament player, psychologist, teacher, filmmaker, innovator, international consultant, entertainer, and philosopher. In the May 10, 1976 *Sports Illustrated,* Frank Deford said, "When he stands up, Vic Braden sounds like a combination of Norman Vincent Peale and Rodney Dangerfield, but attentive students listen—and learn." —E.H.

The Vic Braden Tennis College
22000 Plano Trabuco Canyon Rd.
Trabuco Canyon, CA 92674

Advantage—Yours

What ever happens to all those ski chalets in the summer? Do they just sit there gathering dust under the sun's warm rays?

Big Bear Tennis Ranch's owner-director, Bill Frantz, thought it was foolish to let those chalets go downhill out of season. The California mountains are just as beautiful in the summer as they are in the winter—maybe even more beautiful. The weather is gorgeous: warm enough but not too hot. So Bill decided to give a cluster of chalets a lift. He built 13 tennis courts, 2 clay ones and 11 hard courts, and opened the Tennis Ranch.

The Ranch is open for adults on weekends. Starting Friday and ending Sunday afternoon, tennis lovers can play their hearts out. They can get lessons from pros, individual counseling, and instruction from watching tennis movies in the evening.

All meals are provided by the Ranch. Total cost, including tuition, is $150 per person. That costs includes wine and beer, which are on the house. If you overdo, at least you won't have to worry about injury from a sloppy slalom. A sloppy serve never hurt anyone.

On weekdays, the Ranch serves as a tennis camp for boys and girls ages 7 to 17. —A.L.

Adult Weekends
Big Bear Tennis Ranch
Box 767
Big Bear City, CA 92314

Taos Racquet The people at the Tennis Ranch of Taos say that their tennis clinics are unique. "Why unique?" asks their brochure. "Unique because the emphasis of instruction revolves around one word—'Awareness.' Awareness of your own learning process is the major goal of the clinics, and our tennis pros are committed to increasing your awareness of all phases of your tennis game." The package price is $395-$433.

Tennis Ranch of Taos
P.O. Box Drawer BBB
Taos, NM 87571

Net Gain Learn how to play tennis at the Tennis Institute. And that's not all. You can also learn how to play badminton. The Institute's objective is to make quality tennis and badminton instruction available to all, with emphasis on small group instruction and a friendly environment. Instruction fees are $40 to $240.

Tennis Institute
27 E. 19th St.
New York, NY 10003

Tennis 101? "Our tennis program is designed to suit the individual's need—be it overall practice, specialized work on a skill, or an in-depth strategy lesson to complete a player's game," says the Pala Mesa Resort's College for Tennis brochure. The rates are $63 to $236 for the two-day packages.

College for Tennis
Pala Mesa Resort
2001 S. Hwy 395
Fallbrook, CA 92028

The Net Setters Vacation in comfort and learn how to play tennis—or learn some tips on how to improve your game. John Gardiner's Tennis Ranch on Camelback Mountain offers special week-long tennis clinics for beginners through advanced at various times during the year. The cost is between $775 and $1100 per person.

John Gardiner's Tennis Ranch
on Camelback Mountain
5700 E. McDonald Dr.
Scottsdale, AZ 85253

The only athletic sport I ever mastered was backgammon.
DOUGLAS JERROLD

Fore School

Ben Sutton doesn't believe you can't teach an old dog new tricks. It's not even hard—not when you combine Florida sun, an alluring golf course, and novel teaching techniques. Put in a week at Golf School for Seniors, Sutton's place, and Arnie Palmer, look out!

Straightaway, Sutton clarifies, participants need not be seniors. In most years, the age of golfers ranges from 15 to 85, with an average age of 50. "The young, not-so-young, couples, and singles are all most welcome," says Sutton.

No matter what your age, golf is the thing here. For 22 weeks every year, running from fall through spring, the Golf School for Seniors is open and operating with a single goal in mind—making participants better golfers. But you'll have fun while you're at it.

Individual attention is guaranteed. Attendance at each week-long session is about 75. But there's a teaching pro for every six to eight participants.

Classes start at 9 a.m. and run nonstop through 4 p.m., when optional play commences. Sure, there's a lunch break—but your pro sits, eats, and talks golf at your table.

Sound thorough? It is. Each class lasts one hour, and a typical day includes a clinic, practice on the range, a dose of chipping and putting, a bout with sand traps, and a color TV analysis of your technique. That's right, TV—the little box is a big and important part of the Sutton method.

Instant replay, the School thinks, allows golfers to see exactly what they are doing, both right and wrong. See it and you're on your way to making necessary corrections.

Every student's first class consists of taping his or her swing, followed by detailed examination of the technique. Comes the final day of classes and every student is back to the taping room for another session. This time, the student gets to watch both his entry swing and his new swing. Most see real improvement—improvement reflected on score cards, too.

That TV is running continuously, in fact. The School packages golf lessons for distribution to TV stations across the nation and those lessons flicker on the School's closed-circuit TVs. Students are free to watch and learn at their own pace—and that's in addition to the personalized attention of the pros.

Cost of a week at the Golf School—including room, most meals, greens fees, lessons, and other goodies—is $800 per person. Reduced rates for accompanying spouses who wish to forego the School are also available. —R.McG.

Golf School for Seniors
Golf Schools, Inc.
P.O. Box 9199
Canton, OH 44711

If you watch a game, it's fun.
If you play it, it's recreation.
If you work at it, it's golf.
BOB HOPE

Par for the Course

Golf is a sport that takes a long time to play, but as my father insists, you can play it (even professionally) to a riper, older age than almost any other sport.

Since this is true, it's reasonable that golf should take a long time to learn. This is so, in part, because of the aeronautical and engineering aspects of the game, aspects that are complex and essential. Yet most golfers are unaware of the scientific technology behind their sport.

In fact, sports and science go hand in hand these days. The partnership has been going on for quite some time and has helped topple records in many sports. On the other hand, there has been a slower acceptance of the role of scientific theory as applied to golf. The Golf Academy at Stratton Mountain wants to change that.

That is an argument that could be used by the Academy to coerce you into taking their golf lessons (which take a longer than average time to learn for a game that takes longer than most to play, though you can play it longer than those others).

But the staff at the Academy feels a golfer has to know how and why a golf ball flies where it does, and they feel he must understand how to change his style to accomplish a specific goal.

The Academy is not interested in "patching up" any difficulties. Rather, it wants to study the player's total game and begin at the beginning.

The "Five Laws of Golf" are taught, which deal with arm speed, angle of approach, the "sweet-spot" for best contact, the track of the swing, and the angle of the clubface at contact.

Videotape and still-photo studies of the individual golfer are made to help develop an accurate self-image and provide the kind of feedback students need.

The Academy uses a group system that provides "encouragement and support" and gives ample time to practice.

The five-day golf program offers lodging, breakfast and dinner daily, at least 30 hours of instruction, plus greens fees, carts, free play, "Meet the Pros Welcome," and nightly entertainment. —J.S.

The Golf Academy
at Stratton Mountain
Stratton Mountain, VT 05155

A Runner's Life for Me

Runners can get used to a lot of run-of-the-mill running. For some it might be the same strip of grass down the middle of the same road at the same time every morning. For others it's the same number of laps on the same asphalt track at the same nearby high school. Being a runner, in solitude or in company, offers personal rewards, but—outside of the likes of the Boston Marathon—very few celebrations.

Now there's National Running Week. Sponsored by *Runner's World* magazine, National Running Week is held in the last part of December in Northern California. It's an educational experience, a professional convention, and a joyful celebration of running, all at the same time. Cooperation is the keynote, rather than competition, and thus whole families can participate, as well as runners at every level of ability.

In previous years one-hour clinics were offered in acupressure, beginning running, beginning racing, mountain running, orienteering, ride and tie, *Runner's World* corporate cup, running after 40, and yoga for runners. One- to two-hour workshops were held in diet and nutrition, foot care, marathoning, medical advice, mental attitudes and performance, running style, training advice, weight training, women's running, and ultra marathoning. Film festivals and open houses provided more information and an opportunity for runners to exchange experiences and ideas with one another.

For those interested in the week as a meeting-of-professionals-in-convention, there was a huge exhibit of equipment displayed by major manufacturers. Equipment demonstrations were given by the major suppliers, and special information booths were provided for people with questions about the use of any of the equipment on display.

For those interested in running in order to run, there was plenty of that, too. The week began with the National Fitness Run, an easily-paced (9-10 minutes per mile) 15-mile run, divided into five stages. Runners participated in one or more of the stages, and the idea was to stay together and be part of the group rather than to finish first. There were also noon social runs, fun runs, and a week-closing midnight run, all in the running-for-everyone category. In addition, for those runners who qualified, there was a world-class invitational run.

There was also a banquet at which most participants in National Running Week gathered to hear prominent speakers and to meet well-known proponents and practitioners of the sport. In past years such notables as George Sheehan, Steven Subotnick, Bill Rodgers, Nathan Pritikin, Erich Segal, Marty Liquori, Kathy Switzer, and Senator Alan Cranston have all been in attendance. Future years can hold no less stellar contingents in store. —R.J.

National Running Week
Runner's World
Box 366
Mountain View, CA 94042

And who, 'mid e'en the Fools, but feels that half the joy is in the race.
SIR RICHARD BURTON

Run Away

You needn't run until you drop, but if you do, the Colorado Adventuring Distance Running Camp offers a choice of flops—from flat, dirt mining trails to sand dunes and steep mountain paths. And, no matter what terrain is covered, every participant rapidly learns the value of oxygen, because Colorado Adventuring—located in Westcliffe, Colorado—towers 9000 feet (nearly two miles) above sea level.

Participants are free to set their own mileage quotas, and the training staff of experienced runners gladly works with every participant in developing suitable training programs. Other than a willingness "to accept the challenge of running," there are no restrictions placed on applicants.

But applicants must be prepared to run, run, run. The highlight of each day's activities is a major run covering six to fifteen miles over a wide variety of terrains.

Sound like your idea of a runner's utopia? Twelve days of this fun-on-the-run costs about $200, including meals and lodging. Sessions are scheduled in July and August, with enrollment limited to 25 persons per session. —R.McG.

Colorado Adventuring
P.O. Box 293
Westcliffe, CO 81252

On the Jog Training

I jog. Five or six times a week I get up at 6:00 and I'm out on the streets by 6:30 to do my three miles. Some of you may think I'm a fanatic. Others of you might think my three miles is nothing—a mere trot down the driveway. But I'll say this to all of you—I do enjoy jogging. My legs turn red and my breasts bounce, but I still enjoy my jog.

Which is why the Annual Sea Pines Plantation Jogging Holiday on Hilton Head Island, South Carolina, seems like it would be an enjoyable vacation for me.

The first Annual Holiday was held in February of this year, and I'm assuming that future Holidays will be somewhat the same.

Designed for all levels of joggers, the four-day session had as its panel of instructors such running notables as Gayle and Ben Barron, Amby Burfoot, Ian Jackson, and Joan Ullyot.

The instructors conducted workshops on creative running, women's running, runner's nutrition, and couples' running. And, yes, there were plenty of opportunities for jogging.

Registration was $375 per person double occupany and $445 per person single occupancy. The price for nonparticipating spouses was $320, which included everything except the workshops and discussions. —J.S.H.

The Annual Sea Pines Plantation Jogging Holiday
Sea Pines Plantation Company
Hilton Head Island, SC 29928

The Puck Stops Here

If you think a hockey puck is just a Don Rickles joke, these schools are not for you. But if you've a flirtation with the world of gleaming skates, ice rinks, and rocket-fast pucks, the Canadian Professional Hockey Schools can consummate your romance.

Age, sex, and prior experience are not barriers to entry into the rink's excitement, say the Schools, and courses are tailored to meet just about every need. Separate programs are available for beginners, intermediates, and advanced students as well as for boys and girls. Instruction is by skilled professional teachers and classes often feature appearances by certified National Hockey league stars.

Courses are offered in Minnesota, Illinois, and Manitoba, Canada, throughout the summer months. Cost varies with each program's duration and intensity, with the least expensive course priced at $53 weekly. The Schools recommend that students attend for at least two weeks, and early enrollment is urged. —R.McG.

Canadian Professional Hockey Schools, Ltd.
Box 487
Winnipeg, Manitoba R3C 2J3
Canada

МИЛОСТИ
ПРОСИМ

BIENVENUE

WELCOME

خوش آمدید

ALOHA

歡迎

שלום

BIENVENIDOS

For my part, I travel not to go anywhere,
but to go.
I travel for travel's sake.
ROBERT LOUIS STEVENSON

Footloose

They say the world is shrinking. Maybe it is, but the shrinkage doesn't seem to cut down on the number of fascinating travel destinations available to today's enterprising voyager.

If anything, the "shrinking" world makes possible ever-more-exotic jaunts. But, oh, the choices!

How about a walking tour of the historic Blue Ridge Mountains of North Carolina? Or a pioneerlike covered-wagon trip down the old Santa Fe Trail?

Is something a bit more faraway indicated in this year's plans? We've found an overland encounter that will take you to the legendary land of Katmandu or to Africa within sight of the snows of Kilimanjaro. And we have, of course, hair-raising Amazonian expeditions, climbing parties in the Himalayas and the Andes, plus the inevitable photo safari in Africa, the South Pacific, and so on.

But maybe what you're yearning for is something, well, a bit different from last year. We suggest a trip on the trains of America: the trains that tamed the West, the trains that stretch from sea to shining sea, the trains that still put bud vases on white linen tablecloths in the dining cars.

Still not quite what you were looking for?

Here's one that may be absolutely you: It's called a Champagne Balloon Tour, and it's offered by the Bombard Society. You'll travel by hot-air, gaily striped balloon (you remember Phileas Fogg, don't you?), and you put down for each meal at a different champagne vineyard in France. Tons of bubbly, of course—and food that you'll be talking about 25 years from now.

Have we still not caught you? Maybe what you yearn for is excitement. White water, rapids, dips, spills, laughs, campfires, painted gorges. Does that interest you? If it does, we've gathered a group of river trips that will positively floor you.

That got you *too* excited? Think calm, pretty thoughts, and imagine a cruise in the Greek Isles. Not just a cruise, mind you, but a Swan tour. You'll be accompanied by archaeologists, classicists, actors, musicians. You'll get the history of Lesbos from an Oxford don, and the all-night diversions of Mykonos from Mykonos. Altogether entertaining.

But maybe you're a people person. None of this tour stuff for you; what you like to do is meet people. Well, as it happens, we can place you in a Fiji family if you like.

Face it. We've got you every way from Sunday. Each travel adventure is educational in some sense. And each one is fun in every sense. The prices range from $1(!) to luxuriously expensive.

Which one will you have?

Adventuring in Our Time

Travel the Heights

There might be a travel agency somewhere that offers a wider scope of unusual trips.

Maybe.

There may be one somehow that boasts a more experienced and knowledgeable collection of trip leaders and guides.

Perhaps.

There could be one someplace that allows for a closer look at new territories and different people, cultures, and wildlife.

Possibly.

But if there is one around that can top the promises of Mountain Travel, Inc. of Albany, Calif., please let us know. We'd be amazed to find it.

Definitely.

Founded in 1967, Mountain Travel claims to have pioneered the idea of "worldwide adventure travel." The key to the company's philosophy is expressed so: "We are seeking discoveries which fall outside the normal scope of standard travel itineraries. Our idea of travel is to leave the cities far behind and freely roam (on foot, if possible) through a small and wild corner of the world."

To actualize this philosophy Mountain Travel schedules some 90 different tours covering the planet. Their list includes Europe, Africa, Pakistan, India, Nepal, Siberia, the Orient, the Pacific, North America, South America, Central America, and the Arctic, taking in more than 25 countries overall.

To lead the trips Mountain Travel calls on any of dozens of modern-day explorers and adventurers; men and women with impressive outdoor credentials. (One of their regular guides is Tenzing Norgay, the Sherpa who stepped on the summit of Everest with Sir Edmund Hillary in their famous conquest of 1953.)

Teams of 12 to 15 make up the standard Mountain Travel group, and physical requirements range from the ability to stand up, to easy hiking, to a minimum of six years of mountaineering experience. The company supplies trippers with all the information they need on their selected areas (maps, itineraries, clothing requirements, etc.) and even provides a suggested reading list to further enhance the discoveries. Tours are scheduled the year around and may last anywhere from two to seven weeks. Costs run from $1000 to $4000, not including air fare.

True to its name, Mountain Travel specializes in mountain tours, hikes, treks, and expeditions (including no fewer than 21 different adventures at the top of the world in Nepal). But they travel the lowlands, too, such as in their Sahara Desert crossing by camel or their sailing trip around the Greek Islands.

The company publishes annually an excellent catalog full of pictures and descriptions of its upcoming tours. It's a book worth having—for armchair adventures at least, if not the real thing. —C.McB.

Mountain Travel, Inc.
1398 Solano Ave.
Albany, CA 94706

Wagons Ho

For those pioneering spirits whose pulse beats faster when the Old West and its adventures come to mind, the only solution just may be a quick trip to yesteryear. Wagons Ho makes it happen.

Offering a summertime odyssey in an authentic wagon train, Wagons Ho's mini-vacations cover 55 miles of West Kansas terrain along the historic Smoky Hill Trail. For three full days and nights, contemporary seekers of that Western magic cross prairies and rivers, meet up with Pony Express riders, gather around an evening campfire for tasty grub and sing-alongs, and perhaps encounter a raiding outlaw band. First-hand history lessons are mixed with the generous natural pleasures afforded by the scenic trail.

Cost for the three-day wagon train trip is about $325 for adults; less for children. Food, shelter, and entertainment are included in the package.
—R.McG.

Wagons Ho, Incorporated
600 Main
Quinter, KS 67752

Emergency at Sea

You're miles from shore on a lavish yacht trip and a fellow passenger suffers a heart attack. What *do* you do?

Medical emergencies at sea are no rarer than they are on land, but few sailors come equipped to deal with those life-and-death realities when professional medical attention is many miles, and hours, away. That's why Oceanic Expeditions offers its six-day onboard training program in "Emergency Medicine at Sea." With instruction taking place aboard the *San Juan*, a 50-foot ketch, as it cruises off Santa Barbara in the Channel Islands, participants also find time—between probings of advanced first-aid treatments—to assist in day-to-day sailing and shipboard chores and also for individual recreation. Prior medical and sailing experience is not required, and the cost—inclusive of meals—is $300.

You've no desire to be an at-sea Marcus Welby? Oceanic Expeditions also offers an array of nonmedical sea adventures, with cruises to Tierra Del Fuego, the South Pacific, New Zealand, and like climes on upcoming schedules. Ample instruction in sailing techniques is available for inexperienced mariners, with costs of the packages averaging about $40 to $50 daily. —R.McG.

Oceanic Expeditions
240 Fort Mason
San Francisco, CA 94123

"Great Expeditions" "Great Expeditions" does not sponsor expeditions, great or otherwise. But this newsletter does tell potential explorers and adventurers where they can find companions for their journeys, and about trips that modern-day Lewis and Clarks can go on. Yearly subscription rates are $12 in North America and $16 elsewhere.

"Great Expeditions," Inc.
Box 46499
Vancouver, BC V6R 4G7
Canada

Schooner Bill of Rights Become a 19th-century Yankee sailor for two or seven days while cruising on the Schooner *Bill of Rights.* For an average of $250 you can loll around the deck, learn how to plot a course, or do whatever you wish.

Schooner *Bill of Rights*
Box 477
Newport, RI 02840

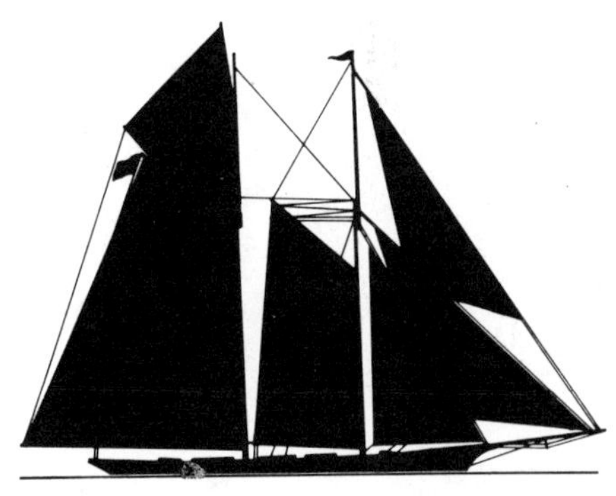

The Great Bus Trip It is neither dangerous nor difficult to travel from Frankfurt to Nepal or Delhi these days. The roads are paved and the people met are friendly. And your bus and accommodations are comfortable on your 63-, 66-, or 47-day trip. But it's not cheap—$950 is the minimum cost, plus air fare.

The Road to Katmandu, Inc.
4 Jones St.
New York, NY 10014

Far and few, far and few,
Are the lands where the Jumblies live;
Their heads are green,
and their hands are blue,
And they went to sea in a sieve.
EDWARD LEAR

Bubbly in the Sky

Shades of F. Scott and Zelda! How about a $3200 "adult Easter egg hunt," one with many, many twists?

Nobody is going to pay $3200 to hunt Easter eggs, we know, no matter how adult. What about hunting huge balloons as they crisscross the French countryside and, for an added dollop to make the search a hair more intriguing, a bottle of Moet & Chandon champagne cracked open to celebrate *every* successful landing and search? Better still, there are lots of successes daily, and that elegant bubbly is pouring aplenty.

You'll get all that and more on the Bombard Society's Champagne Balloon Tour of France, a two-week high-flying adventure including wine tastings, gourmet meals, luxury hotels, and glimpses of France's storied past. Limited to groups of 18, every Champagne Balloon Tour deploys three balloons. Group members take turns gracefully gliding through the air, half making the spin, while the other half tracks down those wandering hot air bags in a search, Bombard says, that's reminiscent of those childhood Easter egg hunts.

Balloon trips last about one hour apiece and cover from two to fifteen miles of French countryside. Worry not. Air time is divided equally.

Wondering if you've made this trek before? Bombard happily provides a full itinerary of their stops in Paris, Epernay, Beaune, Vezelay, Chenonceaux, and Chinon. Along the way, hotel accommodations are chosen with the discriminating guest in mind and none merits fewer than two stars.

All that ballooning works up ravenous appetites, of course, so every noon features a gourmet lunch crafted by Robert Noah, *Chef de Picnic* of the Champagne Balloon Tour. Evening repasts are taken in restaurants specializing in appropriate regional cuisines. And, if the day's bubbly leaves you with a taste for more, Bombard sympathizes. Both lunch and dinner are complemented by wines selected by Steven Spurrier, director of Paris' *Academie du Vin.*

Between the flights and dining, participants are invited to tour local vineyards, castles, caves, and museums. In the Loire Valley, for example, some 120 historic buildings are to be found, says Bombard, and, impossible as many of them are to see from the road, the balloons provide unexcelled vantage points for sightseeing. Chef Noah will also gladly instruct you in the preparation of local cuisines and welcomes guests on his morning tours of local markets.

Total frivolity, you think? Not at all. Some of the inflight time on this trip is accepted by the U.S. Federal Aviation Administration in partial fulfillment of experience qualifications leading to certification as a balloon pilot.

You've no interest in a balloon pilot's license? Then go for the frivolity. There's more than enough to make this one of the most enchanting ways to tour France. —R.McG.

The Bombard Society
c/o AIR FRANCE, NYC-PG
1350 Avenue of the Americas
New York, NY 10019

Encounter Overland

Overlanding. I can remember when I wasn't sure I knew the meaning of the word. And then when I found out what it meant, it was still hard to conceptualize. A bunch of people crossing a continent in a truck. A long-range expedition.

To go, or not to go? No small decision. Sublet the apartment. Table the career. But the magnetism of remote places is strong. The struggle changes to when to go, and how.

Encounter Overland. "A company that combines experience and know-how with spontaneity and adventure." Asia, Africa, and South America. Four-wheel-drive trucks built and equipped in their own workshops.

London to Johannesburg in 15 weeks. Half of the 13,000 miles between the northern edge of Africa and Johannesburg were just a track.

I learned a lot. How to dig a truck out of soft sand. What it's like to sleep under a mantle of stars in the African desert. The history of the Hoggar Massif. How it feels to meet a Pygmy, photograph a cheetah, and attempt a climb of Kilimanjaro.

The trips last at least 11 weeks and cost an average of $1700, not including air fare.

Overlanding. Now I know what it means. —E.H.

Encounter Overland
36 Pine St., Suite 516
San Francisco, CA 94104

Adventures in Scotland

John Ridgway single-handedly sailed from Ireland to Brazil and, in another odyssey, rowed with a partner across the North Atlantic—but he hardly demands such feats from guests at his School of Adventure. Courses instead offer carefully selected introductions to the natural charms and activities found on Ridgway's "campus," a remote setting in Scotland's North West Highlands, where there is ample time as well to reflect on the realities of Ridgway's natural world.

With separate one- and two-week programs for youngsters, young adults, men, women, and co-ed offerings, Ridgway's programs are flexibly structured to allow every participant to fully experience the joys of physical activities and the intellectual stimulation nature itself provides. Activities might include canoeing, fishing, sailing, climbing, hiking—or just strolling amidst the Highlands' splendor.

Prices for Ridgway's courses range from about $175 to $250, with food and lodging included. While there are no prerequisites for enrollment, class size is strictly limited. —R.McG.

John Ridgway School of Adventure
Ardmore, Rhiconich, By Lairg
Sutherland, Scotland, UK

Balloons over Valleys Begin your tour of the Sonoma and Napa Valley wine country in California with a balloon flight. Sunrise Balloon offers one-hour flights that will show you the layout of the valley; you can pick out some of the wineries you would later like to tour. Sunrise also offers balloon pilot flight training.

Sunrise Balloon
P.O. Box 6757
Santa Rosa, CA 95406

Burros as Buddies Learn to understand a donkey. The Sierra Club says the animals are sure to win your heart when you go on one of their Burro Trips. The trips are seven days long, take place mostly in the Sierras, are designed for novices and children, and cost around $200.

Sierra Club
350 Bush St.
San Francisco, CA 94108

Follow Johann "If you have the desire to explore, the spirit of adventure, come hiking or mountain climbing with us," says the Johann Mountaineering Guide Service. Their mountaineering/hiking trips last from four to ten days and cost around $300. They also have beach hiking and camping with survival classes.

Johann Mountain Guides
P.O. Box 19171
Portland, OR 97219

Let's all move one place on.
LEWIS CARROLL

Wagons West

The settlers of America have come full circle—from covered wagon, to '36 Ford, to air-conditioned Cadillac—and back to the covered wagon.

Wagons West lets you explore the wilderness trails of Wyoming in the summer, and Arizona in the winter, from a creaking pioneer wagon, jest as yer grandpappy once did.

There are a few discernible differences. These Conestoga replicas are outfitted with rubber tires and foam seats to relieve aching backs. Civilization is never farther than a holler away. And the cost of reliving the romance of the pioneers is modern-day, too.

The spirit of bygone wagon trains is intact, however. Covered wagons enable youngsters and old-timers alike to have an outdoor vacation without strenuous physical demands. The wagon's canvas cover is a protection against sun and shower, and the driver is a local rancher, well-versed in his territory.

At night the wagons pull into a circle, and grub is dished out under the chuckwagon fly in he-man proportions. After the traditional cowboy's campfire, with singing and yarn-spinning, 20th century pioneers bed down in the wagons, a luxury trail tent, or under the stars.

Saddle horses are furnished for those who would rather straddle cowhide than the wagon bed along the trails. Scheduled side trips on horseback take the riders into the wilderness to photograph deer, coyote, and eagle. Wildflowers are uncovered, identified, and photographed. Inland beachcombers turn up petrified wood and elk antlers.

The crew is agreeable to letting the paying guests help drive the wagons or pitch in with camp chores.

Wagons West offers trip options from two days and one night on the trail, to a full six days and five nights in the open, for those who are zealots in their escape through the fourth dimension. Fares run from $80 to $250.

The summer treks rendezvous each week from June through August at Jackson, Wyoming, and wind through the Teton National Forest in the foothills of the Rockies. Many travelers combine the covered wagon trip with a visit to Yellowstone National Park.

The entire company moves to Arizona for the winter season of November through April in the Sonoran Desert Foothills near Wickenburg. There the wagons retread the old Wickenburg-Phoenix stage road, past ghost towns and abandoned gold mines, and explore the Hieroglyphic Mountains. —J.W.

Wagons West
Afton, WY 83110

Adventures of the Pacific

Inexpensive, intimate, but genuinely wild. That's the successful formula behind every Pacific Adventures wilderness jaunt.

Itineraries change annually, but last year saw Pacific Adventures climbing Mexico's Picacho del Diablo Mountain (five days in total; cost: $95), backpacking for two days on California's San Gorgonio Peak ($35), exploring, over ten days, the Grand Canyon's south rim ($185), touring British Columbia and Vancouver on bicycles for ten days ($480, inclusive of motel expenses), and sailing to the North Shore of Santa Cruz Island ($95).

All Pacific Adventures trips—and there are dozens every year—are strictly limited in size and each tour's price includes meals. Guests provide their own personal gear, such as sleeping bags, where appropriate.

Staffed by professional outdoor specialists, Pacific Adventures prides itself on *gently* prodding guests beyond their self-conceived limits of physical and mental capacities. But, for most tours, there are no prerequisites other than good physical condition—and an eagerness to escape from congested cities and fully enjoy nature's wonders. —R.McG.

Pacific Adventures
P.O. Box 5041
Riverside, CA 92517

Ramblers Holidays

The world's heretofore aimless wanderers can do their rambling with guidance and congenial company amidst some of Europe's most spectacular scenery.

Ramblers Holidays Ltd. of London, which has been guiding footsteps for 30 years, provides a leader, often a volunteer, who takes your party in tow. He, or she, is chosen partly on the basis of enthusiasm.

All the walking holidays, mostly two weeks in duration, have one thing in common: all are among hills or mountains where the walker comes into his own. Fitness and footwear are the watchwords.

Tours are graded on the steepness of the slopes—Grade D for beginners where five hours of walking a day is the limit, to Grade A requiring the use of crampons and ice axes.

Choices include the *Sound of Music* mountaintops of Austria and Alpine summits and meadows in France, Italy, and Switzerland, including the classic *Tour du Mont Blanc* around the highest mountain in Europe. There are also little-known regions of Bulgaria and Hungary, the mountains and fjords of Norway, and stretches of Yugoslavia, Greece, Turkey, Nepal, and Morocco.

The prices are from $350 to $1300 for the two- to three-week trips. —J.W.

Ramblers Walking Holidays
¼ Crawford Mews, York St.
London W1H, 1PT
England, UK

Center for Adventures The Adventure Center offers you the world—Asia, Africa, Europe, South America, and even the US. You'll go by "safari vehicle," and stay in hotels or camp at night while on your 7- to 114-day overland trek. Prices range from $118 to $3050.

Adventure Center
5540 College Ave.
Oakland, CA 94618

Trail Riders of the Wilderness The Trail Riders of the Wilderness Program offers a variety of horseback, backpack, and river trips. These trips are educational—"not in a formal way but by acquainting members with the value, beauty, and wonder of wilderness." These trips are for AFA members only. Dues are $8.50 a year. The trips themselves cost extra.

The American Forestry Association
1319 18th St., N.W.
Washington, DC 20036

Barefoot Adventures Under White Sail It's up to you on Windjammer Barefoot Cruises whether you want to be an extra "hand" or merely a passenger on their ships. Trips on their schooners are six or fourteen days, and prices start at $310 for these Bahamian jaunts.

Windjammer Barefoot Cruises
P.O. Box 120
Miami Beach, FL 33139

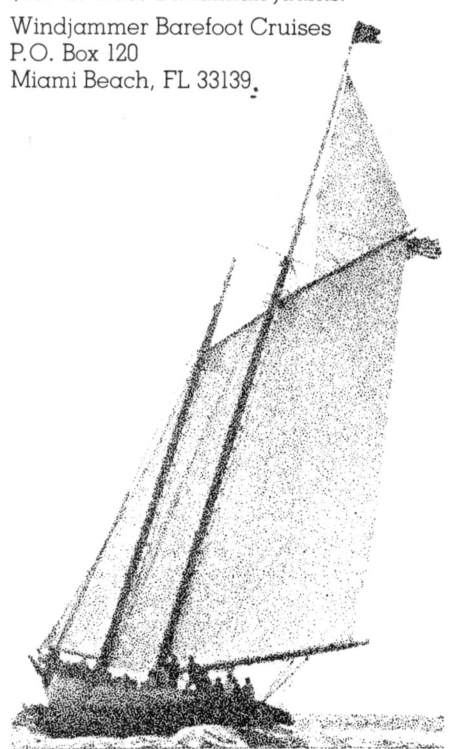

Wind Over Mountain

Travel should be slow but enriching. Anachronistic as that philosophy may seem in the jet age, it is the guiding principle of Sarah B. Larrabee's philosophy—and, since she is founder and director of Wind Over Mountain, each of her carefully planned treks exemplifies that thought.

Slow at Wind Over Mountain sometimes means easy. Sometimes it doesn't. Can you run *four* miles in 36 minutes or fewer? No?—then forget the Mexican Volcanoes climb. Brief and intense, that trip demands top physical performance from participants. For those who can make the grade, they will climb several volcanoes—some still active—in southern Mexico. Prior mountaineering skill is not a prerequisite—all techniques necessary to make the climb are taught beforehand.

Not up for gamboling on active volcanoes? Wind Over Mountain offers numerous trips—many designed to appeal to people of all ages and physical conditions. Even would-be adventurers with serious health problems—diabetes and angina, for instance—are welcome on some Wind Over Mountain tours.

Still, to keep the travel slow, all the treks employ basic transportation modes. Participants walk, ride horses, and, on some treks, paddle canoes or enjoy sailboats.

Time is never the object on Ms. Larrabee's treks—because each participant, she hopes, will find the time during these leisurely tours to discover him or herself. Groups, accordingly, are kept small—usually no more than eight participants. A casual, relaxed atmosphere predominates.

Trek schedules change annually, but recent tours include a three-week exploration of Alaska ($1450); 40 days in Nepal's Annapurna Sanctuary ($2430); a three-week probe of Mt. Everest and its region ($2300); 22 days canoeing and sailing the Caribbean Reef ($1450); and a month in Afghanistan ($2500). Tentatively scheduled treks include a tour of Mongolia involving visits to sites mentioned in the novels of Roy Chapman Andrews; another literary tour—this time to British Isles sites found in the writings of Arthur Conan Doyle and Agatha Christie; and, a joint mountain climb with Chinese women in China.

Most prices include transportation from New York City, meals on the trail, hotels (where available), and local transportation. And some treks qualify for college credit through the University of Michigan and the University of California at Los Angeles. —R.McG.

Wind Over Mountain
Box 1380
Telluride, CO 81435

Down the Amazon

Bored with paddling down your neighborhood stream? Laszlo Berty is the man to see for a sure-fire cure for your blahs.

Berty's stream is the churning Amazon and, for adventurous rafters seeking the maximum in white-water thrills, he offers the challenge of his Rio Maranon Expeditions. Jungle hikes and floating down the Peruvian portion of the Amazon are not for everyone, Berty concedes. But, other than demanding that applicants be in excellent condition, no additional requirements are imposed. A three-day Expedition Training Program is included as a prelude when necessary.

Duration and cost vary with the exact tour package. Three weeks is the typical length at a fee of about $2000. Travel costs to and from Peru are not included, and early reservations are urged. —R.McG.

Amazon Expeditions
310 W. Grandview Blvd.
Erie, PA 16508

Holidays for the Adventurous

God, what an experience. I never would have had the gall to do something like that on my own. Two weeks in Borneo. I'll never forget what it was like going up the Rajang River in that canoe or living in the Iban longhouse. It's lucky we all got along so well. If Jim hadn't been such a great leader, the whole trip might have been different. He really knew the jungle. I don't think we would've been so involved with the local tribesmen if it hadn't been for him.

Even over the roar of this jet I can still hear the noises of the rainforest. It's probably good that we spent those last two days in Singapore. It'll sort of ease the transition between the jungle and my nine-to-five routine.

What if I'd never heard of WEXAS? World Expeditionary Association. I think it was the "expedition" part that appealed to me. They sure offer more than other travel clubs—like a chance to experience some off-the-wall places.

I wonder where I'll go next year? Maybe I'll go to Iceland, or the Sahara. Or perhaps I'll go diving in the Red Sea.

It'll cost me anywhere from $500 to $2500, not including air fare, for a two- to four-week trip. —E.H.

Wexas International, Inc.
North American Office
Graybar Building, Suite 354
420 Lexington Ave.
New York, NY 10017

A New Trend in Travel I'm tired of "bus 'em and feed 'em" tours. Travel Trends says they're different, with hiking, backbacking, and mountaineering tours to India, New Zealand, Switzerland, Nepal, and Africa to back up that statement. Trips last an average of 21 days and cost around $2000, including air fare.

Travel Trends, Inc.
Market Center, Suite 302
1624 Market St.
Denver, CO 80202

Horsey Holidays If you want to explore and learn about the wilderness but your legs tire easily and you don't mind sitting on a horse for hours, AWA has horseback adventures with a saddle just for you. Trips are a week long and cost between $370 and $485.

American Wilderness Alliance
4260 East Evans Ave.
Denver, CO 80222

Arctic Explorers Go with Consolidated Tours "to a land as vast, primitive and magnificent as it is unexplored by the average tourist"—the Arctic. On one of their "tours" you're not accompanied by an escort, but instead one of their representatives recommends excursions. Trips last from one to eight days and cost from $200 to $1500.

Consolidated Tours, Ltd.
188 University Ave.
Toronto, Ontario M5H 3C3
Canada

A tourist is a fellow who drives thousands of miles so he can be photographed standing in front of his car.
EMILE GANEST

Fast or Lazy

Scared? Me?

"And now this next slide shows the area known as New Zealand's Grand Canyon. As you can see, the river runs right through the middle of it. Well, really, it's called Skippers Canyon, and that's the Shotover River. You might say we really *shot over* it too. Heh, heh. I've never seen a rubber raft move faster."

"Gee, Frank, weren't you scared?"

"Me? You gotta be kidding. There were times when our rafts nearly brushed against those jagged walls and the boatmen had a job to outmaneuver the currents. Whole trip only ran 12 miles, and we got through it in less than a day."

"It looks scary to me, Frank. Didn't it kind of take your breath away, being in white water going that fast?"

"Naw, you get used to it. Have a look at this next one, if you want to see something spectacular."

"Oh, my. Oh, my. It gives me chills just to look at it. Where is it?"

"That's the Hunter River. On that trip we hit the Hunter and the Matukituki."

"Frank, tell me. What else did you do in New Zealand?"

"This company, Dane's Back Country Experiences, set out a whole program for us. We did some hiking, some backpacking, and a lot of river running. Now these slides are in Mount Aspiring National Park. We set down near the Dart Glacier, and hiked in from there.

"The beech forests are incredible. Feels like you're the first human being ever set foot there."

"Forests kind of give me the creeps, Frank. I've always been afraid of snakes and creepy-crawlies, like spiders."

"Put your fears to rest, honey. There isn't a poisonous snake or a poisonous spider in all of New Zealand. Close as you can come to paradise, the way I see it."

"Was it expensive, Frank?"

"No, as a matter of fact, it was all pretty inexpensive. That three-day trip I told you about only cost $86—and that included the sleeping bag."

"Oh, Frank, you've done so much. It just stuns me. And that cute little moustache you grew while you were there. Tell me, Frank, are you going back any time soon?"

"Now that you ask, sweetie, I'm planning to go back next year. I'm going to take the trek to the Blue Slip Gooseberry Gully."

"The what?"

"The Blue Slip Gooseberry Gully."

"That sounds like a joke, Frank. I don't appreciate it when guys treat me like a dummy."

"No joke. That's what it's called. The Blue Slip Gooseberry Gully."

"Right, Frank. And I'm Venus de Milo. Good night, Frank."

"Wait a minute, honey, you don't understand. Honey?" —E.H. & J.A.

Dane's Back County Experience
c/o International River Touring Association
2004 Virginia St.
Berkeley, CA 94709

American River Touring Association

Huckleberry Finn was real—as real as men's dreams. Scratch a little boy, or even girl, of any age, and underneath you'll find a secret yearning to run away on a raft down a river.

The Mississippi may have been all right in Huckleberry's day, but in our time the West is the best for river adventures. And the American River Touring Association, which has been called the undisputed champion of white-water adventures, is ready and willing to help you run away on the rivers of the West in a raft of your choosing.

Trips range from single-day excursions costing as little as $44 to nine-day runs priced at $665. Groups of 20 are standard, using oar and paddle rafts that seat four to seven. Individual rafts and inflated canoes are available for advanced river runners.

On all of their trips ARTA provides professional river guides capable of steering a safe course through the

toughest rapids and then whipping up a nifty beef stroganoff for their guests over the evening's campfire.

ARTA also runs white-water workshops, where they teach the tricky techniques of river navigation, and a river classroom experience that is aimed at education-oriented groups. —C.McB.

American River Touring Association
1016 Jackson St.
Oakland, CA 94607

Wild and Scenic

Row or walk, but come to enjoy the wild and scenic terrain that's home to Patrick and Susan Conley, the founders and operators of Wild & Scenic, Inc. But enjoyment, satisfying as it is, is not all Wild & Scenic offers. Every tour includes informal but professional instruction in the nature that surrounds us.

Row yourself down a river, the Conleys urge, and many Wild & Scenic guests do just that in sportyaks, virtually unsinkable seven-foot skiffs. Sounds exciting but baffling? Worry not. Prior experience is not mandatory—whatever skills you'll need are taught.

Row the San Juan River, for example. A major tributary to the Colorado, the San Juan courses through Utah, and the Conleys' trip starts near Bluff. It ends 84 miles later and, along the way, you'll pass through remains of an ancient village that once housed the Anazazi, inhabitants of the area from A.D. 200 to 1260. You will also ride the spectacular Goosenecks, where the rolling river travels eight miles in order to cover an airline distance of a mere two miles. Cost of the trip is $400.

Crave a tad more excitement? Oregon's Owyhee River is your speed.

This cold, fast-running Snake River tributary will host Wild & Scenic for the first time in 1979. Experienced sportyakers *only* are invited to row their own boats. Novices are welcome, but must travel as passengers on the support rafts. Cost of this trip is $475 for six days.

Wild & Scenic offers numerous other trips—ranging from treks into remote southwestern lands to runs down Alaskan rivers. Minimum age for sportyaking is fourteen, although children eight and older are welcome as passengers on the rafts. —R.McG.

Patrick and Susan Conley
Wild & Scenic, Inc.
P.O. Box 2123
Marble Canyon, AZ 86036

Floating Geology Itching to do a little archaeological digging or fossil hunting on your next river trip? Geo-Expeditions offers guided canoe trips in Lake Huron and McGregor Bay-Killarney Provincial Park, Canada. Trips are six days long and cost $135 per person.

Geo-Expeditions
Box 8
Gore Bay, Ontario P0P 1H0
Canada

Conserve Water And you thought all the Sierra Club does is fight to save the wilderness. Not quite. They also sponsor water trips all over the country. The trips are from four days to two weeks and cost an average of $450.

Sierra Club
530 Bush St.
San Francisco, CA 94108

Huck Finn Adventures Float down the Mississippi and other rivers with Spirit Waters. They offer raft, kayak, and canoe trips of two to five days in Minnesota, Wisconsin, and Canada. Prices start at $52.

Spirit Waters
ARTA-North Country Office
5375 Eureka Rd.
Excelsior, MN 55331

Custom-Made Float Trips "We offer a custom white-water trip running from three to seven days, tailored to fit the interests of each party whether they be hunting, fishing, photography, archaeology, scenery, or Indian habitat," says Stanton C. Miller Primitive Area Float Trips. About $300 per person.

Stanton C. Miller
Primitive Area Float Trips
P.O. Box 585
Salmon, ID 83467

The Family That Floats Together Parklands Expeditions provides wilderness adventures suitable for the entire family. Canoe and raft trips on the Snake River near Jackson Hole. The trips are five days long and cost about $385.

Parklands Expeditions, Inc.
P.O. Box 371
Jackson Hole, WY 83001

I am not born for one corner:
the whole world is my native land.
SENECA

Rafting in the Rockies "Listen to the sounds of the wind, water, wildlife, and your companions" as you raft down Colorado's rivers, says Wilderness Aware. They offer one- to five-day trips where you can learn river camping, cooking, and sanitation for a starting price of $30 per person per day.

Wilderness Aware
Box 401
Colorado Springs, CO 80901

Down the River Find both peace and excitement on a river. Arkansas River Tours offers river-running trips on the Rio Grande, Dolores, and Arkansas Rivers. You can help in the paddling on some trips, while on others you can "leave the rowing to them." Prices range from $10 to $175 for the one- to five-day trips.

Arkansas River Tours
c/o O.L.T.S.
P.O. Box 20281
Denver, CO 80220

Float the West Lute Jerstad Adventures' guides know the flora and fauna of the rivers they guide, and are equally familiar with the history and geology of the areas. They float on rivers of the West, and the cost is around $200 for the two- to six-day trips.

Lute Jerstad Adventures
P.O. Box 19527
Portland, OR 97219

Way Down upon the Owyhee River Wilderness River Outfitters say they "strive to create an increased awareness of the challenge, the beauty, and the fragility of the wilderness." Trips on the Salmon, Owyhee, and Snake Rivers, which cost around $400.

Wilderness River Outfitters
P.O. Box 871
Salmon, ID 83467

The river glideth at his own sweet will.
WILLIAM WORDSWORTH

Paddle with O.A.R.S.

The river is a place to find yourself and with O.A.R.S. you've a wide choice of spots for that epiphany. The Outdoor Adventure River Specialists (O.A.R.S.) now conducts float trips, for novices and white-water experts alike, throughout the western United States on rivers such as the Rogue, Toulumne, Salmon, and Middle Fork.

Eager for a taste of white-water travel but not ready for a full course meal? Some trips are as short as a single day. The Stanislaus or American Rivers of California, for example, host one-day tours, with the price per participant set at about $45.

Ready for a complete dinner? Try the five-, eight-, thirteen-, or nineteen-day treks down the granddaddy of them all, the Grand Canyon's Colorado River. Cost for the expedition starts at $345 and escalates to $760 for the full ride.

No age limitations are imposed by O.A.R.S. and every package includes meals and necessary equipment. Participants must supply their personal gear, and prior physical examinations are required for longer trips. —R.McG.

O.A.R.S.
P.O. Box 67
Angels Camp, CA 95222

Torpedo Trips

Ready for white-water adventure? This one is for real—your vessel is a torpedo, and an orange one at that.

But these torpedoes do not blow up boats—they are boats, specially designed kayaks. Deceptive as their moniker may be, make no mistake—this white-water is very real because the rivers are those of the Pacific Northwest.

Try the Rogue River, an aptly named stream that is unspoiled and fully protected—by federal legislation—against encroaching civilization. If that one is too rough, there is the gentler Klamath, recommended by Orange Torpedo for family outings. When the Rogue is not rough enough, Orange Torpedo will gladly show you the turbulent mysteries of the Deschutes and Idaho's Salmon River.

Fear not. Orange Torpedo insists that kayaking, no matter how rough the water looks, is fun and safe. Most trips require no prior experience, although pretrip conditioning exercises are recommended.

Cost averages about $200 for three days of kayaking, with food and necessary equipment included in the package. Transportation to the river site—and a sleeping bag—must be provided by each guest. —R.McG.

Orange Torpedo Trips
P.O. Box 1111
Grants Pass, OR 97526

River Echos

The Call of the Wild. It's as clear today as in Jack London's time—you just have to travel farther to find uncharted territory.

It does exist in the Brooks Mountain Range, and Echo River Trips will take you there. The excursions begin at Bettles, Alaska, a community of 53 people and 214 dogs.

One trip takes you hiking through the tundra of ankle deep moss and wild blueberries to the Arrigetch Peaks. Or you can float down the Kobek River for 12 days, with the same distant peaks on the horizon. Summer daylight is 20 hours long, and the territory is thick with arctic fox, mink, wolverine, grizzly bear, and eagles. The human species is scarce.

In 1978 Yugoslavian and Peruvian rivers were added to the schedule. Rafts on Yugoslavia's River Tara glided past villages untouched by the 20th century. In Peruvian dugouts, groups explored the headwaters of the Amazon.

For the timorous, Echo also sponsors journeys on the more familiar rivers of California, Oregon, and Idaho—occasionally for college credit.

The one- to thirteen-day trips start at $44 and finish at $1200. —J.W.

Echo River Trips
6505 Telegraph Ave.
Oakland, CA 94609

Alaska to Baja

Huck Finn, poling his raft down the Mississippi, could not have imagined the river trips available today.

How would Huck have fared, tumbling through the white-water of the deepest gorge in North America, Hell's Canyon of the Snake River? In some places sheer rock walls rise 7000 feet from the churning water. A quieter river view takes in petroglyphs of prehistoric people, stone shelters, and abandoned mines of past civilizations.

Other river rafts head up the Tatshenshini into Alaska, where bald eagles and grizzly bears patrol the shoreline. At the Alsek Glacier, skyscraper-sized chunks of ice fall continuously into the water with deafening thuds.

James Henry River Journeys sponsors these adventures and a dozen others in the waters of Northern California, Oregon, Idaho, Alaska, and Baja California. University of California Extension credit is offered for several Snake and Rogue River summer trips, where a naturalist is aboard to explain the wildlife.

Prices range from $40 for one-day trips to $475 for a two-week journey. —J.W.

James Henry River Journeys
1078 Keith Ave.
Berkeley, CA 94708

White Water Yearning to take a river trip and learn some natural history? Outdoor Adventures supplies the raft, guide, and supplies; you supply the $35 to $650 for the one- to twelve-day trips.

Outdoor Adventures
3109 Fillmore St.
San Francisco, CA 94123

Return of White Water Henry Falany is worried about ecology. He feels it's important that his guests gain a feeling of personal responsibility to the wilderness. River trips on the Colorado River through the Grand Canyon.

Henry Falany's White Water
River Expeditions
P.O. Box 1249
Turlock, CA 95380

Son of White Water The American Wilderness Alliance says they "guarantee an exciting and informative experience" on their river trips—dory, raft, canoe, and sportyak journeys on the rivers of the West. Prices average at $375.

American Wilderness Alliance
4260 East Evans Ave.
Denver, CO 80222

The Family of White Water
Nantahala Outdoor Center offers one-day raft trips down the Nantahala, Chatooga, and Ocoee Rivers in Tennessee and the Carolinas. No experience necessary; prices run between $10 and $25.

Nantahala Outdoor Center, Inc.
Star Rte, Box 68
Bryson City, NC 28713

I Was a Teenage White Water
Learn to "love, share, cherish, and to protect for posterity this marvelous land," says Outlaw Trails. They'll take you down rivers in Colorado and Utah for around $300 for a five-day trip.

Outlaw Trails
Box 336
Green River, UT 84525

Meeting the People

Pacific Encounters

What is a guided tour of the South Pacific? Sightseeing trips to observe the quaint village culture of the island's natives? Cute people living in grass huts? Tourists watching from behind a tour guide's shoulder?

Forget it.

It's hard to feel like a tourist—an alien—while sleeping, eating, and living in the same house with a Tahitian, Samoan, or Fiji family. Taking part, in full costume, as your hosts teach you their dances is not conducive to staying an outsider. You'll know you aren't just watching from a tour-bus window.

Richard A. Goodman, president of Goodtravel Tours, says, "We're trying to enable travelers to get to know Pacific Islanders on the Islanders' own home ground, and as human beings rather than as stereotypes." Which is why you may find yourself sleeping on an air mattress over a mat-covered lava floor inside a thatched-roof house when you stay in a Samoan village. (When not in a village, you'll sleep in a Western-style hotel.)

You have a number of choices: Goodtravel offers a program called "Exploring Polynesia": 24 days visiting the Cook Islands, Tahiti, Fiji, and Samoa. You'll live with the villagers part of the time; other nights you'll sleep in a hotel.

You can take part in a homestay program. Stay with a Tahitian, Fiji or other island family. Live with them in their modern- or island-style home. If you like, help out around the house. Or don't. It's cheaper than a hotel—and the family receives some extra money.

There is also a "People of the Pacific" tour. In this tour you'll spend only days, not nights, with the villagers, and Goodman himself accompanies your group.

One note: If you are excessively overweight or have heart trouble or chronic asthma, consider spending your money and time somewhere else. These tours require that you be in reasonably good health. If in doubt, your doctor has the final say.

The tours cost around $2000. Homestay costs start at around $30 per day for adults. —J.S.H.

Goodtravel Tours
5332 College Ave.
Oakland, CA 94618

Become Darwin

If you see yourself as a modern Darwin aboard the *Beagle*, or you dream and hunger for travel adventures which celebrate the world of nature, then you might consider Nature Expeditions International. NEI offers educational trips to spots in the United States, Mexico, Central and South America, East Africa, the South Pacific, Scotland, India, Egypt, and Persia.

The more exotic the place, the more pressing is the need for leadership by someone who knows. Each NEI expedition is headed by a well-qualified leader with an advanced degree, experience in college teaching, and knowledge of the language of the host country.

Trips are graded according to difficulty from A (all the comforts) to D (roughing it on camping trips or bona fide scientific expeditions). Transportation depends on circumstances and can include: sailboat, four-wheel-drive vehicle, camelback, elephantback, raft, bush plane, and the always popular shank's mare.

Prices vary from $36 to $105 a day without air fare, and include most food, accommodations, instruction, and leadership. Expeditions range in length from 7 to 30 days. (In addition, NEI offers short courses, lectures, travel symposia, and mini-expeditions within the San Francisco area.) And the University of San Francisco offers college credit for all trips. —A.E.

Nature Expeditions International
599 College Ave.
Palo Alto, CA 94306

Through Understanding, Peace

This summer vacation is not ordinary, but neither is the goal: peace through understanding. That's the aim of the YMCA World Ambassadors program, which provides college students and other adults with the opportunity to live and work in a developing country for six to eight weeks.

Host countries change annually, but this year Young Ambassadors are summering in Taiwan, the Philippines and Hong Kong, Japan and Korea, Kenya and Egypt, and Latin American nations. Travel to neighboring countries is often included.

Enrollment is limited, and applicants are carefully screened for personal qualifications. Participants foot their own costs and demonstration of financial soundness is also required. Costs vary with destinations, but average about $1500 for the summer. Some participants, the YMCA notes, successfully conduct fund-raising projects to meet their expenses.

A plus for students is that several universities award college credit to World Ambassadors. Participating are the University of Cincinnati, the University of Minnesota, and the University of Texas as well as many other schools. —R.McG.

YMCA World Ambassadors
301 W. Lenawee St.
Lansing, MI 48914

Tours with a Twist

"Mr. Lenin, IOU-TV would like your reaction to the current invasion being carried out in your country. Could you give us your views on this siege?"

"Well, two weeks ago a group of Americans arrived in Russia. Before long their behavior began to look suspicious."

"What were they doing?"

"They began attending lectures at the Leningrad State University and going to places like the Russian Museum. This group appeared to want to learn everything they could about our Soviet way of life and they started spending a suspicious amount of time at the Leningrad House of Friendship. This was no ordinary American tour group."

"Do you have any idea who they were?"

"They claimed to be a study tour from the University of California. They said that the University arranges these tours to various parts of the world and that a meaningful learning experience was all they were after.

"We also found that the University arranges study tours to Greece, Japan, England, Canada, and Australia. But the places visited change from year to year. The cost is between $750 and $2700, including air fare, for the one- to three-week trips. And participants can earn UC Extension credit." —E.H.

International Studies
Dept. E-71
University Extension
University of California
2223 Fulton St.
Berkeley, CA 94720

Monumental Expeditions

Worry not if you don't know where Ulan Bator is. The Society for the Preservation of Archaeological Monuments will gladly tell you where it is and, better still, will even take you there—as part of a 22-day Project Mongolia Expedition. Along the way, expedition members—limited by the Society to 20 persons per group—will explore the Gobi Desert, live for several days in the yurt camps of Mongolian peasants, and discuss their experiences with distinguished professionals in archaeology, history, and allied disciplines. The cost? About $2700 plus round-trip air fare to Moscow.

The Gobi Desert isn't your idea of a thrill? How about Antarctica, New Guinea, Easter Island, India-Nepal, the Galapagos Islands, or Patagonia? The Society is currently arranging tours to these and other untraveled locales as part of its ongoing commitment to arranging some of the rarest expeditions in the tour business.

A commitment to the unique is not without risks, and every tour participant is forewarned that itineraries are flexible. Political disturbances, extremely inclement weather, and the like can, and sometimes do, disrupt travel plans. But the Society quickly devises alternatives, and flexibility also means that expeditions can be detoured to capture unplanned treats such as rare native rituals.

Society Expeditions is not for everyone. But good health and an interest in exploring new cultures are the only requirements the Society imposes. Accommodations, while not four-star, are comfortable and physical danger is avoided.

To allow participants a full taste of a new culture, all tours last several weeks and price tags often climb above $3000. But, as the Society points out, participants "enjoy a cultural experience known to few outsiders" as they visit the ancient Easter Island temple of Ahu Tepeu, track wild boars in New Guinea, or study penguins at Punta Tombo. The Society also earmarks a part of its proceeds for nonprofit organizations working to preserve the monuments visited on these tours. —R.McG.

Society Expeditions
P.O. Box 5088
University Station
Seattle, WA 98105

Chez des Amis

Two women in New York are doing more to dispel the image of the surly French than the entire diplomatic corps.

Their Ches des Amis travel service puts Americans into French homes for five days to two weeks, to view the people and the region from the French standpoint.

The Chez des Amis accommodations dot the map of France from Normandy to Marseilles, mostly outside the cities. Houses range from restored farm buildings to chateaux, converted abbeys to villas. Some families take only two guests at a time; others can make room for five or six. None is the ordinary bed-and-breakfast pension.

Dinner with the family is optional, but not for dieters. The dinner table is suggested as a good way to get acquainted with haute cuisine and interesting people.

Some host families can provide a guide who will make arrangements for an escorted day of sightseeing in the region, as the French know it.

Chez des Amis can handle a complete trip abroad, or just a stay in a French home. Clients fill out a questionnaire to match them with a compatible French family. And prices are from $24 per day per person to $47 for two persons per day. —J.W.

Chez des Amis
139 West 87th St.
New York, NY 10024

A good holiday is one spent among people whose notions of time are vaguer than yours.
J.B. PRIESTLEY

All the World's a Classroom

What could be better than studying Italian art in Italy—poking around ruins and seeing masterpieces, not reproductions? Or learning Swahili in Africa? Or probing British social structures in England? So pack your bags and head for the American Institute for Foreign Study's summer school.

Course offerings vary from year to year, but every summer features a full academic slate with programs held in England, Russia, Italy, Africa, and more. Participants need not be currently enrolled college students and linguistic fluency is not a requirement. Students who wish can sample course offerings in English. Others opt for learning the native language in the ideal "language lab."

Cost depends upon the desired course of study, but fees start at about $1000 for four weeks at the University of Salamanca, Spain, and quickly go over $2000 for other programs. Tuition, room, board, and air fare are all included in the package, and college credit can often be arranged. —R.McG.

American Institute for Foreign Study
102 Greenwich Ave.
Greenwich, CT 06830

Civilized Tours to the Wild

Wanted: Adventurers of all ages who are interested in exploring the Amazon Jungle. Applicants should be willing to forego some of the luxuries of plush hotels for the opportunity to visit primitive, unspoiled areas. Accommodation will be in jungle lodges and first-class hotels when available. Fringe benefits offered are: spear fishing in the Amazon from a canoe at night; bartering with the Yagua Indians and watching how they hunt their daily food with poisoned darts; observing hundreds of species of birds from the porches of the lodges and along the river banks; and traveling in small boats down tributaries close into the living, breathing jungle.

No previous experience is necessary. Our guides will provide informal training in the areas of ornithology, botany, zoology, etc.

If you feel you qualify for this position, apply to the Amazon Safari Club. If accepted, you'll pay them from $699 (8 days, 7 nights), to $1299 (14 days, 13 nights). —E.H.

The Amazon Safari Club
R.D. #1, Box 2
Elverson, PA 19520

Bully to You

What's your fancy? Paddling around the Loch Ness in search of its monster, or going to panel discussions with the British press and BBC?

The British Study Center of the University of Wisconsin, River Falls, offers a bully summer programme that could be titled: "Subjects You Always Wanted to Know About but Were Afraid to Ask For."

The whimsical study vacations in Great Britain run for three weeks each August. They are reasonably priced at about $600 per student, plus transportation to London. Charter flights are available to hold down the travel costs.

An eclectic range of courses is taught by qualified academicians, and college credit is offered through the University of Wisconsin at River Falls, or by special arrangement with other universities.

The knottiest problem for most dedicated dilettantes is deciding which of the fascinating offerings to enroll in.

One choice for the scientifically bent is the class that searches for the Loch Ness monster. Besides looking for "Nessie," students can learn about prehistoric creatures, about the history of the countryside surrounding Loch Ness, and about the history of the "monster" itself. Should "Nessie" appear during this expedition to Scotland, the class will present any evidence it has gathered to the Natural History Museum for evaluation.

There's also a study of the government and politics in the United Kingdom where students can hear lectures and participate in tutorials held by a leading British sociologist. And students can also discuss British politics with an eminent member of the House of Commons.

Still another class allows media buffs behind the TV screen or newsprint of the British mass media, in a combination of lectures, discussions, and behind-the-scenes looks at Britain's news network.

Participants in the British study vacations are housed in private rooms in a London university dormitory, and in inexpensive hotels while out on field trips. Meals away from the school are reimbursed at the end of the tours. The class schedule leaves most weekends free to explore the British Isles. —J.W.

British Study Center
Arts and Sciences Outreach
Dept. of Journalism
University of Wisconsin, River Falls
River Falls, WI 54022

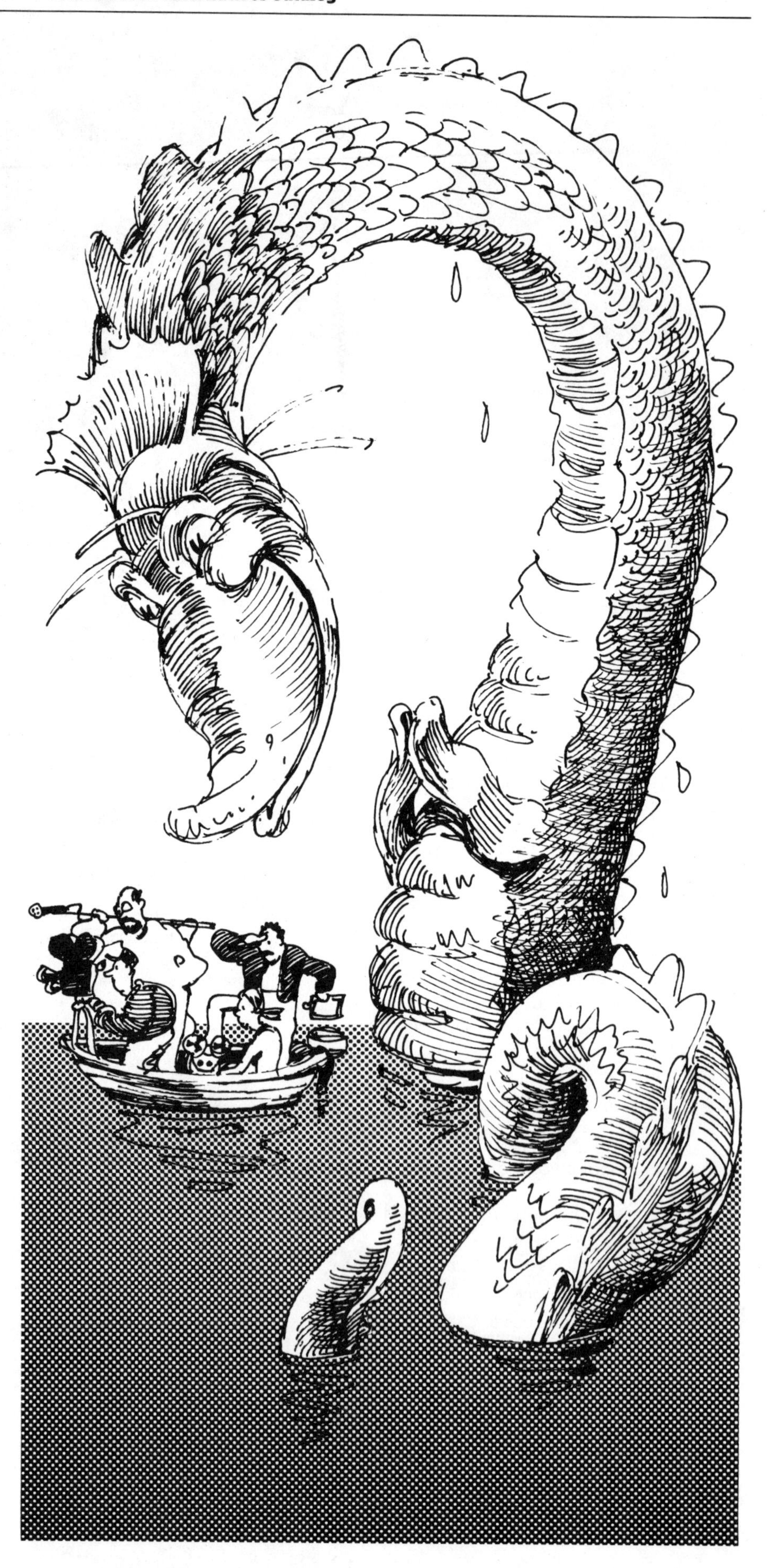

The World as Campus

Enroll at New York University and see the world—through the School of Continuing Education's World Campus Program.

Combining travel with learning, NYU's World Campus Program annually singles out exciting locales for adults to visit—Paris, London, Spain, and Egypt are current destinations.

Group members need not be students, and no age restrictions are imposed. But all members must be eager to learn—about Spain's three cultures, for example, in a tour designed to illuminate the diverse Hebraic, Hispanic, and Arabic influences that merge in modern Spain's art, culture, and society.

Featuring instruction by NYU faculty members as well as seminars and discussions with local experts, all tours also provide ample free time for members' personal investigations and forays.

Cost varies with destination, but NYU stresses that its goal is a reasonably priced travel and learning experience. Two weeks in Egypt, for example, is priced at $1259, inclusive of tuition and travel costs. Other tours are priced between $700 and $2000. —R.McG.

World Campus Program
New York University
School of Continuing Education
2 University Place
New York, NY 10003

Wine Country Safari

If you're heading out for a week's hard tippling, it might as well be under the auspices of one of America's most revered and distinguished institutions, The Smithsonian. With participation restricted to Smithsonian Associates ($12 annual membership contribution), the Associates annually stage a seven-day trek through California's luscious wine country. Cost is $475, inclusive of hotel accommodations, local transportation, some meals, and wine, of course. Air fare to San Francisco is not included.

For Smithsonian Associates with a hankering for more than grapes, the Institution offers a variety of forays into other parts of the world and this nation. All trips are designed to reflect the Institution's pursuits and are staffed by museum curators and other experts.

Most trips are domestic study tours—a weekend in Washington's Hirshhorn Museum, an exploration of Colonial Williamsburg or of Illinois' archaeology—but some are to exotic foreign locales. Full details on all tours are found in the *Smithsonian* magazine, distributed without additional cost to Associate members. —R.McG.

The Smithsonian Associates
Travel Program
Arts and Industries 1270B
The Smithsonian Institution
Washington, DC 20560

Natives who beat drums to drive off evil spirits are objects of scorn to smart Americans who blow horns to break up traffic jams.
MARY ELLEN KELLY

When in Greece

An archaeology class plumbs new depths when it is held on the Acropolis; a workshop in classical theater assumes heightened drama at Epidaurus.

At the Athens Centre for the Creative Arts in Greece, just such experiences await 60 foreign students, most of them from England and America, each summer. Courses and workshops concentrate on Greek studies, theater and dance, and the fine arts.

Americans soon learn to adjust to the Southern European life style. They sit in class from eight in the morning until one in the afternoon, and then are given a four-hour lunch break and siesta. They return at five o'clock for seminars in literature, history, music, and language, and finally disband at eight in the evening for dinner. Concert and theater performances begin after nine at night.

Participants live in apartments staffed by the center, and attend the classes in the city for four weeks. The fifth week is spent on the island of Paros, lolling in the sun and getting acquainted with the local fisherfolk.

Students can earn up to six hours credit at American universities for their summer in Athens. The cost is around $650, which covers tuition, housing, and some other expenses. —J.W.

Athens Centre for the Creative Arts
22 Massalias St.
Athens 144, Greece

Foreign Affairs

"Buenos dias Señorita. Taxi?"

"Si, gracias. Can you please take me to this address?"

"Si. Get in. I'll get your luggage. Have you just arrived in Spain?"

"Yes. I'm from America and I'm going to be living with a family here in Madrid for the summer."

"Are they friends of yours?"

"Well, not exactly. Not yet at least. My stay was arranged by FACETS."

"What is FACETS?"

"It stands for Franco-American Committee for Educational Travel and Studies. It is the New York office of the *Comite D'Accueil*, a nonprofit foundation of the French Ministry of Education. They arrange university study, homestays, on-campus summer programs, and study tours for Americans."

"But, Señorita, this isn't France."

"Oh, I know. FACETS coordinates programs in Canada, Israel, the British Isles, and most Western European countries. It's really nice for people like me who are trying to learn a foreign language or people who are studying world affairs.

"Most of their programs last for about five to eight weeks. On the average they cost about $1300, including air fare."

"Here we are at your new home. Bienvenida a España." —E.H.

FACETS
545 Madison Ave.
New York, NY 10022

Experiment in Living

It's a small world, we often hear, but the Experiment in International Living aims to make it smaller still—by helping to erase barriers between peoples through a program of intercultural living and experimentation.

The pioneering organization in its field, the Experiment opens its programs to everyone from 14 on up. Included in its offerings are group leadership opportunities, academic courses, and homestays. Offer a homestay and a foreign visitor is invited to stay in your home. Take part in a homestay and you'll be the guest in a foreign host's home. Duration is typically one month, but the *International High School Student* program involves opening one's home for a semester or two while a foreign student attends high school in the US.

Experimenters from more than 90 nations have participated in these ongoing programs, and thousands have learned about international living since the program began a half-century ago. Today about 1200 Experimenters are annually involved in programs in 35 countries, and still more participants are actively sought by the Experiment for coming years.
—R.McG.

The Experiment in International Living
Brattleboro, VT 05301

Appalachian Life

Distant as Appalachia may seem from the mainstream of American intellectual life, the American University is bringing it closer—by bringing its students to live and study there. Enroll in AU's course in Appalachian Life and you are speedily transported from the university's Washington, D.C., campus to the Hindman Settlement School in rural southeastern Kentucky where, for three weeks, the many facets of Appalachia's rich culture are explored.

Coal mining, strip mining, weaving, bluegrass, woodworking, pottery—all are included in the course of study as are lengthy conversations with local residents on their views of living in Appalachia. And college students can earn credit. Cost for this Appalachian experience is $541, with meals and lodging included.

Offered in the 1978 summer session, Applachian Life, says AU, will likely be offered in subsequent summers.
—R.McG.

The American University
Division of Continuing Education and Summer Session
Massachusetts and Nebraska Aves., NW
Washington, DC 20016

One song leads on to another
One friend to another friend.
So I'll travel along
With a friend and a song.
WILFRID WILSON GIBSON

The Wondrous World of China

Once upon a time in a land far away there began a strange and mysterious culture. It is the land of the Great Wall, the land of temples and tombs, the land of pagodas, gardens, and majestic mountains.

Marco Polo visited this land in AD 1324, but when he returned to Italy and described what he had seen, hardly anyone believed him.

The people in this land flourished and today it is the world's most populous nation.

For many years it wasn't possible to visit this wondrous land, but recently she has raised her bamboo curtain and begun to allow small numbers of Foreign Friends to get to know her.

Lindblad Travel conducts "Journeys into the Wondrous World of China." They visit Hong Kong, Canton, Kweilin, Shanghai, Soochow, Peking, Mongolia (including the Gobi Desert,

Ulan Bator, and Khujert), and Japan. In many of these places the tour members hear lectures by experts in Chinese culture.

You'll need a little help from your fairy godmother, however. Four weeks in this enchanted land including air fare from the West Coast will be between $4000 and $5000 depending on the time of year and the class of air travel. —E.H.

Lindblad Travel
133 E. 55th St.
New York, NY 10022

Capers 400 Club

Admit it. No matter how jaded you are with travel, there remains one place—or more—you've *always* wanted to visit and there still are things you crave to do. Maybe your dream adventure is chatting with a ghost in a medieval castle. Or riding a yak through Tibet's mountains. Or?

No matter how exotic your dreams, Capers 400 Club will quickly transform them into reality. Specializing in exotic tours, Capers claims fistfuls of travel firsts. It's the first tour group to follow the migratory Qashgai Tribe in Iran. The first to venture up the Baram River to visit Borneo's Punan nomads. The first to travel by yak in the Mt. Everest region. The list goes on, but Capers promises always to be in the forefront of planning new tour experiences.

Tours aren't what you've in mind? Capers can still help. The group gladly assists in designing personalized vacation jaunts—to wherever you wish to go.

"The Adventure Club for Particular Professional People," Capers exacts an annual membership fee of $75 per couple, $50 for a single. Participate in one of Capers' tours, and your membership is free for life. Capers' tours are not inexpensive—most cost well above $3000—but the packages are detailed and exotic, even if that chat with a ghost is subject to his availability. —R.McG.

Capers 400 Club
960 N. Larrabee St.
Los Angeles, CA 90069

The Inca Trail The Incas have come and gone, but they left lots of evidence behind. Holbrook Travel sponsors tours of the Inca "trail" from Cuzco to Macchu Picchu. The price is about $1400 for the two-week trip.

Holbrook Travel, Inc.
3520 W. 13th St.
Gainseville, FL 32601

Friends Overseas It's not easy to meet a Scandinavian if you're merely a tourist. Friends Overseas can supply you with the names and addresses of Scandinavian residents wanting to meet like-interested Yanks. The cost is $20.

Friends Overseas
68-04 Dartmouth St.
Forest Hills, NY 11375

River Safaris Run a river and meet the people of New Guinea, Africa, Alaska, or others. Prior experience is not required, but you must be in good health. Ten days to three weeks; $1200 is the average land cost.

Sobek Expeditions, Inc.
P.O. Box 67
Angels Camp, CA 95222

Expeditions for Understanding Forum Travel offers trips different from traditional tours. Travel with qualified guides and create an understanding of past and present cultures. Past trips have included visits to the worlds of the Incas and Mayas. Prices between $400 and $800.

Forum Travel International
2437 Durant Ave., Suite 208
Berkeley, CA 94704

Estudia en México Take a vacation with a purpose in Leon, Mexico. Vacationists are welcome in their Spanish and Mexican culture programs held throughout the year.

Instituto Moderno de Lenguas Extranjeras
Av. Hidalgo, Num. 206
Leon, GTO
Mexico

I Came, I Saw, I Learned

Walk Your Soles Away

Explore the whole of the nation for $4 or, if money is tight, stick to cheaper regional excursions. Any of the West, South/Southwest, Midwest, or East can be yours for $1—a single, lonely dollar bill.

That price cannot be beat, we know, but we also know you're wondering about the catch. It's a big one: these are do-it-yourself, pay-as-you-go vacations that must be taken on foot.

Send that buck to Walking Tours of America and, in the return mail, you'll get a walking tour for the region of your choice. All tours are authored by local writer-walkers, with each setting out the historical, visual, and cultural delights of a specific, often quite small, area.

Prefer the East? That tour covers New York City, Philadelphia, Pittsburgh, New Jersey, Massachusetts, Washington, D.C., and Virginia. Eighteen individual walking tours in all—none covering more than a few miles.

On the Western tour there are no cowboys but there are, instead, the peaks of Southern California, Northern California, Oregon, Washington, and Colorado. Sixteen individual tours come in this package.

Walk the South/Southwest and you'll cover turf from Miami through Scottsdale, and get 13 individual tours for your money. Thirteen separate tours are also included in the Midwest tour of Chicago, Milwaukee, Detroit, and the rest of our heartland.

Sponsored by Kinney Shoes (no, you've no obligation to replace worn shoe leather at Kinney's shops) in cooperation with the President's Council on Physical Fitness, these Walking Tours aim to get America on its feet and walking again because it's a fun way to explore the country and get exercise, too. Every package accordingly includes a brief essay on the benefits of walking, but purchasers are free to ignore that statement in order to devote still more time to walking itself.

Quibble as we might about the tours' contents—omissions range from old Hollywood with its venerable movie studios and faded elegance, to Cambridge, Massachusetts, home of Harvard University and history galore—there is no denying that every included tour is well researched, walkable in a few hours, and, best of all, well within even the most limited budgets. And, for a buck, it *is* hard to beat. —R.McG.

Kinney Walking Tours of America
P.O. Box 5006
New York, NY 10022

Travel, in the younger sort, is a part of education; in the elder, a part of experience. He that travelleth into a country before he hath some entrance into the language, goeth to school, and not to travel.
FRANCIS BACON

Righto

Davis here. Inspector, Scotland Yard. Seems we've had a bit of a flap about you conducting tours of Britain and claiming they are quite different. Home office wants a full file on this.

Right, then let's have a look at what you've got. I see, you're the American representative for the Swan travel people. Bloody good outfit, that.

Well then, you schedule eight different tours in all. Great Britain. Two weeks at a go, normally. Using motor coaches and staying at the better hotels. Well, all very standard stuff I'd say. Look out the windows, visit a few churches. Nothing too exciting here, mates.

What's that? You send distinguished professors, lords, lecturers, and experts along on the trips, do you. They discuss the histories and high points of the people, homes, castles, theatres, churches, and the like. Better than any university class, you say. Right. I see what you're driving at now.

Well, let's have a look at this one: Scotland's castles, houses, and gardens, seen firsthand and expertly explained, for only $652 plus air fare. Or the leading London and regional theatres for just $966. And six other tours to pick from. Good show, I'd say. —C.McB.

Esplanade Tours
38 Newbury St.
Boston, MA 02116

Journeys into Mexico's Past

Situation: You're really interested in the archaeology and ancient cultures of Mexico, but a bit timid to venture off the beaten track by yourself. You've got two weeks' vacation coming up and a few bucks saved, but you don't know a soul who'd like to do the digs with you. Do you stay home and leaf through the pages of *National Geographic* or summon all your courage and set out on your own?

Solution: You don't do either one. Instead you join one of Wampler Tours' special archaeological trips to Mexico. Joseph C. Wampler is an archaeologist and mountaineer who conducts several moderately priced tours to Mexico every year. He offers the only tours over the entire F. C. Chihuahua al Pacifico railway system. He also leads tours which examine the Pyramids of Teotihuacan outside of Mexico City, the ruins of Mitla and Monte Alban near Oaxaca, and the excavation at Xochicalco, just outside of Taxco.

Prices average at about $800, inclusive of air fare. The tours last from five days to two weeks. —E.H.

Wampler Tours
P.O. Box 45
Berkeley, CA 94701

The Train in American Culture

Take the train to a college degree? Perhaps not the whole degree, but at least part of the requirements can be earned by training across the country in a special program offered by The American University of Washington, D.C.

For 21 days students intrigued by the train and its role in our history and culture visit—by train, of course—Cincinnati, Chicago, Seattle, San Francisco, Los Angeles, La Junta, Kansas City, St. Louis, and New York City. Along the way, local experts—including ones versed in train music and literature as well as railroad workers—meet and speak with the group. And a two-day overview of the Iron Horse and its impacts is provided by American University staff before setting out on this adventure.

Scheduled for the 1978 summer session, The Train in American Culture will likely be offered in subsequent summers. Cost for the course—including tuition, rail pass, and accommodations—is $631. Meals are not included, but college credit is. —R.McG.

The American University
Division of Continuing Education and Summer Session
Massachusetts and Nebraska Aves., NW
Washington, DC 20016

Cruise into History

If you're looking for the "Love Boat East," you would do well to take a pass on this one.

Not that Swan's nine different Hellenic cruises are lacking in mirth and merriment. Not at all. You sail through some of the most beautiful waters in the world on the luxurious *Orpheus*, complete with modern lounges, dining rooms, sun decks, and a swimming pool. An orchestra plays and champagne corks pop in the evenings.

But these are cruises with a difference. The fun and frivolity of boat life is there to be had, but the real emphasis is placed on education and enlightenment through the use of expert lecturers who accompany the passengers during both their ship and shore journeys.

Swan is a London-based travel company that is represented in the United States and Canada by Esplanade Tours of Boston. They started their "lecture" cruises some 25 years ago and have found them to be highly popular and successful.

You can combine several different Mediterranean countries and dozens of various ports and historic sites on the two-week tours. The ship docks in Greece, Turkey, Italy, Sicily, Malta, and the Dalmation Coast. Ports of call include Delphi, Delos, Rhodes, Athens, Istanbul, Naples, Messina, Palermo, Corfu, Olympia, and Zante.

Swan's lecturers are well versed in the history, archaeology, architecture, and religions of the different countries visited, and are also chosen for their ability to communicate and mingle easily with the cruise travelers.

Obviously, it is one thing to stand among the ruins of Delphi and attempt to recall your history of the site, and quite another to be aided by an acknowledged expert who can provide extensive background or interesting tidbits of information. This is the advantage that the Swan tours provide.

An added highlight of the three spring cruises is the inclusion of an expert botanist among the lecturers to discourse on the Mediterranean wildflowers that cover the islands and mainlands along the routes.

Cruise prices start at $1050 and go up to $2030, depending on cabin accommodations. Point of origin is London.

Swan also conducts a 600-mile Nile River cruise aboard the m.s. *Delta*, a treat of a trip for Ancient Egypt buffs. The cruises, staffed with Swan's experts, of course, run from Cairo to Assuan, or vice versa. The 18-day adventures cover the rich history of the river and the country, its pyramids and Pharaohs, its tombs and temples. Prices vary from $1430 to $1715, double occupancy, with London, again, as a starting point. —C.McB.

Esplanade Tours
38 Newbury St.
Boston, MA 02116

Safaris and Treks

Today the Grand Tour of Europe is definitely tame stuff. Inquisitive and experimental travelers now survey the remote. It may be the Arctic, the Himalayas, or the rivers of Indochina. And they wish for more than tacky souvenirs or the "city after dark."

It's not necessary to be a loner to embark on a new adventure—Hanns Ebensten Travel can put you on one of their own. Compatible people are around to join you on everything from a trip up toward Mount Kilimanjaro's icy cap, to a study tour and stay at a nature center in the Northern mountains of Trinidad.

South Pacific lovers set off in privately chartered ships to touch shore on Galapagos Islands where tortoises roam free. Comparative culture buffs visit archaeological sites in Java and Bali including some classical Buddhist monuments built 400 years before Europe's great cathedrals.

Good leadership is one clue to the success of an off-beat trip, and tour consultants come with expertise in needed camping or climbing skills as well as long-time firsthand knowledge of the area you will visit.

Trips last approximately 20 days and price, excluding air fare, can range from $965 for a Trinidad visit to a $3150 tab for a river safari in Borneo. —S.A.

Hanns Ebensten Travel
55 West 42nd St.
New York, NY 10036

To Ancient Times

Don't scoff at time machines: Kurt Bergel *is* one. And he will happily welcome your company as you join in a search for our culture's roots.

The Acropolis, Crete, Corinth, Ravenna, Florence, Gubbio, Rome, and Athens provide the itinerary for Dr. Bergel's time-machine passage into Western Civilization's cradle—a four-week exploration of our pasts. Sponsored by Chapman College, Bergel's Ancient Civilizations Tour stresses a no-frills approach to travel coupled with a well-planned itinerary and the guidance of experts versed in the nuances of our beginnings.

Local guides supplement the tour leaders' expertise and, while the primary focus is on the ancient world, the art, architecture, and achievements of more recent periods are not ignored. Fully contemporary side trips are possible through an optional tour to Paris and London.

Cost of this visit to our roots is about $2000. Air fares, hotel accommodations, surface transportation, and some meals are included. Undergraduate college credit is available, but Dr. Bergel's time machine is not restricted to students. —R.McG.

Prof. Kurt Bergel
Chapman College
Orange, CA 92666

Horticulture Happiness

Recipe for: Horticultural Happiness
From the files of: The American Institute for Foreign Study
Cooking time: Fifteen days
Ingredients: 1. Interest in gardens, castles, homes and chateaux overseas. 2. Fifteen days in which to pursue that interest. 3. Approximately $1400.
Method: Combine the efforts of the American Institute for Foreign Study, The Civic Garden Center of Cincinnati, and Gulliver's Travels of Greenwich, Connecticut. The result will be group tours to foreign countries. The special accent of these tours is an emphasis on horticulture. Guided tours through famous gardens are provided as well as slide shows and lectures on various aspects of gardening. There is a satisfying blend of time spent in the cities with time spent touring the countryside by coach. Homes, chateaux, and castles are visited—many of which are not normally open to the public. In 1978 one group sampled the delights of Northern England and Scotland and another went to France's Loire Valley, Paris, and Brittany. The destinations vary from year to year, but the flavor of the final product is always a success. —E.H.

American Institute for Foreign Study
102 Greenwich Ave.
Greenwich, CT 06830

Questers Tours and Travel

Ever seen a Komodo dragon? A puffin? A wallaroo? A quetzal? Questers Tours and Travel will gladly show you where and how to see these and hundreds of other exotic animals in the Everglades, Death Valley, Greenland, the Outer Hebrides, and scores of other far-from-the-beaten-track locales.

Questers, a packager of worldwide nature tours, annually draws up a list of vacations designed to excite experienced as well as amateur naturalists, and every Questers tour stresses the natural history, culture, customs, art, and wildlife of the selected areas. On the 23-day Nepal Trek, for example, participants explore the art and architecture of the Katmandu Valley; grab an aerial glimpse of Mt. Everest; hike across 150 miles of Nepalese back-country; and briefly poke around jungle foothills. Tigers, rhinos, and varied wildlife may be spied along the way, Questers promises.

Those with a taste for cooler climes might opt for the 11-day Greenland jaunt. Questers again assembles a diverse package, with participants looking for ringed seals, arctic foxes, terns, and eiders. A visit to a crumbling medieval red sandstone cathedral is included.

And for those with a yen for a bit of mystery, Questers offers an Inca experience in the Peruvian Andes. One highlight of the tour is the Nazca Lines, made famous in *Chariots of the Gods*. In an aerial survey of the eerie land drawings, you'll see a dog, an enormous monkey, and a bird with a wingspan of 100 meters.

Or if romantic ruins are your forte, join Questers for an introspective trip to Tintern Abbey in Great Britain. Once you've gazed on that noble ruin, you'll be off to Carmarthen and Caernarvon, then to Hadrian's Wall and Lindisfarne. Finally to Edinburgh for a visit to Holyroodhouse, with its ghostly remembrances of Mary Stuart and her brutal lover, the Earl of Bothwell.

Ranging in duration from 4 to 36 days, Questers' tours aim to provide participants with ample time to explore in detail specific areas of interest—flora or fauna, for instance—while also affording a perspective on life in the region as a whole. Prices start at a few hundred dollars and scale upward to well over $4000 for a 30-day tour of Australia and New Zealand.

Questers happily mails complimentary copies of their thrice yearly *Nature Tour Notes*, and will provide a directory of all upcoming tours as well as detailed descriptions of specific offerings upon request. —R.McG.

Questers Tours and Travel, Inc.
257 Park Ave. South
New York, NY 10010

The Classroom Is Everywhere

The mailing address is New York, New York, but the campus is wherever a yellow school bus goes. And the whole of the United States serves as the science lab.

Make no mistake, the National Audubon Society's Expedition Institute is unique and the stress is decidedly on "expedition." Starting out from home base, the students find their way—with the help of experienced guides and teachers—into and through forests, tidepools, bogs, swamps, everglades, tropical jungles, deserts, and mountain ranges. Along the way, accredited course equivalency is attained in dozens of academic subjects—from astronomy through music.

High school and college students as well as seekers of more advanced accreditation are active participants in the program, and there are no set age limits. Participants are free to spend as little as one week or as long as several academic years exploring the nation.

Cost for the two semesters on the road is $4900; a single semester is $3300; a week, $160. Scholarships and like financial aids are available, and special programs can be developed to meet individual needs. —R.McG.

National Audubon Society Expedition Institute for Environmental Education
950 Third Ave.
New York, NY 10022

Pacific Northwest Sea Trails

Does life in the wilderness breed character? That's what the pioneers preached and city-slickers who crave a dose of that rough-and-ready character find what they are seeking in Pacific Northwest Sea Trails' 14-day environmental journeys across British Columbia's rugged wilderness.

Beginning at Campbell River, PNST's expeditions cover the 150 miles of sea and land separating British Columbia's mainland from Vancouver Island. Travel is by inflatable boat and by foot as participants explore evergreen-dotted terrain, majestic mountains, and pristine waters. Throughout, emphasis is put on learning how to preserve the wilderness as well as better survival in it.

Participants must be in good health and at least 16 years old. Cost of the 14-day PNST experience is $400. Necessary personal items and licenses hike the total to about $600, exclusive of transportation to British Columbia. Current courses are scheduled in June, July, August, and January, with each expedition limited to a maximum of 20 participants. —R.McG.

Pacific Northwest Sea Trails, Inc.
Administrative Center
13062 Caminito Del Rocio
Del Mar, CA 92014

Historical Vail "Learn the stories of those who built Vail and those who came before," says Vail Guides. In their two-hour tour they'll take you through the town and into the valley exploring Vail's past and present. The cost is $7.50.

Vail Guides, Inc.
P.O. Box 1474
Vail, CO 81657

Learn as You Go Want to learn about the everyday life of Medieval England? the Aztec? Russian art? Egyptians? or Persians? A.C.E. offers lecture-filled tours to these and other places for the curious traveler. The two- to three-week trips cost about $900, including air fare.

Association for Cultural Exchange
539 West 112th St.
New York, NY 10025

A Sweet Stop For nearly 85 years Kahuku processed cane from the surrounding fields. Now, instead of sugar, it produces historical tours of its factory for interested travelers. The prices are $3.50 for adults, $2.00 for children.

Kahuku Sugar Mill
c/o Avatar
Connie Wright
Suite 202
835 Keeaumoku St.
Honolulu, HI 96814

Britain with a Flair Visit "magic" Wales. Or listen to the music of England's cathedrals. Each tour is full of lectures for travelers who want to know more than what the tour book says. Prices about $1200, plus air fare, for the two-week trips.

Norman Wilkes Tours
P.O. Box 616
Indian Hills, CO 80454

Subject Index

Index of Programs